RESONANCE
OF VIOLENCE

INDEPENDENCE, DECOLONIZATION, VIOLENCE AND WAR IN
INDONESIA

ESTHER CAPTAIN, ONNO SINKE

RESONANCE OF VIOLENCE

BERSIAP AND THE DYNAMICS OF VIOLENCE IN THE FIRST PHASE
OF THE INDONESIAN REVOLUTION, 1945-1946

TRANSLATED BY VIVIEN COLLINGWOOD

AMSTERDAM UNIVERSITY PRESS

This publication is the result of the research programme *Independence, Decolonization, Violence and War in Indonesia, 1945-1950*. A complete overview of the programme's publications and the acknowledgements can be found at the back of this book.

The research programme was carried out by the Royal Netherlands Institute of Southeast Asian and Caribbean Studies (KITLV-KNAW), the Netherlands Institute for Military History (NIMH) and the NIOD Institute for War, Holocaust and Genocide Studies (NIOD-KNAW), in accordance with the guidelines on independent scholarly research set by the Royal Netherlands Academy of Arts and Sciences (KNAW). The programme was partly financed by the Dutch government.

Cover image: Two Indonesian boys from a local people's militia armed with a spear. Source: Cas Oorthuys, Nederlands Fotomuseum
Cover title page: A parade for the declaration of Indonesian independence, Aug. 18, 1945. Source: ANRI/IPPHOS

Cover design and interior: BVDT – Bart van den Tooren
Image editing: Harco Gijsbers, Ellen Klinkers, René Kok
Maps: Erik van Oosten
Index: Femke Jacobs

ISBN 9789463720892
e-ISBN 9789048557189
DOI 10.5117/9789463720892
NUR 680

Creative Commons License CC BY NC ND (http://creativecommons.org/licenses/by-nc-nd/3.0)

© Esther Captain, Onno Sinke / Amsterdam University Press B.V., Amsterdam 2025
© Translation: Vivien Collingwood / Amsterdam University Press B.V., Amsterdam 2025

Some rights reserved. Without limiting the rights under copyright reserved above, any part of this book may be reproduced, stored in or introduced into a retrieval system, or transmitted, in any form or by any means (electronic, mechanical, photocopying, recording or otherwise).

Content

9   **I. INTRODUCTION**

11   Prologue – The sound of violence
17   1. *Bersiap* in broader context

29   **II. HISTORICAL BACKGROUND**

31   2. Violence from above: the colonial context of violence in Indonesia
63   3. Rising tensions

79   **III. CONFRONTATIONS**

81   4. Power constellations
87   5. The Eastern archipelago: Allied dominance
101 6. Java and Sumatra: rival international power blocks
143 7. The organization of Indonesian violence
153 8. Estimates of casualty numbers

183 **IV. IMPACT**
185 9. The significance of bersiap in the Indonesian War of Independence (1946-1949)

211 V TO CONCLUDE

213 Conclusions
223 Epilogue – The resonance of the sound of violence

227 Notes
263 Abbreviations
267 Glossary
271 Sources
283 Acknowledgements
286 About the authors
287 Index

I.
INTRODUCTION

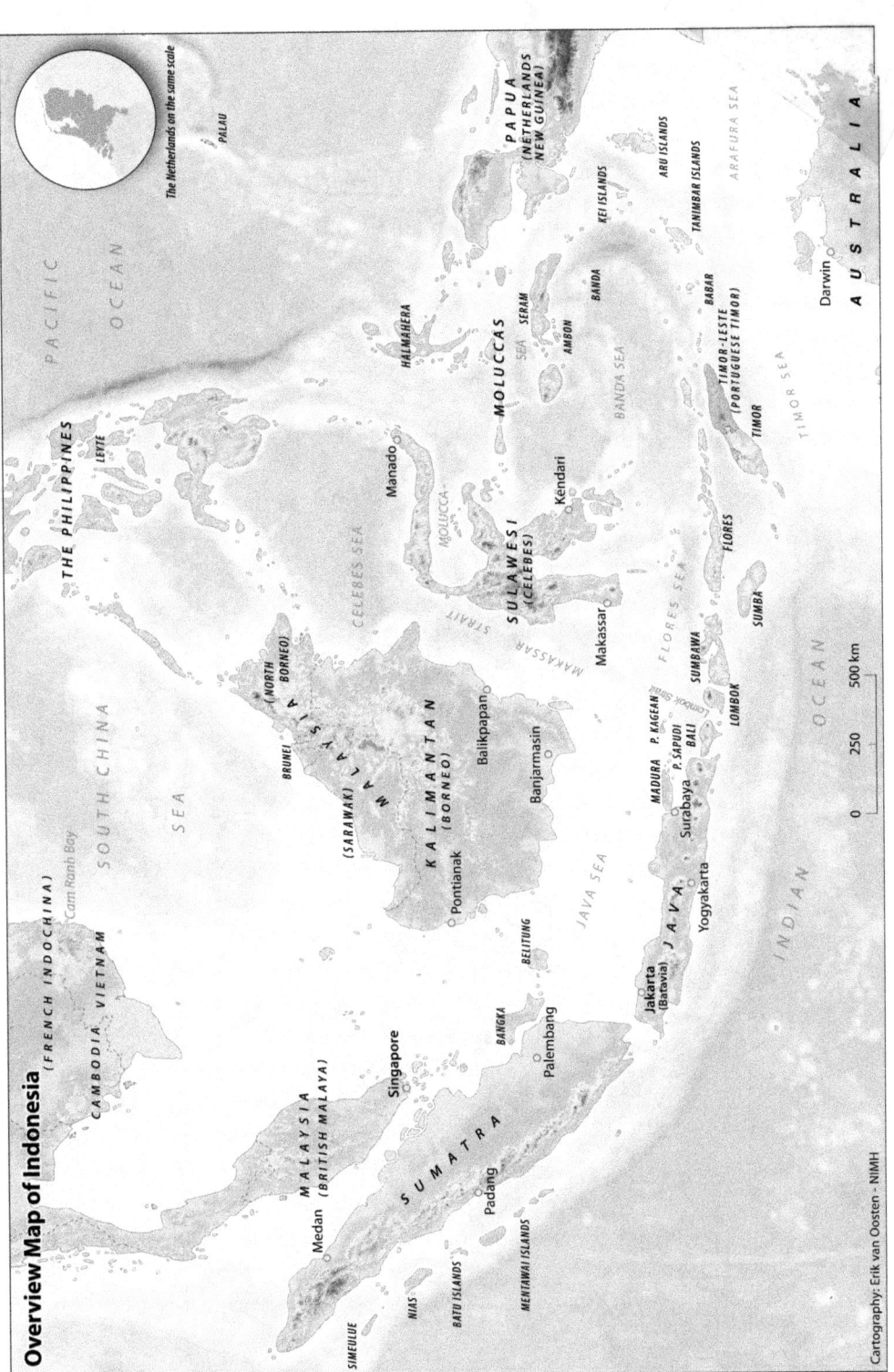

Prologue
The sound of violence

Memories of years gone by, or countries left behind, are often coloured by sensory perceptions. In his novel *À la recherche du temps perdu* (*In search of lost time*), Marcel Proust describes how eating a madeleine, a French cake, catapults the protagonist back to the holidays of his youth. Whilst for Proust's character it is the taste of a madeleine that evokes this association, those visiting Indonesia for the first time or returning to the country mention different, yet similar, sensory perceptions: the taste and smell of durians, the smell and sound of *kretek* (clove) cigarettes, the scent of camphor in wardrobes, the sound of the *muezzin* (crier) issuing the call for prayer five times a day. Tastes, smells and sounds evoke associations with a bygone era and, in the case of the Dutch East Indies, with the former Dutch colony. For some, the tastes, smells and sounds of Indonesia spark feelings of nostalgia or homesickness; for others, they are elements of their daily lives, either in Indonesia or taken elsewhere from there.

In *The sound of violence*, an important role is played by the rallying cry of 'bersiap!' (Indonesian for 'pay attention, ready for action!') in the first phase of the Indonesian Revolution (17 August 1945–31 March 1946). This was the signal for revolutionary young Indonesians to take up arms and defend the independence of the recently founded nation against anyone associated with the former colonial regime. For the KNIL soldier S.M. Jalhay, the danger posed by this rallying cry was so great that he recalled the shelling of Bandung thus:

> The roar of exploding grenades was like music to our ears after the terrifying nights of screams of 'merdeka [independence]' and 'bersiap', which chilled you to the bone and which you were powerless to resist.[1]

The cry of 'bersiap' made a deep impression on many Indo-Europeans, Chinese, Moluccans, Menadonese and Timorese, and on Indonesians who were (allegedly) on the Dutch side.[2] But the Japanese rear admiral Yaichiro Shibata also recalled how a certain sound announced a sudden gathering of Indonesian fighters in Surabaya:

> Since the rioting had first broken out, we often heard the dull sound of two pieces of wood being banged together. On hearing this sound thousands of Indonesians would appear from nowhere, and quietly gather ready for action. That night [3 October 1945] the same dreaded sound of wood banging together could be heard. Where were they going to this time?[3]

It took some effort not to associate the cry of 'bersiap' with this, as well as other sounds that had only recently heralded violence and fighting. In late December 1949, for example, prompted by a so-called 'vendutie' (sale of household goods before leaving the colony), the Indies daily *Nieuwe Courant* read:

> The times are changing, or rather they have already changed, and it thus does us good suddenly to encounter an old thing or sound from the dim and distant past. How often did we listen in times gone by, for instance, to the dull beats of the gong that announced a viewing? Those monotonous beats in the quiet tropical night did not spark memories of mortar or bomb attacks, they did not exhort us to lock or barricade our windows and doors, we did not expect to hear the cry of 'bersiap' at any moment; no, we simply looked at one another and said, 'Shall we?' And we entered a house where many people were wandering around, where all the furniture, paintings and other items were numbered, and we thought about what we liked, and what might be worth taking for the *vendutie* in front of our home tomorrow.[4]

In the Dutch East Indies, holding a public sale before emigrating was the order of the day. This was certainly the case in late December 1949: one week later, on 27 December 1949, the Netherlands would formally transfer sovereignty to Indonesia, which had proclaimed its independence back on 17 August 1945. The beat of the gong thereby regained its earlier meanings: as a way of telling the time or as a warning of fire or another calamity. In pre-war Indonesian society, the word 'siap' had been used in everyday life as an exhortation: 'get ready'. The Indonesian scouts, the Gerakan Pramuka Indonesia (GKI), had also used the term as a command: 'stand ready'.[5]

Certain sounds were typical of social life in the Dutch East Indies, and remain so in Indonesia today. Street vendors, for example, can be recognized from the distinctive sound that each makes to announce their arrival and extol their wares. In an interview in 1999, for instance, Mrs Roon-Koek, born in Bandung in 1924, did not recall the names of the street vendors so much as the sounds they made:

> You could always hear who was in the street, the Chinese; he ticked on a bamboo wood BAMI TOCK TOCK, a special click. BOT-BOTOL, that is the junk dealer. All these small calls.[6]

In a society where much of public life literally played out in the street, for the initiated these subtle signs were part of everyday existence; an outsider might miss them. Sound-imitation (onomatopoeia) plays an important role in the naming of sounds: the beat of the gong speaks for itself. In 'sréét-srot', we hear the slow shuffle of someone wearing *sloffen* (flip-flops, sandals) walking along a *gang* (alleyway); in 'tjies' (the title of the eponymous book by Tjalie Robinson), we hear the crack of a bullet fired from a .22 calibre rifle, the gun that young men in the archipelago used for hunting.[7]

Some onomatopoeic words and sounds – and that is why we called this book *The sound of violence* – refer to the violence that took place during the Indonesian Revolution. At that time, Indonesians used various words to describe revolutionary actions and violence, such as *bergolak* (turmoil), *gedor* (to beat up), *gedoran* (to bang, knock (on a door)), *menggedor* (to loot), *geledah* (to search), *rampok/rampokan* (to rob/raid), *penggarongan* (to loot/raid) and *geger* (Javanese for commotion, uproar).[8] It is in this context that we can also place the word 'tjintjangen' ('cincang' in Indonesian), which literally means 'to cut into bits' or 'dice'.⁹ It evokes the sound of a knife used to cut meat into small pieces. The journalist Hans Moll describes how, when one types the modern spelling of 'cincang' into Google, one is directed to Indonesian cooking sites. He adds: 'With the old-fashioned spelling, we immediately find ourselves back in the *bersiap* period, and then the meaning is less innocent.'¹⁰ In that context, *tjintjang* meant the butchering and merciless killing of one or more people.

It was in that context that the term was recalled by Father Van Beek (1908-1979), one of the congregation of Missionaries of the Holy Family, who worked in Semarang (Central Java) between 1937 and 1967. Several weeks after the proclamation of Indonesian independence, violence broke out between Indonesian nationalists and their (alleged) opponents. This did not stop Father Van Beek from travelling to the church in his mission area. He recalled that the Indonesian sexton had approached him, aghast: 'But *romo* [pastor], why have you come here? It's much too dangerous, it's nothing but *tjingtjang, tjingtjang* [sic] here.'¹¹ The historian Robert Cribb has written a chilling account of how this was experienced by the European and Indo-European civilians who returned to Jakarta after the Japanese surrender:

> Strolling Dutchmen were hauled off the street and strangled or hacked to pieces, their bodies being dumped in one or other of the canals. [...] The already colourful vocabulary of Indies Dutch acquired a new word, *getintjangd*, meaning hacked to pieces.¹²

Another example of onomatopoeia is 'dombreng', a ritual used by Indonesian fighters to expose and humiliate local officials who had previously worked with the Dutch regime. A crowd of fighters armed with bamboo spears and empty kerosene cans would go to the accused person's house and force them to leave. As the fighters beat on the kerosene cans, making the sound 'breng dong breng', the person was shown to and paraded in front of the tumultuous crowd:

> If the person was found, he was taken out, presented to the crowd [...] to the 'breng dong breng' of empty tins and sticks being beaten.¹³

'Dombreng' is a combination of two onomatopoeic words:

...words for the sounds of banging on wood or metal [...]. 'Tong' also refers to the sound of the ketongan, the signal-drum which is sounded in a different way for calling meetings, giving the time or warning of fire, theft and other emergencies.[14]

The public humiliation of (alleged) collaborators, deliberately held in daytime so that it could be witnessed by as many people as possible, sometimes replaced actual physical violence. Whereas 'tjintjangen' resonates within an Indo-Dutch commemorative community, 'dombreng' does so within an Indonesian one.

The origins of 'tjintjangen', however, go back beyond the Indonesian Revolution. Pre-war newspaper ads, for example, contain the phrase 'lapis tjintjang van rundvleesch': chopped slices of beef.[15] Aside from the domestic context, where the sense of dicing or chopping meat was predominant – and already common in the nineteenth century – we also come across the word in the sense of 'merciless killing' in the reporting on the Aceh War (1873-1914). For example, *De Java-bode* wrote in 1878 about 'marauders', fighters who stayed behind on the battlefield to plunder. The newspaper reported that the 'barbaric way' in which a person was dismembered was 'known to the native as *tjintjang* (making them into *frikadel*)'.[16] The Indonesian journal *Historia* nevertheless argued in 2011 that *tjintjangen* had been added to the Dutch dictionary as a new word as a result of the Indonesian Revolution.[17] Just as this word acquired new overtones during this period, for many an Indo-European, Moluccan or Dutch person, the negative meaning of the word 'bersiap' is largely associated with traumatic memories of the extremely violent first phase of the Indonesian Revolution.

I.

Bersiap in broader context

'The sound of violence' refers to the first months of the Indonesian Revolution, after the proclamation of independence on 17 August 1945. As explained in chapter 1, and as will also become clear later in this book, memories of this period of extreme violence are deeply anchored in the Indo-Dutch and Moluccan communities in the Netherlands. To further our understanding of the events, however, we need to view the extreme violence against Indo-Europeans, Moluccans and Dutch in a broader context.

In the extremely violent situation that developed in the first phase of the Indonesian Revolution, intra-Indonesian violence also targeted Indonesian administrators and officials, Indonesian violence was directed against Chinese, Japanese and British civilians and/or captured fighters, and the Japanese, British and Dutch used violence against Indonesian civilians and captured fighters. These acts of violence mostly took place outside of combat action and in the absence of clear military aims or military necessity.

When studying violence in the earliest phase of the Indonesian Revolution, we therefore took a broader approach than has long been customary in the historiography of the *bersiap* period, which has tended to focus on the killing of Indo-Europeans, Dutch and Moluccans.[1] Although this study focuses on extreme violence by irregular Indonesian armed groups against Indo-European, Dutch and Moluccan civilians and captured fighters, we also take a detailed look at the wider context of extreme violence against civilians and captured fighters from other groups and communities in the archipelago between 17 August 1945 and 31 March 1946.

This broader approach is not without its problems, because it requires access to a wider range of sources. Although much is available in the Dutch archives, on the whole this material is limited to violence against victims on the Dutch side, and it is also strongly coloured by the gaze of the colonial occupier. For example, most of the more detailed information about the perpetrators comes from the Dutch archives, which is problematic. It is more difficult to find data on the violence against victims on the Indonesian, Japanese, Chinese, British and British Indian side. The history of the Tumpang murders not only reveals the nature and form of the extreme violence in the earliest period of the Indonesian Revolution, but it is also illustrative of the problems that surround the availability and character of the sources.

The 'Tumpang murders'

On 29 October 1945, ten women and children from the Engelenburg family were murdered by *pemuda* (young Indonesian fighters) in the mountain village of Ngadireso, around 25 kilometres south-west of the city of Malang (East Java). The victims were from an Indo-European family. A total of fourteen people in Ngadireso were violently killed. We do not have any more information about the Simon family.

The bodies of the victims from the Engelenburg family were reburied at the Kembang Kuning Dutch military cemetery in Surabaya. The sight of their final resting place was poignantly described by author Hans Vervoort. He went to the cemetery to visit the grave of his brother, who was six years old when he died of illness and exhaustion in a Japanese internment camp in 1944:

> At the very front are the children. Their crosses are smaller than those of the adults, the girls' crosses end in a flower pattern. [...] Both times I was struck by how many Engelenburg children there were; eight in total, five girls and three boys, ranging in age from three to eleven years. What calamity had befallen them?[3]

Six of the murdered children were from the family of Miene Henriëtte Engelenburg-de Quillettes and Lothar Engelenburg. One daughter escaped the murders: Roos Engelenburg was in Malang on that fatal day. During

Ngadireso: 14 victims[2]

Surname	First name	Male/Female	Place of birth	Date of birth	Date of death	Age
Engelenburg	Benita	Female	Malang	19-02-1935	29-10-1945	10 years old
Engelenburg	Eveline	Female	Malang	19-02-1935	29-10-1945	10 years old
Engelenburg	Irene	Female	Malang	19-12-1940	29-10-1945	9 years old
Engelenburg	Johanna Felicienne	Female	Malang	17-03-1942	29-10-1945	3 years old
Engelenburg	Johannes	Male	Malang	15-08-1934	29-10-1945	11 jaar
Engelenburg	Richard	Male	Malang	24-07-1939	29-10-1945	6 years old
Engelenburg	Robert	Male	Surabaya	03-07-1939	29-10-1945	6 years old
Engelenburg	Wilhelmina	Female	Bodjonegoro	00-03-1937	29-10-1945	28 years old
Engelenburg-de Quillettes	Miene Henriette	Female	Pati	11-05-1917	29-10-1945	28 years old
Engelenburg-van Noort	Annie M.	Female	New Guinea	13-02-1917	29-10-1945	38 years old
Simon	N	Female			'beginning of the Merdeka period'	
Simon (child Mrs N Simon)		Unknown			'beginning of the Merdeka period'	
Simon (child Mrs N Simon)		Unknown			'beginning of the Merdeka period'	
Simon (child Mrs N Simon)		Unknown			'beginning of the Merdeka period'	

the Japanese occupation, father Lothar, a captured KNIL soldier, had been taken to Sumatra, where he died in 1944. After the Republic of Indonesia was proclaimed and unrest broke out in Malang and the vicinity, mother Miene decided to send her thirteen-year-old daughter Roos to Malang for her own safety. She mistakenly believed that nothing was likely to happen to her younger children. Roos Engelenburg found a job as a kitchen assistant in Sawahan hospital. While in Malang, she received the shocking news that her mother and younger brothers and sisters had been killed by *pemuda*.

Only 46 years later did she find out how it had happened. During a trip to Indonesia in 1991, she tracked down her old nanny, who had witnessed the massacre. In the words of Roos Engelenburg:

> My mother was not at home when the children were murdered. She was with our nanny, washing pots at the well. When she got home, she saw what had happened. Our nanny ran away as fast as she could and hid herself for a week. She was scared that she would be murdered, too. Then my mother was murdered. They were all cut into pieces [*getjingtjangd*].[4]

Ngadireso, where the Engelenburg women and children were murdered, is one of four mountain villages situated one above the other at the foot of the Semeru volcano, the highest mountain in Indonesia. As well as Ngadireso, there are the villages of Tumpang, Watesbelung and Poncokusomo, each at a distance of around 5 kilometres from each other. The tenfold murder in Ngadireso on 29 October 1945 was not the only bloodbath to take place in the mountain villages. Between 17 October and the end of October 1945, massacres were the order of the day in the mountain region. The following tables give an overview of the victims in Tumpang and Poncokusomo (separate data for Watesbelung were not found; it is likely that these victims' details were entered in the records of a larger place, such as Tumpang).

Tumpang: 31 victims[5]

Surname	First name	Male/Female	Place of birth	Date of birth	Date of death	Age
Boogaard	Tineke	Female		00-00-1901	17-10-1945	Ca. 44 years old
Deuning-Anthonio, van	Victorine	Female	Yogyakarta	01-03-1882	28-10-1945	63 years old
Goossens	Bobbie	Male			28-10-1945	
Goossens	Joan Willem	Male	Pasuruan	03-06-1892	29-10-1945	53 years old
Goossens-Paath	J.	Female			29-10-1945	
Kriegenbergh, von	Adèle Georgeine Anthonehe	Female	Yogyakarta	16-09-1919	27-10-1945	26 years old

Kriegenbergh, von	Louise	Female	Yogyakarta	26-11-1923	27-10-1945	21 years old
Kriegenbergh-Stralendorff, von	Adèle	Female	Klaten	08-11-1898	27-10-1945	46 years old
Lijnis Huffenreuter-Schröder	Johanna Frederika	Female	Surabaya	14-11-1898	28-10-1945	46 years old
Moormann	Clemens Leo	Male	Malang	24-10-1934	17-10-1945	10 years old
Moormann-Vlaanderen	Marie	Female	Pekalongan	26-10-1896	17-10-1945	48 years old
Noort, van	A.M.	Unknown			27-10-1945	
Noort, van	Robert	Male			27-10-1945	
Noort, van	Johanna Felicina	Female			27-10-1945	
Ruter, (brother of 2 sisters)	B.	Male			27-10-1945	
Ruter, one of the sisters B. Ruter		Female			27-10-1945	
Ruter, one of the sisters B. Ruter		Female			27-10-1945	
Scherius, daughter		Female			Bersiap	
Scherius, fam.		Unknown			Bersiap	
Scherius, fam.		Unknown			Bersiap	
Scherius, fam.		Unknown			Bersiap	
Scherius-van Vollenhoven	Jeannet Christine	Female	Pasuruan	18-06-1864	29-10-1945	81 years old
Schipper	Louis Johan	Male		10-10-1883	27-10-1945	61 years old
Schipper-Heiligers	Josephine Christine	Female	Surabaya	13-10-1886	27-10-1945	58 years old
Schreuder		Female			Bersiap	
Schreuder		Male			Bersiap	
Schreuder		Male			Bersiap	
Schreuder	(son)	Male			Bersiap	

Poncokusumo: 14 victims[6]

Surname	First name	Male/Female	Place of birth	Date of birth	Date of death	Age
Coenen	Rudy Leendert	Male			October 1945	
Coenen	Hugo	Male	Poncukusumo	03-11-1935	27-10-1945	9 years old
Coenen-Kampen	Adriana Johanna	Female	Surabaya	09-07-1904	27-10-1945	41 years old
Haasen-van den Dungen Bille, van	Francine	Female	Wlingi	23-05-1900	29-10-1945	45 years old
Hughan	Alexander Theodoor	Male	Surabaya	13-11-1885	27-10-1945	59 years old
Rossum-Johannes, van	Sophie Catharina	Female	Buitenzorg (Bogor)	20-04-1896	27-10-1945	49 years old
Rossum-Tio, van	Johanna	Male			October 1945	
Werff, van der	Annemarie	Female	Batavia (Jakarta)	15-09-1941	29-10-1945	4 years old
Werff, van der	Clara Antoinette	Female	Ambon	12-05-1938	29-10-1945	7 years old
Werff, van der	Henny Jan	Male	Batavia (Jakarta)	23-02-1934	29-10-1945	11 years old
Werff, van der	Pia Louise	Female	Ambon	21-12-1935	29-10-1945	9 years old
Werff-van den Dungen Bille, van der	Louise	Female	Blitar	21-06-1907	29-10-1945	38 years old
Winter	Ronald James	Male	Malang	28-05-1936	29-10-1945	9 years old
Winter-van den Dungen Bille	Henriëtte	Female	Blitar	31-07-1904	29-10-1945	41 years old

To our regret, we were not always able to find Indonesian sources, including sources specifically on the 'Tumpang murders'. During our research, some sources proved to be missing and some were unavailable (many are not yet accessible online, and some were digitized during our research period), some sources were not accessible (because we had no access to certain Indonesian archives), and due to the COVID-19 pandemic, travel to Indonesia became impossible from early 2020. As a result, the planned archival research, seminars and other exchanges with Indonesian colleagues in the research programme turned out to be impossible, and a series of planned workshops in Depok, Malang, Medan and Semarang unfortunately had to be cancelled.

The sources were recorded from a Dutch perspective, meaning that we know more about how these events were viewed by the Dutch. As historians we are critical of our material, and we try to be maximally aware of one-sidedness or bias. Nevertheless, this does not solve the problem of imbalance in the use of sources. The case of the murders in the four mountain villages east of Malang can be used to illustrate how the limited scope of the sources determines our ability to reconstruct the events. The sources in the Dutch archives provide details about how the murders were carried out. A 1948 report by the Investigation Service for the Deceased (Opsporingsdienst van Overledenen, ODO) states that the victims in Tumpang were buried in a mass grave on the plot belonging to the Schröder family, opposite the mosque. The arms of four bodies had been bound together with dog chains and the bodies had been hacked into pieces. Four other people were buried in a mass grave on the plot belonging to the Indo-European victim Erna Wilhelmina Wetzel-Catherinus. In Poncokusumo, there was a mass grave containing another twelve people.[7] An informant who was interrogated by the Dutch police in Malang stated:

> The following concerns the method of killing. The victims in Poentjokoesoemo were all butchered. Those from Watesbeloeng were both butchered and tortured to death; most of those from Ngadireso were butchered, with the exception of Mrs Deuning, who was hung. Concerning those from Toempang, it is said that most of them were butchered.[8]

According to a statement by the Indonesian informant Dulsaid Gondongan in 1948 to the Netherlands East Indies Forces Intelligence Service, NEFIS, the murderers went to the home of Mrs Scherius two or three days after the Indonesian civilian authorities in Malang had called for a boycott of Europeans and Indo-Europeans (it was no longer permissible to sell them food, for example). They asked her sister-in-law, who was of Menadonese descent:

> Madam, where do your national allegiances lie? If you wish to be saved, you must leave here and stop mixing with the *Blandas* [whites]. If not, then that's up to you.[9]

The sister-in-law refused to leave. A few days later, the men returned and 'slaughtered with blunt *klewangs* [machetes] the Scheerius [sic], Wijtzel [sic] and Schröder women and their relatives.'[10]

Reports from NEFIS also provide information about the alleged perpetrators of the murders in and around Tumpang. After the massacres, the Badan Keamanan Rakjat (BKR: the Republican People's Security Agency, the forerunner of the Indonesian national army) or the Republican police arrested three main perpetrators and locked them up in Lowokwaru prison.[11] However, the sources are ambiguous on this point. NEFIS reports contain multiple and different names and figures, ranging from two to eleven perpetrators.[12] The suspects were said to have been aged between 30 and 40, and were working as a taxi driver, teacher and sugar trader. They were said to have no affiliation with armed groups.[13] In terms of their age and profession, the alleged perpetrators thus did not fit the profile of *pemuda* – young, not yet established fighters who wanted to defend Indonesian independence. A number of sources give an impression of some level of organization: the murderers were said to have driven by truck first to Tumpang, and then to Poncokusomo.[14] Indonesian publications about that time make no mention of the murders in Tumpang and the other villages.

The Dutch sources also reveal a range of attitudes and actions on the part of Indonesians. Bambang Sumadi, the chief of the Republican police in Malang, played an important role in the case of the massacres of European and Indo-European women and children in the four mountain villages.[15] His actions show that the position of Indonesians could be fluid and that the Republican side also offered protection. For example, sources reported that Sumadi had tried to prevent the massacres in Tumpang, but that the police were only able to save two families from the hands of the murderers.[16]

After the violence had broken out in Malang and the Europeans and Indo-Europeans had been taken to Republican internment camps, Sumadi, as the head of the evacuation committee, had apparently been present with his police force as the trains carrying European and Indo-European evacuees left each day. It is said that Sumadi ensured that Europeans and Indo-Europeans had effective, orderly and disciplined protection during the train journey. Regarding Sumadi's role, a Dutch witness claimed that in his absence, 'everything wouldn't have gone so well':

> I myself, and many others besides me, had the impression that B.S. [Bambang Sumadi] did those things because he was pro-Dutch, and

in that case he pulled off a very dangerous feat by playing a double role, and in so doing risked his own life to bring thousands of men, women and children to safety.[17]

Other witness statements confirm this picture. Sumadi is described as a 'moderate nationalist', and his sympathetic attitude to the Europeans and Indo-Europeans is said to have brought him into conflict with 'the extremists'.[18] It seems that Sumadi was able to continue his career with the police; sources indicate that he may have been the head of the Republican police in Jakarta in 1947.[19] In any case, it is striking that even sources from NEFIS, which was supportive of the Dutch authorities and usually portrayed Indonesians unfavourably, give such a positive picture of Sumadi. His name also features in an Indonesian publication about the struggle for independence in Malang, where, in September 1945, Sumadi, as the chief of police, was a member of a delegation that discussed the transfer of power by the Japanese military in Malang to the Republican government.[20] This publication focuses on the armed struggle, and it does not mention the murders in Tumpang. Sumadi does not feature in two other Indonesian historical studies about Malang in wartime.[21]

In the Netherlands, the murders east of Malang became known as the 'Tumpang murders' or the 'Tumpang affair'. The horrific events sent out shock waves that resonated not only at the time, but also decades later.[22] In 2001, a member of staff at Pelita, an Indo-Dutch welfare institution, noted in a report on a conversation with a client:

> In the vicinity of Malang was the village of Toempang [sic.] where the whole Indo-Dutch community was massacred. This event made a great impression on everyone in the area. As a child, the applicant took the story very seriously. He was scared that it might also happen to him and his family.[23]

The group of 59 who were murdered in Tumpang belonged to a much larger group of victims who lost their lives in the first months of the Indonesian Revolution. As in 'Tumpang', there were many massacres of families and relatives, but also of individuals, of all origins.

Central questions, method and approach

This book aims to offer a broad analysis of the extreme violence that took place in the first months after the proclamation of Indonesian independence on 17 August 1945. Our research is not limited to the violence on Java and Sumatra, but extends to the islands beyond.[24] In the case of Java and Sumatra, rather than dealing with this period by city or region, we aim for an analysis that transcends place and region in order to reveal any common characteristics. To do so, of course, is not to deny that local conditions played an important role in the dynamics of violence.

We focus on the following questions:

- What are the characteristics of, and explanations for, the extreme violence against civilians and captured fighters of different nationalities and population groups in Indonesia, which was carried out mainly by irregular Indonesian armed groups in the period between 17 August 1945 and 31 March 1946?
- What were the factors that led to the extreme violence, and who were the most important actors?
- What are the most plausible estimates of the numbers of victims who lost their lives in the extreme violence?

For our analysis in this book, we decided not to use the term *bersiap* as an overarching concept. Though relatively common until recently, we do not consider the term a suitable description of the broad spectrum of violence in the first phase of the Indonesian Revolution. First, in the Dutch historiography and culture of remembrance, the word has long been understood to mean atrocities – mainly racially or ethnically motivated – committed against the Dutch, Indo-European and Moluccan communities in particular. Although ethnicity was certainly a factor in the violence, our study shows that such a simple explanation is insufficient. Second, the use of an Indonesian word can act as a (subconscious) distraction from that broad perspective, because the term may evoke associations with violence on the Indonesian side alone. For that reason, when discussing this period, we prefer to refer to 'the first (or earliest) phase of the Indonesian Revolution'. Third, by doing so, we wish to indicate that this period should be viewed in historiographical terms as an integral part of the Indonesian Revolution, and not as a separate episode in history. None of this alters the fact, of course, that the concept of *bersiap* is extremely important for the Indo-European, Dutch and Moluccan communities of experience and remembrance in the Netherlands, who actually lived through the events that took place in that period. The way in which *bersiap* and recollections of it have been processed by the various groups will be discussed in the epilogue to this book.

Although extreme violence by irregular Indonesian armed groups against Indo-European, Dutch and Moluccan civilians and captured fighters forms the starting point for this study, we also look in detail at the broader context of extreme violence against civilians and captured fighters from other communities in the archipelago between 17 August 1945 and 31 March 1946. This concerns both intra-Indonesian violence against Indonesian administrators and officials and Indonesian violence against Chinese, Japanese and British civilians and/or captured fighters, as well as violence by the Japanese, British and Dutch against Indonesian civilians and captured fighters. This violence was usually perpetrated outside of combat operations and had no clear military purpose or military necessity. This means that we also consider violence by regular soldiers, to the extent that it was directed against civilians or captured fighters.

The violence in these months cannot be viewed in isolation from the preceding oppression by the Dutch colonial regime and the Japanese occupation.[25] That is because the struggle by the Republic of Indonesia and irregular Indonesian armed groups was directed against those, both in and beyond the archipelago, who represented the colonial regime, who advocated the return of the colonial system, and who threatened the independence of Indonesia or were suspected of doing so, rightly or wrongly. Seemingly trivial details could determine whether someone fell victim to ruthless violence: even the possession of a certain (colour combination of) clothing, fabrics or paintings, a preference for Dutch products, or having Dutch contacts or trading relations could mark someone out as a 'traitor' or 'collaborator'. In addition to government officials, many ordinary Indonesians were also victims.

From early October 1945, the violence escalated in several directions: it came from many sides – not only from the Indonesians, but also from the Indo-European, Moluccan, Dutch, British and Japanese – and was directed against multiple targets, including the British, British Indians, Japanese and Chinese. Viewed in this context, we can say that the situation was 'extremely violent', drawing on the concept of the 'extremely violent society' developed by the German historian Christian Gerlach. By this, Gerlach means a society in which different communities fall victim to physical and non-physical violence perpetrated by multiple parties and social groups, often in collaboration with official organizations. We use the term 'situation' to indicate that this was a temporary state of affairs.[26]

The beginning of this earliest period of violence was marked by the Indonesian proclamation of independence on 17 August 1945. Indonesia declared itself a sovereign nation, free of Dutch colonial oppression and the Japanese occupation. The end of this period can be dated to the end of March 1946, when the first wave of Indonesian extreme violence was contained, partly as a result of Japanese and British military interventions, the interventions of the Republic of Indonesia, and negotiations. Intra-Indonesian violence decreased, most Indo-Europeans were taken to Republican camps, some of the *totok* (European) Dutch were evacuated to the Netherlands or elsewhere, the repatriation of the Japanese was almost completed, and Dutch servicemen were allowed onto Java.

This did not mean that the violence directed against specific groups ceased after March 1946, however; on the contrary. The Chinese and Indonesian communities in particular would subsequently suffer many civilian casualties. Most Chinese victims probably died after March 1946, for example, in violence such as that in Tanggerang (West Java) in June of the same year, when local criminal gangs attacked, raped and killed Chinese people.[27] And in the extreme intra-Indonesian violence on South Sulawesi in the second half of 1946, which targeted people who may or may not have been pro-Dutch, hundreds of Indonesian men, women and children were killed, often gruesomely. These events formed the background to the deployment from 5 December 1945 of the special forces, the Depot Speciale Troepen (DST) led by lieutenant – later captain – Westerling, which behaved very violently.[28] Throughout the later period, Dutch, Indo-European, Moluccan and (allegedly) pro-Dutch Indonesian civilians also remained a target, to a greater or lesser extent, of intimidation, abuse and murder. Around the time of the first Dutch offensive ('Operation Product', 21 July–5 August 1947), for example, the extreme Indonesian violence against these groups increased again, to the extent that the American historian William H. Frederick even refers to a 'second *bersiap* period'.[29]

II.
HISTORICAL BACKGROUND

2.

Violence from above

The colonial context of violence in Indonesia

On 8 March 1942, the Royal Netherlands East Indies Army (Koninklijk Nederlandsch-Indisch Leger, KNIL) surrendered to Japan. The Japanese army, commanded by General Hitoshi Imamura, took control of the Dutch East Indies. Imamura moved into the official residence of Governor General A.W.L. Tjarda van Starkenborgh on Koningsplein, Jakarta. The governor general left his palace flanked by a number of Japanese soldiers, who made him carry his own suitcase.[1] It was an unprecedented humiliation. The message was inescapable: under Japanese leadership, the roles of Europeans and Asians in the archipelago had been reversed. The European was no longer the lord and master, the Asian no longer the one who served him.

The image of the most senior figure in the colonial government being unable to order an Indonesian servant to carry his *barang* (luggage) was of great symbolic importance. Imagery played a crucial role in a colonial soci-

Sukarno addresses people to recruit labourers for the construction of defences. Probably in Jakarta, ca. 1944. Source: KITLV

ety: it both reflected and simultaneously shaped unequal structures in various facets of daily life, such as clothing and appearance. General Imamura was well aware of this. By moving into the previous governor's residence, he was indicating that Japan had taken power from the former rulers of the colony, the Dutch. This symbolism represented continuity: after all, the Japanese general had moved into the same palace and surrounded himself with the same wealth and grandeur as the Dutch authorities. Imamura, however, said that this was not his personal choice: 'I personally desired to live and work in a simple residence,' he declared in 1993.² According to the general, Japan had to pursue a policy of simplicity; a deliberate break with '300 years of exploitation of the Indonesian inhabitants, in which both the private homes and the public buildings of the Dutch, as well as the residences of overseas Chinese, had become extravagantly luxurious'.³ But Imamura could not refuse the order from the Military Administration Bureau (Gun Sei Bu) to take up residence in the governor general's palace. It had to be clear to everyone in the colony that Japan had taken power.

Both the Dutch and the Japanese regimes in Indonesia can be characterized as violent systems that were imposed from above by external rulers, with a power apparatus that had a far-reaching impact on the Indonesian population and society. There was a structural power imbalance between the Dutch and the Indonesians, and subsequently between the Japanese and the Indonesians. In order to understand the context of the violence after 17 August 1945, it is important that we reflect further on both the Dutch and the Japanese regimes in the Dutch East Indies. After all, these events were closely intertwined with the colonial context in which the structural power imbalance between the Dutch and the Indonesians, and later between the Japanese and the Indonesians, was anchored. A number of Indonesians perceived a form of continuity between the pre-war Dutch colonial regime and the subsequent Japanese occupation (8 March 1942–15 August 1945). In the words of the future vice-president, Muhammad Hatta: 'We had three and a half centuries of Dutch colonization and three and a half years of Japanese imperialism. That's enough.'⁴ The *New York Times* quoted President Sukarno as follows: '"We proclaimed our independence Aug. 17," said Dr. Soe Karno [sic], president of the republic of Indonesia. "We don't like Japanese oppression and we don't want Dutch oppression either."'⁵ The future prime minister Sutan Sjahrir used the umbrella term 'colonial fascism' to describe the parallels he perceived between the Dutch and the Japanese oppressors:

The Dutch regime sought its strength in the link between modern reason and Indonesian feudalism, and ultimately became the first example of fascism in the world. This colonial fascism was there much earlier than the fascism of Hitler or Mussolini; long before Hitler built the concentration camps in Buchenwald or Belsen, Boven-Digoel already existed.[6]

With his reference to the Boven-Digul prison camp, Sjahrir was speaking from personal experience: he had been exiled there by the Dutch colonial administration. Hatta and Sukarno had also been sentenced to exile.

It is evident from the words of Hatta, Sukarno and Sjahrir that they would not have accepted the return of Dutch or Japanese rule. In chapter 1 we described how, shortly after the proclamation of Indonesian independence, violence had broken out against Indo-Europeans and Dutch. There were also casualties among other population groups. This chapter examines the historical background to the violence after 17 August 1945. By reflecting further on the role of violence under Dutch rule, it becomes clear that an Indonesian 'potential for violence' had been building under the Dutch colonial regime, a process that was further stimulated by the Japanese occupation. This chapter is based on a literature review, and does not offer a new analysis or explanation for the violence during the Dutch or Japanese periods. First, we shall consider violence against the background of the colonial regime, and then the violence during the Japanese occupation.

The late colonial Indies

For the Netherlands as a colonial ruler, the establishment and – in particular – the preservation of power in the archipelago was far from straightforward. The geography of Indonesia alone made the territory difficult to occupy: the archipelago consists of over 13,000 islands and islets, scattered over a region equal in size to the area stretching from Ireland to the Urals.[7] For centuries there was trade in the archipelago between the local inhabitants and Europeans, with the earliest traders founding settlements with limited scope and influence. Even at that time, though, Europeans took territory from the local population, who resisted and challenged the authority of the external invaders. With reference to the period 1510-1970, historian and journalist Piet Hagen has described more than 500 military confrontations between colonial traders, companies, powers and sultanates, and kingdoms and other rulers in the archipelago. He has drawn up a 30-page chronology of resistance, uprisings and war by Indonesian armies, armed groups, sultanates, and religious and political movements against colonial troops of diverse origin, including the Portuguese, Spanish and Dutch.[8] The largest and fiercest confrontations took place between the Dutch and Indonesians.[9] This struggle was not limited to conflicts between colonial and anti-colonial forces; there was also significant infighting between Indonesian dynasties.

Although in early October 1945, Vice-President Muhammad Hatta spoke of more than three centuries of oppression by the Dutch, at the time of the Republic of the Seven United Netherlands, Dutch influence was concentrated in fragmented power centres that were spread across the islands.[10] After 1800, the Netherlands gradually established an overarching central authority in the archipelago; and with the exception of the war in Aceh, the armed struggle between the Netherlands and Indonesia ceased shortly after 1900. The almost impossible design of the Dutch colonial project in Indonesia becomes evident when we compare the population numbers involved. The Dutch, at that time referred to as 'Europeans', made up an absolute minority of the total population. In 1930, the Dutch East Indies was home to 60 million Indonesians and 240,000 Europeans, less than half a percent of the population. In other words, every Dutch person would have encountered Indonesians, but far from every Indonesian would have met a Dutch person. Considering how it was possible for a European power with a relatively small number of officials, soldiers and merchants to oppress tens of millions of Indonesians for so long, Hagen's answer is unequivocal: through a colonial system that was based on military, economic and administrative repression.[11] It was a system that penetrated every aspect of life and from which there was no escape. The use of the inhabitants of the archipelago, including members of local dynasties, was crucial in this regard. A number of the cornerstones of the system are discussed below.

As a colony, the Dutch East Indies was a society based on a hierarchical classification in terms of 'race'. Although race is neither a natural nor a biological entity, but a construction that is both historical and temporal, thinking in terms of 'race' as an administrative and legal category, together with categories such as gender, sexuality, class, age, health and so forth, acquired great significance in daily colonial practice. Race was crucial because it was the main criterion for dividing society into superiors, inferiors and the most inferior of all.[12] At the same time, it was by no means all-encompassing: new racial dividing-lines and categories were created over time.

In the late colonial period, around 1900, the group of 'Europeans' included all those who were of European origin (that is to say, born in and beyond

Europe) and all Indo-Europeans who were recognized by their European fathers, as well as Japanese and a select group of Indonesians, Chinese and Arabs who were 'equal to Europeans'. This motley group of 'Europeans' occupied the highest rung of the social ladder, and as such formed a social and legal category. According to the last census to be conducted in the Dutch East Indies in 1930, this European population group, as mentioned above, consisted of ca. 240,000 people.[13] As we noted, at 0.4 per cent of the total population of the colony, they were by far in the minority. Moreover, as indicated above, this group was ethnically heterogeneous and thus anything but exclusively 'ethnic European' in appearance: they included 137,000 Indo-Europeans (57 per cent) with both Dutch and Indonesian parents and grandparents, and 86,500 Europeans (36 per cent) of non-mixed descent. The remaining 7 per cent of Europeans consisted of other European nationalities and 'European foreigners [*Europese Vreemdelingen*]' (non-Dutch Europeans, Americans, Australians, Africans, Japanese and other Asians who were considered equal to Europeans), as well as Indonesians, Chinese and Arabs who were considered 'equal to Europeans'.[14] As no census was held in the Dutch East Indies after 1930, we can only estimate the number of inhabitants on the eve of the Second World War. It is usually said that in 1940, 250,000-300,000 Europeans lived alongside a population of more than 60 million Indonesians.[15]

SUPERIORS, INFERIORS AND THE MOST INFERIOR

In the colonial hierarchy, the category of 'Foreign Orientals [*Vreemde Oosterlingen*]', which consisted of Chinese and Arabs, was included in the European population group; Chinese and Arabs were the 'inferiors'. In 1930, this category consisted of ca. 1.2 million Chinese and 71,000 Arabs, ca. 2 per cent of the total population of the Dutch East Indies.[16] Most Chinese lived on Java, mainly in the north-western part of the island around the capital, Jakarta, and other urban areas. It is estimated that there were around 1.5 million Chinese in 1945, 700,000 of whom lived on Java, as well as Chinese communities in Bangka, Belitung, Riau and West Kalimantan. There were 150,000 Chinese living in Jakarta, an estimated total of 844,000 inhabitants.[17] Half of the Chinese on Java were born in Indonesia; they were classed as *peranakan* Chinese. Most of them spoke Javanese or another local language; members of the *peranakan* elite spoke Dutch. Chinese who were born in China, known as *totok* Chinese, retained Chinese as their spoken language.

On the bottom rung of the social ladder were the 'Natives [*Inlanders*]', a derogatory colonial term for Indonesians.[18] From a colonial-hierarchical perspective, they were the 'most inferior', but in numerical terms they formed by far the majority of the population of the Dutch East Indies, namely 60 million or 97.6 per cent of the whole.[19] Moreover, the catch-all term 'Natives' concealed the fact that the Indonesian population was extremely heterogeneous and contained more than 300 ethnic groups. There were also major differences within this group: aristocratic members of the numerous dynasties in the archipelago were extremely wealthy, and could be richer than many Europeans and Indo-Europeans. No matter how wealthy they were, however, the term 'Foreign Oriental' (who was actually a 'foreigner' in the archipelago?) and the disparaging term 'Native' reflect the Eurocentrism and sense of superiority with which Dutch and Indo-Dutch colonialists viewed and treated these communities.

Based on the racial constructions outlined above, a colonial reality was created that had real-life consequences, including a dual judicial system: a legal system for Europeans and a legal system for Indonesians, the latter based on traditional *adat* law. This dual system legitimized the legal inequality between European individuals with the status of citizens on the one hand, and Indonesian subjects on the other. The education system was also organized along ethnic lines: the early twentieth century, for example, saw the establishment of the European Elementary School (Europeesche Lagere School, ELS), the Dutch School for Natives (Hollandsch-Inlandsche School, HIS) and the Dutch Chinese School (Hollandsch-Chineesche School, HCS) for primary education. Bapak Hartawan, the son of the aristocratic Bapak Raden Wiryowinoto and Ibu Raden Ismirah, recalls how he went to primary school in Probolinggo:

> I myself went to the Dutch School for Natives [HIS] [...] Not everyone was given access to the HIS. In the past, during the Dutch period, there was discrimination. If you were one of the common folk, you couldn't attend the HIS; only the nobility had access and those who were on a par with the Dutch.[20]

That the division into population groups was not based on 'natural' or 'biological' categories, but on racial constructions, is shown by the fact that it was possible to 'switch' from one group to another. Indonesians who were registered in the colonial classification as 'Natives', as well as Chinese registered as 'Foreign Orientals', could apply for 'European equivalence'; to be eligible, they had to demonstrate their European orientation, for example by having European family origins or a European education. If the government approved a request for European equivalence, its decision was published in the official gazette, the *Staatsblad van Nederlands-Indië*. New Europeans were thus also known as '*Staatsblad* Europeans', which had derogatory connotations.

Especially for those from outside the archipelago who were not familiar with such a motley population, the great variety of population groups could create confusion. The memoirs of soldier C. van Reijnoudt, who served as a conscript in the Z Brigade on Sumatra in October 1946, reveal how the diversity of the population and the multitude of political alliances caused great uncertainty:

> You can't make head or tail of the races here: there are Indo-Chinese, Chinese, Bataks, Acehnese, Javanese, and goodness knows what else. What's more, there are different political groups: for example, the K.N.I.L., which mainly consists of Ambonese, as well as Acehnese, Javanese, Indo-Europeans, Chinese. Then there's the T.R.I. (Tentara Republik Indonesia); these parties apparently cooperate with us (this supposedly does not apply to the K.N.I.L.). Opponents: *rampokkers* [raiders], *Permudas* [sic], communist Chinese and so on. In short: you simply can't make it out.[21]

For those who were born and raised in the archipelago under the colonial regime, the unusually diverse population may have been familiar, but it was not necessarily acceptable, given their often subordinate position in society. Historian Sudjarwo concluded that the social stratification was tantamount to oppression:

> One major cause was the colonial oppression that found its source in Jakarta. The Dutch colonial rule had created a political constellation which resulted in social stratification with the Europeans being the most privileged of all social clusters, followed by the foreign eastern ethnic groups (Indians, Arab, and Chinese), while the indigenous were put at the bottommost of the social structure and were deprived of their rights. While this stratification created extreme difficulties for the indigenous to move both vertically and horizontally, this social

structuring gave the very convenience for the Dutch government to secure their colonial interests.[22]

COLONIAL VIOLENCE

Historian Henk Schulte Nordholt has identified two waves of Dutch violence in the Indonesian archipelago. The first took place at the time of the Dutch East India Company (Verenigde Oostindische Compagnie, VOC) in the late seventeenth century; the second took place in the period between 1871 and 1910, at the time of the Aceh War (1873-1912). At that time, colonial troops, especially the Korps Marechaussee (military police), killed more than 75,000 people from Aceh, ca. 13 per cent of the population.[23] Schulte Nordholt characterizes the colonial government as a regime based on fear, something that continued to resonate in the experiences and memories of Indonesians until the end of the colonial period.[24] Historian Petra Groen concurs with this characterization, and adds that the Aceh War was preceded by numerous colonial wars, expeditions and campaigns, including the Java War (1825-1830), which was extremely violent.[25] This situation was also acknowledged by the Dutch government: a ministerial commission from 1852 was based on the principle that in the Dutch East Indies, one 'should always consider oneself in a state of war'.[26] According to Hagen, the Dutch government established an extensive system of economic, fiscal, administrative and judicial measures to force the population into obedience:

> Monopolism, land expropriation, forced labour, requisitioning, segregation and apartheid, language and education policy, police supervision, restrictions of civil liberties, prison sentences, exile and death sentences.[27]

Historian Remco Raben makes a very rough estimate that from the seventeenth century onwards, the Dutch colonial regime cost the lives of between 600,000 and 1 million people in the Dutch East Indies.[28] According to him, the establishment and exercise of colonial authority went hand in hand with the use of mass violence. This not only included murder, but also the use of coercion (exile and imprisonment) and deprivation of resources (food and medication). Raben describes these as the 'standard ingredients of Dutch expansion in the archipelago, from the beginning to the end'.[29] He also points out that violence was more likely to acquire an extreme character in a colonial setting. According to him, a number of factors that were specific to the colonial situation contributed to the fact that violence in the colonies was used earlier, more quickly and on a larger scale.

First, there is the continuity in the exercise of violence in a colonial context. After all, a foreign oppressor almost always used violence in order to gain a foothold in a territory, and to establish and maintain their power. Second, because the establishment of power was accompanied by violence from the outset, a foreign oppressor could follow a long learning curve in waging colonial wars. Third, the new authority deployed a colonial army, consisting largely of personnel from the subjugated population. Due to the frequent shortages of manpower and the fear of ending up in a guerrilla war, a colonial army was more likely to resort to harsh measures. Fourth, a colonial army was more likely to deviate from norms and protocols designed to prevent excessive violence, because prevention, punishment and control mechanisms in a colony were less developed and less effective than in the metropole. Fifth, the loss of Indonesian soldiers in a colonial army such as the KNIL weighed less heavily than the loss of European or Indo-European soldiers. Rabens concludes that violence, which was inherent to a colonial system, was more likely to have fatal consequences in a colony than in the metropole, not only for the military, but also for colonized civilians.[30]

This is not to say, however, that there was no violence in Indonesian society prior to the arrival of colonial powers. Before the Europeans set foot ashore, Indonesians used violence to settle their internal conflicts. Java, Sumatra and Sulawesi were structured such that royal dynasties ruled their subjects with a heavy hand and fought wars with their rivals.[31] Banditry was also a feature of these societies, such as the Javanese *djagos* – literally 'bantams' – who often operated in gangs.[32]

Local support

Another pillar supporting colonial systems was the involvement, and thus in a certain sense the complicity, of the local population in the implementation of the extensive system of rules for exercising control in the colony.[33] The above-mentioned dual legal system in the Dutch East Indies can be viewed as a weapon in the hands of a colonial power.[34] But the colonial regime also used other organizational structures, such as the deployment of local residents in the colonial administration, the police force and the army, as well as in missionary work.[35] How did this system emerge in practice? From the nineteenth century, the Dutch East Indies was divided into residencies, each led by a European resident who represented the colonial authority. The resident was assisted on Java by an Indonesian regent, who was in charge of the Indonesian population. The resident and the regent collaborated closely to govern a residency. The members of the Indonesian aristocracy and royal dynasties were eligible for administrative positions such as these, although they remained subordinate to Europeans. Furthermore, Indonesians and Indo-Europeans with higher (read: European) education held roles in the colonial domestic administration. A crucial factor in this was their orientation towards the Netherlands and Europe, which they had acquired through schooling or – in the case of Indo-Europeans – inherited through their Dutch-Indonesian parents or grandparents.

As well as the colonial administration, the colonial army was an important occupational group for Indonesians. The KNIL recruited Europeans, Indo-Europeans and Indonesians. From the Indonesian population, mainly men of Javanese, Moluccan and Menadonese (sometimes collectively described as 'Ambonese') and Timorese origin served as professional soldiers in the KNIL. Moluccans were traditionally oriented towards the Netherlands, because the island of Ambon was incorporated early in the seventeenth century by the VOC, after which missionaries converted a large part of the Ambonese population to the Protestant faith. Career opportunities for Indonesians were usually limited to the lower ranks; an Indonesian officer was an exception to the rule. This did not apply to Indo-Europeans, though, who formed no exception in the officer corps. A few managed to rise to the rank of general. Once more, a numerical comparison speaks volumes: the KNIL was a professional colonial army that, despite being built on a European and Indo-European cadre of officers and non-commissioned officers, overwhelmingly consisted of Indonesians, mercenaries and forced labour. In 1929, the KNIL had ca. 38,500 professional soldiers, 43 per cent of whom were Javanese, 20 per cent European and Indo-European, 14 per cent Menadonese, 11 per cent 'Ambonese' (Moluccans), 4 per cent Sundanese, and 3 per cent Timorese and other groups.[36] Although the colonial army command tried to prevent Javanese from being deployed against Javanese or Moluccans against Moluccans, this could happen. Colonial wars thus also involved fighting between Indonesians themselves.

This latter point underlines the crux of the colonial regime: the Dutch benefitted from using various local population groups in the colonial system, and these groups thereby helped to perpetuate the unequal power relations. Hagen also identifies a mechanism whereby the colonial regime

KNIL soldiers of various origin, probably from the 10th Infantry Battalion, return from fighting the Japanese on South Sumatra, February 1942. Source: NIMH

made high-ranking members of the Indonesian elite responsible for the policy, and thus for the perpetuation of colonial structures: 'By making rulers complicit, a foreign power could both maintain and simultaneously camouflage its authority.'[37] Thus, the Dutch not only involved Indonesians in the colonial system coercively, but also 'voluntarily', because this cooperation earned Indonesians prestige or strengthened their power position – which in some cases was aristocratic-elitist, but always subordinate to the Dutch. In the colonial army, it was sometimes merely a question of a higher salary plus a uniform. In short, the colonial regime consisted of a complex of relations and (coercive) cooperation between Europeans and Indonesians, with Indo-Europeans, Chinese and Arabs in between. It was not simply a matter of oppressors versus the oppressed. The use of Indonesian officials in the colonial regime and soldiers in the colonial army created the seedbed for much of the intra-Indonesian violence in the first phase of the Indonesian Revolution. It also backfired, because it was no longer possible to distinguish friend from foe. In the words of the historian Riyadi Gunawan:

After the Proclamation of Independence, our society was painted with agitation, a situation which required excellent orators in order to foster the strong spirits in the Revolution, and to direct hatreds against the colonizers, their accomplices, even though later it backfired as friends and foes could no longer be differentiated.[38]

THE THREAT OF VIOLENCE

Something that makes the study of colonial violence particularly complex is the observation that when it comes to the exercise of power, given the colonial structure of the Dutch East Indies, it is impossible to draw a clear and sharp dividing line between victims on the one hand and perpetrators on the other. That is because the colonial regime relied both on the use or threat of violence against Indonesians (extreme or otherwise), and on the systematic cooperation of Indonesians in that same colonial regime. This collaboration with Indonesians from various social classes was essential for the success of the Dutch colonial project, and had the additional effect of making these people complicit within it.

The Dutch East Indies was based on a fundamentally unequal social structure. The Dutch authorities could actively enforce and protect this hierarchy through the constant threat of so-called police military violence. The colonial state established a layer of controlling institutions between the regime and society, such as the colonial army, the Political Intelligence Service (Politieke Inlichtingendienst, PID) and the colonial police. Historian Marieke Bloembergen has pointed out that this left the modern colonial regime in a quandary.[39] The regime was strong because it could organize and deploy a violent instrument such as the KNIL to counter threats to Dutch authority, but the actual use of force by the colonial authorities simultaneously weakened them, because this violence highlighted the resistance of the Indonesian population to the regime and thereby eroded its legitimacy. This insight was reflected in practice. As well as the colonial army, around 1920 a modern police force was created, after some far-reaching reorganizations in which the old principle of the preponderance of force was supplemented by new principles: the pursuit of cooperation with the population and forbearance, as far as possible, from using violence against them. When we consider the staffing of the police, the racial and numerical ratios again speak volumes: the size of the entire police force was limited in any case. In 1931, the police force had more than 54,000 men of both European and Indo-European and Indonesian origin. Of these, 32,000 worked outside Java, in a population of ca. 60 million Indonesians.[40] The threat posed by the whole colonial apparatus of violence was very significant, yet the actual deployment of the police was limited.

The principles that lay behind the reorganization of the colonial police force were entirely in line with the times. The period from 1901 saw the development and manifestation of the Dutch regime's so-called Ethical Policy. This process unfolded simultaneously and in parallel with Indonesian nationalism as a political movement. The term 'Ethical Policy' reflected the conviction that the Dutch regime was responsible for the archipelago, and that the Dutch should promote the development of the Indonesian population based on the Dutch model, including through education and the construction of infrastructure such as bridges, roads and railways. The fact that this new policy was called the 'Ethical Policy', writes historian Elsbeth Locher-Scholten, is an indication, 'in addition to the usual arrogance [...] of a deep-rooted sense of white superiority'.[41] Moreover, the Ethical Policy in no way excluded the expansion of Dutch authority through military violence outside Java; on the contrary.

After the military subjugation of the archipelago was complete in the early twentieth century, the KNIL was certainly not redundant, either. Although from 1920 the police were given the leading role in the maintenance of order, in line with the ideals of the Ethical Policy of a modern, civilized state, the colonial authorities deployed the KNIL during the communist uprisings of 1926 (West Java) and 1928 (West Sumatra). The KNIL used considerable force in the process, with the government keen to show that there were limits to the Ethical Policy if colonial authority were seriously threatened.[42]

INDONESIAN NATIONALISM

The colonial administration tried to accommodate Indonesian nationalism by allowing people to participate in (Dutch-founded) organizations that promised more political say. One of them was the Volksraad ('people's council'), which was established by the Indies government in 1918 to create more space for participation in the colonial regime. The Volksraad, which until 1935 was a council composed exclusively of men, consisted of 60 partly elected and partly appointed members: 30 of Indonesian origin, 25 of Dutch, and five of Arab and Chinese origin. As the Volksraad had only an advisory role, Indonesians could not expect this body to achieve real change in the colonial system. From 1900, Indonesians thus became active in organizations that were separate from and critical of the colonial government. They organized meetings at which Indonesian nationalism developed further. This development coincided with the Ethical Policy.

In 1912, Sarekat Islam (SI, the Islamic Union) was founded in Surakarta. The organization, which was originally a union for batik-sellers, grew rapidly. In 1918, the year in which the SI's programme promoted full Indonesian independence, it had 2 million members. Two years later, non-Islamic members of the SI with Marxist leanings founded the Partai Komunis Indonesia (PKI).[43] The political call by the SI and the PKI for Indonesian independence was a direct challenge to Dutch authority. The activities of three young men stood out: Sukarno, who would become the first president of the Republic of Indonesia on 17 August 1945; Muhammad Hatta, the first vice-president; and Sutan Sjahrir, the first prime minister of Indonesia. They had different views on the way in which Indonesian independence should be achieved. Hatta and Sjahrir, who were both from West Sumatra and had studied in the Netherlands, were in favour of developing an Indonesian framework organization, which they believed would be more resistant to Dutch repression.[44] Sukarno, on the other hand, who was of Javanese-Balinese descent and had trained at the technical college in Bandung, strove to mobilize the population through a mass organization in the struggle for independence. To this end, in 1927 Sukarno founded the Partai National Indonesia (PNI – Indonesian National Party), whilst Hatta and Sjahrir became the leaders of a party that split from it, the Pendidikan Nasional Indonesia (PNI – Indonesian National Education).

In 1933, the Netherlands banned both organizations and decided to exile Sukarno, Hatta and Sjahrir. Sukarno was banished to Ende on the island of Flores; this was followed in 1938 by a transfer to Bengkulu on Sumatra. In January 1935, Hatta and Sjahrir were interned in Boven-Digul, a prison camp run by the Dutch government between 1926 and 1942 at the headwaters of the Digul River in southern Papua. Located in the jungle, Boven-Digul was an inhospitable place and malaria was a ubiquitous presence. Others who were seen as a threat to the Dutch regime, such as Indonesian officials, intellectuals and communists, also ended up in exile in Boven-Digul. In late 1935, Hatta and Sjahrir were transferred to Banda Neira, the main island in the small Banda archipelago in the southern Moluccas. The Japanese invasion of Indonesia in 1941 ended their exile and created new opportunities for these three leaders of Indonesian nationalism.[45]

The Turnaround

With Japan's attack on the Dutch East Indies in December 1941, the overseas part of the Kingdom of the Netherlands in 'the East' was drawn into the Second World War. Until then, the war in Asia had been limited to the Japanese war against China and armed border conflicts between Japan and the Soviet Union. With the Japanese offensive in December 1941, the Eastern and Western fronts were joined up and the war became truly global for the first time. More than a year earlier, on 27 September 1940, the Axis powers had signed the Tripartite Pact, whereby Germany and Italy recognized Japan's leadership in the establishment of a 'New Order in Greater East Asia'. For Japan, which was poor in mineral and other resources, the shortage of sufficient raw materials was a key factor in the decision to go on the attack.[46] The shortage had become more acute after the US, together with the Dutch East Indies, had responded to Japan's actions in China by freezing Japanese currency in the US and imposing an oil boycott, which the US later extended to other products, including steel. After negotiations between Japan and the US failed, Japan attacked the US Navy in Pearl Harbor on 7 December 1941. One day later, Japan declared war on the United States and Great Britain. On the same day, the Netherlands delivered its declaration of war to the Japanese government. Japan had an interest in the plentiful mineral resources in the Dutch East Indies, and in December 1941 the oil-rich Kalimantan was the first Japanese target. On 11 January 1942, this was followed by a Japanese attack on North Sulawesi. The Second World War in the Dutch East Indies heralded the beginning of the end for the colony. The colonial hierarchy was no longer self-evident; in fact, it had changed radically. Europeans were no longer calling the shots over Asians. For many Europeans, this was an unprecedented turnaround.

For most Indonesians, whether Europeans or Asians were in charge made little difference in practice: the war that Japan waged in Southeast Asia was, according to historian Ken'ichi Goto 'not a war for liberating colonies but rather for reorganizing colonies'.[47] However, Japanese propaganda presented the conquest of countries in Southeast Asia by the Japanese army as part of a campaign to liberate the colonies from Western tyranny. The Japanese-occupied areas would form part of the Greater East Asia Co-Prosperity Sphere: a political, economic, military and cultural order led by Japan. As mentioned above, the need to obtain raw materials, including for warfare, was high on the Japanese agenda in the conquest. The Dutch East Indies, especially Sumatra, was very interesting in that respect, due to the profusion of bauxite, rubber, tin and, above all, oil. Japanese policy during the Pacific War was dominated by the extraction of raw materials and the use of manpower, crucial factors for waging war.[48]

Loss of prestige

The hierarchical structure that had determined pre-war society largely remained intact during the Japanese occupation, with one essential difference: the Japanese replaced the Dutch at the top. The imperial army of Japan, with its rapid victories over the KNIL in December 1941 (Kalimantan), January 1942 (North Sulawesi, Ambon, Bali and Timor) and March 1942 (Java), made a great impression on the Indonesian population, delivering a crushing blow to the prestige of the colonial authorities.[49] During the retreat of the KNIL after the Japanse invasion, Indonesians revolted in a number of places on Java, Sumatra and North Sulawesi. There was an outbreak of *perampokan*: looting of shops, homes and offices that were mainly owned by Dutch and Chinese.[50]

For some, the Dutch colonizers' loss of prestige had an irreversible effect. It made an indelible impression on Adam Malik, vice-president of Indonesia between 1978 and 1983, and 25 years old when the Japanese invaded:

> When they controlled the whole colony from their capital in Batavia [Jakarta], the Dutch were proud, arrogant and cold-hearted. But in Cilacap I saw Dutchmen crawling in the garbage begging for mercy before sword-carrying Japanese. That scene from the collapse of the Dutch empire in the Dutch East Indies is forever imprinted on my mind.[51]

Many Indonesians were initially enthusiastic about the arrival of the Japanese; in many places, the troops were welcomed by the local population. Kenji Oe, who took part in the invasion of East Java as a Japanese soldier, recalled:

> It seemed as if when they saw us and that we have the same skin colour and really resemble them, they became overjoyed and welcomed us with the sense that it was just as if their relatives had come to rescue them.[52]

Indonesians helped Japanese soldiers by acting as guides and offering them food. They also refused to keep obeying the orders of the Dutch, who wanted them to destroy key war materials and infrastructure, such as bridges. With the arrival of the Japanese, local residents who had cooperated with the colonial regime, such as Indonesian civil servants, Indo-Europeans and Chinese, found themselves in a precarious situation. Not only did the Japanese view them as suspicious because they had collaborated with the colonial order, but they also faced resentment from Indonesians.

Japanese leadership

As Japan wanted to eradicate European and Western influence in Asia, it proceeded to isolate the European community and separate Europeans from Indonesians. Outside Java, this also applied to Indo-Europeans by default. The term 'isolation' can be taken literally: the Dutch lost their privileged position and were separated from the Indonesian population by the Japanese by means of internment. In the beginning, General Hitoshi Imamura only intended to intern civil servants, but due to the many anti-Japanese plots among Europeans, he decided to go ahead with a general internment of the entire European population. The Dutch administrative elite on Java, which consisted of civil servants and businessmen, were the first to be interned in March 1942. Japan forced them to move to city districts and buildings that were known as 'protected neighbourhoods'. Subsequently, 100,000 of the ca. 300,000 Europeans and Indo-Europeans – women, men and children – were interned in civilian camps. Around 83,000 of them were interned in camps on Java and 17,000 in camps on Sumatra, Kalimantan, Sulawesi, Australian New Guinea/Papua New Guinea, Ambon, Bali, Lombok, Sumbawa, Sumba, Flores, Timor and other islands in the Pacific. Furthermore, the Japanese took ca. 40,000 European and 25,000 Indonesian men prisoner of war; they ended up in prisoner of war camps. As the internees were isolated for years, they had no insight into what was happening in Indonesian society outside the camps during the occupation.[53]

On the grounds of their Indonesian parentage or grandparentage, in principle the Japanese occupier viewed Indo-Europeans as Asians who, once convinced of Japanese leadership in the Asian world, could be used, just like other Indonesians, in the building of the Greater East Asia Co-Prosperity Sphere. As a result, few Indo-Europeans on Java ended up in the civilian camps; around 160,000 Indo-Europeans spent the Japanese occupation outside the camps. Life outside the camps was by no means free though; 'outlawed' would be a more appropriate characterization, because the Japanese were also in control outside the camps. On the islands beyond Java, a different policy was in place: Indo-Europeans *were* interned there. There were fewer of them than on Java, and for that reason it was logistically easier for the occupying forces to house them in camps. In mid-June 1942, the internment of European men aged between 17 and 60 on Java was complete. They were followed by European women and children and European men aged over 60 who had remained outside the camps. It took until mid-1943 for the whole operation on Java to be completed. A total of 225 civilian internment camps were located in the archipelago: in huts, prisons, city districts, schools, barracks, bivouacs, forts, hospitals, orphanages, hotels, factories, monasteries, cinemas, stables, warehouses, churches and guesthouses.[54]

Not only did the Dutch (and beyond Java, Indo-Europeans) literally disappear from society, but their symbolic presence in Indonesian society was also erased. Statues and monuments dedicated to colonial heroes, such as Governor General Johannes van Heutsz and VOC merchant and governor general Jan Pieterszoon Coen, were removed. The Japanese administration banned Dutch inscriptions on shops, restaurants and hotels, as well as the use of the Dutch language in correspondence and education.[55] It became mandatory to display the Japanese flag, to use the Japanese calendar (2602=1942), and to switch to Japanese time, which meant that the clock on Java was put forward one and a half hours. Dutch influence in the colony made way for the 'Japanization' of Indonesian society.

'THE GREATER EAST ASIA CO-PROSPERITY SPHERE'

In terms of the exercise of power, much of what had been common in the pre-war Dutch East Indies also applied during the Japanese occupation. As we have seen, the new ruler, General Imamura, moved into the official residence of the governor general in Jakarta. As the Japanese commander, he continued to use the existing colonial infrastructure and symbolism. Institutions built by the Dutch, such as the police, were left in place by the Japanese occupier. One should add that this was – and is – by no means unusual in cases of occupation and regime change. In order to maintain public order in many places, the Japanese occupying forces ordered domestic officials and the European police – albeit officially disarmed – to remain temporarily in their posts, so as to facilitate a smooth transfer of power.[56] This 'smooth transition' served a specific purpose, however: as Japan wanted to obtain strategic resources in the conquered areas of Southeast Asia as quickly as possible without upsetting the local situation too much, Tokyo had instructed the occupying military forces to make maximum use of the existing administrative apparatus.⁵⁷ To gather intelligence, the Japanese security services relied on the expertise and networks of the police and intelligence services from the Dutch colonial era. Most members of the Political Intelligence Service (Politieke Inlichtingendienst, PID) were Indonesians. In addition, the Kempeitai (Japanese military police) had an extensive network of informants from all groups and levels in society. It is estimated that 80 per cent of informants were Indonesian, 10 per cent were Chinese, and 10 per cent European and Indo-European.⁵⁸

The Japanese occupying forces promoted a pan-Asian ideal: an 'Asian liberation' with an 'Asia for Asians', living in a 'Greater East Asia Co-Prosperity Sphere'. Japan acted as though it were liberating the other colonized countries in Southeast Asia from Western tyranny. In practice, however, Japan imposed a political, economic, cultural and military order on the occupied countries in which Japanese interests, not the interests of the native population, were paramount. When Sukarno paid a visit to Japan in December 1943, where he met Kumakichi Harada, commander of the 16th Army, and Shinshichiro Kobuku, his chief of staff, the latter remarked:

> ...if the central government in Japan is like a grandfather, the local military government is like a father. A grandfather blindly indulges and spoils a grandchild, but the father has the responsibility to discipline the child, and thus the father will provide strict training and teaching for the child.⁵⁹

Kobuku was referring to the promises that Tokyo had made about early Indonesian independence. According to historian Ethan Mark, among the Japanese in Indonesia there could be:

> Colonial impatience and disdain with regard to native behaviour and practice. Here, the boundary between Greater Asian paternalism and colonial arrogance and superiority was all too often breached.⁶⁰

Mark argues that the 'Greater East Asia Co-Prosperity Sphere' was just a facade, although a minority of Japanese – and Indonesians – sincerely believed in it.⁶¹

Japan had divided the Dutch East Indies into three regions. Sumatra was under the command of the 25th Army, which consisted of ca. 70,000 soldiers. Java and Madura fell under the command of the 16th Army, which also had around 70,000 soldiers.⁶² Both armies were themselves under the command of the 7th Area Army, which had its headquarters in Singapore. The east of the Dutch East Indies, which consisted of Kalimantan, Sulawesi, the Moluccas, the small Sunda islands and Papua, was under the command of the Japanese navy.⁶³ In 1941, the Japanese army and the Japanese government had set three goals for the conquered territories: first, the restoration of public order; second, obtaining raw materials for national defence; and third, making Japanese troops self-sufficient.⁶⁴

The Indonesian wish to appoint more of their own administrators at the provincial level was not satisfied by the occupier. The four main cities on Java – namely, Jakarta, Bandung, Semarang and Surabaya – were given a Japanese mayor.⁶⁵ The office of resident, a position reserved for the Dutch in the colonial era, was also filled exclusively by Japanese – with two exceptions:

> The only exceptions were the two Sultans who remained, as under the Dutch, in charge of the two special royal districts of Surakarta and Jogjakarta in central Java.⁶⁶

Japan made partial use of the institutional infrastructure of the Dutch colonial administration, combined with institutions from the home country.⁶⁷

Nationalism

In contrast to the Dutch regime, Japan did give some scope to Indonesian nationalism, which gained more of a foothold on Java and Sumatra than in Eastern Indonesia. As no central policy guidelines were issued by Tokyo, the extent to which nationalism could develop in a certain area was partly dependent on local Japanese troops. Apart from that, the strength and the size of the Indonesian nationalist movement also differed in each region.

For Japan, the occupation of Sumatra, together with Kalimantan and Eastern Indonesia, was a high priority due to the oil and other raw materials that the country needed for the war industry. In addition, the island was of military-strategic importance, because Japan expected an Allied counterattack to begin on Sumatra (and the Malay Peninsula).⁶⁸ The 25th Army that ruled Sumatra was based in Bukittinggi, including the headquarters Gunshireibu and the civil service Gunseikanbu.⁶⁹ In the first phase of the Japanese occupation, the military administration on Sumatra was tolerant of the Indonesian language, the raising of the red-and-white flag, and the forming of nationalist organizations. After this first phase of full military rule, a period followed in which the course of the war worsened for Japan and a semi-military administration took over, eventually followed by an entirely civilian administration. These two successors took a less favourable approach to nationalism.[70]

As mentioned above, it was not the army, but the imperial Japanese navy that was responsible for Eastern Indonesia during the occupation: Kalimantan, Bali, Lombok, Sumbawa, Sumba, Flores, Timor, Sulawesi, Halmahera, the Sulu archipelago, Buru, Ambon, Seram and West Papua. This sparsely populated area was rich in mineral resources such as oil, nickel, mica and iron. The plan was for Eastern Indonesia, unlike Java and Sumatra, to become a permanent part of the Japanese empire; it would become a colonial possession, similar to Taiwan (since 1895) and Korea (since 1910). The colonial administration there was thus led by Japanese civil servants, who answered to the navy. More junior roles were for Indonesians with administrative experience. Indonesian nationalism had less scope there than on Java and Sumatra. In order to 'Japanize' Eastern Indonesia, the Japanese language was introduced and education was based on Japanese principles.[71] During the Japanese occupation, the people of Eastern Indonesia were also living on what was partly a military battlefield. There was bombing and fighting between Japanese and Allied forces, such as in East Timor in 1942-1943 and East Kalimantan in April-August 1945.[72]

Java, by contrast, was a lower priority for Japan. The occupier largely saw the island, with its 50 million inhabitants, as a supplier of manpower. Because the Japanese authorities realized that it would be impossible to suppress nationalist sentiment altogether, the leaders of the nationalist movement on Java, Sukarno and Hatta, enjoyed a degree of latitude that would have been impossible under the Dutch regime. In this way, the Japanese occupation helped to raise Indonesian political consciousness and spread nationalist sentiment yet further. If the nationalist movement before the war had been more or less monopolized by Western-educated intellectuals, during the Japanese occupation it developed in the direction of a mass movement, supported by Indonesians from almost all walks of life.[73]

The idea of a nation

Under Japanese rule, a number of measures were introduced that reinforced the idea of an Indonesian nation, history and social and political situation. The use of the Indonesian language in education, the media and government institutions facilitated contact with people from other parts of the archipelago. Through radio, posters, free film screenings and education, Indonesians came into contact with Japanese ideology, which also stirred up anti-colonial feeling.[74] Japan replaced the colonial press system, in which a wide range of newspapers had co-existed, with a system with a single newspaper for a particular (urban) community, such as *Asia Raja* for Jakarta and *Sinar Baroe* for Semarang. As a result, a much smaller number of dailies was published during the occupation, all linked to a Japanese publisher.[75] And even though Japan applied all kinds of restrictions during the occupation – for example, Indonesians were not permitted to use the red-and-white flag or sing the nationalist song *Indonesia Raya*, which would later become the national anthem, until September 1944 – Indonesia had more opportunities than ever to shape its national identity.[76]

The nationalists had varying views on the way in which the new state should be formed. For example, after the Japanese occupation, Sjahrir was sharply critical of Sukarno, who had collaborated with the Japanese occupiers, without specifically mentioning his name:

> our revolution [must] be led by revolutionary, democratic groups and not by nationalist groups, which once allowed themselves to be used as the servants of fascism, whether it was Dutch colonial or Japanese military fascism. [...] our own fascists, as the accomplices and tools of Japanese fascism, bear a heavy burden of guilt and have betrayed our struggle and our popular revolution.[77]

However, Sukarno enjoyed much more support among the Indonesian people than Sjahrir had hoped. In his principled and public rejection of collaboration with the Japanese regime, Sjahrir was an exception. Sukarno and Hatta sought reform of the social and political order that had taken shape under colonial rule, but gave priority to the defence of Indonesian independence and the building of the young nation. Radical nationalists, including many *pemuda* (youths), also wanted a social revolution, which would bring an end to the structure in which the Indonesian aristocracy had lorded it over their more humble compatriots. That desire for social reform was also fed by their experience with the Japanese, who promoted staff on the basis of skills and competences, instead of racial origin or (aristocratic) family descent. During the Japanese occupation, education and work experience played a greater role, as well as proficiency in the Japanese language and knowledge of Japanese culture, loyalty and courage. Whilst in the Dutch era administrative positions had automatically been granted to members of Indonesian royal dynasties, in the Japanese era commoners were appointed to these positions.

The school system also ceased to be a dual system under the Japanese occupation. In the Dutch period, there were separate schools with a Dutch curriculum for the Indonesian elite (the Dutch School for Natives or Hollandsch-Inlandsche School, HIS), and Indonesian village schools with fewer years of lower-quality education for pupils of non-aristocratic descent. The Japanese school system was unitary and based on a Japanese curriculum, with former HIS pupils sharing school benches with pupils from village schools. This, too, contributed to the emergence of a new form of leadership, in which a person's origins were no longer the deciding factor.

THE FOUNDING OF ORGANIZATIONS

The Japanese occupation saw the founding of organizations that were based on Japanese military principles and broadened the perspectives of Indonesians. There were large gatherings at various levels – residential, provincial and national – at which nationalists came into contact with Indonesians from different classes and regions. From April 1942, under the slogan of the development of the Greater East Asian Co-Prosperity Sphere, Japan began to set up various organizations. On Java, the Japanese propaganda service created the Gerakan Tiga-A ('3A Movement'): Japan as Asia Tjahaja, Asia Pelindoeng, Asia Pemimpim ('Light of Asia, Protector of Asia and Leader of Asia'). 'Light of Asia' was a reference to Japan's military victories; 'Protector of Asia', because Japan protected other countries in Asia like its children; and 'Leader of Asia', because Japan would educate and lead these Asian countries. At first, a range of social and political groups from the Indonesian social elite embraced this new movement; each saw opportunities to shape it in line with their own interests and gain influence with the Japanese command. The 3A Movement thus got off to a successful start. But the Japanese command was internally divided: the Kempeitai and the Japanese military distrusted the 3A Movement and viewed its meetings with suspicion. They saw the organization as a disguised independence movement that might seem pro-Japanese, but that could turn against Japan. Corruption and mutual conflicts between different Indonesian groups resulted in the eventual disbanding of the 3A Movement in late 1942.[78]

In early 1943, a movement was formed in which Japan managed to involve prominent nationalists, such as Sukarno and Hatta, among others:

Pusat Tenaga Rakjat ('Centre of the People's Power'), better known by the abbreviated name Putera. This organization focused exclusively on Indonesians; Chinese, Arabs and Indians were excluded.[79] The movement was also hampered by Japanese distrust of Indonesian nationalism, however. This prevented Putera from growing into a mass movement, and its leaders were only allowed to produce propaganda for Japanese purposes. When Putera was disbanded in February 1944, it became clear how limited the size of the movement had been: in the large cities, Putera had just ten branches.[80] According to historian Sudjarwo, Japan also repeatedly dissolved nationalist youth organizations if there were suspicions that they might harm Japanese interests.[81]

After their experiences with the '3A Movement' and Putera, the Japanese decided to take charge of two new mass paramilitary organizations that they founded in early 1943: Keibodan, a kind of auxiliary police or vigilante patrol (known in Sumatra as Bogodan) and Seinendan, a youth 'labour service'. In 1945, Keibodan had 1.3 million members and Seinendan 700,000. In total, around 2 million Indonesians, including youths, received paramilitary training on Java and were intensively exposed to Japanese ideas.[82] On Sumatra, the 25th Army founded the Giyugun, a youth organization in which the Japanese ideology of the Greater East Asian Co-Prosperity Sphere was combined with Indonesian nationalist ideas and tough military training. This paramilitary youth organization, similar to PETA on Java, which will be discussed further below, consisted of 7,000-9,000 young men. After the Japanese surrender, Giyugun officers formed the core of the militias of the Badan Keamanan Rakyat (People's Security Agency).[83]

In the meantime, the tide of the war had turned for the Japanese. On 4 June 1942, at the Battle of Midway, an atoll in the Pacific Ocean, the Japanese armed forces had suffered a heavy – and, in retrospect, decisive – defeat. Japan then decided to focus on defending the territory it had already won. The worse the war went for Japan, the more necessary and urgent it became to secure the cooperation of people in the occupied areas. In 1943, for this reason, Japan allowed armed groups to be created from the local population in the occupied territories.[84] As a result, on 3 October 1943, as well as Keibodan and Seinendan, the (Sukarela Tentara) Pembela Tanah Air – abbreviated as PETA, the Volunteer Defenders of the Homeland – was founded on Java, Madura and Bali, recruited entirely from Indonesians.[85] Yanagawa Motoshige, the founder of PETA, and many other Japanese PETA instructors, saw their pupils as the cadre of the future Indonesian army and trained them as freedom fighters. After the proclamation of Indonesian independence on 17 August 1945, PETA officers would indeed form the core of the Indonesian army. For example, Sudirman, the future commander-in-chief of the Indonesian armed forces, was the battalion commander of PETA in Banyumas on Java.[86] Battalion commanders were selected from local notables who enjoyed the respect of the local population, including religious scholars, government officials, doctors, teachers, and members of aristocratic and royal families.

PETA had strong local ties: after a short period of training in Bogor or Singaraja, PETA officers returned to their hometowns to form local battalions and recruit fighters. PETA also had its own hierarchy and was in theory only subordinate to the commander of the Japanese 16th Army. In this sense, PETA was different from the Heiho: Indonesians who were attached to the Japanese army as auxiliaries and mainly did labour. The Heiho were included in the Japanese military structure, however, and also received combat training from 1944.[87] The 16th Army on Java allocated around 40 per cent of its firearms to PETA, mainly weapons that had been taken over from the KNIL. At the end of the Japanese occupation, PETA on Java, Madura and Bali consisted of 69 regular battalions with 37,812 Indonesian men and a few guerrilla units with 922 men. PETA's main enemy was the former colonizer, the Netherlands, which was expected to try to follow in the footsteps of the Allied armies.[88] As well as a military objective, PETA had a political objective, in line with the Japanese attempts to persuade the Indonesian population to cooperate with Japan. For example, on 16 June 1943, the Japanese prime minister Kuniaki Koiso promised that the inhabitants of the Dutch East Indies would be able to participate in the political administration.

In addition to these military and paramilitary organizations, other armed and semi-armed local units were established, trained by PETA officers: in June 1944 the Gakutotai (Student Corps), and in August of that year the Barisan Pelopor (Vanguard Corps). In February 1945, Hizbullah (the Party of Allah) was founded, the armed branch of Masjumi and an umbrella organization for Islamic groups on Java. In 1945, this was followed by the founding of the Barisan Wanita (Women's Corps), an organization for secondary-school-age girls. Ethnic groups also formed their own armed organizations: for example, the Chinese founded the Kakyo Leibotai (Civic Guard of Overseas Chinese). Finally, the Japanese occupying forces gave military training to officials and other Indonesians in towns and in rural areas. By means of all of these organizations, the militarization of Indonesian society penetrated to village and neighbourhood level during the Japanese occupation.[89] In an interview in 2002, for example, *bapak* Hartawan looked back on this period thus:

> In the Japanese time we were trained. At that time, it was good for us to be physically and mentally trained by the Japanese. Of course, the mindset then was that we had to serve Japan. Each time, a flag ceremony had to be held. That flag ceremony was at a school, we had to face the direction of Tokyo, precisely towards Tokyo. We also had to sing the Japanese national anthem the whole time [...] that was all during the three years of occupation.[90]

The Japanese occupier also tried to maximize the involvement of the Indonesian population in other territories. In January 1945 on Java, the new organization Djawa Hokokai was founded, the successor to Putera, which had been disbanded in February 1944. The top positions were held by Japanese, whilst Indonesians – Sukarno, Hatta and two leaders of the Masjumi – were merely 'advisers'. The movement was not a great success, however, and exacerbated the differences between In-

Japanese recruitment poster for the Heiho, Indonesian auxiliaries. Translated from Indonesian, the poster reads: 'I am a Heiho with the navy. Come and join the defence of the homeland'. Source: NIOD.

donesian nationalists and the Javanese administrative aristocracy. The latter saw Djawa Hokokai as an undesirable meddler that was dominated by nationalists.[91]

As well as these more military-style organizations, in January 1944 Japan added a kind of neighbourhood watch system, known as the *tonarigumi*, also based on the Japanese model. Local Indonesian society was thereby divided into a neighbourhood system in which ten households – on Java, usually slightly more: ten to twenty households – were made collectively responsible for maintaining social order, collecting taxes and carrying out various community tasks, such as food distribution. But it did not end there: the neighbourhood units were also responsible for the maintenance of norms and values, as well as loyalty to the Japanese regime.[92] Finally, the *tonarigumi* were also used for the mobilization of semi-forced labour, the *romusha*.[93] The neighbourhood system was an influential disciplining system that shaped the daily lives of everyone outside the Japanese prisoner of war or civilian camps. According to the daily *Asia Raja* on 20 June 1944, there were 50,000 *tonarigumi* units on Java.[94]

The other side

As well as or in contrast to these developments, which furthered Indonesian emancipation and contributed significantly to the achievement of independence, as the war progressed the Indonesian population faced growing hunger, poverty and Japanese oppression. For example, in October 1943 Japan began to recruit *romusha*, Indonesian forced workers who had to carry out heavy labour. In theory, they were recruited on a voluntary basis via campaigns using speeches, posters and films, but in practice most of them were set to work under false pretences. The *romusha* were used on Java for the construction of aircraft hangars, sheds for tanks, weapons and troops, loading and unloading ships and trains, and digging tunnels and caves.

On Sumatra, most *romusha* worked as dock labourers. Japan also used them for the conversion of rubber plantations into market gardens for growing vegetables and the construction of roads and forts. On Kalimantan, *romusha* worked in the ports, as well as in petroleum plants and sawmills. On the Moluccas and in Eastern Indonesia, *romusha* not only built houses, forts, hangars and airstrips, but they also worked in factories producing soap, coconut oil, spices, clothing and other daily necessities.[95]

The population also suffered greatly under the Japanese rice policy. In order to feed both the *romusha* and the Japanese military, from 1943 the occupier obliged every residency to deliver a certain quantity of rice to the Japanese administration. As a result, the extensive pre-war rice trade between the residencies ground to a halt. The forced labour and the requisitioning of produce such as rice caused social disruption, large-scale famine, and shortages of all kinds. Bapak Hartawan recalled in an interview in 2002:

> During the Japanese time, we all had shortages and the situation was extremely difficult [...] especially when it came to foods such as coconut or rice [...] We had no fabric for clothes, so we made clothes out of used bedding, and from the pillowcase that remained we made dresses and trousers.[96]

It is estimated that 4 million people on Java were forced to work for the Japanese, under extremely harsh conditions.[97] This led to mass mortality: according to historian Ethan Mark, in the period 1943-1945, 3 million people died on Java alone.[98]

Whilst the *romusha* were mostly men – and occasionally children – from the Indonesian population who became mass victims of the Japanese regime, women, and the occasional man, faced a system of forced prostitution. The Japanese 'jugun ianfu', the Indonesian 'gadis-gadis penhibur' and the English 'comfort woman' are all euphemistic names for the victims of this system.[99] In occupied Indonesia, but also in Korea, Taiwan and Japan itself, the occupier established a system of military brothels to provide 'sexual services' to Japanese soldiers. Japan recruited women in the occupied territories for this purpose; some of them were already prostitutes or had been forced into prostitution by wartime circumstances, others were lured in under false pretences. Many of them, however, were simply forced to work in brothels. This was the fate of Indonesian, Indo-European and Dutch women, including women in the civilian internment camps. In Jakarta, there were four military brothels with a total of 30 women; there were also four military brothels in Semarang. On Sumatra, there was a military brothel in Padang; in Eastern Indonesia, there were brothels in Borneo/Kalimantan, Halmahera, Ambon and Timor, among other places.[100]

Tensions

The phenomena of *romusha* and *jugun ianfu* – the press-ganging of Indonesian men and women for forced labour and forced prostitution – cast their shadow in two ways. In the first place, the oppression of Indonesians by the Japanese created, to a greater or lesser degree, a seedbed for later Indonesian violence against the Japanese in the first phase of the Indonesian Revolution. Disappointment and resentment grew with regard to the earlier promises about Indonesian independence made by the Japanese. In the second place, the authority of local Indonesian administrators was eroded by their cooperation with Japanese policy.[101] It became increasingly clear that the Japanese were not the longed-for liberators from Dutch colonial rule, but were instead oppressors in a similar vein:

> The population of Java, however, was deprived from its wealth for the benefit of the Japanese. In this colonial constellation, the Japanese replaced the former privileged group, while the indigenous group remained in the lowermost position.[102]

The result was that the Indonesians increasingly detached themselves from the Japanese occupier. For example, Japanese influence on *pemuda*, the youngest generation of nationalists, waned. The attitude of *pemuda* was typical and could be summarized as:

> If one was outraged by the increasing misery of the population, disgusted by the complicity of the older politicians and officialdom in the face of the *romusha* and compulsory rice-delivery programmes, and cynical about the Japanese promise of independence, one was already in the underground.[103]

During the revolution, the *pemuda* did not belong to the regular armed forces. Having started out in street fights in the *kampongs*, they had a preference for radical action. 'Merdeka atau mati', was their slogan: freedom or death. They chose armed struggle and formed local, autonomous *laskars* (militias), separate from the older generation of nationalists in and around Jakarta, who were in favour of diplomacy.[104] The revolutionary basis of the *pemuda* movement – the roots of which can be traced back to pre-war anti-colonial student associations, such as Perhimpunan Indonesia (the Indonesian Association) and Pemuda Betawia (Young Batavia) – lay in the *asramas*, which traditionally provided Islamic education. In the cities, the *asramas* functioned as lodgings where *pemuda* could organize their resistance.[105]

Three important *pemuda* groups were active in Jakarta, all linked to an *asrama*.[106] The first was at the medical faculty at Prapatan 10; it consisted of an elite group of (often Dutch-speaking) Indonesian students around Sutan

Sjahrir. They had a more Western orientation; Sjahrir, for example, refused to cooperate with the Japanese on principle. The second group, the Asrama Angkatan Baru Indonesia (Asrama of the New Generation Indonesia) at Menteng 31, which had around 50 members, was more outspokenly anti-Dutch. As well as law students, it also included less educated youngsters. The third group, known as the Asrama Indonesia Merdeka (Independent Indonesia Asrama), was located at Kebon Sirih 80 and had around 50 active Indonesian students. The membership of and relations between supporters of an *asrama* were fluid: they were at most a quarter of an hour's walk from each other. Sukarno's bodyguard was composed of *pemuda* from all three *asramas*. *Asramas* were also founded in smaller towns.[107] According to the journalist and Asia scholar Frank Palmos, Surabaya was the birthplace of the nationalist youth movement, which spread outwards from the city during the Indonesian Revolution.[108]

Indonesian nationalists had competing visions of whether to cooperate with the Japanese administration, which came to the surface with violence:

> Many of the leaders who were considered to have misused their authority were condemned for their excessive collaboration with the Japanese. In extreme cases anger toward those leaders resulted in kidnapping, physical violence, and even murder.[109]

The phenomenon of intra-Indonesian violence was known as 'kedaulatan rakyat' (sovereignty of the people); in the Indonesian historiography, it is known as 'revolusi sosial' (social revolution).[110] Local administrators and even nationalist leaders were known as 'anjing Jepang' ('dogs of Japan') for cooperating with the policies of the Japanese occupier.[111]

Having fought a losing military battle since the naval Battle of Midway in June 1942, after the atomic bombs were dropped on Hiroshima and Nagasaki on 6 and 9 August 1945, Japan surrendered to the Allies. Emperor Hirohito announced the Japanese surrender in a radio broadcast on 15 August 1945. This news only formally reached the Japanese authorities on Java on 21 August, however, almost a week later.[112] Moreover, no fewer than six weeks passed between the reporting of the news of the Japanese surrender

Photos 1a-1f: Portraits of pemuda (Indonesian youths), photographed in a photo studio on Java. They carry a combination of Dutch and Japanese weapons and equipment. Source: KITLV

on Java and the arrival of the first Allied (British) troops on the island in late September 1945. In the meantime, Sukarno and Hatta, under pressure from *pemuda*, proclaimed the independent Republic of Indonesia on 17 August 1945.

The consequences of this step were mainly felt on Java and Sumatra, which still lay beyond the Allied troops' reach for the time being. The situation was different in Eastern Indonesia, where Australian troops were able to move in rapidly; in fact, the Allies had landed there long before the Japanese capitulation. American troops occupied Hollandia in New Guinea on 22 April 1944, Australian troops arrived in Morotai on the northern Moluccas on 15 September 1944, followed by Tarakan, Balikpapan and other places in eastern Kalimantan in May and July 1945. This led to a rapid restoration of Dutch authority. Following in the wake of the Australian troops was the Netherlands Indies Civil Administration (NICA), which was formally subordinate to the South East Asia Command (SEAC).[113] The NICA was set up by the Netherlands Indies government in exile in Brisbane, Australia, with the aim of rebuilding the administration in areas that had been liberated from the Japanese.

As the head of NICA, it was the task of Lieutenant Governor General Van Mook to restore the Dutch administration. NICA staff and KNIL troops were able to establish themselves relatively easily in Eastern Indonesia, despite Indonesian declarations of independence in at least three cities in East Kalimantan and Sulawesi. Indonesians who viewed NICA with suspicion often simply lacked the means of power to make things difficult for these officials.

In the long process of Indonesian state formation, the Japanese occupation can be seen as a 'point of no return'. Although it was inconceivable for by far the majority of the Dutch, for Indonesians, a return to the earlier colonial relations was unthinkable. The social disruption, the mobilization of Indonesians by both Japan and their own organizations, as well as the anti-Western propaganda at the end of the Japanese period and the many Japanese weapons that became available afterwards, contributed to the creation of a 'potential for violence' from below that erupted in late 1945. On Java, and to a lesser extent on Sumatra, older and younger generations wanted to right the wrongs done to Indonesian society under Dutch and Japanese rule, and were prepared to fight against the reoccupation of their country.

3.
Rising tensions

The chaotic days leading up to the Indonesian declaration of independence on 17 August 1945 revealed the tensions that had existed from the outset between the *pemuda* and older nationalists, such as Sukarno and Hatta. After the Japanese capitulation, the latter still wanted to declare independence through the Panitia Persiapan Kemerdekaan Indonesia (PPKI), the preparatory committee for independence that had been established shortly before the Japanese surrender. The committee represented the whole country, in their view, because it was composed of prominent individuals from different regions. They thereby hoped that the revolution would proceed peacefully, without any disorder or violent intervention by the Japanese.[1]

The *pemuda*, by contrast, thought that independence should be declared immediately after the capitulation by the Indonesians themselves, without any involvement from the Japanese authorities. They attached less importance to an orderly transfer of power; independence would be achieved by force if necessary. At a hastily organized meeting of the various *pemuda* groups in Jakarta on 15 August 1945, the *pemuda* decided to dispatch a delegation led by one of their leaders, Wikana, to convince Sukarno of their position.[2]

Emotions ran high that night. Wikana threatened Sukarno with bloodshed if the proclamation was not made that same evening: the *pemuda* would kill everyone they suspected of being pro-Dutch, such as the Moluccans. But Sukarno and Hatta, who later joined, refused to give in. They did not want to risk provoking the Japanese military authorities, and therefore wanted the proclamation to be made later through the PPKI. Wikana felt that he had not been taken seriously. When he reported back to the assembled *pemuda*, the attitude of the older leaders was interpreted as an insult. In response, the *pemuda* decided to abduct Sukarno and Hatta and take them to Rengasdengklok, while simultaneously preparing the capital for an uprising or coup, if necessary.[3]

The abduction of Hatta, Sukarno, the latter's wife and their nine-month-old son on the morning of 16 August 1945 was successful, but it did not have the desired effect. Sukarno and Hatta stuck to their guns and there was no uprising in the capital. The assurances from the Japanese Admiral Maeda Tadashi, that the Japanese would fully cooperate with the proclamation of

Parade to celebrate the proclamation of Indonesian independence, 17 August 1945.
Source: ANRI/IPPHOS

Indonesian independence, convinced the *pemuda* to call off their action and bring both leaders back.⁴ In the end, Sukarno, at a hastily convened ceremony in the grounds of his house on 17 August 1945, made the following proclamation: 'We the people of Indonesia hereby declare the independence of Indonesia. Matters concerning the transfer of power and other matters will be executed in an orderly manner and in the shortest possible time.' The *pemuda* found the moderate, factual text, drafted in consultation with Maeda's advisers, difficult to accept. They had wanted a more militant statement, but had lost the argument.⁵ The proclamation and subsequent developments meant that the Allies, upon their arrival in Indonesia six weeks later, were met by a completely different situation from the one they had anticipated.

The first weeks: the Dutch, the British and the Japanese

Although the Allies had won the Second World War, they were unable to dispatch troops immediately to the key islands in the Indonesian archipelago. During the war against Japan, Indonesia – with the exception of Sumatra, which was in the British area – had been in the American operational area, the South West Pacific Area Command of General Douglas MacArthur. When the Japanese surrendered on 15 August 1945, the area was immediately handed over to the British South East Asia Command of Vice Admiral Lord Louis Mountbatten, along with French Indochina south of latitude 16° north. This meant that Dutch troops also fell under the command of the British commander on the ground.⁶

The British agreed with the Australians that the latter would initially cover a large part of Eastern Indonesia. Before the Japanese surrender, part of this area had already been recaptured by Australian troops. Dutch units from NICA and the KNIL followed in their wake and took over the administration. In the months after the Japanese capitulation, the Australians were able to occupy Eastern Indonesia in a short time, disarm the Japanese and the Indonesians, and restore Dutch authority.⁷

When Indonesia had been added to his operational area after the Japanese surrender, Mountbatten had been instructed by the British General Staff to accept the Japanese surrender and to disarm and repatriate the Japanese. He also had to free and repatriate the Allied prisoners of war and internees from the prisoner of war and internment camps. The organization known as Recovery of Allied Prisoners of War and Internees (RAPWI) was founded for this purpose. Finally, his troops had to reoccupy Java and

KNIL soldiers patrol the streets of Jakarta, October-November 1945. Source: Desmond Davis, Imperial War Museum

Sumatra, so that these areas could eventually be handed over to the Dutch colonial government.[8]

However, the arrival of British and British Indian troops on Java and Sumatra was delayed. MacArthur had ordered that the Allies first await the official signing of the general Japanese surrender on 2 September 1945 in Tokyo Bay, before Allied operations in occupied territory could be carried out and regional surrenders be accepted. Moreover, Mountbatten could only deploy a limited number of troops in Indonesia, due to the many other commitments of his South East Asia Command.[9]

Indonesia was also a low priority for the British. First it would be the turn of Britain's own colonies in the region, after which some strategic locations, including in Indonesia, would be reoccupied. Jakarta and Surabaya were almost at the bottom of the list of strategic locations; the first landings would take place in Jakarta in late September 1945, after which Surabaya on Java, and Medan, Padang and Palembang on Sumatra were occupied in October and November, respectively. Only then was it the turn of other strategic locations in the interior, with the aim of maintaining public order on the islands until the Dutch arrived. Thus, the British did not initially consider it necessary to occupy the entire archipelago to keep sufficient control of the situation on the ground.[10]

In their absence, the Allies had made the Japanese responsible for the maintenance of public order and the assistance and security of Allied prisoners of war and civilians (mainly Dutch, but also Indo-Europeans). On Sumatra, the Japanese 25th Army largely complied with these demands, but on Java, some units of the Japanese armed forces did not resist the Indonesian takeover of the administration, public services and arms.[11] The commanders of the 16th Army on Java faced the dilemma of how to carry out Allied orders while at the same time fulfilling the promise of Indonesian independence. In any case, the army command wanted to avoid being accused of failing to carry out Allied orders, as this would have threatened the emperor's position. They considered an independent Indonesia important for Japan, however, not only as a market, but also for its raw materials.[12]

In addition, some Japanese had genuine sympathy for the Indonesian struggle for self-determination. They felt bound by the promises of independence that had been made during the war, and wanted to offer the Indonesians the opportunity to achieve this, but without actively participating in it themselves.[13] Six to eight hundred Japanese soldiers on Java, however, decided to join the Indonesian armed forces or militias and not return to their homeland.[14]

On 17 August 1945 and in the following days, the Japanese first disarmed and disbanded the Japanese-founded and Japanese-trained Indonesian PETA units and Heiho (auxiliaries) on Java and Bali, to prevent them from taking up arms against Japan or the Allies. On 21 August 1945, the Japanese army command on Java then decided that the combat troops should self-intern in remote mountain areas, in order to avoid problems with the Allied armed forces, which were expected at any moment. In the eastern part of the archipelago, this was done on the orders of the Australians. The Japanese thought they could leave enforcement of the order to the Indonesian police, supported by the Kempeitai (military police) and some small infantry detachments that remained in the cities. Self-internment started in early September 1945 and was complete by the end of that month. However, Japanese troops continued to guard the internment camps in which the Dutch, Europeans and Indo-Europeans were still staying. Japanese weapons were collected in depots, to be handed over to the Allies in due course. Japanese soldiers were not allowed more than five cartridges per weapon.[15]

On Sumatra, the Giyugun – similar to PETA on Java – was disbanded on 22 August 1945.[16] The Japanese troops on Sumatra did not self-intern, as they did on Java, but initially took responsibility for maintaining public order, with the exception of an air force division in the south. They also helped considerably with the evacuation of the Allied internees and prisoners of war, and with guarding arms and ammunition depots.[17] The internees were mainly Dutch and Indo-European, as the Japanese had interned all Indo-Europeans outside Java. During the Japanese occupation of Sumatra, hardly any Dutch or Indo-Europeans had remained outside the internment camps. Only a small number of Europeans from countries friendly with Japan and neutral countries had been able to move around freely at that time.[18]

The first RAPWI party, led by the South African Major G.F. Jacobs, landed in Medan on 2 September 1945. After a first inspection of two internment camps, Aek Pamienke and Si Rengo Rengo, Jacobs asked the Japanese commander on Sumatra, Lieutenant General Tanabe Moritake, to evacuate the prisoners of war and internees from the isolated camps to neighbourhoods in Medan, Padang and Palembang, where they would be guarded by the Japanese. This was because Jacobs had noticed that the Indonesian nationalists were increasingly turning against the Japanese and the Allies. In late October 1945, the evacuation was complete.[19]

Even after 15 August 1945, the Dutch remained interned in the Japanese camps for some time. It was some days after the capitulation, in some cases even two weeks, before they were officially informed by the Japanese authorities about the end of the war. This did not bring an immediate end to their life in the camps, however. Mountbatten advised the internees to stay there for the time being, for their own safety. The Indies authorities were not yet present; the colonial government in exile was still in Australia and Dutch military units had yet to arrive. After all, the Dutch government had only a limited military force at its immediate disposal, and the Dutch lacked their own transport ships, as these formed part of the Allied shipping pool until February 1946.[20] The absence of the British and the Dutch, along with the self-internment of the Japanese, gave the Republic of Indonesia the opportunity to strengthen its base after the proclamation of independence on 17 August 1945.

The First Weeks: The Republic of Indonesia

Proclaiming independence was one thing; establishing the authority of the Republic of Indonesia was quite another. The Indonesians used the six weeks between the declaration of independence and the arrival of the Allies on Java to build up the power apparatus of the Republic. On 22 August 1945, the Komité Nasional Indonesia Poesat (KNIP) was founded in Jakarta. With 137 members, it would function as a parliament. It consisted mainly of nationalist politicians, *pangreh pradja* (the Indonesian bureaucratic elite), and other professionals who had belonged to various bodies and organizations during the Japanese occupation. Islamic leaders and *pemuda* were relatively underrepresented. On 4 September 1945, President Sukarno and Vice-President Hatta presented the first cabinet of the Republic of Indonesia.[21]

In the meantime, the *pemuda* were becoming increasingly impatient. Adam Malik, one of the leaders of the *pemuda*, later wrote about the formation of the first cabinet:

> But that formation consisted only of writing down names on paper, which were then passed on to the newspapers. There was no sign of action at all. At most, meetings were held in the building on Pegangsaan 56 [Sukarno's home address]. The *pemuda* saw and observed absolutely no attempts by the government to develop a meaningful form of government. There was no activity, no plan, no decision, everything was adrift.[22]

It was not true, however, that the government was doing nothing. In exchange for their support, the *pangreh pradja* received assurances from the government that they – as they had under the Dutch and the Japanese – would continue to play an important role in the polity. For example, all but one of the Indonesian vice-residents were promoted to resident, replacing their Japanese superiors, and the three governors of the provinces of West, Central and East Java were also included in the traditional Indonesian layer of governance. The government also secured the support of another traditional power base, the four princes in Surakarta and Yogyakarta in Central Java.[23]

A power apparatus was needed in order to maintain civil authority. The most obvious bases for a national army – PETA, Heiho and the Giyugun – had been disarmed and disbanded by the Japanese. On 22 August 1945, the Indonesian leaders therefore founded the BKR, the Badan Keamanan Rakjat (People's Security Agency), which would have local branches across Indonesia and could be joined by former members of PETA, Heiho and Indonesian KNILsoldiers. In order to avoid offending the Allies, the government deliberately refrained from calling the organization a national army.[24]

So as to root the authority of the Republic of Indonesia at the local level, too, the national government in Jakarta also called for the founding of local 'national committees' everywhere. There was a massive response. In late August and early September, Komités Nasional Indonesia (Indonesian National Committees, KNIs) were formed in almost all major cities and sometimes even in villages. These KNIs often consisted of local notables and a few *pemuda*; on the whole, the most important roles were reserved for members of the pre-war nationalist movement. The immediate function of the committees was symbolic, rather than practical, as a declaration of support for the Republic and expression of the desire to unite the Indonesian people.[25]

The symbolic struggle for power

All across Java, Indonesians symbolically claimed public space in order to show their support for the Republic of Indonesia. Buildings, walls, bicycles, carts, cars and buses were decorated with red-and-white flags and posters; many Indonesians wore red-and-white badges on their clothing.[26] Walls and vehicles were daubed with anti-imperialist and pro-independence slogans, such as 'Better to Hell, than be colonized again', 'V.d. Plas/Mook, what are you doing', 'Indonesia merdeka!' (Indonesia free!), 'Jagalah Kemerdekaanmu' ('Protect your freedom') and 'Milik Republik Indonesia' ('Property of the Republic of Indonesia'). NICA was renamed 'No Indonesian Cares About'.[27] 'Merdeka' ('Independence') became the national greeting.[28]

Large meetings were held in several places on Java. On 11 September 1945, for example, a committee led by local *pemuda* in Surabaya (East Java) held a meeting at the Tambaksari sports ground, attended by thousands of youths. In Bandung (West Java), the local KNI and BKR took the initiative to hold parades and mass meetings with speeches. Every 17th day of the month, Salatiga (Central Java) held a large parade in honour of the founding of the Republic. In Jakarta (West Java) on 19 September 1945, tens of thousands of people descended on a meeting on Ikada Square (formerly Koningsplein, now Medan Merdeka) organized by the Angkatan Pemuda Indonesia (API), despite a Japanese and Allied ban on large meetings and the presence of Japanese tanks and armoured personnel carriers. Fearing a large-scale confrontation that might result in many casualties, Sukarno urged the crowd to stay peaceful and maintain order. He ordered them to go home, which they duly did.[29]

Tram 1 in Jakarta with slogans for an independent Indonesia: 'We the people of Indonesia want peace/youth, your blood is hot'. Source: NIOD

Like similar meetings in other cities, the mass meeting on Ikada Square was of great symbolic importance. For the first time, the Indonesian people were able to show their support for the Republic of Indonesia. The fact that they had defied Japanese tanks on Ikada Square and a ban by the Kempeitai only increased their self-confidence and hope. The Ikada meeting was also of personal significance for Sukarno. He had shown that no one could afford to ignore him; he could inspire Indonesians like no other, and they obeyed him *en masse*.[30]

In those first weeks of September 1945 in some cities on Java, Indonesians decided to occupy strategic buildings that symbolized the power of the oppressors and collaborators. In Jakarta, some of the more radical youths, united in the API, led the takeover of train, tram and telephone companies, as well as a growing number of private and public institutions.[31] In September 1945, Indonesians already controlled a substantial number of public services, such as the gas and electricity companies, the railways and the postal services on Java.[32]

It was increasingly the *pemuda* in cities who took the lead, followed by the rest of the population. The Japanese tended to hand over these institutions without resistance, because they were focused on the return to Japan and wanted to avoid any difficulties in the meantime. The older nationalist politicians and the *pangreh pradja* functioned as a kind of buffer between the *pemuda* and the Japanese. For the time being, it was sufficient for the *pemuda* if symbols of power, such as public transport and government institutions and buildings, came into Indonesian hands, even if these were the hands of older, more moderate Republicans. This situation would change after the first Allied landings on 29 September 1945.[33]

In the meantime, more and more Dutch were leaving the Japanese internment camps and searching for their relatives and abandoned homes, despite the call from the Allied high command to stay in the camps. There was already a considerable Dutch community in Jakarta in late August 1945, for example, trying to resume their pre-war lives. At that time, the size of the Allied presence was very limited. Between July and September 1945, only a few small commando units and relief contact teams had been dropped over Java and Sumatra.[34]

The 15th of September 1945 saw the arrival of the British cruiser *HMS Cumberland*, the flagship of Rear Admiral Wilfred Patterson, and the Dutch cruiser *Hr.Ms. Tromp* in Jakarta, the vanguard of the Allied forces. On board the *Tromp* were, among others, Charles Olke van der Plas, the Dutch delegate to the Allied high command and former governor of East Java, and some representatives of NICA. NICA was to function as the civilian administration in the Dutch East Indies under the Allied military commanders, until full authority over the archipelago could be transferred to the Netherlands.[35]

The Dutch who were present saw the proclamation of independence and the establishment of the Republic of Indonesia as a Japanese fabrication, and thus not to be taken seriously. 'The Japanese have taken all kinds of devious measures. They had Sukarno proclaim the Republic and gave all the offices to Natives', noted the 39-year-old mechanical engineer L.R. Oldeman in his diary on 2 September 1945, in the Baros 6 internment camp in Cimahi.[36] People were unwilling or unable to believe that relations had changed.

This was evident, among other things, from an interview that Van der Plas gave to the *New York Times* before his arrival in Indonesia:

> Mynheer van der Plas said it was 'beyond question' that the Indies would achieve Commonwealth status, but expressed the fear that it would take 'several more generations' before the Indonesians could

'adequately operate a Commonwealth without Western assistance'. He declared that most of the seventy million people in the Indies had not yet been 'adequately introduced to modern civilization', although they had produced great leaders.[37]

At the time when Indonesia was added to Mountbatten's operational area after the Japanese surrender, people on the Allied side were hardly aware of what had taken place during the Japanese occupation of Indonesia. The same was true of the developments in the weeks immediately after the Japanese capitulation. The only information that the Dutch authorities in Australia had received during the war had come from Japanese radio broadcasts, and reports from a small number of people who had managed to flee occupied Indonesia. Attempts to get information about the situation in Indonesia via intelligence operations had largely failed.[38]

As a result, the Dutch in Australia had an overly optimistic view of the situation in Indonesia. Although Lieutenant Governor General H.J. van Mook was well aware during the war that the 'difficulties would only really start with peace', he nevertheless believed that order could quickly be restored after the Japanese surrender.[39] That was also the opinion of his right-hand man, Van der Plas, when the latter set foot in Jakarta once more on 15 September 1945. Although the Dutch in Australia had underestimated anti-Dutch sentiment, they believed that the resistance would soon collapse in the face of a rapid Allied occupation, the dissolution of the Republic of Indonesia, and the rounding up and arrest of the leaders.[40] The British likewise had little or no information about the situation in the Dutch East Indies. 'Little was known about the situation in that area of Java,' wrote Captain A.I.D. Prentice – who formed part of a small team that landed in Surabaya on 19 September 1945 – in a later report. 'We were told that the Javanese would be pleased to see us, and that the Japanese would provide us with anything we need, information [sic] that proved to be not entirely true,' he added wryly, with a feeling for understatement.[41] By the end of the British occupation of Indonesia on 29 November 1946, the British had suffered 620 dead, 1,331 wounded and 402 missing.[42]

This latter development was a consequence of the fact that the British and the Dutch were soon confronted with mass support for independence among the Indonesian population. This inevitably led to clashes between Indonesians and Dutch, Indo-Europeans and Moluccans, as well as between Indonesians and Chinese and Japanese; clashes that initially focused on a struggle for symbols of power. And what could have more symbolic meaning than a flag? In several cities on Java in September 1945, disputes arose over who could claim government buildings and other centres of power with which flag. It was, in the words of Mohammad Hatta, a 'war of the flags'.[43]

The best known of these is the so-called flag incident in Surabaya (East Java) on 19 September 1945. This began with the hoisting of a Dutch flag by Dutch former internee Jack Boer and reserve officer candidate Joost Lansdorp, who belonged to a British/Dutch RAPWI team, above the Yamato hotel (formerly the Oranje hotel), where the RAPWI team was staying at the time. Young Indonesians saw this as a gross provocation. They stormed the building, tore off the blue stripe so that only a red-and-white flag remained, and hoisted it again. During the scuffle that subsequently broke out between Dutch and *pemuda*, the Indo-European W. Ploegman sustained injuries that proved fatal several days later. Four *pemuda* are also said to have died in the incident.[44]

Such incidents involving flags took place all over Java; for example, in Bandung in West Java (14 September 1945), at the internment camps near Semarang in Central Java (10 September 1945), and in the residency of Pekalongan on Central Java. These incidents not only involved clashes between Indonesians and Dutch, but also with Chinese, Japanese and other Indonesians.[45]

In Tegal (Pekalongan residency), there were outbreaks of violence between Chinese and Indonesians. The Chinese were accused of not wanting to raise the Indonesian flag and of using it inappropriately. This was because the makeshift flagpoles were originally intended for knocking ripe mangoes out of tall trees, but the Chinese did not always take sufficient care to remove the flags from the poles before using them for this purpose.[46]

In the city of Pekalongan, local *pemuda* took down the Japanese flag from the resident's office in front of a group of enraged Japanese officers and the furious Japanese resident. Although the local authorities supported the action of the *pemuda*, they were also trying to handle armed Japanese who were still in shock due to the surrender, and not in a mood to suffer even greater loss of face. When the *pemuda* refused to lower the Republican flag and hoist the Japanese one again, the situation became very tense. In the end, a few youths from the residency office lowered the Indonesian flag to avoid escalation. The Indonesian and Japanese authorities then agreed to stop hanging flags altogether, so as to prevent incidents. This lasted a week, until the Japanese gave in and allowed the Indonesian flag to be hung from all buildings.[47]

On the other islands, it seems that this symbolic struggle sometimes took place later or lasted longer than on Java. On Sumatra, it was not until 23 September 1945 that the Badan Pemuda Indonesia (BPI) was founded. Seven days later, it organized a meeting in Medan, attended by a thousand people. From that time onward, the situation developed rapidly. Within a few days, there were branches of the BPI in Karoland and in the regencies of Langkat and Asahan. Youths in all large cities began to wear red- and-white insignia.[48]

Teuku Mohammad Hasan, the Republican governor of Sumatra, began issuing the first orders on 3 October 1945. Civil servants were only allowed to obey orders from the Republican authorities, and workers had to down tools in all offices where the Indonesian flag was not allowed to be hung. The following morning, the *pemuda* followed his instructions and raised the red-and-white flag above the post office, the station and several other places without any difficulty. Only at the police station and the town hall did they encounter resistance from the Japanese. The red-and-white flag was soon on display everywhere. In Medan, there were various demonstrations and marches to show support for the Republic. The largest parade, on 9 October 1945, is said to have drawn 100,000 people.[49] 'The air is electrified,' wrote the Dutch lieutenant C.A.M. Brondgeest about the atmosphere in those days.[50]

The flag incident in Surabaya.
Source: NIOD

In South Sumatra, the power struggle occurred on 8 October 1945, when the resident of South Sumatra, A.K. Gani, together with Japanese officials from the military administration, hoisted the red-and-white flag at a ceremony. The red-and-white flag was then raised at all government offices. On the same day, it was announced that the Republic of Indonesia was the sole legitimate authority in the residency of Palembang. The struggle in Palembang took place without incident, because the Japanese avoided the demonstrations.[51]

In Balikpapan on Kalimantan in mid-November 1945, according to J.C.C. Haar, the local commander of NICA, 'quite a large demonstration' took place, which is otherwise said to have gone peacefully.[52] On Bali, where there were no Allied troops in the autumn of 1945, an – incorrect – radio report about the recognition of the Republic of Indonesia by China, the Soviet Union and the United States on 1 October 1945 provoked a spate of public meetings. At the end of the week, a large meeting was organized at which the Japanese transfer of power was demanded.[53]

A few weeks later, on 27 October 1945, there was a meeting in Singaraja on the north coast of Bali, between the Indonesians, Dutch and Japanese.

Children selling red-and-white badges, place and year unknown. Source: *National Archives of the Netherlands/Archive F.J. Goedhart.*

According to an Indonesian eyewitness, a unit of Dutch soldiers from the minesweeper *Hr.Ms. Abraham Crijnssen* came ashore in Buleleng, the port of Singaradja, and replaced the Indonesian flag with a Dutch one.[54] They also demanded, via the Japanese, that the Republican governor, Ketut Pudja, come on board the Dutch ship to negotiate. If he refused, armed soldiers would arrest him. Pudja refused and was arrested not long after. Humiliated and desperate *pemuda* then took down the Dutch flag, provoking a counter-action from the Dutch. When a dozen *pemuda*, armed with daggers, swords and bamboo spears, removed the blue stripe from the flag and re-hoisted the red-and-white remains, the Dutch fired on them from the ship with machine guns. In this incident – which was remarkably similar to the 'flag incident' in Surabaya – the sixteen-year-old Ketut Merta was killed.[55]

After the shooting, a group of soldiers came ashore. Armed with machine guns and hand grenades, they drove the Indonesians from the shore and in doing so, according to the English-language report by the commander of the Heemskerck, caused 'some casualties'.[56] When a small boat carrying Indonesians armed with spears came too close to the ship, in the Dutch view, machine guns were fired again. This struggle for the flag strengthened the resistance on Bali. The nurse Jero Wilaja, then fourteen years old, was so furious that she decided to fight for independence. 'We were so angry because they evidently didn't understand that we had declared independence, and we were also shocked that they behaved so badly', she told journalist and historian Anne-Lot Hoek in 2014.[57]

Disagreements about flags, graffiti and arguments in markets, sparked riots and incidents between the different population groups in various cities on Java, sometimes with fatal consequences. In Jakarta and Bandung, armed groups were formed on Java in September 1945, consisting of former Moluccan, Menadonese and Dutch KNIL soldiers and Dutch, Moluccan and Indo-European youths. These groups wanted to protect Dutch civilians, take revenge for Indonesian violence and restore colonial authority, and acted harshly in the process.[58] Also on Sumatra, in Medan, a pro-Dutch armed group was founded that behaved in a similar way. This 'police force' ultimately amounted to around 600 men, mainly Moluccans, and was led by Lieutenant Raymond Westerling.[59]

In the course of September 1945, the tensions on Java mounted further. On 23 September 1945, the Japanese 16th Army's *Intelligence Bulletin* read: 'Prevailing tendency is that rivalry between Indonesians and others is becoming so acute that just a trifle friction may lead to furious impulsive explosions at any moment....'.[60] On 18 September, three days after his arrival on the *HMS Cumberland* in Tandjong Priok, Rear Admiral Patterson also noted an increase in the political tension and violent incidents. In his view, only the rapid arrival of the Allies would prevent the situation from getting out of hand.[61] That would prove to be a grave misconception: it was in fact the landing of the first regular Allied units on Java that set relations on edge. The arrival of the Allies on 29 September 1945, and in particular the arrival of the Dutch, heralded the end of a phase of what was mainly a symbolic power struggle on Java, and ultimately proved to be the immediate cause of the explosion of violence in the following months.

III.
CONFRONTATIONS

4.

Power constellations

The landings in 1945 of the first British and Australian units in Makassar (Sulawesi, 21 September), Jakarta (Java, 29 September) and Medan (Sumatra, 10 October) acted as a catalyst, and soon put relations between different groups and nationalities on edge. What had been a symbolic struggle for power with a relatively limited number of casualties, especially on Java, was transformed from late September 1945. More or less at the same time, an armed struggle for power unfolded on the three islands between different ethnic groups and nationalities; a struggle that was accompanied on all sides by many casualties, most of them civilians or captured fighters.

PATTERNS AND CONSTELLATIONS OF POWER
The arrival of the Allies did not lead to an immediate outbreak of violence against civilians and captured fighters everywhere. This was the case in New Guinea, the Moluccas and Kalimantan, for example; islands with areas that had never been occupied by the Japanese, or that had been taken by the Allies before the end of the war or shortly after the Japanese capitulation. In short, local conditions played an important role. For our analysis

Laskar Puteri (women's armed group) holds a parade on Jalan Malioboro, Yogyakarta, date unknown. Source: ANRI/IPPHOS of the extreme violence against civilians and captured fighters in the first six months after the Japanese surrender, it is therefore important to analyse the power constellations in the archipelago, conceived as the relations between different actors on certain islands, in certain regions, at certain points in time.

These power constellations largely determined when the extreme violence against civilians and captured fighters began and ended, and who the perpetrators and victims were. For example, was there one dominant party that could effectively exercise its authority? Or did a party rule an area in name only, with mainly symbolic power? Did several actors contest each other's power? Broadly speaking, we can identify three power constellations in the months shortly after the Japanese surrender.

The first kind of constellation covered areas where there were different competing national and international power blocks. This was the case on much of Java and Sumatra. Java was the most densely populated island and the political and military epicentre of the archipelago, the administrative and economic heart in the colonial period. It was both the seat of government of the Republic of Indonesia and the island where the British and the Dutch focused the lion's share of their military and political efforts. The defeated Japanese were the fourth party that was able to tip the balance from one side to another, particularly in August-November 1945, depending on the attitude of the local Japanese military authorities to the Indonesian struggle for independence.

Second, there were areas where a single party was dominant. For example, this constellation existed on the islands in the eastern part of the archipelago, with the exception of Bali and large parts of South Sulawesi. Here, the Allies – in this case, the Australians and the Dutch – had the upper hand, both militarily and politically. In the approach to the *bersiap* period that prevailed in the Dutch and Anglo-Saxon historiography until recently, no or hardly any attention was generally paid to these islands, because they were the site of less extreme violence against Dutch, Indo-European, Moluccan and (allegedly) pro-Dutch Indonesian civilians. Nevertheless, an analysis of the developments on these islands can aid our understanding of the extreme violence against civilians and captured fighters on other islands. Why was there much less extreme violence against Indo-European, Dutch and (allegedly) pro-Dutch Indonesian civilians there, at least until mid-1946? Was there violence against civilians or captured fighters of other nationalities and/or ethnicities? And if so, who was responsible for it? Studying this violence can reveal certain general characteristics that may also have been present on other islands.

Third, there were areas where none of the national or international power blocks could exercise effective authority; not because they were rivals, but because they had insufficient resources for this purpose. In these areas, local armed Indonesian groups fought one another for power. This was the case, for example, in the residency of Pekalongan (Central Java), Banten (West Java), Aceh in the north of Sumatra, the East Coast of Sumatra and on Bali. This kind of violence is often described as *berdaulat/daulat* action or 'social revolution'.[1]

These three power constellations can help us to understand and analyse various forms of violence against civilians and captured fighters. At the same time, some important caveats should be made. Although the balance of power played a determining role in the excessive violence, it was not the only factor that influenced the use of force. The local impact of the Japanese occupation, such as the mass mobilization of the population, the militarization of large number of youths on Java and Sumatra and more specific, local events, or the impact of propaganda and rumours on the behaviour of various actors, also played a role, for example. Moreover, the power constellations changed constantly as a result of the shifting alliances and the course of events.

It is thus important to take account of shifts in power relations during this first phase of the Indonesian Revolution. In addition, it is not always possible to draw a clear dividing line between the different power constellations, which could overlap in some periods and in some areas. Although South Sulawesi was part of the power constellation in which the Australians and the Dutch were the dominant party, on the island, that dominance did not initially extend much further than the capital, Makassar. On Java and Sumatra, where there was a power struggle between rival national and international power blocks, as mentioned above, it was sometimes impossible for these parties to enforce their authority at the local level during a certain period. When that was the case, local armed Indonesian groups and individuals seized their chance. These two power constellations will thus be addressed together in this analysis.

A further caveat concerns the fact that there were sometimes (major) differences between the Japanese, Dutch, British and Indonesians themselves. On the side of the Republic of Indonesia, for example, there were tensions between the central government in Jakarta, which took a moderate line against the Dutch and put the emphasis on diplomacy (*diplomasi*), and *pemuda* groups that wanted to defend independence by force of arms (*perjuangan*). The official army of the Republic of Indonesia, the TKR, was sometimes diametrically opposed to a wide range of armed groups of a religious, political or other nature, but sometimes it also rejected the diplomatic approach of the political leaders of the Republic. These armed groups also fought one another, too. For all parties, the personality and attitude of the political and military leaders on the ground had a major influence on the local course of events.

It is also important to take account of socio-economic differences that transcended the islands, such as those between urban and rural areas. Historian Audrey Kahin highlights the distinction in the nature of the violence in the cities and in the rural areas beyond. In her opinion, there were more similarities between the developments in Medan, Makassar and Jakarta than with those in their hinterlands. In the cities, it was the *pemuda*, especially those who had received paramilitary training during the Japanese occupation, who took the lead in (violent) actions against the authorities (whether they were Japanese, Dutch or Republican). Another characteristic of urban areas was the presence of older, more moderate nationalists who supported a gradual path to Indonesian independence.[2]

According to Kahin, the relations in rural areas, by contrast, were much more polarized. It was there in particular that attempts were made during the Indonesian Revolution to push through major social, political and sometimes economic changes. In those regions, the farmers were the main catalyst for revolutionary action, often because they rebelled and seized food supplies and toppled, drove away or killed the local Indonesian authorities. On Sulawesi, in Aceh and in other rural areas of Sumatra, too, youths often took the lead in the struggle, but they had a different background from that of their peers in the cities. They had been educated at Islamic schools and belonged to Indonesian organizations.[3]

However different the local conditions may have been, we can nevertheless identify some relatively general characteristics and patterns in the extreme violence against civilians and captured fighters in the first phase of the Indonesian Revolution. As explained in chapter 1, the violence was simultaneous, often intertwined, multiform and extreme, and the leaders of the diverse parties were unable – and sometimes unwilling – to curb violence by regular units, armed groups and individuals.

'Simultaneous' refers to the fact that the extreme violence against Indonesian, Moluccan, Dutch, Indo-European, Japanese, British and Chinese civilians and captured fighters erupted more or less simultaneously on Java, Sumatra and some other islands. Violence in one place or region or another, or on an island, often led, besides local interactions, to a violent reaction in other areas. It is therefore important to take account of the intertwined nature of this violence.

The extreme violence was also multiform, in the sense that it took a wide range of forms. From robbery, extortion, intimidation, torture, rape, forcible removal or eviction, to arson, mass internment, bombing that caused many civilian deaths, and murder. This study will focus in particular on murder, partly in view of the necessary limits of the research. The inability, and sometimes also the unwillingness, of the political and military authorities to curb regular units, armed groups and individuals was also a recurring pattern in these situations, both in relation to the Indonesians and in relation to the British, Dutch, Moluccans and Japanese.

Much of the violence against civilians and captured fighters in the first phase of the Indonesian Revolution was also generally characterized by exceptional cruelty. The 'tjintjangen' – the literal dismemberment of the victims – occupies an important place in Dutch memories of the Indonesian extreme violence, but Indonesians killed others in this way, too, including Japanese and British.[4] The Dutch and British also used excessive violence in the first months of the revolution, such as the shooting of civilians or prisoners without trial, or the torching of *kampongs*. However, as far as is known, no methods such as dismemberment (*tjintjangen*) were used. The Japanese, on the other hand, are known to have decapitated opponents as a form of deterrent.[5] The characteristics and patterns described above will be addressed in detail when discussing the different power constellations in the following chapters.

5.

The Eastern archipelago: Allied dominance

Large parts of the archipelago beyond Java and Sumatra had already been captured by American and Australian troops during the Second World War. In the other parts of Eastern Indonesia, with the exception of Bali, the Australians had arrived relatively soon after the Japanese surrender, although the occupation was initially limited to the larger towns. On New Guinea, the Japanese occupation had not extended beyond a few places on the north and west coasts, whilst parts of the south and the interior had remained in Allied hands. On 22 April 1944, the Americans captured Hollandia, followed by several other places on New Guinea. On 15 September 1944, the Australians occupied the island of Morotai in the northern Moluccas, and in May and July 1945 this was followed by Tarakan, Balikpapan and other parts of Eastern Kalimantan.[1]

One exception in Eastern Indonesia was Bali, where Dutch troops would not land until much later, on 2 March 1946. Due to the absence of the Allies, the initial aloofness of the Japanese troops present and the weak position of the official Republican authorities on the island, power fell into the hands of local aristocratic families and *pemuda*. Local aristocrats were divided between supporting the Republic of Indonesia and staying loyal to the Dutch, leading to infighting. According to Geoffrey Robinson, the revolution on

Bali could better be described as a local civil war than a regional manifestation of a national liberation war.[2]

Along with the Allied troops, the first months after the Japanese surrender also saw the arrival of the first NICA units on the other islands in Eastern Indonesia, accompanied by KNIL soldiers, to take over the civilian administration.[3] Unlike on Java and Sumatra, Dutch rule was restored there relatively early. After all, not only had the Australians arrived earlier than the British on Java and Sumatra, but they were also present in much larger numbers. At the time of the Japanese surrender, they already had 50,000 men on Kalimantan. By contrast, until 16 October the British had only 24,000 soldiers on Java, a number that would later grow, including Sumatra, to around 65,000.[4]

Due to their early arrival and relative strength, the Australians were soon able to assemble and evacuate the former Allied prisoners of war and internees, and they did not have to call on Japanese troops to help them keep order, as the British later had to do on Java and Sumatra. The Australians ordered the Japanese commanders in their operational area to gather their troops in certain places where they would subsequently have to provide for themselves. In these remote locations, the Japanese received no or little protection from the Allies. As the Australians had sufficient capacity to maintain order, Japanese self-internment in Eastern Indonesia played very little role in the dynamics of violence, as it did on Java and Sumatra.[5] As a result, with the exception of Bali, the Japanese did not come face to face with Indonesian armed groups that demanded their weapons to defend themselves against the Allies.[6]

What is more, the 170,000-plus Japanese troops in the eastern part of Indonesia generally appear to have taken a more cooperative line with the Allies than the Japanese on Java and Sumatra. As a result, the disarmament of the Japanese went smoothly.[7] For example, Brigadier F. Chilton, the Australian commander of the Makassar Force on South Sulawesi, spoke of the 'utter correctness' of the Japanese on the island, especially the Japanese Vice Admiral Ohsugi. The latter expressed great appreciation for the Australian armed forces and wanted to do everything in his power to help; and he stayed true to this, in Chilton's opinion.[8]

As a result, the Japanese on Sulawesi did not transfer any weapons, ammunition or other equipment to the Indonesians.[9] The few weapons that did fall into nationalist hands were apparently taken from the several hundred Dutch KNIL soldiers present, or provided by or bought from Australian soldiers. Arms were stolen from the Japanese, too; after the transfer of authority from the Australians to the British (February-July 1946), nationalists fished weapons out of the sea that had been dumped by the Australians.[10] There does not appear to have been any underhand Japanese support for the Republic in Eastern Indonesia, although the Dutch believed this to be the case – without providing any concrete evidence for it.[11]

As well as the relatively speedy arrival of the Australians, a number of other factors facilitated the restoration of Dutch colonial authority. Some parts of Eastern Indonesia had traditionally been oriented towards the Netherlands, such as the Moluccan islands and the Minahassa, the peninsula of North Sulawesi. Both islands had large Christian communities, whilst the local population had traditionally been a source of recruitment of soldiers for the KNIL and for the (lower) ranks of the colonial bureaucracy. The Allies thus generally received a warm reception on the Moluccas. Groups that had traditionally been loyal to Dutch rule soon regained dominant positions on the island, whilst nationalists who had collaborated with the Japanese during the war kept a low profile. Local *pemuda* organizations played only a minor role.[12]

Moreover, Indonesian nationalism in Eastern Indonesia was generally less developed than on Java. It was a vast, sparsely populated region that had fallen under the responsibility of the Japanese navy during the Japanese occupation, and had been destined to remain a Japanese colony. Unlike the Japanese 16th Army on Java, the Japanese navy had done little to mobilize the population or support the nationalists. Only very late in the war did the navy start encouraging Indonesian nationalism, in an attempt to enlist the population in the defence. There was no large-scale mobilization of young nationalists, either, as there was on Java and Sumatra. This is an important explanation for the limited nature of the nationalist violence in much of the Eastern archipelago. After all, it was these youths in particular, with their (semi)-military training, who played a key role in the violence on Java and Sumatra.[13]

Violence against civilians and captured fighters

As mentioned in previous chapters , the first phase of the Indonesian Revolution saw violence against Indo-European, Moluccan, Dutch and (allegedly) pro-Dutch Indonesian civilians outside Java and Sumatra. This was not the case on Ambon, where the Dutch were particularly dominant. The few acts of violence that took place there were perpetrated by Dutch units, and mostly targeted pro-Republican Indonesians and interned Japanese.

One of the first actions taken by Dutch officials returning to Ambon was to remobilize former KNIL soldiers who had been held as prisoners of war. These KNIL soldiers soon became embroiled in confrontations with Javanese and Madurese soldiers, and they undertook revenge attacks against interned Japanese soldiers and those whom they believed had collaborated with the Japanese.[14] For example, some former KNIL soldiers on the island of Saparua, who had been ill-treated by the Kempeitai during the war, went to the nearby island of Seram to attack and disarm the Japanese there. There were some fatalities in the ensuing gun battles.[15]

There was also sporadic unrest on New Guinea. Allied dominance was not absolute, even there, as shown by the fact that the inhabitants of the hinterland of Genyem rebelled against the Dutch administration, whilst there were also incidents in the town of Merauke.[16] In the last months of 1945, major tensions arose in the capital Jayapura – then called Hollandia – between Javanese and Menadonese KNIL soldiers, in response to the reports of violence on Java. The Javanese in the city – including a large number of recruits from the police school – supported the pursuit of independence and turned against the Menadonese KNIL company stationed there. The fiercely pro-Dutch Menadonese were extremely agitated, because they feared for the lives of their women and children on Java. In October 1945, they could still be kept in check by the threat that, in the case of riots, the Papua battalion, which was made up of local soldiers, would not only fire at Javanese, but also at them.[17]

Tensions remained high, however. When a large quantity of weapons was stolen from an army depot, the rumour immediately went round that the Javanese on the island were planning an uprising on 15 December 1945. In response, in the night of 14-15 December, Menadonese KNIL troops not only arrested all Javanese present, but also those members of the police force whom they considered untrustworthy. The Menadonese 'went completely wild during the operation', in the words of the SONICA (Senior Officer NICA) J.P.K. van Eechoud.[18] During the arrests, there were nine deaths among the Javanese and police officers in so-called escape attempts. Although the order was given to shoot in such cases, Van Eechoud believed that a calmer approach would have prevented fatal confrontations.[19]

Kalimantan demonstrates yet another aspect of the violence against civilians in this early phase of the Indonesian Revolution. It was mainly the site of tension and violence between Chinese and Indonesians, in which foreign relations – in this case, pro-Chinese nationalist sentiment – played an important role. Although various places, including Balikpapan and Tarakan, had been captured by the Australians before the end of the Second World War, the latter were not able to occupy the entire island until mid-September 1945. The advance began with the arrival of the 7th Division in Banjarmasin on 17 September 1945. The Australians were accompanied by a contingent of 160 NICA staff. At first, the Indonesians on Kalimantan welcomed the Australian soldiers as liberators and paid little attention to NICA. When they realized that NICA was planning to restore Dutch colonial rule, however, their attitude turned to fear and uncertainty, and then to hostility. NICA was joined by KNIL soldiers who had just been released from Japanese internment camps; in Banjarmasin, they were 70 strong.[20]

The Australians – like the British on Java and Sumatra – generally wanted to return home as soon as possible, and thus tried to minimize their involvement in local politics. Some Australian soldiers in Banjarmasin were sympathetic to the Indonesian struggle for independence and supported the local freedom fighters with information, weapons and, in one case, the distribution of pamphlets calling for all Indonesians to unite and expel NICA. Nevertheless, on 24 October 1945 the Australians formally transferred authority to NICA.[21]

NICA faced a range of nationalist, mostly underground paramilitary organizations that carried out armed attacks, committed sabotage, and/or urged the population to oppose the Dutch and support the Republic. In Banjarmasin on 10 November 1945, for example, around 50 Indonesian youths armed with hand grenades and an Australian rifle attacked the police station. According to the Commanding Officer of NICA (CONICA), C.C. de Rooy, the attack was repulsed by the municipal police without any losses, whilst there were ten dead and wounded on the attacking side; later that evening, other clashes resulted in another four dead and wounded.[22] In Balikpapan, unknown parties threw two Australian hand grenades at the power plants and the home of the CONICA; there were also disturbances in Pontianak.[23]

In Pontianak (Western Kalimantan), Indonesians and Chinese founded a joint security organization, the Pendjaga Keamanan Oemoem (PKO). The Chinese in the PKO formed part of an underground organization that had resisted the Japanese during the Second World War, and they had firearms. In August 1945, they took action against Chinese they viewed as collaborators, due to their cooperation with the Japanese. Nevertheless, problems soon arose within the PKO between Chinese and Indonesians, due to the more assertive attitude of the former. This was because rumours were circulating among the Chinese that ships with troops from General Chiang Kai-shek's Kuomintang were en route from China to occupy Western Kalimantan. At that time, the Kuomintang was embroiled in a civil war with the communists in China. The rumours fuelled nationalist sentiments among the Chinese. They hung up posters of Chiang Kai-shek, displayed Kuomintang flags, and announced that the Province of Western Kalimantan would become part of nationalist China. The Chinese in Pontianak, the provincial capital, no longer wished to be addressed by the Indonesians as 'cina' – which they believed to have derogatory overtones – but as 'tionghoa': a name that referred to Tiongkok, the Chinese republic that had emerged as one of the winners of World War Two, and the idea that all ethnic Chinese, including those abroad, formed part of the Chinese nation. If Indonesians failed to use this term, they were reprimanded or beaten.[24]

Although the Chinese troops did not arrive, tensions rose in the meantime, because the Indonesians felt threatened and indignant. Fighting broke out between Chinese and Indonesians in various places. There were also confrontations between the two groups in Pontianak. The Chinese PKO members controlled the market, whereas the Indonesians held power in the surrounding *kampongs*. Many Chinese who lived in the *kampongs* were stabbed and beaten to death. Chinese merchants who wanted to bring their fresh produce to market were stopped; if they refused to cooperate, they were murdered and their bodies were thrown into the water. In the end, Indonesians set fire to the market and Chinese homes in the city. The *dayaks* – a community on Kalimantan – did the same in villages around Pontianak and Singkawang. NICA capitalized on the mutual animosity between the different communities, and managed to get the province firmly under control in September.[25]

On Kalimantan, however, the violence against civilians came from many sides: here, too, KNIL soldiers asserted themselves. On 30 November 1945, a KNIL patrol in the Chinese quarter of Bandjermasin fatally shot a Chinese man during the arrest of two Formosans (from modern-day Taiwan), who had been mistaken for Japanese soldiers. During the later investigation, the soldiers stated that the Chinese man had been acting aggressively. According to civilian witnesses, though, he had been sitting peacefully on his front porch when he was hauled out by the soldiers and shot; he was unarmed and not acting aggressively. The Dutch judge advocate (public prosecutor for the court martial), E. Bonn, initially went along with the witness accounts and saw sufficient reason to prosecute the soldiers. He eventually decided against prosecution, however, despite protests from the Chinese consul general in Jakarta.[26] In a letter to the Chinese consul, the attorney general to the Supreme Court of the Dutch East Indies gave the following reason for the decision:

> The present case was essentially dropped on very opportunistic grounds, whereby, in view of the extremely special circumstances under which the action took place, the initiation of criminal proceedings would have affected the self-confidence – and the mood – of the heavily burdened Dutch troops in an undesirable way. [...] Under these special circumstances, it can be necessary to drop criminal cases that in normal times would undoubtedly be brought to court, on purely opportunistic grounds.[27]

It seems that this action by the KNIL on Kalimantan was not exceptional. On 11 March 1946, E.O. baron van Boetzelaer, the first government secretary to Van Mook, wrote to General Spoor, noting with regard to a Chinese objection to excessive action by Dutch soldiers in Jakarta: 'several complaints of violent action by our military were also received from the outer provinces, especially from Western Borneo and Bandjermasin [South Borneo].'[28]

In South Sulawesi, where the Allies were less dominant and were mainly limited to Makassar and the immediate vicinity, there were more victims among civilians and captured fighters on both the Dutch and the Indonesian side. In the first months of the Indonesian Revolution, this region saw more armed resistance to the restoration of pre-war Dutch rule than the other islands in Eastern Indonesia. The region had a long tradition of resistance to the Dutch; colonial rule had only been established in 1910 after five years of fighting. The memory of this was thus still alive in 1945. The aristocrats who had taken the lead in the resistance in those days did so once more. Due to their low level of education, they had not been involved in governance under the pre-war Dutch colonial regime and the Japanese occupation. As a result, their legitimacy was not corrupted in the eyes of Indonesian nationalists, unlike that of the nobility on Java.[29]

At first, the picture was somewhat divided. Some older Indonesian officials, from the Ambonese and Minahassan Christian minorities, welcomed the arrival of the Allies and helped them to take Makassar. Other residents of South Sulawesi opposed their arrival, however. Although the leadership and organization of the nationalist movement was initially weak on South Sulawesi, many red-and-white flags and garments were also on display there, as a sign of support for the Republic.[30]

Like their colleagues on Kalimantan and the British on Java, the Australians noted that at first, they generally received a warm reception from the Indonesians on South Sulawesi. One rare exception was a reconnaissance mission to Palopo, but the dismissive attitude of the residents there appears to have had more to do with the presence of NICA representatives.[31] As on Java, many nationalists on South Sulawesi were suspicious of NICA. Indonesians interpreted the presence of NICA officials as writing on the wall that the old colonial regime was being reinstated. The reputedly arrogant, pre-war attitude of the Dutch in the NICA unit also contributed to this. As on Java and Sumatra, local nationalists and pro-Republican aristocrats initially tried to make a distinction between NICA and the foreign military occupying force, in this case the Australians. They wanted to work with the latter, but categorically not with the former.[32] This was like inserting a wick into a powder keg, not least because in addition to the NICA officials, in early October 1945 around 500 Moluccan KNIL soldiers were in Makassar who had been in prisoner-of-war camps during the Japanese occupation.

From October 1945, a dynamic of mutual provocation and violence emerged in Makassar and the surroundings, between Moluccan soldiers and *pemuda* and other Indonesians. There were dozens of civilian deaths on both sides in various actions. The first incident took place on 2 October 1945. At five in the afternoon, a truck carrying Moluccan soldiers left their barracks at the nautical training school on Mariso, now Jalan Rajawali 35. The first victim fell when the Moluccans fired without authorization on a group of Indonesians youths wearing red-and-white badges, in front of the mosque of the *kampong* in Maluku. People in three other locations were also killed when the Moluccans shot at groups of Indonesians. An hour after it left, the truck returned to the barracks. The number of fatalities is not known.[33]

What ensued has gone down in history as the 'Ambon Murder' or the 'pembalasan terhadap kekejaman KNIL Ambon' ('revenge for the atrocities by the Ambonese KNIL').[34] In the night of 2-3 October 1945, *pemuda* and civilians from Makassar and the surroundings left for Ambonese *kampongs* armed with anything that might serve as a weapon, and killed dozens of Moluccan civilians, according to Indonesian sources. In doing so, they made no distinction between pro-Republican and pro-Dutch Moluccans. For example, relatives of fighters from the pro-Republican Moluccan armed group Kebaktian Rakyat Indonesia Maluku (KRIM) were also killed. And Latumahina, whose entire family was pro-Republican and whose father formed part of the circle around Governor Ratulangi, was wounded; she survived the massacre.[35]

Australian troops managed to bring an end to the massacre in the early hours of the morning. The tensions continued in the following days and nights, however, and there were reportedly more casualties. The Australian commander Ivan Dougherty and the NICA officers asked Governor Ratulangi to intervene to calm the situation. At a meeting in Budi Langgeng Budi Suworo, Maricaya, he appealed to the population to stop the attacks and restore order. Manai Sophiaan, the leader of the *pemuda* in Makassar, and influential nationalist leaders such as Latumahina and Syaranamual, also made great efforts to reduce the tension and explain the situation.[36]

On 13 October 1945, there was another incident in which two Moluccan soldiers shot wildly at Indonesians wearing red-and-white badges. According to a Dutch source, 'unfortunately, Chinese and even an Australian were also killed or wounded'.[37] Two days later, disturbances erupted again in Makassar, following a 'declaration of war' on the Dutch, Indo-Europeans and Ambonese by the Indonesian People's Army on Java. A Moluccan sentinel was killed by an unknown group at a water reservoir. Some soldiers rushed up, shot at the fleeing attackers and killed two of them. After that, Moluccan soldiers roamed the city in search of their enemies, bent on revenge. They said they were shooting at gatherings of people who wore red-and-white insignia. An unknown number of people were killed in the shootings. In the evening, an unspecified number of Indonesians in the Moluccan neighbourhood went from house to house and killed any residents who had not fled. The Chinese were told that they would be next if they did not throw their lot in behind the Republic.[38]

According to an Australian source, that day and evening, eighteen people were killed and fourteen wounded in the violence between the Moluccans and 'local tribes', although the nationality or ethnicity of the victims was not reported. A Dutch source mentioned 50-60 Ambonese (Moluccan) fatalities: men, women and children.[39] From the casualty lists that were drawn up for this study using diverse sources (see chapter 9), it can only be concluded that on 15 and 16 October 1945, at least one Moluccan soldier and four Moluccan civilians were killed in Makassar and, one day later, another Moluccan civilian in the same city.⁴⁰ Notably, only one Indonesian source appears to refer to the murders of the Moluccan civilians on 15 October 1945. Other Indonesian sources only report the killings on 2 October and the following days.⁴¹ In the night of 18-19 October 1945, there was also violence in Paré-Paré: a Menadonese man was attacked in his bed by a group of Indonesians, and died as a consequence of the stab wounds he endured.⁴²

Ivan Dougherty, the Australian commander in Makassar, evidently believed that the Moluccans were chiefly responsible for the violent incidents in Makassar. On 16 October 1945, he ordered all KNIL soldiers to be confined to barracks until further notice. No one from NICA or the KNIL was allowed to confiscate badges or emblems from the Indonesians, or to interfere with them. KNIL soldiers were only allowed to carry arms when on guard and when they had received approval from the Australians.⁴³

Three days later, the Australian commander-in-chief General T.A. Blamey had the Moluccan soldiers transferred to Balikpapan on Kalimantan. It is said that while out walking, Blamey had seen with his own eyes how the Moluccans had shot Makassans or Buginese out of the trees as they gathered coconuts.⁴⁴ As will become clear below, the provocative actions of the KNIL units in Jakarta (Java) and Medan (Sumatra) also resulted in the British commanders there removing these units from the city, and in Medan they were even disarmed.⁴⁵

The fact that the Moluccan soldiers were undisciplined did not go unremarked by the Dutch military and civilian authorities. The civil servants G.J. Wohlhoff and H.J. Koerts acknowledged the need to 'moderate and control them'.⁴⁶ Colonel C. Giebel, the liaison officer from the KNIL at the Australian headquarters on the island of Morotai, wrote in his memoirs that in early October 1945 a number of KNIL officers were present, but they were unable to keep the Moluccan troops 'in check'. He also pointed out, though, that they had been 'extremely handicapped' by their internment as prisoners of war on Kalimantan, and that they were therefore unable to assert their authority.⁴⁷

In any case, the harsh conduct of these Moluccan KNIL troops – like the actions of their European colleagues who were present in the archipelago at that time – can partly be explained with reference to a long colonial military tradition that aimed to intimidate the Indonesian population with a great show of force and violence. Violence – extreme or otherwise – against warring parties and the population as a whole was a structural feature of colonial warfare in Indonesia prior to 1942.⁴⁸

Other circumstances may also have contributed to the violent actions of KNIL units in the first months of the Indonesian Revolution. After three and a half years of imprisonment in Japanese prisoner-of-war camps, the KNIL soldiers were often mentally and physically exhausted, but this evidently did not prevent the Dutch army leadership from re-deploying them without delay. KNIL soldiers' concerns about the fate of their relatives may also have played a role, as well as the desire for revenge among those whose loved ones had been killed.[49]

The colonially-rooted extreme violence by the military on the Dutch side on South Sulawesi had its counterpart on the Indonesian side, as local Republican leaders were unable to curb the extremely violent attacks by *pemuda* and others on civilians. This was the case on 29 October 1945, when *pemuda* in Makassar attacked two radio stations, a hotel, police barracks and the NICA headquarters. Australian forces eventually drove the attackers away.[50] The attack was planned in secret by the more pro-active members of the *pemuda* movement, without the knowledge of the Republican governor G.S.S.J. Ratulangi and the official leader of the *pemuda*, Manai Sophiaan. The *pemuda* were inspired by the heroic descriptions of the deeds of *pemuda* in Surabaya and Semarang by the journalist St. Mohammed Jusuf Sama, who had just arrived from Java.[51]

The Australian Commander Chilton responded by issuing a proclamation of severe penalties for anyone found guilty of carrying or being in possession of all kinds of weapons, holding parades and demonstrations, or perpetrating acts of violence. Anyone guilty of sabotage, destruction or obstructing public services or Allied equipment could be shot dead on the spot.[52] Chilton was thereby following in the footsteps of his British colleague on Java, General Douglas Hawthorn, who on 13 October 1945 had proclaimed that any Indonesian who was caught looting, sabotaging or carrying weapons could be shot on the spot without trial.[53]

Pro-Republican Indonesians outside Makassar were also guilty of violence and intimidation against pro-Dutch Indonesians, Chinese, Indo-Europeans and Japanese. On 20 October 1945, an estimated 50 Indonesians attacked Japanese civilians who were working at a cement factory near Makassar. The manager and his assistant were killed, two other Japanese were wounded, and goods were stolen, including typewriters.[54]

Sometimes the Japanese used violence, too. For example, on 4 October 1945, Japanese had tied up and beaten two Javanese in their encampment. In response, in the evening a large number of Indonesians forced their way into the Japanese barracks and attacked the Japanese with stones, sticks, knives and other weapons, severely injuring some of them. An Australian company had to come and rescue the Japanese.[55]

Allegedly pro-Dutch Indonesians also fell victim to violence. The expansion of the range of the Australian troops and the reoccupation, together with Dutch NICA officers, of various places outside Makassar gave rise to tensions. Almost every place now had an active, strong youth movement that was led or had contact with the Indonesian leaders and the circle around Governor Ratulangi. In the Bonthain section, for example, anti-Dutch groups wandered around, looting and attacking people. On 23 October 1945, for instance, the director of the post office in Bonthain, the headquarters of the eponymous section, was killed.[56]

The Indonesian leaders and princes were internally divided. A significant number of them initially supported the Republic; another group wanted to cooperate with the Dutch. The attitude of the princes – and, at a lower level, of the *lurahs* (village chiefs) – was important, because they traditionally determined the position of their subjects, which was why their support was sought and/or exacted by both the Dutch and the Indonesian nationalists. In late 1945, NICA increasingly gained the upper hand on South Sulawesi. Although the Australians limited the deployment of their troops because they wanted to repatriate them as soon as possible, the KNIL units present on South Sulawesi were strengthened at the end of 1945 by two infantry battalions. These mainly consisted of former Dutch and Indo-European prisoners of war.[57]

In November 1945, the Australians allied themselves squarely with NICA. Local administrators were now under significant pressure to accept the Dutch. Several of them were removed from their positions by the Australians, because they did not want to work with NICA. A number of them were arrested and imprisoned. In late 1945, the great majority of the princes, including Governor Ratulangi and his people, appeared to opt for cooperation with the Dutch in exchange for far-reaching concessions, such as the creation of a provisional administration. After the Australians transferred their duties to the British on 1 February 1946, however, this cooperation amounted to little in practice. The Dutch refused to grant the promised concessions, and the princes turned out to have been largely coerced into cooperation by the Australians.[58]

After the failed attack on Makassar at the end of October 1945, the armed Republican resistance fled to rural Sulawesi and to Java. Outside Makassar, the situation remained unsettled. In January 1946, two KNIL units managed to take Palopo, the capital of Luwu, after two days of fierce fighting. Given that the Republican resistance was badly armed, they mainly focused on civilian targets, such as pro-Dutch Indonesian civilians.[59] On 26 January 1946, for example, a local *pemuda* group killed a certain Latang and ten others accused of being NICA accomplices in his house in the Surutanga district near Palopo.[60]

Conversely, in the same period the KNIL in the region also used extreme violence against captured *pemuda*. According to a statement – under oath – by the Indonesian district judge Hadji Sinapati, who was not pro-Republican, in early 1946 KNIL soldiers hauled dozens of *pemuda* who had been given prison sentences out of prison and shot them. There were 30 victims in Palopo alone.[61]

Conclusion

On New Guinea and Ambon, Australian and Dutch authority was so strong and Indonesian nationalism so weak that the extreme violence was perpetrated almost exclusively by KNIL soldiers against – allegedly and actual – pro-Republican Indonesians and self-interning Japanese troops. On these islands – as in the whole of Eastern Indonesia, with the exception of Bali – the Japanese were rarely involved in the violence against civilians and captured fighters, either as perpetrators or as victims. The relatively rapid arrival of the Australian troops, the cooperative attitude of the Japanese towards the Allies, the initially weak nationalist movement, and the almost complete absence of young people mobilized by the Japanese meant that there were no confrontations between the Japanese military and Indonesian armed groups over the transfer of weapons, as there were on Java and Sumatra; there, such fights were often accompanied by extreme violence against civilians and captured fighters.

The Australian and Dutch presence in South Sulawesi was initially limited to the capital, Makassar. As on Java and Sumatra, the arrival of NICA and KNIL soldiers also gave rise to major tensions there. In October 1945, this resulted in extreme violence against civilians and captured fighters. On this part of the island, the extreme violence mainly involved *pemuda* against Moluccan civilians and KNIL soldiers against pro-Republican Indonesians. There are no known cases of extreme violence committed by Australian units against civilians or prisoners of war or disarmed military personnel.

The events on the islands of Eastern Indonesia in the first seven months after the Japanese surrender reveal a pattern in the dynamics of violence that could be observed on Java, Sumatra and other islands, too: the inability – and also the unwillingness? – of moderate Indonesian nationalists and the Dutch civilian and military authorities to control the *pemuda* groups and KNIL units, respectively. This, in turn, set in motion a spiral of violence in which civilians and captured fighters on both sides would become victims.

6.

Java and Sumatra: rival international power blocks

It was not until 29 September 1945 that the first 2,000 British troops arrived in Indonesia, at the port of Jakarta. Their numbers would eventually swell to around 50,000, the great majority of them in the British Indian Army. On 10 October 1945, the first 5,000 British troops also landed at Belawan, Medan. The British (Indian) contingent on Sumatra eventually came to 15,000 men. In late September 1945, Louis Mountbatten, the commander-in-chief of all Allied forces in South East Asia (SEAC), concluded on the basis of new information that the nationalist movement was much stronger and enjoyed much more popular support than he had previously assumed.[1]

In order to prevent bloody confrontations with the Indonesians and avoid endangering the aid to Allied prisoners of war and internees, the British would occupy only a limited number of strategic sites, so-called 'key areas': initially Jakarta and Surabaya on Java, and Padang, Palembang and Medan on Sumatra. Semarang, Bandung and Bogor on Java were added later. The aid to Allied prisoners of war and internees and the disarming and evacuation of the Japanese would take precedence over the restoration of Dutch colonial rule throughout the archipelago. In the cities that were appointed key areas, a British military administration would be set up with supreme authority, under which NICA would govern. Outside the key areas, it was up to Dutch – not British – troops to attempt to restore Dutch authority.[2]

The arrival of the Allied troops precipitated a chaotic situation on Java. A letter from a Dutch planter from Bandung reveals the extent of the confusion:

> We don't really know who's in charge anymore, either. In different places you come across the strangest arrangements. In Batavia, there are Englishmen, Dutch, Indonesian militia, regular police, special police, a kind of extremist vigilante group and even some Japanese among those keeping order. All the parties are ready to cut each other's throats at the first opportunity. No one knows whose word is law, because while certain decrees have been made, each party decides for themselves whether they apply, so when it comes to carrying out and monitoring certain orders, confusion reigns.[3]

The situation in Jakarta was different from that in other cities or rural areas, of course, but disorder often prevailed in the other areas where the Allies had not ventured. For example, Abu Hanifah, the chair of the Komite Nasional Indonesia in the residency of Bogor, based in Sukabumi (West Java), reflected somewhat cautiously in his memoirs: 'I must confess that sometimes the administration was in a confused state in my region.'[4]

Hanifah was left more or less to his own devices, because he had no contact with the national government of the Republic of Indonesia. According to Hanifah, communication between and within the provinces was poor. The Republic still lacked a real army, and there was a shortage of police officers and soldiers. Later on, Indonesian armed groups were often better armed than the official Republican army (TKR). Moreover, it could be difficult to keep the *pemuda* in check, certainly when they allied themselves with new political parties.[5]

Mutual distrust and fear

The arrival of the Allies was viewed with suspicion by Indonesians in the archipelago. The sense of distrust was heightened by the harsh conduct of the first KNIL units in Jakarta. The resulting reports and rumours fuelled the suspicion that the Dutch had hitched a ride on the British wagon and come to re-occupy their former colony. The combined landing of British

The Laskar Wanita (Laswi: women's armed group) in Surakarta receives military training. The photo shows women receiving instruction in the use of weapons, including a KNIL revolver, c. 1946. ANRI/IPPHOS

and Dutch troops reinforced existing fears of 'the NICA' to such a degree that there was talk of 'NICA-phobia' among Indonesians.[6]

Time and again, the British on Java and Sumatra, like the Australians on South Sulawesi, observed that the Indonesians were extremely distrustful of the Dutch and NICA. 'Every action of the Indonesians is based on fear of NICA penetration and in order to maintain our position we have to maintain the most strict neutrality,' wrote the British RAPWI Lieutenant Commander A.J. Leland from Semarang (Central Java), for example, on 3 November 1945.[7]

If the Indonesians even got the impression that the British were helping the Dutch or if there were Dutch servicemen in British units, their attitude turned to hostility and armed groups went on the attack.[8] The *pemuda*, in particular, were deeply resentful of NICA and thought they saw NICA spies everywhere. They body-searched people in the street and in trains, hunting for signs of red, white and blue in their clothing or possessions. Sometimes this alone was enough for them to commit murder.[9]

In October 1945 and the ensuing months, many reports were published in the Indonesian-language press about the robbery, torture and murder of Indonesians by NICA soldiers, sometimes accompanied by the Japanese. The name 'NICA' thereby became synonymous with both civilians and the military, and with both KNIL soldiers and British Indian troops. On 18 October 1945, for example, *Merah Poetih* published an article about two Moluccans (at that time called 'Ambonese') in 'NICA uniform'. One of them shot a woman dead and the other killed two men at Jatinegara market in Jakarta. Both Moluccans sustained severe injuries when they were subsequently attacked by a crowd. At other markets in the capital, attacks were said to have been carried out by 'Indian' (British Indian) NICA troops.[10]

The rumours circulating about extreme violence by the enemy were not limited to the Indonesian side. On 5 November 1945, for example, the above-mentioned British RAPWI officer Leland, based in Semarang, wrote in a letter to his wife:

> The good old atrocity stories are getting around. One brought in today from an agent in Sourabaya [sic] was that the Indonesians were openly boasting that they had broiled the flesh of Indians on skewers and had eaten it.[11]

Stories circulated among the Dutch in Bandung that human flesh was being sold at the *pasar*, and in and around Jakarta, according to Dutch reports, *hadji* had fed the hearts of young abducted and murdered Chinese to militia to make them stronger, whilst the rest of the body was sold as meat at the market. Although these reports appear to have been propaganda, sources that were sympathetic to the Republic also reported similar cases of cannibalism as an attempt to absorb the enemy's spiritual power.[12]

Although the possibility that such incidents actually took place cannot be ruled out, reports such as these are very similar to the kinds of stories that often circulate during periods of revolution, war and mass violence, regardless of whether they were deliberately disseminated in order to demonize the enemy. In those first chaotic months after the Japanese capitulation, rumours and reports about the misdeeds of the enemy, true or otherwise, could intensify the fears that always lay dormant in the various groups in the former colony. In short: the indigenous population's fear of the power of the colonial regime, as opposed to the latent terror felt by Europeans at the surrounding, largely unknown colonized world.[13]

The fear of the other could magnify the sense of vulnerability and lower the threshold for violence. In addition, from October 1945 violence was often encouraged by local Indonesian propaganda. After the declaration of independence, propaganda initially emphasized a peaceful transfer of power. In October 1945, however, there was public approval of the use of force by local leaders, in response to the increasing skirmishes between armed Indonesians on the one hand and retreating Japanese troops on the other and, subsequently, Allied and Dutch troops.[14]

Whereas the Allies had initially been depicted as potential allies of Indonesia, they were now portrayed as foreign occupiers and enemies of the Republic, just like the Japanese and the Indo-Europeans. One of the best-known Indonesian propagandists was the journalist Sutomo ('Bung Tomo'), who from mid-October 1945 used his Radio Pemberontakan Rakjat ('Radio People's Revolution'), based in Surabaya, to call for action against the Dutch and later the British (although Sutomo also called for restraint, according to historian Marjolein van Pagee).

From early November 1945, the Republican government in Jakarta also began to justify the use of violence against the Dutch on the grounds that it was inevitable, in view of the many armed incidents between Indonesians, British and Dutch. At the same time, it continued to stress its preference

Sutomo, founder of Radio Pemberontakan in Surabaya, February-March 1947. Source: Cas Oorthuys, Nederlands Fotomuseum

for a peaceful solution.¹⁵ In an official declaration on 17 November 1945 in *Berita Repoeblik Indonesia,* for example, the government of the Republic of Indonesia stressed that it would never use violence to achieve its aims, but that when Indonesians resorted to violence, this was because the Dutch felt it necessary to use force against the Indonesian nation in order to bend it to their will.¹⁶

The growing willingness to use violence, motivated by a sense of vulnerability and sometimes reinforced by propaganda, applied not only to Indonesians and Dutch, however, but to all parties, including the British.¹⁷ A dynamic arose in Indonesia that is similar to a more general process described by the French historian and political scientist Jacques Sémelin:

> the instrumentalization of an *imaginaire* of fears, fed by both shocking and revolting images with a high emotional charge, literally enables the perpetrators to shift from fantasy into action: from the fear of being viciously destroyed to the concrete action of destroying viciously.¹⁸

THE INDONESIAN ATTEMPT TO TAKE POWER: THE FIRST ARMED CONFRONTATIONS

Although the first armed groups (*badan pejuangan*) were formed in August and September 1945, it comes as little surprise that it was mainly after the Allied landings on Java and Sumatra that a large number of armed groups spontaneously formed and frantically developed all kinds of activities. The *pemuda* and armed groups believed that it was essential to take action before they themselves became a target. The armed groups were often difficult to define. There were large *pemuda* organizations with a more formal structure, such as the API (Angkatan Pemuda Indonesia), founded on 1 September 1945, but many more marginal groups also emerged from existing social networks, such as particular *kampongs*, schools, professions or professional associations, and there were many youth groups that had been established by the Japanese or that were gathered around a religious leader or local criminal.¹⁹

There were also armed groups for specific ethnic minorities, such as the Chinese (Angkatan Muda Tionghoa in Malang), Moluccans (Pemuda Indonesia Maluku) and youth from Sulawesi (Kebaktian Rakyat Indonesia Sulawesi). They aimed to demonstrate the loyalty of these minorities to the Republic of Indonesia; a loyalty that was in doubt among Indonesians, due to their privileged position in the prewar Dutch colonial order. They also served to protect their own communities against attack.²⁰

Many of the armed groups did not even have a name or belonged in name only to a large organization. They were often loose associations that frequently entered into and broke alliances with other armed groups, and it was not always clear who the members were. The smaller groups were often held together by a personal bond with the individual leaders. Only a few had a clear political orientation, aside from being nationalist. Due to the lack of mutual communication, the different armed groups were mostly unaware of each other's activities, attempts at organization and contacts.[21] More coordination gradually emerged between the different armed groups at both the national and local levels. In Bandung in mid-November, a coordinating body was founded for all armed groups, the Markas Dewan Pimpinan Perdjangan (MDPP). At the national level, the seven largest *pemuda* groups united on 10 November 1945 in Yogyakarta at a national *pemuda* congress as the Pesindo (Pemuda Sosialis Indonesia), including the PRI (Pemuda Republik Indonesia) and the API (Angkatan Pemuda Indonesia).[22]

On the whole, the armed groups tended to be private rather than official, consisted wholly or largely of *pemuda*, and were primarily engaged with the struggle (*perjuangan*). They also shared a strong desire to propagate and defend the idea of the Republic and independence – two concepts that were inextricably linked in their view – against anyone who threatened them. And this seemed to be at stake after the landing of the first Allied units on Java in late September 1945 and on Sumatra in early October 1945. The *pemuda* needed weapons to defend the newly gained independence and protect the Republic of Indonesia, as the groups were barely armed and often only had sharp weapons such as bamboo spears.[23] The Japanese occupying forces had the greatest potential as a source of weapons. If the Japanese were unwilling to hand their arms over without further ado, force would have to be used. The *pemuda* regarded the prudent, conciliatory attitude of the Republic's leaders with increasing incomprehension.

After the Allied landings on 29 September 1945, however, Sukarno and his cabinet had become even more cautious and even keener to make a good impression on the Allies. They wanted to show the world that the Republic of Indonesia was capable of maintaining peace and order and overseeing an orderly transfer of power. Chaos and uncontrolled violence would tarnish this image.[24] For this reason, national Indonesian propaganda initially focused on campaigning for a peaceful transfer of power.[25] At the local level, too, there were often tensions between Indonesian armed groups that were more inclined towards action and the more cautious civil authorities.

Whilst the arrival of the Allies on 29 September 1945 had increased the urgency of the *pemuda's* arming themselves, ever since the arrival of the Allied vanguard on 15 September 1945, the Japanese had been under heavy pressure from the Allies to take a tougher line against the Indonesians. Previously it had been possible for the Japanese to assume a relatively accommodating stance vis-a-vis the Indonesians; now they were expected to act more harshly, and to use force if necessary. Direct confrontations between Japanese troops and Indonesian freedom fighters became increasingly frequent.[26]

Japan thereby became an enemy of the Republic, as Sukarno – who had cooperated with the Japanese during the Japanese occupation – wrote on 30 September 1945 to the Supreme Commander of the Farther East regions (probably Mountbatten, the Supreme Allied Commander of the South East Asia Command):

> Every inhibition from the side of the Japanese Military Government increased the strong desire to be free and affected a psychological sphere among the population, namely that Japan was the barricade of bringing Indonesia's independence to perfection.[27]

The Indonesian press published more and more negative stories about the Japanese during this period, with the general import that the latter were attacking the Indonesian people and undermining the Republic.[28] The deterioration in the Indonesian attitude to the Japanese is also reflected clearly in the number of Japanese victims. Whereas there had been eighteen victims in September 1945, in October of that year there were probably 415, including 86 barely armed navy personnel and at least 96 civilians.[29]

A contemporary report, probably compiled by the Japanese 16th Army on Java, records a stream of looting, robberies, abductions, attacks and murders on Java after the surrender on 15 August 1945, including dozens of casualties among Japanese civilians and unarmed or captured military personnel. A few examples suffice to give an impression. On 1 September 1945, the administrative and stock warehouse of the office of the Japanese navy in Jakarta was plundered. Two days later in the same city, two non-commissioned officers from the telegraph service went missing in *kampung* Bali in Matraman. On 15 September, a Japanese naval carbide factory was attacked and one person was injured. On 28 September 1945, a Japanese civilian in military service who was wandering around Kediri (East Java) was injured in an attack. On 4 October, a motor vehicle depot was looted in Cilandak

(West Java). On 10 October, 30-45 Japanese were killed at Preanger Bontweverij weaving mills in Garut (West Java). On 20 October, there were 53 fatalities among the Japanese employees of the Oji paper factory in Kaliung near Malang (East Java).[30]

Some cases also involved extreme violence. In Sukabumi, Japanese civilians – so-called *sakura* – were ambushed by small groups of *pemuda* as they left the city. During the war, they had engendered local hatred by looting under the threat of the Kempeitai, seducing young girls and pretending to be Muslims. The *pemuda* cut off their hands, arms, heads and legs. Some Japanese also claimed to have converted to Islam. The *pemuda* then checked their genitals to see whether they had been circumcised. If this proved not to have been the case, they were tortured by the furious and indignant youths and hung up by their ankles.[31] There were similar reports from other places. A Dutch eyewitness reported that Japanese in Ambarawa prison were 'getjingtjangd' (chopped into pieces) in front of the Europeans.[32] During or as a result of fights with Indonesians for weapons, equipment or control of organizations, there were dozens more Japanese casualties among civilians, prisoners of war and disarmed soldiers in October 1945.

From late September 1945, the Indonesians made an increasing effort to take the civilian administration and public services from the Japanese, if necessary by force. On 25 September 1945, shortly before the Allied landings, the central government of the Republic of Indonesia determined that all officials who had hitherto fallen under Japanese authority were henceforth formally officials of the Republic. Furthermore, it was announced that as many governance tasks as possible should be taken over from the Japanese.[33] On the following day, 26 September 1945, government buildings and businesses that had been managed by the Japanese in Yogyakarta (Central Java) were taken over by Indonesians. The takeover in Bandung (West Java) began two days later, and on 30 September 1945 the most important government and public buildings in Malang (East Java) and Surakarta (Central Java) were transferred from the Japanese to the Indonesians.[34]

The Indonesians also tried to get hold of Japanese weapons, motor vehicles, military hospitals and other Japanese provisions and equipment. Buildings and weapons were often handed over through negotiations, sometimes under the pressure of (threat of) violence from large crowds armed with makeshift weapons and units from the Badan Keamanan Rakjat (BKR), the Republican people's security organization. In some cases, actual fighting broke out.³⁵ Eventually, at least two thirds of Japanese weapons on Java were in Indonesian hands.³⁶

The quantity of weapons and the ease with which they were obtained varied by region, and this depended on the attitude of local Japanese commanders. In Surabaya – the headquarters of the Japanese navy – an enormous arsenal of Japanese weapons eventually fell into Republican hands, accounting for an estimated half of the total weapons stockpile of the Republic of Indonesia on Java. Around 50 per cent of the arms were obtained by the local department of the PRI, the Pemuda Republik Indonesia.³⁷

From late September 1945, there were increasing confrontations in Surabaya between Japanese and *kampong* residents, in which the former fled or were killed and their weapons taken by the latter. On 1 October 1945, the Japanese were told that the Indonesians would take over the governance of the whole of Surabaya with immediate effect. In doing so, the local branch of the Pemuda Republik Indonesia cooperated with official Republican organizations and representatives such as the BKR, het Komite Nasional Indonesia Daerah (the regional arm of the KNI), resident Sudirman, the population of Surabaya, and what historian William

Young Indonesian fighters in a train with Japanese officers' swords, Surabaya, 1945.
Source: KITLV

Frederick calls the 'new *priyayi*', a new social class of intellectuals. Large numbers of Indonesians, armed with swords, firearms and bamboo spears, took to the streets. After two days of negotiations, actions involving large numbers of Indonesians and with what was often fierce fighting, in which dozens of Japanese were killed and thousands put in detention camps and prisons, the Indonesians forced the Japanese military and civilian authorities to surrender.[38]

On 3 October 1945, however, Vice Admiral Shibata Yaichiro and Major General Iwabe Shigeo surrendered the last Japanese weapons to the Dutch Captain Huijer, as the Allied representative. Huijer had made an agreement with the Indonesian resident Sudirman and the local Komite Nasional Indonesia that the Indonesians would refrain from confiscating these weapons as a result of the transfer. Huijer did not have enough soldiers to keep the weapons in Allied possession, however, meaning that they fell into the hands of the *pemuda* and armed groups. Iwabe also ordered that not only his units in Surabaya, but all units in his command area of East Java were not allowed to use their weapons. They had to leave the maintenance of public order and the guarding of Japanese army property to the Indonesians. As a result, the weapons of the Japanese garrisons in Besuki, Surakarta and Malang also fell into Indonesian hands.[39]

The situation was different in Bandung on West Java; there, the local Japanese commander, Major General Mabuchi, intervened by force, having spent two weeks assessing the situation. After the Japanese had officially transferred governance of the city to the Indonesians on 27 September 1945, every important building fell into Indonesian hands in the ensuing two weeks. *Pemuda* undertook large-scale actions to obtain Japanese weapons, cars, trucks, warehouses, (arms) factories, arms stores and cattle. On 8 October, Andir airfield fell into Indonesian hands and the Japanese there were disarmed.[40] When a large crowd of Indonesians subsequently attacked the Kempeitai building on 10 October 1945, Mabuchi sprang into action, possibly on the orders of the Allied headquarters in Jakarta.[41] In the following days, the Japanese recaptured the city and the airfield. The *pemuda* were driven to *kampongs* on the outskirts of the city, but they were not defeated. The Japanese ensured that the Republican food boycott of Europeans was lifted, removed red-and-white symbols and confiscated weapons.[42] In West Java, the Japanese would never be disarmed on a large scale, meaning that the number of weapons in Indonesian hands was more limited than in Central and East Java.[43]

Typical of the interconnectedness of the events was that the large-scale violence between Japanese and Indonesians in West Java now spilled over into Central Java, as the Japanese intervention in Bandung reinforced the conviction of the *pemuda* in Central Java that they had to act swiftly to obtain Japanese weapons. In the first days of October 1945, Japanese units in Central Java that had not self-interned came under increasing pressure to give up their weapons to the Indonesians.⁴⁴ The Japanese in Yogyakarta and Surakarta (mostly) surrendered on 5 and 12 October 1945, respectively, whilst in Semarang, some of the Japanese weapons were transferred to the Indonesians on 4 and 5 October 1945.⁴⁵

On 12 October 1945 in Semarang, a crowd of thousands of Indonesians surrounded the barracks of the troops of the local commander, Major Kido, and demanded their complete disarmament. Kido refused, because he had been ordered by Lieutenant General Nagano, the Japanese commander-in-chief in Jakarta, not to hand over Japanese weapons to the Indonesians

On 29 November 1945, Indonesian nationalists murdered 80-120 Indo-Dutch – men, women and children – in Indisch Bronbeek, a residential area in Northwest Bandung for retired KNIL soldiers. Many of these soldiers' families had sought refuge there. Photographer unknown, 1945. Source: NIMH

under any circumstances, even if this meant using force.⁴⁶ In response to Kido's refusal, representatives of the Angkatan Muda *pemuda* organization from across Central Java, together with Wongsonegoro, the governor of Central Java, decided to take action.⁴⁷

In the night of 13-14 October 1945, the Indonesian attack on the remaining Japanese troops in Central Java began with thousands of partly armed Indonesians surrounding the headquarters of Major General Nakamura Junjiro in Magelang. Nakamura surrendered without a fight; he did so, he explained, to avoid endangering the security of the thousands of Dutch who were still in Japanese internment camps in Magelang and Ambarawa.⁴⁸ On 15 October 1945, the Japanese unit of Major Kido in Semarang counterattacked. Four days later, Kido had Semarang under control again, and the First Battle of Semarang came to an end. At least 2,000 Indonesians are likely to have died in the five days of battle. One hundred and eighty seven soldiers were probably killed on the Japanese side.⁴⁹

Dozens of civilians and captured fighters also fell victim to the violence in this first battle. For example, the Japanese executed captured *pemuda* without mercy. In retaliation, *pemuda* killed at least 99 Japanese in Bulu prison in Semarang with a pistol machine gun and bayonets. Another 75 tortured and murdered Japanese were later found in the trenches at the Semarang-Joana Stoomtram Maatschappij tram company.⁵⁰ Moreover, to avenge the murdered *pemuda* in Semarang, on 19 October 1945 86 virtually unarmed Japanese navy personnel, who were travelling from Semarang to Jakarta by train, were hauled from the train near Cikampek and tortured to death.⁵¹

In the areas that would shortly experience Indonesian violence against civilians, such as Banten and Pekalongan, local coalitions attacked Japanese troops around the same time, when the latter proved unwilling to hand over their weapons peacefully. On 4 October 1945, for example, in the city of Pekalongan (Central Java), a fight broke out between the Kempeitai and the Indonesians in which 32 Indonesians and 13 Japanese lost their lives. After negotiations brought an end to the fighting, the Japanese departed, leaving a power vacuum. The same happened in Banten (West Java), where the Japanese left the region after fighting in Warunggunung (near Rangkasbitung) and Serang on 7 and 9 October 1945.⁵² In both regions, the absence of the Japanese, Allied troops or strong representatives of Republican authority created space for alliances between local Indonesian groups to deal with anyone who was believed to be standing in the way of the Republic of

Indonesia, either because they were suspected of wanting a return to the old colonial order or because they were unwilling to side with the Republic, for whatever reason.

On Sumatra, by contrast, there was initially little Japanese armed resistance to the Indonesian takeover of power. The *pemuda* had more trouble with senior Indonesian officials who were reluctant to defy the Japanese and the Dutch. It was only in November 1945 that the *pemuda* sought more confrontation with Japanese troops, in order to get weapons to fight the British. Anti-British feeling grew rapidly among some *pemuda* at that time, mainly due to the reporting about the Second Battle of Surabaya (10-29 November) on Java between the British and the Indonesians.[53]

Increasing violence against civilians and captured fighters

In the course of October 1945, the extreme violence against civilians and captured fighters of diverse origin intensified on Java and Sumatra. Whereas on Java mainly Japanese civilians and disarmed soldiers had initially fallen victim to the Indonesian extreme violence, the violence now targeted other groups who were suspected of standing in the way of independence. At the same time, these groups were not always defenceless victims, and they too sometimes resorted to violence themselves.

Shortly after the first Allied landings on Java, a phase began in which particularly Indo-Europeans who had remained outside the internment camps during the Japanese occupation, but also *totoks*, were isolated, excluded and eventually interned. Between 4 and 12 October 1945, there was an Indonesian boycott of 'Europeans' in several places on Java. It seems that this action was mainly aimed at Dutch and Indo-Europeans, and to a lesser extent the British – and not against other Europeans who happened to be in Indonesia at the time.

According to the *pemuda*, Indonesians and Chinese were no longer allowed to sell food to the Dutch, Indo-Europeans and British at the *pasar* (market) or other places. Servants had to stop working for their Dutch masters. There was a general cessation in the provision of services to the Dutch. For example, *betjak* (trishaw) drivers in Malang were no longer allowed to transport Dutch clients. Moreover, in Malang, like in many other cities on Java, the electricity and water supply to European houses was cut off. Here and there, Indonesians and Chinese lent a helping hand, but they had to do this in secret, because the *pemuda* enforced the boycotts with intimidation and violence if necessary. Anyone who did not cooperate was at risk of being killed.[54]

The exclusion of the Dutch and Indo-Europeans on Java and Madura was followed by the internment of these two groups. These two phases flowed almost seamlessly into one another. Whilst the boycotts were announced in the period until 12 October, the period between 11 and 19 October saw the first wave of internments of men and older youths, mainly Indo-Europeans. Almost at the same time, a group of women was interned. The remaining women, children and elderly and sick men were imprisoned in internment camps on Java in November and December 1945.[55] The local Komite's Nasional Indonesia (KNIS) organized the internments. After this, the local police, the Republican BKR and other pemuda groups picked up people from their homes or assembled them in prescribed places and took them to the camps.[56] Only in Jakarta was there no internment, due to the presence of the British, whilst in Bandung there was no general internment. In the end around 46,000 people, including 4,500 *totoks*, were interned in the 398 so-called Republican or *bersiap* camps on Java and Madura. The great majority of them were thus Indo-Europeans.[57]

At around the same time, from the beginning of October 1945, a wave of extreme violence against Dutch, Indo-Europeans and Moluccans broke out across the whole of Java and Sumatra. One of the first massacres on Java took place on 7 October 1945. A group of eighteen 'Europeans' who were travelling by train from Jakarta to Bandung were taken off the train at Krandjie. Fourteen of them were murdered in nearby *kampongs*; four survived.[58] On 11 October 1945, *pemuda* then attacked Depok (West Java), where many Christian Indonesians lived, and killed 33 residents.[59] In mid-October, the intensity of the violence increased.

One of the most notorious massacres took place on 15 October 1945 and on the following days at the Simpang Club in Surabaya (East Java), since 4 October 1945 the headquarters of the Pemuda Republik Indonesia. Before the Japanese occupation, the club had been a society that had exclusively admitted white Dutch; it was also where the arch-conservative political party known as the Vaderlandsche Club was founded in 1929. On 15 October, c. 3,300 Dutch men and boys were arrested in Surabaya and taken to Kalisosok and Bubutan prisons. Some of the prisoners were assembled at the Simpang Club. The PRI wanted to hold a tribunal to establish the extent of their involvement in NICA. The process quickly got out of hand. Impatient *pemuda* guards and residents of surrounding *kampongs* gathered

KNIL *lieutenant R. Dunki Jacobs in Depok (West Java), where many Christian Indonesians lived. Pemuda killed 33 residents here. The well is said to contain the corpses of a man and a woman; photo from 11 April 1946.* Source: W. van de Poll, National Archives of the Netherlands

outside the Simpang Club and began to shout 'Merdeka' and 'Death to the whites'.⁶⁰

The Europeans who were brought in were body-searched by the *pemuda*. Anyone who had NICA money or a red, white and blue pin on them was killed on the spot. According to eyewitnesses, they were first beaten, and then mutilated and decapitated.⁶¹ One of those present recalled having seen piles of flesh from severed limbs, amongst which the wounded still lay.⁶² Others recounted women being tied to a tree in the Simpang Club's back yard and being stabbed in the genitals with *bambu runcings*.

The heart-wrenching screams and writhing and jerking of the unfortunate woman's body, wracked with excruciating pain, seemed only to intensify the brutes' murderous rage. They stabbed the place in question in the lower body with their *bamboo runcings* until the unfortunate woman died of her injuries and loss of blood.⁶³

It is likely that between 40 and 50 Dutch and Indo-European prisoners were murdered at the Simpang Club.⁶⁴

Coincidences could make a difference between life and death. For example, lieutenant first class W.J.M.W. Timmers was interrogated at the Simpang Club in Malay by an Indonesian officer who accused him of being a Red Cross spy, because Timmers was carrying a pass from the International Red Cross, which he had been given by the Swiss consul in Surabaya. It was clear that things were not looking good for him:

Until he asked, 'Where did you study?' 'Leiden', I replied. And at that moment he dismissed the guard, the door closed, and suddenly he started speaking Dutch, saying, 'I studied there too!' It turned out that he had done civil service training there. The atmosphere changed immediately.⁶⁵

The officer ensured that Timmers had a guard, so that he could reach Kalisosok prison on Werfstraat unharmed.

The notorious murderer Zainuk Sabaruddin (b. 1922) was active in the vicinity of Surabaya. He had received PETA officer training during the war, and in early October 1945 he founded a Polisi Tentara Keamanan Rakyat (PTKR, military police) unit in Sidoardjo. Between 11 October and December 1945, he is said to have murdered more than 100 Europeans and Indonesians in Pacet, a holiday resort in the mountains; many of his victims were tortured to death.⁶⁶ For example, a fifteen-year-old boy recalled witnessing the execution of eight Moluccans – four men and four women from Surabaya. First the women were killed with teak clubs:

Then the men were interrogated by SABAROEDIN, during which he ordered them to hold the blade of his sword, which he then jerked towards him, meaning that all of their fingers were cut off. They were then tied together by the legs to the back of a truck, and dragged through the city in front of everyone as a deterrent example. When it turned out they were still alive, they were wrapped in mattresses, doused with petrol and set alight.⁶⁷

On 14 October 1945 in Kuningan near Cirebon, West Java, a number of Indonesians who probably belonged to the Islamic umbrella organization Masjumi and the socialist youth organization Pesindo used *bambu runcings*, axes and other weapons to attack twelve Indo-Europeans who had been interned by the Indonesian police, when the police wanted to transfer them from the police station to prison. Only a few of them reached the prison alive. The next day, the Indonesian police picked up another eleven Indo-Europeans from Cilimus and other places in the vicinity of Kuningan. According to a report drawn up around two years later by the Netherlands Forces Intelligence Service (NEFIS), 'the people' also attacked these eleven men on the way; they did not kill them immediately, but began by cutting off their hands and stabbing them with *bambu runcings*. The bodies were taken to the prison, where the prison governor ordered the other prisoners to dig a pit and throw the total of 23 victims into it. Those who were still alive were stoned or beaten with a shovel. According to the report, some of them were buried alive.⁶⁸

Unlike on Java, the Indonesian violence against civilians on Sumatra appears to have been directed mainly against the Chinese in the first months of the Indonesian Revolution. Relatively prosperous and highly visible in society, the Chinese were regularly targeted by *pemuda*, who attacked them and looted their shops and storehouses. According to a Dutch source, for example, the Chinese in the town of Pematang Siantar (North Sumatra) were attacked by a 400-strong group of Batakkers armed with sharp weapons and clubs every day between 15 and 25 September. In response, the Chinese in larger towns formed militias in their own neighbourhoods. There were increasingly clashes between these militias and *pemuda*.⁶⁹

The first major violent incident against Dutch and Moluccans on Sumatra took place on 13 October 1945 at the former 'Pensiun Wilhelmina' on Jalan Bali in Medan, the club of Westerling's Moluccan police officers. That eruption was preceded by a period of rising tensions. Two months earlier, on 15 August 1945, the Dutch commando officer C.A.M. Brondgeest had been dropped in Medan, and had subsequently established a police force there consisting of Moluccans, Menadonese and Indo-Europeans, including many ex-KNIL soldiers and former police officers. When Lieutenant Raymond Westerling arrived on 12 September, Brondgeest handed the leadership over to him. In September 1945 the police force numbered around 600 men, 150 of whom were armed. The Moluccans guarded the most important places in the city, such as the water tower, the electricity company and the hospitals, and later also the camps and buildings in Medan where the former Dutch internees from the Japanese camps were being housed. When the atmosphere deteriorated and the *pemuda* started pressing for violence, Westerling also sent patrols into the city. He also brought threatened Moluccan and Menadonese families from the *kampongs* to safety. The Moluccan police force and the *pemuda* groups provoked one other, and there were daily shootings.[70]

According to some Indonesian sources, the mood in the city had been tense for some time. The last straw was a parade by KNIL soldiers and NICA on 12 October 1945, which began and ended at the Wilhelminahuis. The next day, the events rose to a climax. According to Indonesian publications, a KNIL soldier is said to have arrested a banana-seller at a checkpoint in Jalan Bali, insulted the Republic, and removed a red-and-white badge from the seller's chest and trampled it. A *pemuda* present began to hit the soldier and a fight broke out. Another KNIL soldier shot at the banana-seller and injured him in the leg. The sound of shooting drew *pemuda* from the immediate vicinity, who forced their way into the building. Ahmad Tahrir, the leader of the Badan Pemuda Indonesia, and Japanese troops initially managed to calm the situation.[71]

Once they had left, however, the violence flared up again. The *pemuda* attacked the former 'Pensiun Wilhelmina' once more. According to a Dutch source, five people were killed in the attack, but according to Indonesian sources, seven KNIL soldiers, a Swiss family and a Dutchman who was managing the hotel were killed, and 96 men and women on the Dutch side – probably Moluccans and Menadonese – were injured. The difference in numbers appears to stem from the fact that Indonesian publications confuse the fatalities in this incident with another incident in Pematang Siantar that took place two days later. It is a striking illustration of the fact that the two incidents have been merged in the Indonesian historiography and are seen as the beginning of the Battle of Medan – a standard part of the Indonesian narrative that is completely absent from the Dutch historiography.[72]

That other incident, which took place on 15 October 1945 in Pematang Siantar, 140 kilometres away, concerned an attack on another hotel, Hotel Siantar, owned by the Swiss H. Suerbeck. At that time, there were a number of guests at the hotel and a four-man RAPWI party, to assist and evacuate Allied prisoners of war and internees. Due to the grim atmosphere in the town, a group of Moluccans and Menadonese had sought protection with the RAPWI party and had moved into some houses next to the hotel.[73]

As happens more often, the Dutch and Indonesian sources differ on the cause of the attack. According to a Dutch *post facto* reconstruction, based on the accounts of the survivors, on 15 October 1945 at 12 midday, a Moluccan came running into the hotel because the Indonesians had tried to take him out of his house.[74] By contrast, an Indonesian publication tells of how a KNIL soldier, when passing the office of the Barisan Pemuda Indonesia, emptied his carbine without provocation and then fled to the Hotel Siantar.[75] This version should not be discounted, given the provocative KNIL behaviour in other places, but it is not confirmed by other sources.

An hour later, in any case, a Japanese truck arrived at the hotel carrying Indonesians armed with spears, sabres and clubs, demanding that all Moluccans and Menadonese be handed over. The Swiss hotel employee, Bauer, managed to persuade them to leave without taking anyone. Later that afternoon, a large number of Indonesians came back. This time they attacked the hotel and set it on fire. The Japanese soldiers present did nothing. In the attack, two members of the RAPWI party died fighting, while at least four guests and a hotel employee were killed. Two Swiss men who were taken away from the hotel were also killed. Ten to twenty Moluccans were also reported killed. The remaining guests who were captured were freed by the British on 19 October 1945.[76]

The Indonesian extreme violence also triggered a counter-reaction. Dutch, Indo-Europeans and Moluccans sometimes took individual revenge for the killing of relatives. In Kuningan on Java in mid-October 1945, 23 Indo-Europeans were killed, including some members of the Loriaux family. One male member of the family, whose father and brother had been killed, escaped the same fate because he no longer lived at home. According to his cousin, he later returned to Kuningan and killed six Indonesians after interrogating them.[77]

Father Jan van der Pol described a similar incident in Bandung:

The base instincts of self-defence... back and forth, back and forth. I experienced how an Indo, who knew his family had been killed, he – I was there and this is true – simply asked a British Indian for a revolver and bullets and went away and then, it was around eight or seven o'clock, he came back and said: 'So, that's settled. I got 21 of them.'[78]

In Jakarta and Bandung, Dutch, Indo-European, Moluccan and Menadonese former KNIL soldiers and youths formed armed groups. In Surabaya, the *pemuda* dispersed such armed groups before they could really take action. The armed groups on the Dutch side wanted to protect the Dutch, Indo-Europeans and Moluccans against the many murders, looting and abductions by pro-Republican groups and individuals.

From the Dutch perspective, the British stance was too passive. For example, Indonesian armed groups in Jakarta pursued a campaign of terror against Europeans. Dutch people taking a walk were hauled from the street and strangled or chopped into pieces, and their bodies were dumped in one of the canals. Houses where European families lived were surrounded at night and the inhabitants murdered.[79] According to historian Herman Bussemaker, patrolling pro-Dutch armed groups rescued hundreds of Indo-European families in Jakarta.[80]

The armed groups on the Dutch side not only offered protection, however, but they also took revenge for the Indonesian violence and tried to

The destroyed house or office of a European, Java, year unknown. Source: KITLV

restore colonial rule. In doing so, they often used brute force. In Jakarta, a group of soldiers from an armed group, which operated from the barracks of the pre-war 10th battalion of the KNIL, arrived just too late to save the Bokelaar family in Cawang. One of the soldiers saw that his sister was still alive, but the well she was in was too deep to rescue her. He then shot a random number of Indonesians in the nearest *kampong*.[81]

From late September 1945, the first regular KNIL units active on Java also contributed to an escalation of the violence in the early phase of the Indonesian Revolution. Hendrik Wehmann formed part of the support company of the KNIL battalion infantry V (a unit with the nickname '*Andjing* NICA', 'NICA-dogs'), which was officially founded on 10 December 1945 and moved to Cimahi not long afterwards. There the battalion took over the guarding of the former internment camps from the Japanese. Later he said in an interview:

> I experienced what the Indonesian population did to their own Indo population. I saw how they impaled a pregnant woman from a camp on bamboo. Another was stabbed in the chest with a bamboo spear. I couldn't forget that, and therefore I wanted to cool my revenge on the people who did it. It didn't just happen to the *blandas* [White Europeans/Dutch], but also to Indonesians who were on our side. They were also slaughtered by those people. That's why I said I felt revenge and frustration, because I saw it.[82]

According to Wehmann, the sight of these atrocities and their own experience of combat meant that the KNIL men acted more harshly. When it came to Indonesian fighters, it was a case of: 'Catch, shoot, job done'.[83] The entire family of a sergeant from the same Andjing NICA was reportedly killed. He is then said to have forced confessions from *pemuda* by making them stand in the sun on a zinc plate, and setting fire to their genitals with petrol.[84]

British and Dutch eyewitnesses were critical of the aggressive, provocative conduct of the armed groups and remobilized KNIL soldiers, who shot at everything that seemed suspicious to them. The war diaries of the British and British Indian units in Jakarta contain many references to incidents in which Dutch and Moluccan (then still known as Ambonese) troops behaved provocatively and appeared to shoot first. 'Trigger happy Ambonese started firing in xth Bn area [10th Battalion] close to own barracks,' noted the 1st Patialas on 20 November 1945 in their unit's war diary. 'It is apparent that the Ambonese are completely irresponsible and are a danger to the lives and property of all nationalities.'[85]

The Dutch writer Jan Fabricius believed that the British were right:

> The Tommies, with their years of war experience, accused our soldiers of being 'trigger-happy'; that is, being too quick to shoot. And when I saw our men driving past in cars, pale and thin, gun at the ready, the fear came over me that the accusation was well-founded. They did not comprehend the dangerous state of nervous exhaustion in which they found themselves. The suffering they'd endured was still burning in their eyes. For years, they'd had to swallow humiliation after humiliation: they'd been beaten, kicked, half-starved and hadn't been able to defend themselves. Now they held a carbine in their hands; this weapon meant power, authority; now they didn't have to take anything anymore. And they had a score to settle.[86]

The senior civil servant Van der Plas also recognized this behaviour. He described an action by KNIL troops in Jakarta: 'Near my house, for example, some of those soldiers in a truck shot dead a Javanese walking in the street in the middle of the day. He turned out to be the driver of a doctor who lived there, who'd had the courage, despite the ban on working for the Dutch, to keep working.'[87] It was certainly not the case that the irregular armed groups and soldiers on the Dutch side were only responding to Indonesian violence. Sometimes they resorted to extreme violence on their own initiative, without a direct or with a fabricated cause, by (randomly) shooting at or abusing Indonesians without trial, for example. In doing so, they were partly responsible for the escalation of violence in the early phase. The extreme violence by regular units and armed groups on the Dutch side – which worked together – was condoned by local commanders, but also by the army leadership.[88]

According to the British, there were so many shooting incidents in which the KNIL soldiers were the first to open fire that on 15 October 1945, Lieutenant General Christison decided to remove all KNIL units from the centre of Jakarta and concentrate them south of the city.[89] Moreover, on 2 November 1945, Mountbatten decided to allow no additional Dutch troops onto Java and Sumatra until the security situation had been improved through negotiations. Mountbatten and other British commanders feared that the arrival of new Dutch units would escalate relations further. For the Indonesians, their presence alone was like a red rag to a bull. The British also wanted to focus on maintaining order in their key areas, and the trigger-happy troops on the Dutch side were unhelpful in this respect.[90]

His colleague on Sumatra, Brigadier T.E.D. Kelly, took a similar measure. Soon after his arrival, he observed that the Indonesian population were boycotting the Dutch and viewed the English as preparing the way for the restoration of Dutch colonial rule. The aggressive behaviour of Westerling's police force merely made the situation worse, in his opinion. He therefore disarmed the police officers and only allowed them to carry *klewangs* (sabres). He then had them removed from Medan and placed in a camp halfway between Medan and Belawan, where they were guarded by British soldiers. When the Indonesian police in Medan increasingly turned against the Dutch and the protected camps, they were also disarmed by the British. The British likewise attempted to bring a halt to the escalation of the violence in Padang and Palembang by disarming the Republican police in October and November 1945.[91]

Confrontations between the Indonesians and the British

Lieutenant General Philip Christison, commander-in-chief of the British troops in Indonesia, had declared on arrival that the British would limit their actions on Java to liberating the Allied prisoners of war and disarming the Japanese. The British armed forces would not get involved in the internal affairs of the Dutch East Indies. He expected the Indonesian government to maintain the civilian administration outside the key areas occupied by the British.[92] In other words, this was a *de facto* recognition of the Republic of Indonesia. In addition, the British Secretary of State for War, John Lawson, had declared in Singapore that the Allied obligations did not commit the British to waging a war for the Dutch against the Indonesian nationalists.[93]

In the meantime, the Indonesians had the feeling that the British were nevertheless helping to restore Dutch rule. For example, Sukarno wrote to Christison on 9 October 1945:

> When you first came here we really believed that you would not involve yourself in internal politics. We still believe that that is your intention. Nevertheless, accumulating evidence makes us wonder if the Dutch are not, while hiding under the skirt of the Allied Army of Occupation,

being afforded the necessary cover to establish and strengthen themselves in this country.⁹⁴

Indonesian suspicions were reinforced by the expansion of the British presence on Java. Not long after the British had landed in Jakarta, they were forced to press further into the interior of West Java, to Bandung and Bogor. These two cities were important due to the large number of Dutch internees and their strategic location: Bandung as a railway junction, Bogor because it was on the road from Jakarta to Bandung.⁹⁵

In Central Java and East Java, the British were likewise confronted with the unforeseen consequences of their obligation to protect and evacuate the Allied internees. As explained above, the British had not originally intended to go to Central Java. They had to revise their plans, however, after teams from RAPWI, the Allied organization for the relief of prisoners of war and internees, discovered in September 1945 that there were still 24,750 internees from Japanese internment camps on Central Java. Reports that Indonesians had surrounded the camps and were refusing to allow food in made it even more urgent to protect the internees, from the Allied perspective. On 19 October 1945, the day that the First Battle of Semarang ended, British troops arrived in Semarang, and they arrived in Surabaya six days later.⁹⁶

In the last three months of 1945, the arrival of the British in Central and East Java led to large-scale armed confrontations between British and Indonesians: on Central Java in Magelang (29 October-2 November), Semarang (18-21 November) and the camps in Banjoebiroe and Ambarawa (19 November-1 December), on East Java in Surabaya (28-29 October, 10-29 November), and on West Java in Bandung (24-29 November). The British were often in a perilous position in this fighting, because they faced superior numbers. In Surabaya in late October 1945, for example, 4,000 British had to take on 10,000-20,000 trained and armed Indonesians with tanks, armoured vehicles and light and heavy artillery, and 70,000-140,000 civilians.⁹⁷

Only with the support of Japanese combat troops and with the aid of air strikes and reprisals, such as the torching of whole *kampongs*, were the British able to hold out in these large-scale battles. Moreover, the British in both Magelang and Surabaya had to enlist the help of Republican leaders to engineer a cease-fire. The fighting claimed a large number of victims, particularly on the Indonesian side. During the Second Battle of Surabaya, there were an estimated 14 fatalities and 59 wounded on the British side, while the number of victims on the Indonesian side probably ran into the thousands. It is likely that the latter also included many civilians.[98]

The skewed ratio of the number of victims on the two sides during the Second Battle of Surabaya suggests that the British use of violence was disproportionate, but it also shows that the Indonesians could do little with all the heavy weaponry at their disposal. Revenge played a role in this; not only for the death of Brigadier A.W.S. Mallaby, the commander of the 49th Indian Infantry Brigade, op 30 October 1945 during the First Battle of Surabaya, but also for the extreme Indonesian violence against British and British-Indian soldiers and Dutch and Indo-European women. The soldiers of the 5th Indian Division who landed in Surabaya in November heard stories from the survivors about how some of their colleagues had literally been slaughtered in October 1945: how all of their limbs had been chopped off, one by one.[99]

The so-called Gubeng transport is a notorious example of extreme violence against civilians and British-Indian troops. Twenty British-Indian servicemen were escorting a convoy of twenty trucks carrying around 200 Dutch women and children from camp Gubeng to camp Darmo; the Allies thought that they could be protected more effectively there as they awaited their final evacuation. On 28 October 1945, at around 4:30 p.m., the convoy encountered a barricade. The first half of the convoy came under heavy fire from uniformed Indonesians from the TKR with rifles, light machine guns and grenades. The TKR took this action because it had agreed to the evacuation of former internees from the Japanese camps, but not of the Indo-Europeans and Dutch who remained outside the camps. Four British-Indian soldiers, including the commander, were killed immediately, while several trucks caught fire. Some of the British-Indian soldiers opened up the trucks and took around 40 women and children to some empty houses. Other British-Indians stayed in the street to defend the convoy.[100]

This was followed by a massive attack by Indonesian men from the surrounding *kampongs*, armed with rifles, spears and clubs. The TKR now had to shoot at other Indonesians in order to rescue the women and children. The British-Indian troops in the street were eventually forced to retreat to the houses. 'As soon as the men on the road were withdrawn, the mob swarmed over the lorries looting and flinging the dead bodies of women and children into the road,' the 49th Indian Infantry Brigade reported afterwards:

Members of the Chinese Red Cross in Surabaya stand ready to pick up the wounded from battle, probably in the autumn of 1945. Source: Sergeant Bert Hardy, Imperial War Museum

Owing to the necessity of conserving ammunition, the few INDIAN troops defending the women could not open fire. Wounded Sepoys were seen to be dismembered by JAP swords. Two women and children were seen to be butchered with swords by the crowd.[101]

Four trucks carrying around 27 women and children, including three dead and six wounded, managed to get away and reach British posts. The remaining troops held out until the next evening, but they had to surrender when their ammunition ran out. They and the women and children they were defending were severely mistreated. The soldiers were taken to the prison, where three of them were murdered. The women and children were taken away in handcuffs.[102] In total, dozens of women and children died, possibly even more than a hundred. In addition, most of the British-Indian soldiers lost their lives.[103]

For the British and British-Indian troops, the mission in Indonesia was largely a question of survival and minimizing risk. They were greatly outnumbered, and they were overburdened mentally by a struggle that was not their own. The torching of villages and towns, the abuse and shooting of prisoners, and the excessive use of heavy artillery and aircraft were routine elements of this; a strategy that was condoned or even suggested from above. The ambushing and murder of British soldiers was followed by harsh reprisals that, in turn, provoked counter-reactions from the Indonesian side, resulting in a vicious circle of extreme violence.[104]

In particular, the Battle for Surabaya and the murder of 24 passengers of a British military aircraft in Bekasi, as well as the large-scale fighting elsewhere, led to a hardening of British behaviour and an approach focused on the use of violence as a form of deterrence.[105] During the heavy fighting for Semarang – at the same time as that in Surabaya – the aforementioned British RAPWI officer Leland did not mince his words in a letter to his wife:

> We will try all we know to prevent useless bloodshed on either side, but the timehas [sic] come to take the glovesoff [sic] to a certain extent, and make the most of our very small forces by using a certain amount of 'terror tactics'. The shoot-up of yesterday [aerial bombardment] and the odd *kampong* burning has, I am sure, been very economical in life of Indonesian civilians. The effect is tremendous. They are at present quite bewildered and the cohesion has gone out of them.[106]

Sumatra

From the British perspective, the situation on Sumatra was relatively peaceful at first. In mid-November 1945, however, the security situation deteriorated there, too. Padang, according to a NEFIS report, was afflicted by a 'reign of terror' that prevented pro-Dutch Indonesians from daring to go to work. There were stabbings and abductions of Chinese, Dutch and Moluccans on a daily basis.[107] The 21st of the month saw the murder of 21 people who had gone to live outside the part of Pandang that was enclosed with barbed wire and guarded by British-Indian soldiers.[108]

Around the same time, anti-British sentiment among *pemuda* on Sumatra rose rapidly as a result of the reporting of the large-scale fighting between British and Indonesians in Surabaya from 10 November 1945. This led to a series of skirmishes between *pemuda* and British troops in late November and the first half of December 1945. The number of clashes with Japanese troops also increased, mainly because *pemuda* were trying to get hold of the weapons they needed to fight the British.[109]

By means of negotiations, bluff and the assistance of Japanese deserters, possibly about 350 of them, the TKR 'B' – an armed group affiliated with the TKR – and *pemuda* from Pesindo in the vicinity of Medan and the rest of the East Coast of the province of Sumatra managed to obtain Japanese weapons on various occasions. On 13 December 1945, the fighting between British troops and Indonesians caused the British commander, Brigadier Kelly, to limit Allied operations to an area of 8.5 kilometres outside the city limits of Medan and Belawan. Anyone found carrying weapons inside this zone would be shot on the spot.[110]

Until then, Japanese commanders had reacted relatively mildly to Indonesian actions. The most senior Japanese commanders had made tacit or explicit agreements with the Republic of Indonesia that weapons would be handed over in order to avoid fighting. Even the killing of one or two Japanese did not prevent the demoralized Japanese troops handing over their weapons without resistance.[111] The situation changed in early December 1945. In the first ten days of that month, *pemuda* in Tebing Tinggi and the surrounding area killed dozens of Japanese soldiers in various places. According to the Japanese liaison officer Takao Fusayama, the large number of Japanese victims, especially the 60 dead in Tebing Tinggi itself, whose bodies were hacked into pieces, was the immediate cause of a large-scale Japanese revenge action on 13 December that claimed hundreds, if not thousands, of Indonesian lives.[112]

Indonesian sources, on the other hand, place more emphasis on a specific incident as the immediate cause of this revenge attack. Around 10 December 1945, a group of c. 300 *pemuda* from Pesindo, led by Amir Taat Nasution, stopped a train at Tebing Tinggi station. The train was carrying Nakashima, the former Japanese governor of North Sumatra, his family, staff and an armed escort, from Medan to Kisaran. The *pemuda* asked the Japanese to hand over their weapons. The latter initially refused to comply with the demand, saying they had promised the Allies not to give up their arms. At first the negotiations between the Japanese and Indonesian representatives of the Republican government, the KNI and Pesindo yielded nothing. After hours of standing still in the hot sun, the Japanese eventually decided to hand over their weapons in exchange for food and drink. Meanwhile, a Japanese commander from the escorting troops was abducted by other *pemuda* and taken to the headquarters of the TKR. When attempting to escape, he was killed by an Indonesian policeman who was helping Pesindo.[113] It was then that the Japanese took action, according to this reading.

It seems more likely that it was not this incident alone, but the sum of several incidents involving dozens of victims that led the Japanese to believe that it was time to set an example in order to prevent further violence against their own people. On 13 December 1945, in the course of the afternoon, a Japanese battalion advanced to Tebing Tinggi. Small units cut off the four entrances to the city, while the main force entered the city with two tanks. In the following days, there was fighting throughout the city between *pemuda* and Japanese. It was an unequal battle, as only a few *pemuda* had a rifle or pistol; most were armed only with spears, machetes and suchlike. Here and there, this led to outright massacres. More than a thousand lightly armed *pemuda* from outside the city attempted to enter Tebing Tinggi across a hanging bridge over the Padang River near Bulianstraat. The Japanese concealed themselves at the end of the bridge, however, and shot a hundred of them, perhaps even hundreds, on the bridge.[114]

The Japanese used extreme violence during their punitive expedition. According to Dutch sources, they shot anyone they encountered. They also decapitated around 60 Indonesians and displayed the heads on stakes as a deterrent example.[115] Indonesian publications report prisoners with bound hands being shot or bayoneted by the Japanese on the banks of the Bahilang River or in the bushes. Japanese troops are also said to have stopped a train on 13 December and killed the male passengers.[116] The violence came to an end on 17 December. The estimate of the number of Indonesian deaths in Tebing Tinggi varies from 500-800 to several thousand. It is very likely that these figures also include civilians.[117]

The events had a major impact, not least on Tebing Tinggi itself, where the population was terrified and the national movement was crushed. Political activity was now out of the question, and red-and-white emblems disappeared from the streets. Carrying weapons was prohibited, and anyone who infringed this was arrested and their weapons were confiscated.[118] But the events also had major consequences outside Tebing Tinggi. The Republic could not afford any large-scale confrontations with the Japanese and the British. The Japanese punitive expedition brought the leaders of the Republic of Indonesia and the British military leaders on Sumatra back to the negotiating table. Major General H.M. Chambers, the Allied commander on Sumatra, promised that the TKR outside Medan would be given the status of an official peacekeeping force and that the Indonesian police in Medan would be re-armed. The Japanese and British would also refrain from interfering in the civilian Republican administration unless strictly necessary. In turn, Governor Hassan pledged to cooperate with the Allies. With the aid of the British concession, he managed to convince the *pemuda* that it was essential for them to restrain their actions against the British. As a result, it was relatively peaceful for several months.[119]

The intra-Indonesian struggle for power

In parallel with the widespread violence in the rest of Java and Sumatra, there was also violence against civilians and captured fighters in areas where not one of the four national or international parties prevailed. For example, in the first months of the Indonesian Revolution, in Banten and Pekalongan on Java and in Aceh, North Sumatra, among others, there were uprisings and actions against local administrators, police officers and other representatives of the established order, which became known as 'berdaulat', 'daulat' or 'dombreng' actions. These events also became known as the 'social revolution', although several Western historians consider this an over-generalization, and thus a misleading term for very different regional changes of power and embryonic socialist revolutions.[120]

The power upheavals in Banten and Pekalongan clearly reveal the artificial nature of the division between so-called *bersiap*, understood as extreme violence in cities against 'foreign' groups, and *(ber)daulat* as 'internal' Indonesian violence in the countryside.[121] Indo-Europeans, Dutch and Moluccans were also murdered in rural areas, often in intra-Indonesian violence that was directed against representatives of the ruling order. Characteristic of much of the violence against civilians and captured fighters from various backgrounds in the initial months was that it was directed, as mentioned above, against anyone who stood in the way of the Republic of Indonesia or who was suspected of doing so. But the disruption in both Banten and in Pekalongan (the Tiga Daerah affair) clearly shows that additional factors were at stake.

The Northwest-Javanese region of Banten was known for its strong desire for autonomy, the religious fervour of its people, and its anti-colonial disposition. In 1926, Banten had already been the scene of an uprising by the PKI, the communist party. The communists were aided by *ulama* (Islamic scholars) and *jawara*, local bandits, who were united in their hatred of Dutch colonial rule. The harsh suppression of the uprising in 1926 intensified the groups' dislike of the Dutch and the *pangreh praja*, the Indonesian bureaucratic elite who often came from outside the region.[122]

By cooperating with the Japanese regime, the *pangreh praja* had made themselves more hated still. Even before the end of the Japanese occupation, major shortages of food and clothing and accusations of corruption had led to social unrest. This unrest only increased after the Japanese surrender. As in 1926, the communists, *ulama* and *jawara* took the lead, while the majority of the revolutionary movement consisted of peasants. Indonesian nationalism had gained only a limited foothold in Banten, while *pemuda* played a minor role due to the absence of large cities and a significant middle class and intelligentsia.[123]

As elsewhere on Java, the Japanese were the primary target, due to their weapons. On 7 and 10 October 1945, there were confrontations with Kempeitai soldiers in Warunggunung and Serang, respectively. The Japanese managed to fight their way out of Serang, and then left Banten. In this way, the revolutionary movement of *ulama*, *jawara*, communists and peasants seized power. Their next victims were the loathed bureaucratic elite and the Indonesian police. Throughout the residency, the revolutionaries replaced officials at all levels – from the *camat* (deputy district head) to the regent – with *ulama*. Some administrators were imprisoned. The transfer of power was sometimes violent, and police agents and administrators were killed. In general, however, the violence against Indonesian officials was limited, if only because the most senior police officers and administrators had already fled to Bandung and Jakarta in early October.[124]

Dutch civilians and captured soldiers were also the target of revolutionary action. Strikingly, Indonesian sources only report a foiled attempt to carry out a massacre in the missionary hospital in Rangkasbitung, where all of the Dutch citizens from the Lebak region had been taken for their protection. Local authorities and leaders prevented the *pemuda* from carrying out their plan. The next day, the Dutch were taken to the prison in Rangkasbitung. This was followed by an attack by people from Ciomas, who demanded the Dutch people's property, among other things. With the aid of the local Komite Nasional Indonesia (KNI) and a telephone intervention by Ce Mamat, the leader of the newly established people's council, the Dewan Rakyat, the attackers were dissuaded from carrying out their plan.[125]

The violence against 'Europeans' in Serang, especially in the city's prison, is not mentioned in Indonesian sources about the events in Banten.[126] An eyewitness report on the events that took place in Serang after the departure of the Japanese, however, drawn up by an Indo-European, clearly and movingly illustrates the interconnected and simultaneous nature of the extreme violence against different communities and nationalities:

> The people were hopping mad and set out to kill anyone who was Japanese, and eventually move on to those Europeans who were still living in Serang, especially Indo-Europeans (for there was a report in Serang that in Batavia, the Indos were fighting hand in hand with the Japanese against the Indonesians). The people were openly urged to slaughter any Europeans.[127]

The prison was now in the hands of the *jawara*, with fatal consequences for the six Europeans who were imprisoned there; a lieutenant and five employees of the Billiton Maatschappij mining company. These employees had crossed from Belitung – formerly known as Billiton – to Serang in a proa, and had been arrested as 'NICA accomplices' by the BKR and handed over to the police. In the morning of 12 October 1945, the naked lieutenant was forced to leave the prison, where a crowd with *bambu runcings* awaited him. When he dared not step forward, a bucket of hot water was thrown over him from behind. He then took a few steps, whereupon he received two slashes from a *golok* in his shoulder and his thigh. He fell forward and was dragged into the street. His genitals were cut off and his belly was slashed open. His body was left at a crossroads for three days, until the Chinese buried it in a cemetery. That night, the five others were also murdered one by one with assault weapons in the prison garden.[128]

The revolution in Banten came to an end after a few months. In addition to the civilian administration, which was now dominated by *ulama*, local communists established a people's council or Dewan Rakyat, supported by peasants and the *jawara*. They set up their own *laskars* (militias) and a police force that was aptly named the 'polisi-jawara'. The Dewan Rakyat ruled Banten between October 1945 and early January 1946. The lack of administrative experience and tensions between the *ulama* and the communists and among the left-wing revolutionaries, however, undermined the work of the Dewan Rakyat. There was also a lack of support at the national level. The government of the Republic of Indonesia feared that the social unrest would spread to the hinterland of Jakarta, and that this would be used by the British and Dutch as proof that the Republic was unable to maintain peace and order in its own territory. Moreover, the *jawara* were difficult to control; they continued to commit murders and robberies. There were several clashes between the armed gangs and the Indonesian army, the TKR. In early 1946, the TKR intervened and brought an end to the Dewan Rakyat and the local revolution.[129]

The local revolution in Pekalongan took place at the same time as in Banten, but it ended a little earlier. The revolutionary movement there consisted of a coalition of *pemuda* and veterans of the nationalist and communist movements. Japanese soldiers were initially the target, as they were in Banten, but they were not prepared to hand over their weapons without a fight. When the Japanese left the region following negotiations, the extreme violence was directed against Indonesian, Chinese, Indo-European, Moluccan and Menadonese civilians. From 8 October 1945, so-called *lenggaong* – similar to *jawara* in Banten – carried out actions against the ruling authorities. In a few weeks, they ousted almost all of the local Indonesian administrators, including the regent; some of them were murdered. The *lenggaong* also took the lead in anti-Chinese violence: Chinese shops were set on fire and Chinese rice mills were confiscated. Between 11 and 14 October 1945, leaders of the *pemuda* organizations API, AMRI and AMRI-I were involved in the murder of more than 100 Indo-Europeans, Moluccans and Menadonese in the residency, who were accused of betraying the revolution.[130]

In Balapulang, not far from Tegal in the Pekalongan residency, leaders of Angkatan Muda Republik Indonesia, according to a report by the Netherlands Forces Intelligence Service (NEFIS), gave the order on 11 October 1945 that all 'Europeans' in Balapulang and the surrounding area be killed. Around midnight, eighteen Indo-Europeans from four different families were picked up and taken to an empty building opposite the local hotel. They included five children of F.M. van Wijk, aged between two and fourteen years old. Van Wijk had been the superintendent of the plantation of a sugar mill in Balapulang that had closed for good during the Great Depression. He had then launched a soya bean business and bred horses. He had apparently mistreated the Javanese coolies on the plantation, and had done business with the Japanese during the occupation.[131]

The eighteen Indo-Europeans were taken to the backyard of the house the next morning, to loud jeering and shouts of 'merdeka' and 'kita moesti minum darah blanda' ('We must drink Dutch blood'). A kind of bamboo scaffold was built there, to which the red-and-white flag was attached. The victims had to bow three times to the spectators, honour ('hormat') the flag and ask for forgiveness from the Republic. Then, one by one, they each received a blow with an iron rod. Anyone who did not die immediately was finished off with *bambu runcings*. Two of the Van Wijk children were grabbed by their legs and thrown against the wall of the well. They were then tossed into the well, on top of the bodies of the other victims. The two children did not die, however; the rising groundwater restored them to consciousness, and they managed to escape. One of them died of his injuries several days later. In late 1947, when the area was occupied by the Dutch, their father returned to Balapulang on horseback with two colleagues, to take revenge for the murder of his children. He randomly shot dead eleven Indonesians in the city and another four outside.[132]

The revolutionary movement in Pekalongan was eventually brought to an end relatively quickly. On 16 November 1945, a popular front was formed in Tegal, known as Gabungan Badan Perjuangan Tiga Daerah (GBP3D), which took power in the residential capital of Pekalongan on 10 December 1945. Less than four days later, units from the TKR, the Indonesian Army, and Islamic militias – both of which were at loggerheads with the popular front, for different reasons – retook the capital Pekalongan. They then put an end to the Tiga Daerah movement elsewhere, too.[133]

Unlike on Java, the violent upheavals in Aceh (December 1945–March 1946) and on the East Coast of Sumatra (March 1946) only claimed victims among Indonesian civilians – men, women and children. They were the target of extreme violence because they were seen as collaborators with the Dutch.[134] In Aceh, the *ulèëbalang* – traditional local rulers – faced a coalition of supporters of PUSA, a reformist Islamic organization, much of the *pemuda* movement (which had a clear Islamic character, unlike elsewhere), and peasants who wanted land and justice. The *ulèëbalang* wanted to restore their pre-war authority and punish those who had attacked them during the Japanese occupation. Apart from Mohammad Daud from Combok – the most outspoken and feared *ulèëbalang* – they did not wish openly to challenge the Republic of Indonesia. Some of the traditional leaders even sup-

Men from Laskar Bambu Runcing standing ready with spears to take on the Dutch. Two men in front have firearms. Place unknown, 1946. Source: ANRI/IPPHOS

ported the Republic. Nevertheless, after some hesitation, the official civilian and military authorities eventually turned against the *uleëbalang*.[135]

On 4 December, there was a first skirmish in Sigli over the ownership of Japanese weapons, between armed supporters of the *uleëbalang* and the PRI and thousands of villagers who were armed only with spears and *parang* (knives). According to Japanese sources, hundreds of people were killed in several days of fighting. The violence only deepened the gulf between the two parties, and led to mutual attacks and skirmishes. Although the *uleëbalang* were strongest in the Pidië region, they finally tasted defeat in January 1946 after the arrival of two well-armed militias from outside Pidië, the Barisan Mati from Tangsé and a group from Peudaya. They were supported by large numbers of *mujahidin*, villagers and, in the final attack on Daud Combok himself, by contingents of the special police and the TKR. Hundreds of *uleëbalang* and their relatives and supporters are likely to have been killed after the fighting.[136]

Subsequently, in mid-February in Langsa, in the east of Aceh, a purge of the police and the *uleëbalang* took place. Several hundred *mujahidin* led by

Husain Almujah moved to the north coast of Aceh to oust all *ulèëbalang* from their positions. It eventually came to negotiations, and all of the *ulèëbalang* in Aceh Besar were interned to prevent further violence. Officials were replaced at every level of government, resulting in the *ulama* gaining power and great influence. Most of the land of the *ulèëbalang* was given to peasants, while much of their money went to the government. By late March 1946, the local revolution was over.[137]

In the province of Sumatra's East Coast, with its capital Medan, there was also extensive violence against the rajas and sultans, the aristocratic rulers. The gap between the *pemuda* armed groups and conservative administrators had widened, but the moderate leaders of the Republic of Indonesia, who had few means of exercising power, were unable to mediate between the two sides. After reports of the murders of the *ulèëbalang* in Pidie spread to Sumatra, the princes still only half-heartedly supported the Republic. The news of the founding of the Persatuan Perjuangan by the legendary unaffiliated communist Tan Malaka, which spread to Medan in mid-January 1946, legitimized and focused the demands of many *pemuda* for more revolutionary change. The central leadership of the Persatuan Perjuangan (with representatives from Pesindo, the PNI and the PKI) on Sumatra eventually spearheaded the action against the princes from 3 March 1946.[138]

For the leaders of the Persatuan Perjuangan, the 'social revolution' was subordinate to the elimination of the princes. Most of the leaders had no plans for a democratic or socialist form of government; a more important motive was the rajas' sympathy for the Dutch and the threat they posed to independence. Nor did the prospect of acquiring the princes' legendary wealth play an insignificant role. The violence varied, depending on local ethnic differences and the extent to which the princes could call on armed support. The princes were seen as a symbol of oppression and collaboration. There were hundreds of casualties. Around ten days after the beginning of the 'social revolution', the counter-reaction began. It was the fall of the Langkat dynasty in particular, in which seven prominent members were decapitated and the two daughters of the sultan were raped, that convinced doubters that the 'social revolution' had gone too far. With the aid of three national government ministers, who came over from Java, regional Republican leaders managed to get the situation back under control. In doing so, the ministers appealed to the more radical revolutionaries to prioritize the national revolution over the socialist revolution.[139]

The interventions by the TKR in Banten and Pekalongan and the Republican authorities on East Sumatra ensured that the intra-Indonesian violence in these areas was curbed somewhat. The arrest of Tan Makala and some radical supporters on 17 March 1946 also strengthened the authority of the Republic of Indonesia.[140] In addition, as we shall explain in the conclusion to this chapter, there were other reasons why the intensity of the violence against civilians and captured fighters on Java and Sumatra fell after the peak in October and November 1945.

Decreasing violence against civilians and captured fighters on Java and Sumatra

The Japanese attack on Tebing Tinggi on 13 December 1945 led, as mentioned above, to a relative decrease in violence against Dutch civilians and Japanese and British troops on Sumatra. In November and December 1945, Indonesian regular units and armed groups on Java had suffered defeats against the British and Japanese in Surabaya, Semarang, Magelang, the camps in Ambarawa and Banjoebiroe and Bandung. In addition, the British gradually gained control of the situation in and around Jakarta and Bogor.

On 27 December 1945, the British began a successful ten-day operation ('Operation Pounce') with the aim of creating a cordon around Jakarta, blocking the exit roads, and combing *kampongs* for weapons and suspicious individuals. The electricity and water supply and other public facilities were brought under British control, and the barricades in the city were removed. The British arrested hundreds of Indonesians whom they accused of being involved in 'extremist' activities, and purged the local police of nationalist influences. As a consequence of these actions, the operations and the terror campaign by the Indonesian armed groups became increasingly ineffective and the city became safer for Europeans. For the time being, the Republic had lost the battle for Jakarta. After Prime Minister Sjahrir withdrew the TKR from the city on 19 November, the most important militia, Laskar Rakyat Java Raya, decided to remove all but one of its units from the city. Moreover, on 4 January 1946, the government of the Republic, with the exception of Sjahrir, left for the safer Yogyakarta.[141]

At the same time as Operation Pounce, the British also launched a two-week purge operation in Bogor (West Java) and the surrounding *kampongs*, which included searching for weapons and suspicious individuals. Almost 100 people who had been held prisoner by the Indonesian nationalists were released, and large Japanese arms stockpiles were destroyed.[142]

An elderly Chinese man is supported after being beaten by pemuda, *Cilimus, Cirebon, West Java, 1945-1946.* Source: NIMH, Rups Collection

It took longer to get Bandung under control. North Bandung, where the Dutch were staying, was relatively safe due to the protection from British troops. In early 1946 in the south of the city, which was under Indonesian control, Chinese increasingly found themselves the target of abductions, intimidation, looting and murder. On 23 March 1946, the British announced that all armed Indonesian men within a radius of 11 kilometres in all directions of the city had to make themselves scarce. The *pemuda* complied with this order, but as they left the next day they set fire to South Bandung, transforming the district into a sea of flames ('lautan api'). Even after that, however, road travel between Bandung, Jakarta and Bogor remained a risky business.[143]

Another factor that contributed to the decrease in violence was the fact that there were fewer obvious 'targets' available. Most former internees from the Japanese civilian camps had been evacuated by the British in December 1945, sometimes at risk to their lives, and shipped to Singapore, Bangkok and Ceylon, modern-day Sri Lanka. Others were relatively safe in camps in Bandung, Cimahi and Jakarta, which were under Allied control. Moreover, by the early spring of 1946, half of the planned 50,000-60,000 evacuations to the Netherlands had already taken place.[144] In addition, in the period between October and December 1945, around 46,000 individuals, mainly

Indo-Europeans, were interned in so-called Republican camps, where they were in any case safe from attacks by *pemuda* and others. On 9 January 1946, the TKR and the British agreed that all former prisoners of war and internees from Republican camps would be brought to Jakarta. The first test transport of 156 women and children was taken by train from Malang to Jakarta in late January 1946. Nevertheless, the evacuations would not really get under way until 20 May 1946, partly because the British made transport aircraft available at that point.[145] Finally, the same period of May-July 1946 saw the repatriation of more than 90 per cent of the 300,000 Japanese who were still in Indonesia.[146]

In the last two weeks of March 1946, a start was made – under British leadership – on the first official talks between the Indonesians and the Dutch. This paved the way for allowing regular Dutch units onto Java and Sumatra from April 1946. After all, British commanders had decided on 2 November 1945 that no new Dutch troops would be permitted to land on Java and Sumatra until the military situation had been improved through negotiations. This provided more protection for civilians on the Dutch side.[147]

However, the relative decrease in violence against civilians and captured fighters did not mean that Dutch, Indo-European, Moluccan and (allegedly) pro-Dutch Indonesian civilians were no longer the target of intimidation, assault and murder after March 1946. At times, such as around the first Dutch offensive (21 July-5 August 1947), the level of Indonesian violence against these groups rose sharply – so much so, indeed, that the historian William H. Frederick even refers to a 'second *bersiap* period'.[148]

Finally, it is important to note that the fall in the number of civilian fatalities after the end of March 1946 did not apply to the Chinese and Indonesian communities. It is likely that most Chinese casualties occurred after March 1946, in outbreaks of violence such as that in Tangerang (West Java) in June of that year, where Indonesians turned on the Chinese *en masse*, resulting in 1,085 deaths. In the years that followed, the Chinese were targeted by regular and irregular Indonesian armed forces, especially during the two Dutch military offensives.[149] And in the fierce intra-Indonesian violence on South Sulawesi in the second half of 1946, which was directed against people who were pro-Dutch or suspected of being so, hundreds of Indonesian men, women and children were murdered in what was often a gruesome manner. These events gave rise to the deployment, from 5 December 1945, of the special forces (Depot Speciale Troepen, DST) under Lieutenant – later Captain – Westerling, who are known to have used extreme violence on a large scale.[150]

Conclusion

On Java and Sumatra, a combination of factors led to violence against civilians and captured fighters on a larger scale and of a fiercer intensity than on the other islands. Java, and to a lesser extent Sumatra, functioned as the heart of the archipelago, and it was there that the Republic of Indonesia, the British, the Dutch and the Japanese struggled for power during this period. None of these parties had sufficient dominance, however, to impose its will by force on the others, or was willing to pay the necessary price of such hegemony in human lives.

As a result of the arrival of the British and the Dutch on Java and Sumatra from late September 1945, an already tense situation escalated. The reports and rumours going back and forth about the actions and atrocities contributed to an atmosphere of distrust and fear. At first, Indonesian violence was directed against the Japanese, due to the desire to obtain their weapons in order to defend themselves against the British and the Dutch. As a result of this, and on the sidelines, dozens of Japanese civilians and captured soldiers were also killed.

From early October 1945, an extremely violent situation developed in which force could be used in all directions and assume extreme forms. Indonesian *pemuda* and other armed groups attacked Dutch, Indo-European and Moluccan civilians, killing several thousand people. Places where neither the Allies, nor the Japanese nor the Republic were able to assert their power were often the site of violent social uprisings by local Indonesian alliances. They got even with anyone who was associated with the colonial elite or with whom they had another score to settle.

The Japanese played a key role and, depending on the attitude of the local commanders, could tip the balance towards the Indonesians or the British and the Dutch. They were closely involved in the extreme violence as a result, both as victims and as perpetrators. Armed groups on the Dutch side and the first KNIL soldiers also contributed to the escalation of violence by taking revenge, and sometimes by shooting Indonesians without any provocation. The more the British were drawn into the conflict, the more harshly they acted, ultimately resulting in the deaths of many thousands of Indonesians.

On the whole, there were many more civilian casualties on Sumatra and on Java because there were many more potential targets. Java was the most populous island in Indonesia. Moreover, most Indo-Europeans were more vulnerable on Java, because – unlike on the other islands – they had not been interned by the Japanese during the Second World War, and were therefore unable to stay in the relatively safe internment camps after the Japanese surrender. The escalation of the violence was also facilitated by the fact that national and international parties were unable to curb the violence by the various armed groups, individuals or regular units. Indeed, as we shall see in chapter 7, they often condoned it.

7.
The organisation of Indonesian violence

Gerlach introduced the concept of the 'extremely violent society' to describe a society in which different population groups fell victim to mass physical violence perpetrated by different social groups – sometimes in cooperation with official bodies, sometimes not – for a range of reasons. From this perspective, Indonesian society in the first phase of the revolution can be described as 'extremely violent', with the caveat that it did not involve a single state, but competing parties fighting for state power.

There was a multiplicity of violence, in other words, targeting different groups for diverse reasons; but that does not answer the question about who was responsible for all of these fierce, often extremely bloody outbursts of violence. It is on that question that we shall focus in this chapter, which addresses Indonesian extreme violence against civilians and captured fighters, and in particular against Moluccan, Menadonese, Indo-European and Dutch civilians in the first phase of the Indonesian Revolution. Our starting point, after all, is research on the *bersiap* period, as it is known in the historiography and the Dutch culture of remembrance, during which violence against these groups played a key role.

Who were the perpetrators, and to what extent was the violence organized? Sources from this period often refer to Indonesian perpetrators in very general terms. The reports of the Australian units active on Sulawesi, for example, often mentioned the 'Free Indonesian Movement' or its members.[1] In Dutch newspapers in Indonesia, such as *Het Dagblad*, Indonesian perpetrators were often described in general terms, such as 'extremists' or 'pemoeda'/'pamoeda'.[2] Indonesian publications also made relatively frequent reference to 'pemuda' or 'the people' who attacked the Dutch, Indo-Europeans and Moluccans. Sometimes, these publications also gave the names of *pemuda* or armed groups.[3]

The most detailed information that we have about the perpetrators and the organization of the violence, however, comes from interviews and reports by the Netherlands Forces Intelligence Service (NEFIS). It is clear that these sources, which were produced by a Dutch intelligence service, are biased and should therefore be examined with great caution. In other words, we cannot make any representative or quantitative statements based on them. When examining the NEFIS reports, one is struck by the diverse backgrounds of potential perpetrators: from a *soto* (soup) salesman, a *wayang* (shadow play) player and a hairdresser to a village head (*lurah*) and other officials.[4] According to NEFIS reports, the number of perpetrators who belonged to an organization was limited. When organizations are named in reports, they tend to be the Pemuda Republik Indonesia and the Republican police.[5]

Very occasionally, the Republican-founded people's security agency, the Badan Keamanan Rakjat (BKR), is mentioned. It is claimed, for example, that the murders of eighteen Europeans in Cibatu (West Java) were committed by members of the BKR under the leadership of Ambas, the *kepala* (head) of the local branch of the BKR.[6] However, there were clearly considerable differences in the attitudes of local branches of the BKR. In Garut (West Java), according to a Dutch eye witness, the local BKR unit protected European and Dutch civilians against the violence by 'leaderless gangs'.[7]

To what extent were the killings coordinated at the national, regional or local level? It is striking that in every case, the killings began almost simultaneously on Java, Sumatra and Sulawesi – in the first and second weeks of October 1945. This might indicate a certain level of coordination, although there are also other explanations (imitation, the availability of weapons, and so forth). Rumours that the attacks and murders on Java and beyond were organized were already circulating among the Dutch at the time. For example, the senior government official Van der Plas wrote in a memo on 11 November 1945 – without adding any hard evidence – that the terror campaign that targeted the Dutch in particular was planned. According to him, the central government of the Republic of Indonesia had approved the actions, or in any case would have been able to stop them. He attributed this to the quandary in which Sukarno found himself. The latter had to make concessions to the *pemuda*, the BKR and the Tentara Keamanan Rakyat (TKR), because they were his only means of power. At the same time, he had to promote himself and his position to the Allied armed forces and the rest of the world.[8]

No evidence has yet been found of an explicit central order to carry out the killings.[9] However, it should be noted that access to Indonesian material has been limited and much material may have been lost. Below, we return to the question of the existence or otherwise of orders to use violence. First, we consider the likelihood of the killings having been organized centrally by the government of the Republic. There are two aspects to this question: first, we can ask how far Sukarno and the Republican government were able to control the *pemuda* and other armed groups, and whether the situation was different on each island. Second, we can ask why the government might have had an interest in the extreme violence.

The fact that Sukarno could exert influence over the *pemuda* and armed groups is shown, among other things, by the events in Surabaya (29 October) and Magelang (2 November), when he managed to achieve cease-fires, although the cease-fire in Surabaya was ultimately short-lived. At the same time, though, the situation around the 'declarations of war' in mid-October 1945 shows that some *pemuda* and armed groups on Java went their own way, taking few of the Republican leaders with them. From 11 October 1945, these 'declarations of war' or calls for violence appeared in pamphlets and various Indonesian and international media. The 'declaration of war' that drew the most attention was one in which the Tentara Rakyat Indonesia (the Indonesian People's Army) called on all Indonesians to engage in a guerrilla war against the Dutch, the Indo-Europeans and the 'Ambonese', using all possible means, from firearms to poison and even wild animals.[10] In *Merdeka*, the newspaper that functioned as Sukarno's mouthpiece, two articles appeared on 12 October 1945 in which Islamic scholars were called upon to issue a *fatwa* against NICA and calling for a war against NICA, the Dutch and the colonial oppressors.[11]

While these calls initially appeared to have come from the Indonesian government, it soon turned out that they and other statements had been issued by *pemuda* groups.[12] The Republican government subsequently attempted to correct the false impression. On 17 October, a government statement was published in *Merdeka* banning expressions such as 'declaration of war' and 'holy war' in the struggle for Indonesian independence, mainly because of the impression they would make abroad. According to this statement, only the government had the right to declare war. To underline this, in the same issue of the newspaper a statement was published by the Masjumi, the national Islamic umbrella organization, that only the Republican government could declare a holy war.[13] The Republican government continued to find it difficult to control the media, however. For example, the radio station in Yogyakarta broadcast a new declaration of war on 18 or 19 October 1945. It was withdrawn again shortly afterwards at the behest of the Republican Minister of Information, Amir Sjarifuddin.[14]

Further signs that official Indonesian bodies were able to coordinate on a larger scale were the boycotts on the sale of goods and provision of services to Dutch and Indo-Europeans, and the internment of mainly Indo-Europeans on Java in October 1945. How these events unfolded could be considered an indication of the extent to which official bodies were able to impose their will on the various armed groups.

Between 2 and 12 October 1945, Indonesian boycotts were put in place against the Dutch, Indo-Europeans and British in various places on Java. According to President Sukarno, this happened spontaneously. Officials at the local level, for example in Bandung, denied that they were responsible.[15] The Dutch side, however, pointed an accusing finger at the Republican authorities. Some Dutch people claimed that the central Republican government had declared a food boycott on 4 October 1945, whilst other Dutch – in Bandung, for example – thought that the boycott had been called by the Komite Nasional Indonesia, and that the actions against the Dutch and Indo-Europeans were supported by the official Indonesian police.[16] As early as 23 September, a Dutch agent had informed the British RAPWI officer Tull about a full boycott on Java of Indo-Europeans, Dutch, Moluccans and Menadonese, and about confiscation of their property, which would start on 1 October 1945.[17]

In any case, it is striking that the boycotts were declared in different places on Java – from Malang in East Java to Jakarta in West Java – over a period of around ten days. That is not to say, however, that the boycotts were indeed organized centrally; it could also indicate contact between *pemuda* groups or other armed groups in different regions and cities, or imitation after reports of such actions in Indonesian media, such as the announcement of the boycott on 2 October in Jakarta in the newspaper *Merdeka,* or Sutomo's broadcasts on Radio Pemberontakan.[18] The latter took advantage of radio as the new mass medium of the age. In addition to Bahasa Indonesia and English, the broadcasts by Radio Pemberontokan were given in various regional languages, such as Javanese, Madurese, Sundanese, Balinese, Buginese, Ambonese and Batak.[19] By capitalizing on this, *pemuda* were able to expand their influence rapidly over the rest of the archipelago.

The same organizational question arises with regard to the Indonesians' internment of Indo-Europeans and Dutch in camps. This followed almost seamlessly from the boycotts, and took place only on Java and Madura. Whilst the boycotts were announced in the period up to 12 October 1945, the first wave of internment of Dutch and in particular of Indo-European men and older boys took place between 11 and 19 October 1945. Almost at the same time, a group of women was interned. The remaining women, children and elderly and sick men were imprisoned in internment camps on Java in November and December 1945.[20]

Here, too, the question is whether the actions were organized centrally. The historian Mary van Delden, who has written a standard work about the Republican camps, considers it 'highly likely' that the internment was triggered by a central order,[21] as the action tended to follow a fixed pattern. Local Komite's Nasional Indonesia (KNIs) organized the internment everywhere; the local police, the BKR and other *pemuda* groups then collected people from their homes or assembled them in prescribed locations and took them to the camps.

In Van Delden's opinion, the rapid and largely orderly way in which the internment took place suggests that it was organized centrally, in the form of an order from a senior authority with significant power.[22] The historian Herman Bussemaker also believes that the internment on Java around 15 October 1945 was centrally managed. According to him, it would have been too great a coincidence had the internment begun spontaneously all over Java. He suspects that after the murders in Depok and the Pekalongan residency (the 'Tiga daerah affair'), the national government instructed the field police to start arresting people.[23] According to Rémy Limpach, on the other hand, there is much to suggest that this presentation of events was a *post facto* attempt by Sukarno to justify the large-scale actions by the *pemuda* police.[24]

All things considered, Van Delden makes a convincing argument that it is highly likely that the internment was managed centrally. Partly in the light of the boycott and Sukarno's intervention during the fighting in Surabaya and Magelang, it is probable that the national government also had at least a certain degree of control over the *pemuda* and other armed groups when it came to the internment. At the same time, the matter of the 'declaration of war' shows that this control was limited; and it would have been even more limited on the more distant islands.

This brings us to our second question: to what extent did Sukarno and his government have an interest in the killings? A strong case is made in the scholarly literature, as well as in some contemporary sources, that the government of the Republic of Indonesia wanted to show the Allies and the rest of the world that the Republic was able to maintain order and govern the country effectively. In doing so, it hoped to gain international recognition in a peaceful way. Large-scale, fierce violence against civilians and captured fighters would hardly have advanced this cause.[25]

President Sukarno and Vice-President Hatta made several public appeals to the people to refrain from using force and from taking the law into their own hands. On 30 October 1945, for example, a government statement was published in *Merdeka,* calling for discipline on the part of the Indonesian people. Uncoordinated action would only lead to anarchy and harm the Republican cause.[26] Sutan Sjahrir, prime minister of the Republic from 14 November 1945, also publicly condemned the killings. In his pamphlet *Perdjuangan kita* (*Our struggle*), published on 10 November 1945, he wrote that whilst the zealous actions of the youth provided momentum, they did not work to the Republic's advantage. 'This is the case, for example, for the provocation and the hostile treatment of foreigners that weaken our position in the eyes of the world', argued Sjahrir.[27]

Such statements can be dismissed as attempts to make a good impression on the outside world, of course, but minutes of the Indonesian Council of Ministers seized by the Dutch show that Sjahrir and his ministers also maintained behind closed doors that confrontation with the Allies must be avoided. In doing so, they were acknowledging the difficulty of keeping the revolutionaries in check.[28] At the same time, there seems to have been a certain degree of equivocation among Republican leaders about the violence, the boycotts and other actions against civilians and captured fighters. They may have condoned them in order to keep more radical groups on board, or they may have used the violence and other actions as a means of pressure in the negotiations. For example, in letters to the British commanders Christison (9 October 1945) and King (11 October 1945), respectively, Sukarno and Hatta warned that imminent violence by Indonesian youths against Indo-Europeans and the Dutch could only be prevented if a number of measures were taken.[29] In his letter to Christison, Sukarno outlined several minimum demands to prevent bloodshed, including Allied recognition of his government as the *de facto* government of the Republic of Indonesia.[30]

In a letter to the British commander in Jakarta in early October, Hatta pointed out that Dutch provocations were stirring up the popular mood:

> One of these days some foolish Indonesian youths will start hitting back at the Dutch, the trouble will soon spread throughout the city, and in a short while we will be in big trouble. This I want to avoid. If I may make a suggestion, would it not be better for the time being to restrain all activities of Dutch soldiers?[31]

Even Sutan Sjahrir, who had strongly condemned the extreme violence of the *pemuda* in the pamphlet *Perdjuangan kita*, condoned the violence at times. In an English-language broadcast on Radio Free Indonesia on 8 February 1946, whilst emphasizing the need for discipline, he explained that the extreme violence was a response to the violence that the Indonesians had suffered for centuries, violence that was many times worse:

> You know that the cruelty and the force I have mentioned are something extraneous to our real nature, something foreign to our normal existence, something forced upon us by the environment in which we find ourselves today. You here know how and why our people have come to do these things, albeit with feelings of revulsion, but these in the wide world outside cannot understand this. They do not have enough understanding of the factors involved. They do not realize that much of the cruelty and [words missing] though it might appear, is far, far less than it has been our lot to experience over a period of centuries.[32]

Nor can we rule out the possibility that some authorities were involved in the incitement to violence, for example by radio. For example, General Sudirman, the commander of the Indonesian Army, is said to have helped the journalist Sutomo to set up Radio Pemberontakan Rakjat in October 1945. As mentioned above, as 'Bung Tomo' Sutomo would gain prominence and notoriety among the Dutch for his passionate radio speeches, in which he called for action against the British and the Dutch.[33] Sutomo's role was also controversial on the Indonesian side at the time, according to historian Marjolein van Pagee.³⁴

Local Indonesian authorities sometimes took a permissive attitude – or looked the other way – when it came to violence against civilians and captured fighters. In the Eastern Javanese city of Sidoarjo in early October 1945, for example, Zainul Sabaruddin formed a military police unit, the Polisi Tentara Keaman Rakyat, which quickly gained a reputation for sadism and bloodthirstiness. No Indonesian authority had the courage or means to deal with him. Yet his actions were also condoned, because of his ruthlessness and because his police force was one of the best-armed and best-equipped groups in East Java, making him a useful tool for leaders and commanders who wanted to strengthen their position of power. For example, Sabaruddin developed a close relationship with the young aristocrat Raden Mas Yonosewoyo, commander of a unit of the TKR in Surabaya, who used Sabaruddin to eliminate his military rivals.³⁵

Dutch sources also indicate that here and there at the local level on the Indonesian side, the violence against civilians and captured fighters was organized to a certain degree. The reports by NEFIS sometimes make reference to victims being taken to a 'markas' (post), or an order from a 'markas' to go to a particular *kampong*, without it always being clear whether it was actually a headquarters, which organization the headquarters belonged to, or who might have given the order.³⁶

In other cases, NEFIS reports do mention the names of organizations or specific orders to kill Dutch people and Indo-Europeans, such as in the case of the massacre in Balapulang. In that city, not far from Tegal in the Pekalongan residency, a branch of the Angkatan Muda Republik Indonesia (AMRI) was founded in September or October 1945 by Indonesian government officials. In October 1945, one of the six local leaders – we do not know which – reportedly gave the order for all 'Europeans' in Balapulang and the vicinity to be killed. Some hours later, eighteen Indo-Europeans from four different families were taken from their homes. Just one child survived the subsequent massacre. The same leaders of the AMRI also gave the order for the murder of a total of six people from two families in Durensawit, two kilometres away.³⁷

In Semarang in November 1945, too, an explicit local order was probably given to kill people. On 11 May 1946, the 22-year-old Javanese Slamet-Depok was interrogated about the murder of the family of a pharmacist, Flohr, in Semarang on 19 November 1945, during the Second Battle of Semarang.

Slamet-Depok had just joined the 'Angkatan Moeda' (probably Angkatan Pemoeda Indonesia). When asked about the orders during an attack on the city, he replied that at the organization's office he had overheard Djojoprajitno, the leader of the Bahagian Penjerboean branch of Angakatan Moeda, say to his group leader, Jatin: 'Soedah tangkep itoe njonja blanda di Doewet, bikin mati' ('Good, pick up those Dutch women at Doewet [a pharmacy in Semarang] and kill them').[38] According to his group leader, Jatin, Djojoprajitno even ordered that in the event of an attack by *pemuda* on Semarang, all Europeans should be killed.[39]

According to the record of the interrogation, Slamet-Depok and seven other *pemuda*, led by Jatin, went to the pharmacy and picked up the mother, the three daughters and a son. They were taken from Doewet to a house on Peloran 48. There, Jatin is said to have given the order for the four women and the little boy to be killed. The four women were first raped twice by four *pemuda*, including the group's leader, Jatin. Then two women and the little boy were shot and killed with a *golok*, a machete. The other two women were shot dead. Their bodies were thrown in the well, which was then filled with earth.[40] Questions remain, of course, about the reliability of Slamet-Depok's statement. In any case, this type of interrogation should be read with great caution, not least because in such an interrogation, the perpetrator might have wanted to shift responsibility by referring to an order. Moreover, the intelligence services would have been keen to identify a perpetrator.

Although it is difficult to establish the extent to which people followed orders, it can be said for sure that *pemuda* and other Indonesians engaged in spontaneous violence. For example, the sight of armed Indonesians cordoning off European neighbourhoods in Surabaya and taking fearful, helpless Dutch and Indo-Europeans by truck to the prison provoked the residents of the surrounding kampongs to take spontaneous, violent action. At Kalisosok prison (Werfstraat), the *kampong* residents, armed with bamboo spears, knives and a rifle, managed to force the guards from Pemuda Republik Indonesia (PRI) to hand over the Dutch and Indo-Europeans. Most of the latter were killed or injured while trying to reach the prison from the trucks. Officers from the PRI and TKR units were eventually able to re-establish some control.[41]

Mainly on the basis of sources from the Dutch intelligence service – which should be read with caution – it can thus be concluded that most Indonesian perpetrators of the violence during the first phase of the revolution do not appear to have been affiliated with an official organization, and that in many cases the extreme violence was not directed from the centre. However, this does not alter the fact that the killings were sometimes ordered and coordinated at the local level. Finally, it is likely that the national and regional authorities sometimes condoned the violence to a greater or lesser degree, either for strategic or political reasons, or out of impotence.

8.
Estimates of casualty numbers

In this book, we have explicitly placed the extreme violence against Indo-European, Moluccan and Dutch civilians and captured fighters in the first phase of the Indonesian Revolution in the context of the extreme violence against civilians or unarmed soldiers of other nationalities and ethnicities. That is why we have attempted to estimate not only the number of Dutch, Indo-European and Moluccan victims, but also to report what is known about casualties among the Indonesians, Chinese, British and Japanese. The amount of information that is available about the number of victims and their backgrounds differs from group to group. Some groups have hardly been investigated at all; in those cases, determining the number of casualties is more a question of giving impetus to further research than providing a well-founded estimate.

When writing about the categorisation of the casualty estimates, it is important to note that distinguishing between different groups was an integral part of the colonial system. The distinction was based on a combination of factors, such as appearance and ethnic origin, gender, class, family relations and wealth, as well as education, language, cultural background and career. Moreover, these criteria could affect and strengthen – or weaken – one another. The classification also varied according to location and period.[1]

This colonial perspective also shaped the way in which data on victims were recorded in the second half of the 1940s. It is therefore all too easy to reproduce the old colonial dividing lines in research on the various groups of victims. One way to break through these dividing lines – partially, in any case – is to record as much information as possible about the individual victims; their gender, place of residence and age, for instance. In this way, anonymous catch-all terms such as 'European' and 'Indonesian' are supplemented with more detailed individual and personal information, allowing us to do greater justice to the person behind them. We only partially succeeded in doing this, due to the lack of information in the sources.

In practice, the categories and fault lines are more diffuse in some respects than they appear at first sight – which presents the researcher with an entirely new set of challenges. In the colonial context, the category of 'Europeans' included not only *totoks*, but also many Indo-Europeans (if they were recognized by their European fathers), Japanese, and Indonesians, Chinese and so forth who were seen as being on a par with Europeans.[2] Properly speaking, if a report states only that a certain number of Europeans were killed, this tells us little: were they Dutch, Indo-Europeans, Japanese or another nationality? Thus, it is not always possible to give a precise indication in practice.

Before turning to the estimates themselves, it is important to note various other complications that arise when estimating casualty numbers. In doing so, we often give examples of Dutch and Indo-European individuals, because more is known about them. However, a number of these complications also apply to other groups.

Compiling casualty numbers: complications

First of all, there may have been under-reporting. The first months after the Japanese surrender were a chaotic, dangerous period in which it was not always possible to register victims. The state apparatus of the Republic of Indonesia was still under construction, which hardly favoured meticulous registration. In addition, the Indonesian side was more focused on the military victims of the independence struggle than on civilian casualties. For example, it appears that the Indonesian honorary cemeteries one finds in every city mostly contain those who fought in the army or related militias. There are civilian victims, too, but they are mainly administrators.

On the Dutch side, in those first few months there were no organizations present – or present to any significant degree – that focused on gathering information about the victims of violence, something to which we return below. This was the case on both Java and Sumatra, where most of the victims on the Dutch side died. If organizations were already active, they were concentrated in certain places. On 21 December 1945, the senior Dutch civil servant Van der Plas noted that the office of the police of the commander of the Allied Military Administration Civil Affairs Branch, the new name for NICA from early 1946, had only an incomplete record of abductions, murders and suchlike. 'It was remarked', he wrote, 'that it was such a daily occurrence to see bodies floating past, especially for those who live by the Bandjir canal [in Jakarta], that most cases were not even reported anymore.'[3]

Furthermore, according to Van der Plas, members of the public were uncertain about which agency to report victims to. Due to the lack of action on the English side, people had failed to make reports in some instances, as the commander of the military police would only take up a case if an abducted person had been freed.[4] If this was the situation in Jakarta, which was more or less under Allied control, it is likely that registration in other cities or beyond was even less well organized. In addition, there was another potential cause of under-reporting, mentioned in an article in the *New York Times* on 16 November 1945: fear of reprisals. Relatives may have failed to report abductions for this reason,[5] and the same may have applied to reporting murders.

Over time, the registration of casualties on the Dutch side was organized more efficiently. The Deceased Persons Investigation Service (Opsporingsdienst van Overledenen, ODO), was established on 5 December 1945 as part of the Displaced Persons Office. The purpose of the ODO was to collect reliable information about all Dutch individuals and Dutch subjects who had been in the Dutch East Indies on 7 December 1941, and who had since died in Japanese prison camps or on transport ships. In practice, the emphasis seems to have been on 'Europeans' (in this case, presumably Dutch and Indo-Europeans), not Dutch subjects (Indonesians). The service also carried out research on persons who had been abducted and/or had died after the liberation.[6]

Another complicating factor was that the on-site investigations took place months, and in many cases even years, after the event. This means that in many instances, evidence and/or witnesses would have disappeared in the meantime. Moreover, the ODO only had offices on Java and Sumatra: in addition to the headquarters in Jakarta on Java, there were branches in Surabaya, Semarang and Bandung, and one on Sumatra in Padang. Thus, with a single exception, no research was done on victims who died on islands other than these two and on the nearby island of Madura.[7]

Finally, it is highly questionable whether the ODO reports survived in their entirety. The service's dossiers are spread over several archives; most of them can be found in the archives of the NEFIS intelligence service (National Archives of the Netherlands) and the Netherlands East Indies Collection (NIOD). The majority concern the killings on East Java.[8]

OVER-REPORTING AND OTHER COMPLICATIONS

While it is thus likely that there was under-reporting of casualty figures, over-reporting should not be ruled out, either. Almost from the beginning of the Indonesian War of Independence, the victims on the Indonesian and Dutch side were the subject of a propaganda battle. The extreme violence by Indonesians against the Dutch or against fellow Indonesians was deliberately ignored by the Indonesian media, because it was at odds with the story of the legitimate struggle against the Dutch. Dutch extreme violence against Indonesians, by contrast, was highlighted in detail in Indonesian propaganda, which emphasized that large numbers of Indonesians were victims of Dutch atrocities. These Dutch atrocities, it was claimed, gave the Indonesians the right to defend themselves by any means, including by force.[9]

Casualty numbers were also used for propaganda purposes on the Dutch side. For example, Van der Plas' above-mentioned attempts to improve victim registration on the Dutch side were not motivated exclusively by concern for the fate of the victims' families. He also wanted to improve registration in order to counterbalance Indonesian propaganda, which hammered away constantly about excessive 'enemy' violence against innocent Indonesian civilians. The immediate cause of Van der Plas' initiative was a speech by the Indonesian prime minister, Sutan Sjahrir. In a radio broadcast by 'Allied radio' from British Malaya (presumably a reference to the British Eastern Broadcasting Service), on 15 December 1945 Sjahrir reportedly said that the atrocities that were being committed by Indonesians were the result of enemy atrocities and misdeeds that were ten times worse.[10]

Propaganda considerations also led to one of the first estimates of the number of murdered Dutch people in 1947 (see below). The specific reason for this was the need to provide a counterbalance to the reputational damage that the Netherlands faced after the so-called Bondowoso affair. During a train transport from Bondowoso to Surabaya on 23 November 1947, 46 of the 100 Indonesian prisoners who were being transported in closed goods wagons died by asphyxiation. This issue threatened to have international consequences. E.N. van Kleffens, the Dutch ambassador to Washington, heard that Australia wanted to call for a debate in the United Nations Security Council about the events in Bondowoso. Van Kleffens thus considered it 'useful' to have an estimate of the number of Dutch and Chinese killed by Indonesians.[11]

Accurately counting the number of victims is further complicated by other factors. Sometimes there is insufficient information to identify a victim, for example due to the lack of a name or the date and place of death. It frequently happens that reports only state that a certain number of (Indo-) Europeans or 'Ambonese' (Moluccans) were killed. In other cases, the names of the victims are spelled incorrectly. Indonesian victims of Islamic origin without family names are also difficult to trace. Finally, in the chaotic conditions in the months immediately after the Japanese surrender, it is extremely unlikely that the registration of persons who had been reported missing but nevertheless later proved to be alive was corrected by the agencies concerned.

Numbers of Indo-European, Dutch and Moluccan casualties

In the period 1945-1949, there were estimates circulating of the number of victims who had died on the Dutch side in the first phase of the Indonesian Revolution. What is presumably the first estimate dates from 6 December 1947. A coded telegram from the Far East Department in Jakarta (an agency of the Ministry of Foreign Affairs in Indonesia) to the Ministry of Foreign Affairs in The Hague states: 'The number of Dutch killed by the extremists since August 1945 amounts to 3,500; 3,400 of these are known by name. Data regarding other nationals to follow as soon as possible.'[12] It is unclear which documents were used to arrive at this number. In 1950, in his book *The stakes of democracy in South-east Asia,* Van Mook opted for a slightly lower number: probably around 2,000-3,000 murdered Dutch and Indo-Europeans. In his view, the number of non-Dutch victims could not be estimated with any precision.[13]

It is likely that the figures from this book were also the source of the estimate that Loe de Jong made in 1986, in volume 11c of his *Koninkrijk der Nederlanden in de Tweede Wereldoorlog* [*The Kingdom of the Netherlands in the Second World War*]; namely, that 3,000 Dutch, Dutch Indos and 'Ambonese', as well as an unknown number of Chinese, were killed during the so-called *bersiap* period.[14] Two years later, De Jong arrived at a higher estimate: 3,500, of whom 3,400 were known by name. The above-mentioned 1947 telegram from the Far East Department was probably the source for his calculation. De Jong made the caveat that it was unclear whether this number also included 'Ambonese' victims. In any case, according to him, this estimate was probably too low, because murdered persons were only reported if they had relatives who could do this. Many 'Indo-Dutch' men and women were married to Indonesians and lived isolated lives in the interior. It was therefore likely, according to De Jong, that there were many more unknown victims in addition to the hundred who had been named.[15]

In an appendix to the same volume of De Jong's *Koninkrijk*, retired lieutenant general F. van der Veen added that the number of Chinese killed was many times higher than the 3,500 murdered Dutch. No data were available about the number of casualties among the 'Ambonese' and Menadonese, but these, in his view, should be estimated in the hundreds, if not the thousands. Van de Veen also named the many Indonesian civil servants who had been killed.[16] In the decades following the publication of De Jong's book, the estimates of the number of civilians killed in the first months of the Indonesian Revolution increased enormously, both in academic publications and in social debates. On closer examination, however, many of these estimates are based on extrapolations or unclear and rather unreliable sources.

In his standard work *Bersiap! Opstand in het paradijs. De bersiap-periode op Java en Sumatra 1945-1946* [*Bersiap! Revolution in paradise. The bersiap period on Java and Sumatra 1945-1946*], published in 2005, Herman Bussemaker wrote that estimates ranged from 3,500 to 20,000 casualties on the Dutch side. He himself was inclined to assume the higher figure, certainly if it included the Dutch elderly and children who had died prematurely of hunger and exhaustion in the *bersiap* camps. He offered no further substantiation for this. The time frame that he used ran from August 1945 to November 1946.[17] In 2012, the publicist and historian Bert Immerzeel challenged Bussemaker to substantiate his figures more precisely. In response, Bussemaker explained the basis for his estimates in a blog on Immerzeel's website, *Javapost*. First, he named the 3,500 victims who, according to him, had been documented by the ODO. He then added an estimate of excess mortality – deaths above the normal mortality rate – of 1 per cent (2,500 people) in the so-called *bersiap* or Republican camps. Finally, he added the 14,000 abducted and missing persons. He believed it likely that those reported missing had been killed, because few later reported themselves alive.[18]

The number of 14,000 victims on the Dutch side was based on an extrapolation of the figures for Jakarta, where, according to Bussemaker, the number of individuals killed or abducted during the period between 1 October 1945 and 25 December 1945 amounted to around 300 and 400, respectively. If there were such numbers in Jakarta, one of the key areas controlled by the British, what was the situation like elsewhere on Java? Bussemaker therefore extrapolated these figures to the rest of Java, and in doing so arrived at a figure of more than 10,000 missing. In view of the many abductions and murders, he preferred to use the figure of 14,000 abducted and missing persons. Incidentally, he was the first to admit that his figures were not wholly based on hard facts: 'They are estimates, and anyone who has better figures is welcome to come forward.'[19]

Bussemaker's arguments have been criticized by historians on various points. Mary van Delden, the author of a book about the Republican camps, argued that children and the elderly did not die of malnutrition in their thousands in the camps. The conditions in some camps were admittedly miserable, but they were not nearly as dramatic as Bussemaker made out.[20] Immerzeel argued that there was no reason to believe that every missing person was equivalent to a murder.[21] He later added that the large number of missing persons on the Dutch side was a consequence of the chaotic situation shortly after the war, when many people were separated. Most returned, but the same chaos meant that records were not always kept of which missing persons had resurfaced.[22]

In the years that followed, higher estimates became increasingly common; in some cases, possibly because Moluccans, Menadonese and Timorese were also included. In 2008, the Australian historian Robert Cribb wrote in an article that there may have been 25,000 deaths: around 5,000 registered deaths – a number he based on the number of corpses found – and an estimated 20,000 Indo-Europeans who were registered as missing by the time the Dutch authorities were able to compile records. He allowed for the possibility, however, that many of the missing did in fact survive.²³ For the figures mentioned, he referred to a 2001 book by Okke Norel, *En,... hoe was het daarbuiten*, a bibliography about the Japanese occupation and *bersiap*. Norel cited a spokesman from the Indies pensions union (Indische Pensioenbond), who referred to 8,000 dead – thus, not the 5,000 mentioned by Cribb – and 20,000 missing. How the Indische Pensioenbond arrived at this figure is unclear, because there are no source citations in Norel's book.²⁴

Four years later, the American historian William H. Frederick proposed even higher numbers: 25,000-30,000 Dutch and Indo-Europeans in the period between 1945 and 1949 on Java and Sumatra. His calculations probably included Moluccans, Menadonese and Timorese.²⁵ He also based his estimate on an extrapolation. A total of 11,262 confirmed deaths was obtained from an ODO report from May 1947. That report was published at a time when the ODO was far from completing its work, and the service did not yet have access to most areas in East Java; and it was in East Java in particular, according to Frederick, that there were many deaths. He believed, for reasons he did not specify, that there may have been 6,000 victims in East Java before March 1946. According to him, at least several hundred victims of the 'second *bersiap*' around Surabaya in July 1947 should be added to this number, and there were also the many victims who had died unnamed.²⁶

In an interview with the Dutch newspaper *Trouw* on 18 November 2013, Frederick adjusted the lower limit to 'at least 20,000'. Later in the interview, he stated that he feared, 'intuitively, after years of research in papers that are available', that higher numbers were more likely, and that he had thus arrived at an estimate of 28,000. This number was again based on the Indische Pensioenbond's figure of 20,000 missing and the 8,000 whom we can be sure, in his view, died during *bersiap*; this latter figure probably came from the Indische Pensioenbond too, as shown in the above-mentioned book by Okke Norel.²⁷

Discussions about high casualty estimates

Immerzeel had good reason to argue that Frederick's interpretation of the number of fatalities in the first phase of the Indonesian Revolution, which Frederick based on the ODO reports, was incorrect.²⁸ That is because the ODO reports of the number of people who were entered in the Civil Registry's monthly record of deaths cover fatalities from both the Japanese occupation and the post-war period; wholly in line, in other words, with the remit of the Investigation Service. Moreover, they concerned both (Indo) Europeans and Chinese and Indonesians, and both civilians and the military.[29]

By December 1949, when the ODO was presumably disbanded, a total of 21,181 people had been recorded in the death register. For the reasons explained above, however, this number cannot be used as such to estimate the number of casualties in the first phase of the Indonesian Revolution, nor can the figures from the monthly reports on which it is based. At the time when the ODO was disbanded, around 2,000 applications were still pending, including those for missing persons.[30] Completely in line with this, on 3 February 1948 the Minister for Overseas Territories, J.A. Jonkman, spoke in the House of Representatives of the 2,000 persons who had disappeared during *bersiap* and who were known by name.[31]

The fact that many hundreds of missing persons did turn up later is shown by a newspaper report that was published precisely nine months earlier. On 3 May 1947, the *Nieuwe Courant* quoted H. van der Hart, head of the ODO, who stated that from the time of the Japanese surrender, 2,700 Europeans could be considered missing during the 'extremist turbulence, disregarding the Chinese.'[32] That was in May 1947 – which shows that in nine months' time, 700 people who had been considered missing had resurfaced. All of this casts doubt on the numbers of between 14,000 and 20,000 missing persons mentioned by Bussemaker, Cribb and Frederick.

For this reason, Immerzeel preferred to speak of 'possibly more than 10,000 victims'. According to him, the word 'possibly' left more space for other calculations, whilst the word 'victims' could be interpreted more broadly than 'civilian deaths' or 'murders'.[33] NIOD historian Jeroen Kemperman agreed with many of Immerzeel's criticisms, and in 2014 arrived at an estimate of at least 5,500 victims: the 3,500 documented victims plus the c. 2,000 people who were still registered as missing at the ODO in December 1949. Finally, Kemperman concluded that it could not be ruled out that the death toll may have been somewhat higher, perhaps even by several thousand in the most extreme case. However, he could find no convincing reason to believe that the number of victims exceeded 10,000.[34]

Perhaps partly on the grounds of his high estimates, Cribb was the first to introduce the word 'genocide' in relation to the murders of (mainly)

Identification of the remains of Europeans and Indo-Europeans killed in the earliest phase of the Indonesian Revolution, Bandung 1947. Source: NIOD

Indo-Europeans. In his 2008 article, he proposed that the murders of Indo-Europeans be described as a 'brief genocide'. In his explanation, he argued that the murders were committed not so much on the grounds of skin colour or ethnicity – although the latter was important – but due to an alleged lack of loyalty to the Republic. Remarkably enough he does not address the question of why the violence against Europeans and Indo-Europeans should be classified as 'genocide', but not that against other opponents of the Republic, alleged or otherwise.[35] The use of the term is also problematic, because persecution on the basis of political loyalty does not meet the definition in the 1948 Genocide Convention.[36]

Frederick therefore questioned Cribb's definition of *bersiap* as a 'brief genocide', both for its brief nature and above all for the use of the term 'genocide' itself. He pointed out that it was not easy to categorize either the perpetrators and their motives, or their victims. Nevertheless, he seemed reluctant to abandon the concept altogether. 'It draws needed attention to an episode and type of violence too long hidden from not only world view, but the view of Indonesians themselves.'[37] As such, the use of the term 'genocide' acquires a new meaning: not as a way of describing the violence against Europeans and Indo-Europeans in line with a legal and/or historical definition, but as a way of highlighting this episode.

In his 2008 article in the *Journal of Genocide Research*, Remco Raben also points out that it is difficult to provide a precise classification of the violence during the revolution in Indonesia. 'Not truly genocidal in systemic, intent and quantification, nor clear in its ethnic or class labelling of victims and perpetrators, it [the situation in Indonesia] refuses to be pinned down on one type of violence or another.'[38] Nevertheless, Raben perceived 'strong genocidal overtones' in the Indonesian violence against Europeans and Indo-Europeans. These were ruthless murders in which soldiers and paramilitaries used violence indiscriminately against civilians. 'The essence is their murderous intent and deadly results, aimed at or resulting in killing as many members of a specific (or not so specific) community as possible, or crippling their livelihoods.'[39] Strikingly, Raben leaves open the possibility of random violence, yet it is a characteristic of genocidal violence that the victims are *not* selected at random. Nevertheless, according to Raben, viewing the violence in the first months of the Indonesian Revolution through the lens of genocide could help to raise awareness of the mechanisms that underlie large-scale massacres.[40]

It is questionable whether the approach taken by Frederick, Cribb and Raben truly clarifies our understanding of the dynamics of violence in Indonesia. To start with, there are a great many conflicts in which soldiers and paramilitaries use violence against civilians, whether or not these are specific groups. On these grounds alone, there is much to be said for caution about using terms such as 'genocide' and 'genocidal traits', precisely because the terms are so heavily loaded and controversial.[41] On this point, Gerlach's concept of an extremely violent society seems to offer more potential for a clear analysis of the dynamics of the violence, including against specific groups, as we have shown in the previous chapters.

Towards a new estimate of casualty numbers

It should by now be clear that the estimates proposed by Bussemaker, Cribb and Frederick are not without their drawbacks. For this reason alone, it is important to consider which data are available in the archives, something that has never been done systematically. Not all of the problems can be solved in this way; we are aware that these data are incomplete. Moreover, it is important to consider who compiled the lists, when, and for what purpose.

Table 1

Ethnicity	Number
Arabic	1
Armenian	1
Asian	1
Buginese	1
Dutch	1
Madurese	2
Batak	2
Sundanese	4
European/Chinese	5
Indo-European	8
Timorese	15
Chinese	48
Javanese	61
Menadonese	93
Indonesian	98
Unknown	138
Moluccan	226
European/Chinese	3.018
Total	**3723**

Table 2

Gender	Number
Child	27
Unknown	610
Woman	935
Man	2.151
Total	**3723**

The most complete records of victims on the Dutch side in the Second World War and subsequent violent conflicts are held by the Netherlands War Graves Foundation (Oorlogsgravenstichting). This organization was founded on 1 September 1946 to provide graves for war victims on the Dutch side. For this purpose, the War Graves Foundation needed as much data as possible about those on the Dutch side who had died during the Second World War. A small staff and a team of volunteers searched the archives of the Ministries of War and Social Affairs, the National Institute for War Documentation (today's NIOD) and the Netherlands Red Cross. In addition, they searched for next of kin and cross-checked the data that were available in municipal archives.[42] A total of 180,000 war victims are registered in the War Graves Foundation's file. These are people who died in the Netherlands, Indonesia or elsewhere between 9 May 1940 and the present day, who are classified as war victims in accordance with the statutes of the War Graves Foundation.[43]

The data from the War Graves Foundation were compared to a list that was compiled and updated until 2016 by retired colonel Jan Willem de Leeuw. The 'De Leeuw list' mainly contains the names of soldiers in Dutch service who died during the Second World War and the war in Indonesia in the period between 1945 and 1949. The De Leeuw list contained 37,162 names on 1 November 2016, and is based on other, older lists, archives, literature, the commemorative books of military units and interviews.[44] We supplemented the combined list – the information from the War Graves Foundation plus the De Leeuw list – with data on fatalities from the ODO reports in

Table 3

Citizen/military	Number
Unknown	372
Military	511
Citizen	1.016
Presumably citizen	1.824
Total	3723

Table 4

Island/region	Number
Madura	2
Bali	2
Timor	4
New Guinea	4
At sea	5
Nusa Tengarra	7
Bangka/Belitung	8
Moluccas	31
Kalimantan	63
Sulawesi	64
Unknown	200
Sumatra	274
Java	3.059
Total	3723

the National Archives of the Netherlands and NIOD, other lists in the National Archives of the Netherlands, and newspapers.[45] This information concerns people who were reported murdered. People who were reported missing were not included, as a large proportion of them eventually resurfaced, as explained above.[46]

The archives of the Red Cross are a potentially interesting source of victims' names, which is why the employees of the War Graves Foundation used them to compile their file. Unfortunately, the apparently extensive archives of the Netherlands Indies Red Cross disappeared without trace shortly after 27 December 1949.[47]

The archives of department A of the Information Office of the Netherlands Red Cross did survive, however. At first, this department focused exclusively on the military in and around Indonesia, but it soon widened its field of activity to include civilians. The archive includes correspondence about the fate of people in Indonesia during the Japanese occupation and the so-called *bersiap* period. There are also four card index boxes containing thousands of names of people who went missing and who were murdered during the *bersiap* period. From this, we selected the cards of those people who were reported murdered.[48]

Furthermore, thousands of dossiers at the Pelita Foundation were searched for relevant terms. Pelita assists individuals, mainly Dutch Indos and Dutch of Moluccan descent, who wish to apply for financial or psychological support under the various war-related acts, on the basis of mental or physical complaints that can be traced back to their experiences in the Second World War and the violence in 1945-1949. For each application, Pelita staff prepare what is known as a 'social report', in which the applicant tells his or her life story. The applicant is always asked about any experiences in the first months of the Indonesian Revolution.[49]

Table 5

Period	Number
17-31 Aug-45	550
Sep-45	627
Sep-oct-45	2
Oct-45	1086
Oct-nov-45	7
Nov-45	554
Nov-dec-45	3
Dec-45	308
Jan-46	189
Feb-46	159
Mar-46	167
'Bersiap'	54
'during proclamation …'	10
'beginning of Merdeka period'	4
'after the Japanese capitulation'	1
'just after capitulation'	2
Total	3723

The file from the War Graves Foundation, the De Leeuw list, the ODO reports in the National Archives of the Netherlands and NIOD, the archives of the Netherlands Red Cross and Pelita, and other lists in the National Archives of the Netherlands, yielded a total of 3,723 registered deaths for the period between 17 August 1945 and 31 March 1946. Of these, 1,344 undoubtedly died as a result of violence and 967 died of causes unrelated to violence, such as disease, exhaustion, deprivation, internment, malnutrition and starvation. The latter category probably includes people who died as a result of the suffering they experienced during the Japanese occupation. Three drowned and 36 died in accidents. Finally, the cause of death is not known for 1,373 deaths in the above-mentioned period.

The number of 3,723 deaths corresponds relatively well to the initial estimate of 3,500 that was given in 1947, although that earlier estimate related only to Dutch people, including Indo-Europeans. The number of victims we have identified to date includes Moluccans, Chinese, Menadonese, Timorese and Indonesians. Moreover, the figure of 3,723 deaths is a lower

Table 6

Cause of Death	Number	Total
UNKNOWN		1373
NOT VIOLENCE RELATAD		1006
Drowned	3	
Deprivation	7	
Famine/malnutrition	34	
Accident	36	
Exhaustion	58	
Internment	165	
Disease	703	
VIOLENCE RELATED		1344
Attack	1	
Burned	1	
Buried alive	1	
Possibly murdered	2	
Shot	2	
Tjintjang	4	
Decapitated	9	
Suicide	12	
Tortured	14	
Mines/Bombings	17	
Injuries	18	
Abuses	19	
Execution	85	
Killed (fight)	114	
Murdered	1.045	
Total		3723

limit: after all, not every death was registered in wartime, and sufficient information was not always available. In the sources we used, for example, we found more than 125 people for whom the date of death remained unknown. Thus, it cannot be said with certainty that these individuals died in the period between 17 August 1945 and 31 March 1946, and for this reason they were not included in our file of registered victims. If, allowing for a certain margin, these 125 people are added, and we assume that all 2,000 pending applications (including those for missing persons) in December 1949, when the ODO was disbanded, indeed involved 2,000 persons who died – even though a report of a missing person is not by definition equivalent to a death – then the estimated number of deaths on the Dutch side in the period between 17 August 1945 and 31 March 1946 would be almost 6,000. There is no reason to assume that the number of dead was much higher than that; in any case, certainly not the figures of 20,000-30,000 dead that are in circulation today.

Most of the 3,723 deaths occurred on Java (3,059), followed by Sumatra (274) and Sulawesi (64) and Kalimantan (63). Men make up the majority of the dead, namely 2,151, compared to 935 women.[50] The great majority of them were 'Europeans' (3,018), which probably includes Indo-Europeans, as for only six deaths in the file is there a note that the ethnicity was 'Indo-European'. For the rest, the largest categories are Moluccans (226), Indonesians (168) and Menadonese (93). It is known that 511 of the dead were members of the military, while 1,016 were certainly civilians. It is likely that 1,824 of the remaining dead were civilians.[51]

Finally, it is clear that the deadliest month was October 1945 (1,086 deaths), followed by September (627 deaths), November (554 deaths) and December (308 deaths). In the first three months of 1946, the intensity of the violence against the Dutch, Indo-Europeans and Moluccans fell markedly, with 189, 159 and 167 deaths, respectively. The strikingly large number of deaths in September 1945 – in a month when the violence was still limited – was probably due to the fact that more than half of the people died as a result of their poor physical condition, presumably a direct consequence of the Japanese occupation, not of revolutionary violence.

Table 7

Island/period	Number	Total
SUMATRA		274
17-31 Aug-45	83	
Sep-45	76	
Oct-45	27	
Nov-45	40	
Dec-45	23	
Jan-46	12	
Feb-46	6	
Mar-46	7	
BANGKA/BELITUNG		8
Feb-46	7	
Mar-46	1	
JAVA		3059
17-31 Aug-45	429	
Sep-45	491	
Sep-oct 1945	2	
Oct-45	987	
Oct-nov 1945	7	
Nov-45	456	
Nov-dec 1945	2	
Dec-45	244	
Jan-46	138	
Feb-46	118	
Mar-46	117	
'Bersiap'	51	
'during proclamation ...'	10	
'beginning of Merdeka period'	4	
'after the Japanese capitulation'	1	
'right after the Japanese capitulation'	2	
MADURA		2
Oct-45	1	
Nov-45	1	

Table 7 *(continuation)*

Island/period	Number	Total
BALI		2
Mar-46	2	
KALIMANTAN		63
Aug-45	15	
Sep-45	8	
Oct-45	6	
Nov-45	5	
Dec-45	3	
Jan-46	9	
Feb-46	8	
Mrt-46	9	
SULAWESI		64
Aug-45	7	
Sep-45	15	
Oct-45	6	
Nov-45	2	
Dec-45	7	
Jan-46	10	
Feb-46	5	
Mrt-46	12	
NUSA TENGGARA		7
Oct-45	2	
Nov-45	4	
Jan-46	1	
TIMOR		4
Aug-45	1	
Sep-45	1	
Oct-45	1	
Nov-45	1	

Table 7 *(continuation)*

Island/period	Number	Total
MOLUCCAS		**31**
Aug-45	5	
Sep-45	6	
Oct-45	5	
Nov-45	5	
Dec-45	2	
Jan-46	3	
Feb-46	3	
Mar-46	2	
DUTCH NEW GUINEA		**4**
Oct-45	1	
Jan-46	2	
Mar-46	1	
AT SEA		**5**
Oct-45	2	
Jan-46	1	
Feb-46	1	
Mar-46	1	
UNKNOWN		**200**
Aug-45	10	
Sep-45	30	
Oct-45	48	
Nov-45	40	
Nov-dec-45	1	
Dec-45	29	
Jan-46	13	
Feb-46	11	
Mar-46	15	
'Bersiap'	3	
TOTAL		**3723**

Japanese victims

A document from the headquarters of the Japanese 16th Army on Java shows that until the end of November 1945, 58 civilians in military service and 235 civilians on the Japanese side died – more than the number of soldiers who were killed during the same period (231). It is not known how many of the killed soldiers were prisoners or disarmed. The latter group, in any case, must include the 86 disarmed naval personnel who were taken off the train at Cikampek and murdered in October 1945.[52]

Between 15 August 1945 and June 1946, a total of 1,057 Japanese soldiers died on Java, including the 231 soldiers in the above-mentioned report. How many of them were prisoners or disarmed at the time is also unknown.[53] The number of Japanese military personnel who died on Sumatra and the other islands after the end of the war is unclear, but in view of the situation there, it will have been limited. It should be possible to find more information about Japanese victims, civilians and military personnel in Japan itself, although that would be no easy task, as no central records were kept of Japanese people killed in Indonesia.[54]

British victims

The estimates of the number of British casualties vary only sightly. In the official publication on the military history of the war in Japan by Major General S. Woodburn Kirby, the numbers of British and Indian victims on Java and Sumatra until the British departure on 30 November 1946 are given as follows: 655 killed, 1,663 wounded and 325 missing.[55] In his book, *The British occupation of Indonesia*, the historian Richard McMillan presents slightly different figures: 620 killed, 1,331 wounded and 402 missing. The majority of these victims were British Indians, which may support the thesis that the violence was not (exclusively) ethnically motivated.[56] These numbers cover the whole period of the British presence, thus until the end of November 1946. The number of dead is probably a lower limit, as there is a reasonable probability that (many of the) missing persons died, but were not found or identified. The above-mentioned numbers include both military personnel who were killed in combat and military personnel who were captured and killed, such as the British and British Indian passengers on the aircraft that crashed near Bekasi. The precise balance between these groups is not known.

Indonesian Victims
Western sources

There are no well-founded estimates of the number of Indonesian victims who were active as fighters in the first months of the war of independence, let alone the number of Indonesians who did not participate actively in the struggle themselves. What applies to the first months also applies to the war as a whole: we cannot say with certainty how many Indonesians were killed as a result of violence, regardless of who the perpetrators were.

In the Dutch historiography, Loe de Jong was again the first – as far as is known – to venture an estimate of the number of Indonesian victims in the Indonesian War of Independence. In 1988, in a footnote to volume 12 of his *Koninkrijk der Nederlanden in de Tweede Wereldoorlog,* he wrote that it was assumed in Indonesia that the Republican armed forces lost a total of around 100,000 men in the period between 1945 and 1949. According to De Jong, Dutch military historians considered this to be a reliable figure, but he mentioned neither the source nor the names of the Indonesian or Dutch historians whom he had consulted on this point. The Dutch military historians presumably hailed from the circles of experts who formed the readers' committee for this volume of De Jong's *Koninkrijk*, or from the staff of the Military History department, one of the predecessors of today's Netherlands Institute of Military History.[57]

In 1991, Petra Groen, one of the readers, herself arrived at an estimate of 49,000 Indonesian deaths, but this only concerned victims who had died during much of 1949.[58] More recently, historians Gert Oostindie and Rémy Limpach called the figure of 100,000 Indonesian victims a 'wild guess' and a 'crude estimate', respectively.[59] One of the problems with this estimate is that it is unclear whether the figure of 100,000 covers only Indonesian victims of Dutch violence or also includes intra-Indonesian violence. De Jong seems to have steered a middle course, whilst some later historians, such as Remco Raben and Gert Oostindie, suggest that the figure of 100,000 also includes victims of violence among Indonesians themselves.[60]

Other figures are also in circulation. In an article in 1997, the Leiden historian Vincent Houben referred to the 'several hundred thousand Indonesians' who were killed in the years 1945-1949 – without mentioning a source.[61] According to the Australian historian Adrian Vickers, between 45,000 and 100,000 Indonesians were killed in combat during the Indonesian Revolution (1945-1949). The number of Indonesian civilian victims in that period, according to Vickers, must have amounted to at least 25,000,

After a British Dakota aircraft came down near Bekasi (West Java) on 25 November 1945, the 24 passengers, including 20 Indian infantry, were killed by the Pemuda Banteng Hitam (the youth militia known as the 'Black Bull'). The British army subsequently torched the houses in Bekasi and ordered the local population to bury the bodies of the killed soldiers. Source: NIOD

but possibly even 100,000. Seven million people on Java and Sumatra had to leave their homes.[62] The only person explicitly to address the number of Indonesian deaths in the first months after the Japanese surrender was Herman Bussemaker: 'The number of deaths on the Indonesian side during *bersiap* cannot be approximated. Estimates range from 30,000 to 100,000 *pemuda* killed across Java'.[63] Incidentally, he did not name a source for these estimates.

In 2017, KITLV researchers Bart Luttikhuis, Christiaan Harinck and Nico van Horn published the first well-founded estimate of the number of Indonesian victims in the Dutch weekly *De Groene Amsterdammer*. Based on the 'enemy losses' reported in the periodic operational overviews produced by the Dutch armed forces, available at the National Archives of the Netherlands, they arrived at a figure of 97,421 Indonesian deaths for the entire war. According to Luttikhuis, Harinck and Van Horn, it is 'highly likely' that this is only a lower limit. How many of them were fighters or civilians is, according to them, 'utterly' unclear. What is certain, however, is that this number of almost 100,000 only covers the Indonesian victims who died as a result of military violence by the Dutch side, and not victims of intra-Indonesian violence.[64]

As mentioned above, these estimates of numbers of Indonesian victims relate to the entire war of independence; the question remains as to the precise situation regarding the number of Indonesian victims in the first months of the Indonesian Revolution. It is possible to say something about this. At the website of the KITLV, a table is available that forms the basis of the article in *De Groene Amsterdammer* by Harinck, Luttikhuis and Van Horn. Even though, as the authors point out, the regional periodic overviews of Indonesian casualty numbers have not survived in their entirety for the months September-December 1945, because hardly any Dutch troops were present at that time, some figures are known for *parts* of this period.[65]

We know, for example, that 410 Indonesians were killed on Java between 11 October and 30 November 1945. Figures for December 1945 are missing, but we do have figures for the period between 1 January and 28 March 1946; namely, 1,212 Indonesians killed across the archipelago. Thus, during the period under investigation, at least 1,622 Indonesian victims fell across the whole archipelago as a result of violence on the Dutch side. Here too, however, how many of them were military personnel or civilians remains unclear.[66] It is more than likely that this figure is also a lower limit. No casualties are listed in the category 'Other' (islands), for example, yet it is known that nine people were killed by a Menadonese KNIL unit in New Guinea in the night of 14-15 December 1945.[67]

Considering the number of Indonesian victims of military violence by the Dutch side in the first months of the Indonesian Revolution, ranked by island, the number of Indonesian deaths on Celebes/Sulawesi stands out in particular: 704 over roughly two months (26 January–28 March 1946). This was before Captain Raymond Westerling's special forces went into action on South Sulawesi, which happened in the period between December 1946 and February 1947. Sulawesi is followed, in order of magnitude, by Java, with 669 victims; Bali/Lombok, with 127 victims; Sumatra, with 82 victims; Kalimantan, with 40 victims.[68]

The total number of Indonesians who were killed during the first months of the Indonesian Revolution was much higher. In this early phase of the revolution, the number of Indonesian victims killed as a result of Dutch military action was limited compared to the number of Indonesians killed as a result of British and Japanese action. During the Battle of Surabaya alone (10-29 November 1945), at least 6,000 Indonesians are thought to have died as a result of the use of force by the British.[69] It is impossible to establish how many of them were fighters, if only because they were joined by tens of thousands of often rudimentarily armed Indonesian civilians. According to their own estimates, prior to their departure in November 1946 British troops killed a total of 13,441 Indonesians. Again, the number of Indonesian civilians or captured fighters among the dead is not known.[70]

The Japanese also used excessive violence. The number of Indonesian civilian victims as a consequence of Japanese action is likely to have been considerable. As became clear in the previous chapter, in Tebing Tinggi on Sumatra alone there were probably hundreds if not thousands of Indonesian deaths in a matter of days. These would undoubtedly have included civilian victims, but we cannot establish how many. Finally, it is not possible even to approximate the number of victims of intra-Indonesian violence.[71]

Indonesian sources

As far as is known, no accurate or reliable estimates of the number of Indonesian victims during the struggle for independence – either civilian or military – have been produced by Indonesian historians.[72] The standard Indonesian work on Indonesian national history does not provide any overviews of victims during the war of 1945-1949.[73] Some actions are described, however, with reports of the number of casualties they claimed. On 7 October 1945, for example, eighteen Indonesians were killed in an attack by youths from the Badan Keamanan Rakyat and the Special Police on the Japanese barracks in Kota Baru in Yogyakarta.[74]

In addition to the standard work on Indonesian history, there are other publications that describe episodes from the Indonesian Revolution, such as *Arus revolusi Sulawesi Selatan* by the writer Sharita Pawilo, in which she paints a picture of the war in South Sulawesi. She gives what is sometimes an almost daily report of all the fighting that took place throughout the period of the Indonesian Revolution. For example, she reports that around 12 October 1945, KNIL troops patrolling the city shot anyone they came across displaying red and white Indonesian national symbols. Dozens of young people are said to have been killed or injured as a result.[75]

Finally, there are the published diaries and memoirs of people who lived through the independence struggle in the period 1945-1949, such as the works of Hario Kecik, alias Suharjo Padmodiwirjo (1921-2014). During the *bersiap* period, he was the commander of the military police in Surabaya. In *Pertempuran Surabaya,* Kecik describes the Indonesian resistance that rose up against the Allied troops in late October 1945, after the British commander Brigadier A. Mallaby was killed in combat. Kecik dedicated his memoirs to the 20,000 unnamed citizens of Surabaya who reportedly died in the fighting with the British army in Surabaya in late 1945.[76] Nowhere, however, does he mention the sources on which this casualty figure is based. Further on in the book, he refers to 25 Indonesian and 15 Japanese victims who died in September-October 1945 in fighting between *pemuda* and the Japanese Kempeitai in Surabaya.[77] He appears to have based these latter figures on what he himself observed. In short, the information from the Indonesian literature is fragmentary and difficult to verify, as it is unclear on which sources it rests.

There are a number of other options, however, for gathering more information about the Indonesian victims, although an exhaustive study of such sources would require more time. One point of departure, for example, is the Indonesian governmental war cemeteries body, the Taman Makam Pahlawan (Heroes' Cemeteries).[78] These special cemeteries are the burial place for Indonesians who were granted the official title of 'Gelar Pahlawan Negara Indonesia' ('Indonesian hero') or who received certain honours. Although it is not entirely clear who is buried in the cemeteries, they include administrators and veterans from the army and related militias who fought in the Indonesian War of Independence. The honorary cemeteries are spread across Indonesia, with a headquarters in Jakarta: the Pahlawan Center.[79]

Until December 2019, a website could be accessed via the Internet that contained a list of all the cemeteries in Indonesia, with both the victims' names and the dates and places of their death.[80] Until then, this website – which was subsequently taken offline – formed the best digital source of data on the Indonesian victims during the war of independence and, more specifically, the first months of the Indonesian Revolution. A total of 6,595 graves are located in these cemeteries, of which 348 can be identified with certainty as those of people who died during the period under investigation (17 August 1945 to 31 March 1946). In addition, there are a number of victims who are known to have died in 1945 or 1946, but there is no further indication of the date. These deaths should perhaps be counted, too, but this cannot be confirmed.[81] Nor is it known who killed these victims.

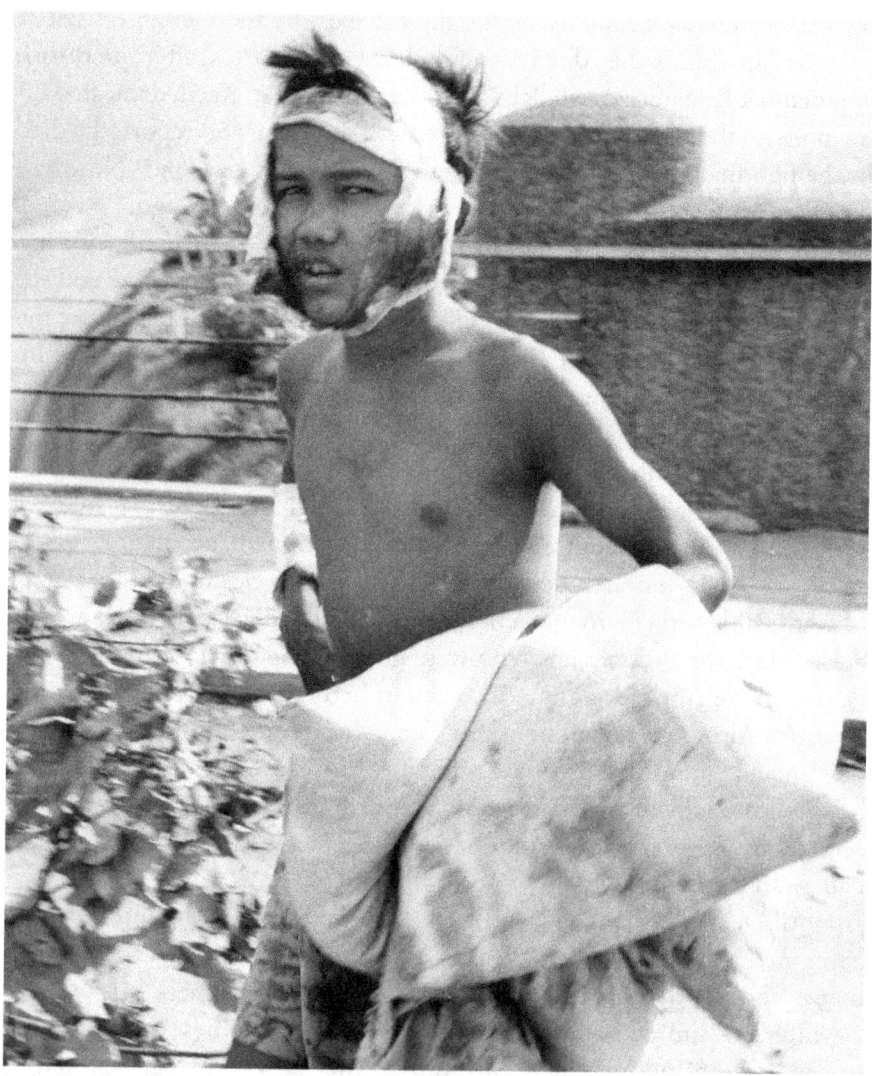

Wounded and bound pemuda *fighter captured by the British, Surabaya, November 1945. On the back is written: 'Extremely young, they neither showed nor received much mercy'.*
Source: *Imperial War Museum*

Another potentially important source is the so-called Legiun Veteran Republik Indonesia (LVRI), the Veterans' Legion of the Republic of Indonesia, a governmental body. This national organization, which was founded on 1 January 1957, manages the personal data of veterans in Indonesia, including veterans of the revolution. As well as the name of each veteran, it also records where they fought, their rank, whether they received a pension or allowance, and when and where they died.

New, additional research would be necessary in order to ascertain what data the LVRI has on casualties in the first months of the Indonesian Revolution, however. At present, we do not know the extent of the Jakarta-based LVRI's records of veterans who lost their lives during the Indonesian Revolution.[82] Should the office lack a central database of victims, it may still be possible to collect a lot of information about Indonesian victims at the local level. There are usually several local branches in each province or district (*kabupaten*), and a total of 334 branches are spread across the whole of Indonesia.[83] Such an exercise would be very labour-intensive, of course.

All in all, based on the currently known Indonesian sources, it is virtually impossible to arrive even at a somewhat substantiated estimate of the number of Indonesian civilian victims or captured fighters in the first months after the Japanese surrender. In any case, it can be said with certainty that there were many thousands.

CHINESE VICTIMS

Many thousands of Chinese citizens in Indonesia were probably killed as a result of extreme violence in the years between 1945 and 1949, but the exact number is unknown. The most notorious massacre alone – in Tangerang in May 1946 – cost the lives of 1,085 Chinese. For weeks on end, armed groups and individuals beat the Chinese, raped women and circumcised men, locked them in burning houses or murdered them in brutal fashion.[84] In the scholarly literature, only Mary Somers Heidhues has dared venture a cautious figure for the entire period between 1945 and 1949. She has estimated that there were 10,000 Chinese victims on Java alone.[85] The file that we compiled on the basis of our research in the archives, in combination with the file of the War Graves Foundation and De Leeuw list, contains the names of only 48 Chinese, just a fraction of the suspected number of deaths.[86] It is not known whether the local archives of Chinese organizations contain more information about Chinese victims during the Indonesian Revolution.[87]

Further indications can be found in memoirs and more journalistic sources that contain fragmentary information about the Chinese victims. One such example is that of the memoirs of Kwee Thiam Tjing, who published an account of the experiences of the Chinese in Malang in the years 1945-1947 under his alias, Tjamboek Berdoeri. Tjamboek reported extensively on the events in Malang in the first months of the struggle for independence, without mentioning numbers of victims. Tjamboek's account of the subsequent period is more comprehensive. He writes about the Chinese victims killed by Indonesian nationalists and provides a name-list of victims. He also provides numbers of victims who were killed in nearby places. However, his focus is mainly on those who died in 1947.[88]

Elsewhere in the literature, too, there are regular reports of Chinese victims in the first months of the Indonesian Revolution. These are often descriptions that do not give precise numbers, but discuss the many victims on the Chinese side in more general terms. In his chronicle of the Indonesian Revolution for the year 1945, for example, writer Pramoedya Ananta Toer cites a radio address that Sukarno gave on 12 November 1945. In this, Sukarno said that not only had thousands of Indonesian victims – including women and children – died in the British bombing of Surabaya, but also hundreds of Chinese, Arabs and traders who came from outside Indonesia and who had nothing to do with the conflict.[89]

Conclusion

In summary, it can be said that the number of fatalities among British and British Indian soldiers in Indonesia remains the best documented, although it is unclear how many died in combat and how many lost their lives in captivity. Establishing this will require further research, in which the conditions of their deaths are mapped out on a case-by-case basis. When it comes to the Japanese, the situation is less clear. Although it is known how many military personnel died on Java until June 1946, in this case, too, we do not know how many of them died after they had been captured. The number of Japanese civilians killed in the period between 17 August 1945 and 31 March 1946 likewise remains unclear.

The number of Indo-European, Dutch and Moluccan civilians who lost their lives in the above-mentioned period has been mapped out reasonably well and is estimated at nearly 6,000, although a certain margin remains. There were not between 20,000 and 30,000 victims, in other words, although this does not alter the fact that 6,000 is a large number, in view of

A grave containing the bodies of murdered Chinese is filled in. The torched canning factory is visible in the background; Malang, July 1947. Source: photographer unknown, Army Contacts Service, National Archives of the Netherlands

the short period in which the violence took place. The major outstanding question remains the number of Indonesian and Chinese civilians and captured fighters who lost their lives.

IV.
IMPACT

9.

The significance of *bersiap* in the Indonesian War of Independence (1946-1949)

In mid-November 1945, airmail was restored between Indonesia and the Netherlands. As a result, more and more families in the Netherlands received letters from their relatives about the precarious situation in Indonesia. Those with loved ones in Indonesia were deeply concerned, and asked Prime Minister Schermerhorn's cabinet to use military means to end the violence as soon as possible. However, the Minister of Overseas Territories, Logemann, opposed the use of force and prioritized negotiations with Indonesia.[1] Against this background of clashing political and personal interests, this chapter addresses the question of how the earliest acts of violence were perceived in the Dutch public domain in the years 1945-1949. This can be divided into two sub-questions. First, how was the violence discussed, regardless of whether 'bersiap' or other terms were used? Second, to what extent did reports of the violence play a role in public opinion, in political and military decision-making and in other areas, as a motive for retaliation or as a spur for intervention? To answer these questions, we address different domains: military information, information provided by the Dutch government, military magazines, journalistic reporting, film productions and, finally, Indies, Dutch and Indonesian newspapers.

Premeditated action

In September 1946, Tj. de Cock Buning, the secretary of the KNIL's field court martial in Jakarta, reported to the director of the Department of Justice about a 'premeditated assault' on an Indonesian who was suspected of having raped and murdered several European women. In his letter, De Cock Buning wrote of the perpetrator, H.F.M. Gereke, who as a KNIL soldier was in charge of guarding the Hoofdwacht, a building that served as a military prison: 'Gereke, whose relatives were also murdered by the extremists, could no longer contain his rage and beat the Indonesian with a hard object.'[2] Twenty years later, the Gereke case appeared in the *Memorandum on excesses* (*Excessennota*): 'While on guard, beating a detainee in his cell with a belt and the butt of his rifle, a premeditated assault resulting in death.'[3] Gereke was sentenced to seven months in prison. The judgment was based on the following consideration: 'Taking account of the youth of the accused and the fact that his father, little sister and nephew were murdered very recently in Semarang by a similar type to the beaten man.'[4] Thus, it did not count as a 'direct retaliation', because the Indonesian Gereke killed was not the same individual who had allegedly killed his relatives. For the military court, however, the association with this Indonesian ('a similar type to the beaten man') was sufficient to reduce the sentence.[5]

After March 1946, violence against Indonesians by Dutch, Indo-Europeans and Moluccans, often KNIL soldiers, frequently took place as a form of revenge on the armed groups or individuals who had murdered their loved ones in the earliest phase of the Indonesian Revolution. In this context, the historian Rémy Limpach has suggested that the Indonesian violence in the first phase of the revolution caused some KNIL soldiers to undergo a psychological change that led them to seek revenge. He points to the role played by the Dutch authorities in spreading incendiary messages; these provoked a desire in many prisoners of war, who had just been released from the Japanese camps in and beyond the archipelago, to take revenge on Indonesians.[6]

Wall posters featuring 'incendiary language against Indonesians' and alarming reports about the situation on Java, fed by army propaganda and informally spread via rumours, fuelled anxiety among former prisoners of war. This provoked a desire among KNIL soldiers to 'go home' and protect their families, even though many of them were still in poor physical and mental health as a result of having been held captive by the Japanese. Finally, preserving their homeland as part of the Kingdom of the Netherlands was an important motive for this group. They regarded the Dutch East Indies, not the Republic of Indonesia, as their birthplace; this was not only the case for Moluccans, Chinese and Indo-Chinese Dutch and the majority of Indo-Europeans, but also for part of the Dutch community, some of whom had settled in the Indonesian archipelago several generations ago.

Training and contact officers

The KNIL soldiers who were already in Indonesia and who had experienced the earliest phase of extreme violence during the Indonesian Revolutions personally, or via their relatives, wanted to take revenge on individuals or armed groups. This personal motivation did not apply to the conscripted soldiers and war volunteers who left the Netherlands for Indonesia in 1945 and 1946. It is therefore questionable whether the revenge motive was a factor in the Dutch violence that took place between mid-March 1946 and December 1949. In order to investigate this, we first need to consider the military training the troops received: did the military provide information that could have sparked feelings of revenge? In early December 1945, the Ministry of Overseas Territories took the initiative to establish an Indies Training squad (Indische Vorming, IV) and an Indies Instruction Battalion (Indisch Instructie Bataljon, IIB). The former was charged with providing general training on the country, the language and customs in Indonesia; the latter provided military training for Dutch troops.

This resulted in the first contingent of KNIL 'training and contact officers' in 1946, albeit very modest in size; there were just 30 Dutch information officers. They gave Indies training to the men on the voyage out to Indonesia. However, the officers had a minor impact, as not every ship had such an officer, and not every commander considered the Indies training to be useful.[7] Even more importantly, the training and contact officers were themselves taught by teachers who had come to the Netherlands as retired KNIL officers before the Second World War. This sparked internal criticism: how could these men, who had not experienced the developments in Indonesia between 1942 and 1945, provide adequate information to Dutch servicemen? The answer was to use Indonesian 'contact men': Indonesian non-commissioned officers from the KNIL, who together with the Dutch KNIL contact officers would provide information to the Dutch troops. This system only got going in mid-1946 and involved a limited group; the first batch consisted of 60 contact men. There was a constant shortage of suitable Indonesian contact men. Later, a few smaller groups came to the Netherlands to teach the soldiers undergoing training and then travel with them to Indonesia. In the period between 1946 and 1949, a maximum total of 100 contact officers will have made the journey.[8]

April 1947 saw the founding of the Army Information Service (Legervoorlichtingsdienst, LVD), with departments in The Hague and in Jakarta; in the East Indies it was known as the Army Contacts Service (Dienst voor Legercontacten, DLC). It amounted to a more or less structured information service.[9] Conscripted soldier J.A.A. van Doorn travelled to Indonesia in the summer of 1947. On board his troop-ship was a KNIL sergeant who, as an experienced expert, was charged with providing information to the new troops. According to Van Doorn, he made it 'absolutely clear that whites were needed to govern Indonesia, because the "natives" were incapable of doing so'.[10] Van Doorn also describes how the instructional films about the recent war in the Pacific, which he and his fellow soldiers had watched in the barracks, only took on an emotional charge when they heard KNIL soldiers' stories about their own experiences in the archipelago:

> The abstract discussions about the 'Indonesian question' that had overwhelmed us in the Netherlands now materialized in the personal experiences of the Indo-Dutchmen, with their stories of murders and disappearances that had happened only a few years ago, and could by no means be excluded from their vision of the future. Like the 'peloppor', the 'Jap' or the 'Nip' was given a face, and that face was alarming.'[11]

The word 'peloppor' refers to Indonesian 'insurgents' and the extreme violence in the first phase of the revolution, with the express fear that the atrocities could be repeated. The information that was provided to the conscripts and war volunteers via the military information services in The Hague and Jakarta could therefore have contributed to the creation of feelings of revenge or hatred towards Indonesian fighters.[12] Furthermore, it is plausible that KNIL soldiers who already lived in the archipelago, some of whom were born and raised there, shared their experiences of extreme violence early in the Indonesian Revolution with newcomers after the arrival of the Dutch troops. This may have created a seedbed for feelings of superiority and revenge, as suggested by the quote from Van Doorn.

Military magazines

Studying magazines published by the DLC in Jakarta reveals what was known about the extreme violence in the earliest phase of the Indonesian Revolution. In the period between 1946 and 1949, the DLC published a number of magazines to inform Dutch servicemen, of which *Wapenbroeders* ('brothers in arms', distributed on Java) and *De Klewang* ('Indonesian cutlass', for Sumatra) are the best known. The Indo-European journalists Jan Boon and Lily van Zele (later better known by their pseudonyms Tjalie Robinson/Vincent Mahieu and Lilian Ducelle) were associated with *Wapenbroeders*, the former as editor-in-chief. They resigned in late 1948, because they sympathized with the Indonesian struggle for independence.[13]

The weekly *Wapenbroeders* had a print run of 10,000 (1947) and was printed in small format on 32 pages, while *De Klewang* – '*The weekly for the troops on Sumatra*' was published each week in newspaper format over twelve pages.[14] Both magazines highlighted Japanese influence, which was said to have 'made the Indonesians' heads spin'. Long into 1947, Japanese propaganda was presented as the evil genius behind the 'terror' and the 'hatred of whites'.[15] In addition, because small numbers of Japanese soldiers fought on the Republican side against the Dutch, the idea became established that Japan was responsible for Indonesia turning against the Dutch.

Wapenbroeders and *De Klewang* were accompanied by the magazine *Pen Gun*, an initiative by Prince Bernhard as the Commander of the Dutch Armed Forces (Bevelhebber Nederlandse Strijdkrachten, BNS). His staff's Information unit was initially tasked with publishing the magazine. When the BNS's role was wound up in September 1945, *Pen Gun* was transferred to a private foundation. The magazine was aimed at a wider readership, and was read both in the armed forces and beyond.[16] *Pen Gun* contained articles that appear to have been taken directly from the paternalistic ideas in the Ethical Policy of half a century ago. For example, a passage on the political position of the colonizer and colonized reads as follows:

> The maintenance of that [political] order is the historic right of the Netherlands. [...] Given that lacking a helmsman who can steer a fixed

course, and who has the resources to keep to it, the peoples of Indonesia would create unsustainable weaknesses in the world economy, and given that Indonesia itself is still unable to provide that leadership, it is obvious that the Netherlands will fulfil that task.[17]

Pen Gun also described the nationalist struggle against the Netherlands not as an Indonesian desire, but as an after-effect of Japanese influence. The article 'The Netherlands and the Japanese legacy' testifies to this:

> Behind every bloodbath, every robbery, every crime, a yellow, slit-eyed Japanese face smirks at our men. The Japanese act as the leaders of these gangs, giving military instruction and supplying arms.[18]

From late 1945, however, *Pen Gun* – and as such it was an exception – published a number of articles about the possible consequences of violence during the first phase of the revolution. The word *bersiap* was not used. In November 1945, a passage in *Pen Gun* read:

> A people who are unable to bear the burden of responsibility, who succumb to it, fall into disarray and make easy prey for their enemies. Such a people stumble from revolution to revolution.[19]

Pen Gun also described this violence as Japanese-inspired 'terror, murder and banditry [*rampokken*].' In March 1946, *Pen Gun* warned of the emergence of a spiral of violence, partly due to a lapse in discipline among (Indo-) Dutch KNIL soldiers:

> There is deep hate here, as one might encounter in a civil war, such as in Spain. [...] There is danger, something I have also witnessed for myself; the danger of retaliatory excesses, of the hard law of an eye for an eye and a tooth for a tooth. All the more so because discipline has suffered in battle and beyond, due to captivity during the war and the precariousness of existence.[20]

Pen Gun thus highlighted the risk that not only Indonesian, but also Dutch and Indo-Dutch troops, might go beyond the pale. It is likely that *Pen Gun*, together with *Wapenbroeders* and *De Klewang*, influenced the war volunteers and the first batches of conscripts, if only because in the first months of their stay in Indonesia they would have had hardly any other newspapers or magazines to read. Later, the Dutch illustrated family weeklies associated with particular social and religious communities became available, such as *De Spiegel* (Protestant), *Katholieke Illustratie* (Catholic) and *Panorama* (non-religious).

The military information magazines for Dutch troops in Indonesia that were published between 1946 and 1949, such as *Wapenbroeders*, *Ik zal handhaven*, *De Klewang* and *Het lichtspoor* (the successor to *Pen Gun*), make no reference to 'bersiap'.[21] However, these military magazines do contain general justifications for the presence and deployment of Dutch troops, who were said to be helping the 'well-meaning Indonesian population' against the Japanese-inspired terror from the Indonesian side. According to historian Rémy Limpach, through the military magazines, the DLC influenced the thinking of Dutch conscripts and war volunteers by presenting polarized and simplistic images of the enemy that legitimized violence. The DLC portrayed Indonesian military opponents largely as terrorists or criminals, whilst no mention was made of the Indonesian struggle for independence. This was accompanied by statements from the DLC in which Dutch troops were presented as harbingers of 'peace and order' or 'law and order', or even 'freedom and law' in Indonesia.[22]

The Army Contacts Service

The DLC had an external task as well as an internal one: its aim was to make civil society sympathetic to the army. The DLC therefore tried to manipulate the press, so as to contain any criticism as much as possible. It succeeded in keeping journalists and editors from the key papers from being overly critical of the armed forces. In doing so, it was assisted by the law-abiding attitude of many publishers and editors at the time. Furthermore, the DLC impeded the work of the few journalists who did take a critical stance. The Dutch authorities did not allow journalists from left-wing and independent newspapers, who were known to have opposed the previous colonial policy, to enter Indonesia. Journalistic agencies, such as the General News and Telegraph Agency (Algemeen Nieuws- en Telegraaf-Agentschap, Aneta) and the General Netherlands Press Bureau (Algemeen Nederlands Persbureau, ANP) were wholly dependent on the DLC and usually reproduced official reports and images uncritically. As a result, the Dutch home front was only partially, and sometimes incorrectly, informed about the political and military situation in Indonesia.[23]

The DLC thus left a deep impression on the way in which people in the Netherlands were informed about the situation in the archipelago. The service was under the direct control of army commander-in-chief Simon Spoor. Retaliation and responding to violent provocations were at odds with the picture that senior military leaders wanted to present to the outside world. Spoor knew that leaving a trail of routine orders, guidelines and protest memos calling for moderation of the violence could play a key role in rebuffing accusations of unlawful violence by Dutch units.[24] Moreover, he knew that modern wars were fought not only on the battlefield, but also in the public arena. He played a crucial role in the design and execution of the army's information and communication strategy in Indonesia, drawing on many years of experience. Prior to becoming the head of the DLC in Jakarta, Spoor had led the Netherlands East Indies Forces Intelligence Service (NEFIS) in Australia. Under his leadership, this service had grown into the largest independent Dutch organization on Australian soil, consisting of 355 servicemen and dozens of civilian employees. The DLC in Jakarta alone had 160 employees, who made themselves heard via radio broadcasts, brochures and publications.

Spoor's vision of the role of the Netherlands in the archipelago shaped the content and the functioning of NEFIS and the DLC. Many years before the outbreak of the Indonesian Revolution, he had set out his military-strategic ideas about the future of the Dutch East Indies. Speaking about the restoration of authority in the 'liberated Indies', Spoor considered one thing to be of utmost importance: power should rest firmly in the hands of the military.[25] For him, a (more or less) independent Indonesia was unthinkable. Spoor assumed the undisputed return of Dutch authority in the archipelago, which he considered to be justified both morally and in international law.[26] Having become commander-in-chief of the Dutch troops in Indonesia in January 1946, he was already pressing for a 'more far-reaching occupation' by early February. In his diary, he wrote that he did not yet consider a war of conquest possible, due to the lack of resources, the political atmosphere of the age, and 'all of our modern-ethical thinking'.[27] Together with his chief of staff, Dirk Cornelis Buurman van Vreeden, he developed an operational plan. 'The reoccupation of Java', the latter wrote, 'will have to be fought for'.[28] Other high-ranking military personnel were also of the opinion that it would be necessary to 'recapture' the archipelago.[29] 'Reoccupation' became the common term in military circles, as can be seen from the backs of the photos taken by servicemen in late 1945 and early 1946. These refer to 'the reoccupation' of the Minahassa (North Sulawesi) and 'the reoccupation' of Timor by 'a delegation of the reoccupying Allied force (NICA officers)'.[30]

JOURNALISTIC REPORTING AND FILM PRODUCTIONS

In addition to providing information for servicemen, for the Dutch government it was extremely important to reach civilians in the Netherlands and the archipelago. Besides the above-mentioned DLC, this was the remit of the Government Information Service (Regeringsvoorlichtingsdienst, RVD). The RVD's department in Batavia was located on the capital's Koningsplein. Its aim was to paint a positive and optimistic picture for the Netherlands of the developments in the archipelago after 15 August 1945. In the period between 1946 and 1949, the policy focused on securing both Dutch and Indonesian support for the Dutch political approach in the archipelago, and giving the impression that the Dutch were working with the Indonesians to rebuild the country. The RVD believed that the best way to achieve this was by responding calmly to the Republic of Indonesia and the violence by armed groups. Focusing attention on the proclamation of Indonesian independence and the subsequent violent embroilment, which targeted the Dutch and everyone associated with them, was at odds with this strategy. The RVD hoped that the Netherlands would thereby make a reasonable impression, not only in Indonesia itself, but also abroad.[31]

The RVD also viewed the Japanese occupying forces, not the Republic of Indonesia or its supporters, as the instigator of the violence against the Dutch regime.[32] In early September 1945, the RVD in Batavia still believed that 'publicity remained undesirable at this stage'.[33] For this reason, the RVD did not initially support the efforts of the Java-born Dutch journalist Johan Fabricius, who worked as a war correspondent for the BBC and *The Times*, to write about the young nation. He described this as 'typical Indies distrust of publicity'.[34] When, in late September 1945 Fabricius and other foreign reporters finally gained permission, it struck him that world opinion had turned against the Netherlands in the meantime:

> We stood in the shadows, and the full light fell on the leaders of the revolution. I heard American journalists, who had just arrived by plane, immediately asking for the address of Sukarno or Sjahrir.[35]

On 4 October 1945, for example, Sukarno warmly welcomed the world's press to his home. Almost the whole cabinet was present, and Subarjo, the

Indonesian Minister of Foreign Affairs, served tea. The foreign war correspondents, dressed in uniform, came from India, China and Australia, among others. They included a number of Dutch reporters who worked for various press agencies: Dolf Verspoor on behalf of Agence France-Presse, Robert Kiek on behalf of the Dutch ANP, and Jan Bouwer on behalf of America United Press. The Indonesian photographers Alex Mendur and Frans Mendur, who would found the Indonesia Press Photo Service (IPPHOS) press agency in October 1946, were also present.[36] The 'sobriety' of 'our' information service and the 'rigidity of press-shy senior officials contrasted with the warm welcome that the press received from the nationalists', Fabricius wrote:

> While the Dutch Information Service saw it as its duty to maintain a strict neutrality towards all foreign correspondents [...] on the Indonesian side, everything was more friendly and thus more attractive to many, because journalists are only human beings, after all.[37]

There were few Dutch journalists on Java in the first phase of the revolution: in addition to those mentioned above, they included Alfred van Sprang and Jan Stevens.[38] As reporters, they wrote press releases and supplied articles for national and international papers and (family) weeklies. A number of them would later publish their memories in book form.

Jan Stevens, for example, a lieutenant 3rd class, was a photojournalist for the Naval Information Service and published the photo book *Vrij* [Free] in 1946, with texts by Ben Grevendamme. The latter described becoming caught up in the violence at the Simpang Society in Surabaya on 15 October 1945, which was the prelude to the extremely bloody Battle of Surabaya between the British and the Republicans. Grevendamme had to run the gauntlet on the square in front of the prison in Werfstraat:

> Then all hell broke loose. We were forced with spear-thrusts to get out of the car, and then we had to walk through a thousand-strong throng, who jabbed at us with spears and knives. There were 25 men on the car when we left the society. Six of them reached the gate seriously injured. Two of us had deep spear-wounds, my front teeth were knocked out, another had deep wounds from cleavers and swords.[39]

In the days that followed, around 40 Dutchmen died. In *En Soekarno lacht..!* [*And Sukarno smiles!*] (1946), Alfred van Sprang wrote about bamboo spears and '*bersiap... bersiap!*' as a slogan and as an 'ominous word' used by young Indonesian men and women. His use of the term 'bersiap' at that time is striking; it was not yet in common parlance as a description of the period of extreme violence in the earliest phase of the Revolution.⁴⁰ This impression corresponds to ANP radio bulletins in the period 1940-1949, which do not mention 'bersiap', but do make frequent reference to 'terror'. In this period, the term 'rampok' was mentioned three times in ANP radio bulletins.⁴¹

Van Sprang also remarked that the Ministry of Information of the Republic of Indonesia was much more effective in its handling of the foreign press, consisting of English, Australian, American, Belgian, French and British-Indian journalists: 'The Dutch were not welcome'.⁴² In his memoirs *Hoe ik Indië terugvond* [*My encounter with the Indies*] (1947), Johan Fabricius reported extensively on the massacre by *pemuda* of 30 or so Christian Indonesians in Depok in mid-October 1945. The journalist noted that it created 'some sensation' in the world, but that the news was swiftly overtaken by other events, such as the killing of the British brigadier general Mallaby two weeks later during the Battle of Surabaya.⁴³

Reports and photos of the violence against the Dutch and all those associated with them hardly reached the Dutch media, due to the actions of the RVD; the aim was to give the public in the Netherlands the impression that pre-war relations would soon be restored and that peace would return.⁴⁴ For example, the Dutch and the British handled publicity issues in the Anglo-Dutch Publicity Committee. In early March 1946, they discussed the previously agreed guideline of 'suspension', which meant that they would only report reasonably substantiated statements about 'atrocities'. At the meeting, it was argued that the guideline did not go far enough, and there was a proposal to ban articles about the atrocities. Only in exceptional cases, such as the murder of the British and British-Indian passengers, could such events be reported. The suspension was aimed only at 'normal run of the mill, day to day atrocities'.⁴⁵ The senior civil servant Charles van der Plas, the successor to governor-general Van Mook, agreed to the proposal. The episode shows how common the violence – and its cover-up – had become.

Dutch journalists who had been given permission to cover the situation in Indonesia were received upon their arrival in Jakarta by the RVD, which provided all facilities, together with the DLC. This meant that the correspondents, almost all of whom stayed together in the capital, were taken to the same locations or situations by press officers. As a result, they were dependent on information from the Dutch government, which was biased, propagandistic, and often difficult to verify. Because rebuttals and expressions of criticism did not yet form part of the standard journalistic repertoire, there was hardly any thorough or critical reporting on the situation in the archipelago.[46]

This also applied to productions by filmmakers who worked for the RVD in Batavia. In 70 minutes, the 1947 film *Door duisternis tot licht* [*Through darkness to light*] presented the course of the Japanese occupation in the archipelago, followed by images of Indonesia in the first months after the Japanese surrender. The final part of the film addressed the Indonesian Revolution with a series of nationalist slogans ('Respect our constitution of August 18 '45. We are a free nation conceived in liberty and dedicated to the proposition that all men are created equal'), plus a closing image that became a shocking icon of the earliest violence: a half-decayed corpse floating in a canal in the capital. The presentation of these images provoked objections from Jan Jonkman (Labour Party), the Minister of Overseas Territories. In response to the film, he told the head of the RVD in Batavia:

Protest in English by Indonesians on the quay wall. Source: NIOD

> I would like to draw your attention to the fact that showing the last part in its present form [in Indonesia] is certainly irresponsible in view of the current negotiations. Although the aim is to reject violence and achieve a cooperative solution [...] the edited film makes an impression on outsiders of the utter rejection of the republic in any form [...] Isn't more positive material pointing to the potential for cooperation available for insertion after the terror scenes?[47]

After showing Indonesian violence directed against the Dutch, Minister Jonkman wanted to show images of partnership with the Indonesians: 'Co-operation that is not forced, but built on mutual understanding', as it was optimistically put in the first part of the film. According to historian Gerda Jansen Hendriks, an independent commercial operator such as Filmfabriek Polygoon, which provided the content for cinema newsreels and thereby made a crucial contribution to the way in which the Dutch public were informed about the situation in the archipelago, was also influenced by this principle:

> As journalists they had to show what was going on in the world, but at the same time, as a newsreel company, they had to ensure that no viewer would take offence at what was being shown.[48]

Nevertheless, there was an increase in the number of images and reports about (extreme) violence against the Dutch and those who supported the colonial regime (or were suspected of this), despite the efforts of the RVD to prevent it. Early publications, such as those by Stevens, Van Sprang and Fabricius, were of some importance in this respect, but most photos and reports of early (extreme) violence that reached the Netherlands were produced by military photographers and reporters from the British army, despite all the efforts of the Anglo-Dutch Publicity Committee.

Egodocuments by soldiers

Whether the military information campaign had an impact on the troops who were dispatched to the archipelago can be investigated using egodocuments, in which war volunteers and conscripts wrote about their experiences. The NIMH data base 'Diary Project Dutch military personnel in Indonesia, 1945-1949' contains more than 6,600 quotes from diaries written by Dutch servicemen between 1945 and 1949. The database mainly contains

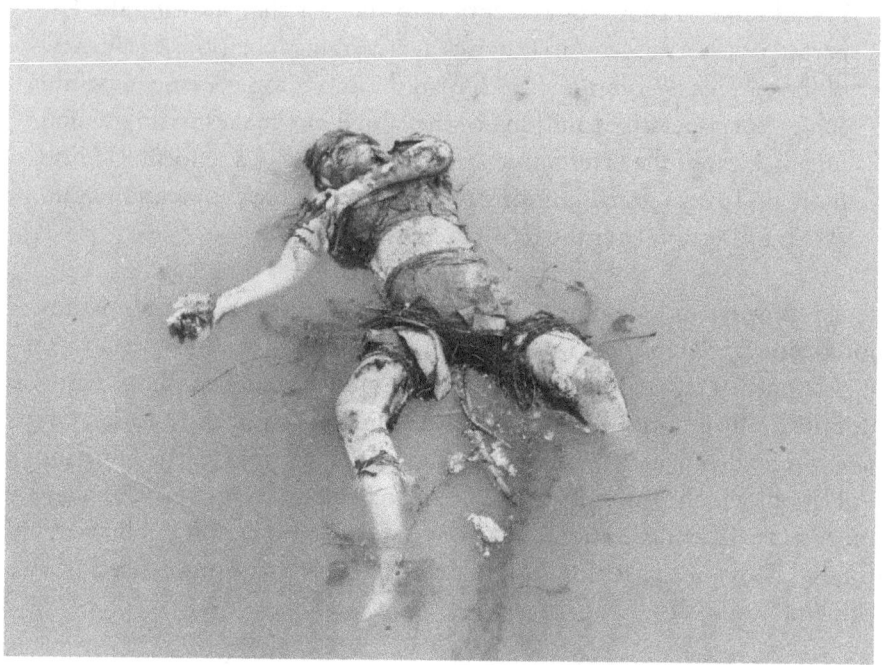

The body of a mutilated Indo-European woman in the Ancol Canal in Jakarta, 1945. Source: photographer unknown, KITLV

the diaries of (conscript) soldiers of all ranks and roles in the Royal Netherlands Army (Koninklijke Landmacht, KL).[49] In order to answer the question above, an inventory was made of keywords that might yield hits about the so-called *bersiap* period, such as 'bersiap', 'pemoeda [pemuda]' and 'bende [gang]'. The results confirm the conjecture that the term 'bersiap' was rarely used at that time; the search yielded only two hits (from 1946 and 1949).

Based on relevant quotes from the first search, new search terms were formulated that expanded on the terms in the quotes. In the end, eleven search terms yielded useful results: 'bende [gang]', 'rampok', 'terreur [terror]', 'evacu', 'kamp[spatie] [camp (space)]', 'kampen [camps]', 'extremist', 'pemoeda [pemuda]', 'moord [murder]', 'indo', 'ambon'. Although these search terms yielded a total of 808 hits, only 23 quotes from the diaries written between 1945 and 1949 related to the *bersiap* period; a remarkably small number.[50] Further analysis of the veterans' diaries revealed that the word 'bende [gang]' appeared by far the most often, followed by the Indonesian words 'peloppor'/'plopper' and 'rampok'.[51] These terms were closely followed by their Dutch equivalents, such as 'rover [robber]', 'extremist', and, to a lesser extent, the word 'terrorist'. In the period between 17 August 1945 and 27 December 1949, a relatively small number of memoirs was published by soldiers and journalists, among others, including the above-mentioned works by Johan Fabricius, Alfred van Sprang and Jan Stevens. In the memoirs as in the diaries, 'bendes [gangs]' is the most commonly used word to describe the Indonesian opponent, followed successively by 'rover [robber], 'rampok', 'p(e)lopper), 'extremist' and 'terrorist'. The term 'bersiap' appears nine times as an entry in memoirs that were published during the Indonesian Revolution.[52] The observation that war volunteer Jot Polman made in his memoir *De brutale reis* [*The bold voyage*], published in 1947, is a striking example of how the meaning of the word had developed and would continue to develop even more strongly in the decades to come:

> Only when the bloody massacres caused by the young revolutionaries, which went down in history as 'bersiap', made the front pages and the Polygoon newsreel did the gravity of the situation dawn on the people and the violent images become firmly established in the minds of many Dutch. It was thus considered a humanitarian act when our first military volunteers embarked to restore order in Indonesia.[53]

In the case of the Indo-Europeans, Dutch, Chinese, Indo-Chinese and Moluccans, including KNIL soldiers, who had experienced the initial phase of the Indonesian Revolution at first hand, these acts of violence often remained hidden in a private world. Their diaries can offer a glimpse into this. Sometimes they were shared, often with their companions in adversity. Although (extreme) violence in the first phase of the Indonesian Revolution was frequently described by servicemen in diaries, for example, they did not use the term 'bersiap'.[54] In any case, experiences and memories of (extreme) violence would remain invisible to the outside world for a long time to come. Many of the Indo-Europeans, Dutch, Indo-Chinese, Chinese and Moluccans did not yet feel a need to talk to outsiders about their past and the (extreme) violence in the archipelago. There also seemed to be little wider social interest in these memories and themes. As in the diaries, the Dutch troops are presented in memoirs as bringers of 'calm and peace', or 'peace and order' in Indonesia. It was with the later rediscovery of 'bersiap' in the public domain that this term would become the name for the period of extreme violence in the first phase of the Indonesian Revolution.

Het Dagblad

Dutch newspapers published in the Netherlands and Indonesia in the period 1946-1949 usually referred more frequently to the violence, although at first it was rarely described as 'bersiap'. An analysis of the Indies newspaper *Het Dagblad,* managed by editor-in-chief Willem Belonje, offers more insight in this regard.[55] This newspaper, founded by the Nederlandsche Dagbladpers in Jakarta, emphatically presented itself as independent, explicitly stating that it was not an RVD publication, 'even less so an offshoot of the Netherlands Indies government': '"Het Dagblad" was founded with the sole objective of meeting the general need for reliable reporting and calm information provision.'[56] Despite this claim, much of the reporting in *Het Dagblad* came directly from the Aneta news agency, which in turn was entirely dependent on the RVD for its news-gathering. As the editorial board was based in Jakarta, news about Java prevailed; there were very few reports about the situation beyond Java.

An analysis of *Het Dagblad* between 23 October 1945 and 31 March 1946 shows that the paper paid ample attention to the Indonesian violence against all who opposed Indonesian independence, desired the return of the colonial regime or who were associated with the Netherlands. The first issue of *Het Dagblad* appeared on 23 October 1945, around the nadir of the violence in the first phase of the revolutionary struggle. This first issue refers unequivocally to 'rampokkers':

> From Sunday to Monday, it was generally quiet in Batavia. There were a few clashes with rampokkers, thirteen of whom were killed. Tanah-Abang camp came under gunfire for half an hour. There were no casualties.[57]

In October and November 1945, a series of articles about the violence was published, entitled 'The situation on Java'. In December 1945 and January 1946, this was followed by the column 'De eindelooze rij' ('The endless list'; also: 'De eindelooze reeks', 'The endless series'), an inventory of the names of Indo-Europeans, Dutch, Moluccans, Chinese and Indo-Chinese who were thought to have been abducted.[58] Under the headline 'Shocking crime', a short news report appeared in *Het Dagblad* on 18 February 1946: 'On Saturday morning, the body of a European girl aged approximately eighteen was found in Tandjong-Priok harbour. It was nailed to a raft and had been horribly mutilated.'[59] A few days later, *Het Dagblad* reported, under the headline 'Crimes in Batavia':

Newspaper report in Trouw, *15 November 1945. Source: Trouw*

We understand that bodies are still being found in the Ancol Canal on a daily basis. On Wednesday, an informant told us that, upon returning from Priok, he had seen no fewer than thirteen bodies floating there. Three were spotted yesterday, probably a family; a man, a woman and a child were seen.[60]

Between 23 October 1945 and 30 March 1946, *Het Dagblad* used terms such as *pemoeda* (102 times), 'extremis[-me/-ten]' (138 times) and 'terroris[-me/-ten/-eren]' (54 times) and 'ontvoer[-ing/-den/-en] [kidnappings/

abductions]' (159 times), 'kidnapp[-ing/-en]' (30 times) and 'moord [murder]' (183 times).[61] The word *bersiap* appeared in *Het Dagblad* for the first time on 26 January 1946 as 'Bersiapan!' ('Get ready!'), in an eyewitness account of a train transport in which former internees were taken by the Tentara Keamanan Rakyat (TKR) from Malang to Jakarta. After that, there are two more mentions of 'bersiap' in the newspaper. On 8 February 1946, a report read:

> It began on the day of the capitulation, before the Allies arrived, with the daily 'bersiap', through to the farthest corners of the city. [...] The Ambonese Tanalepe was the first victim. [He was] detained by a group of Indonesians, who were certainly 'bersiap [ready]'. When the car stopped, Tanalepe was hauled from the car and killed with *goloks* [machetes]. His body was mutilated in every possible way, his stomach was pierced with bamboo spears, and the 'Police of the Republic of Indonesia' did nothing, knew nothing, did not in fact exist. That was the beginning.[62]

On 16 February 1946, this was followed by a report about tensions in the city of Bandung.[63] In these two reports, *bersiap* refers on the one hand to the call to get ready to defend Indonesian independence, and, on the other hand, to the Indonesian state of mind at the time. Furthermore, *bersiap* appeared in *Het Dagblad* from mid-1946 as a term to describe revolutionary violence against different groups: for example, in reporting about the search for information on missing persons, the discovery of the (mass) graves of victims, and announcements about lawsuits against Indonesians suspected of having committed violence during the early phase of the Indonesian Revolution. After that more articles appeared, including in other newspapers, suggesting that *bersiap* was increasingly being incorporated into everyday language to describe the historical period from around October 1945 to early 1946. One example is a newspaper article in which resident M. Klaassen awards the bronze star of merit to Mas Kartawinata, who worked for the Water Management Department:

> Kartawinata earned his award for his exemplary performance during the *bersiap* period after the Japanese surrender, as a result of which key irrigation areas and the accompanying engineering works in the vicinity of Radjamandala were saved from destruction and neglect.[64]

A WARNING

After March 1946, the situation in Indonesia changed when Dutch troops landed on Java and Sumatra and the news supply became somewhat normalized. In addition to *Het Dagblad*, in the course of time more and more Dutch-language newspapers appeared, including *Nieuwe Courant, Algemeen Indisch Dagblad, De Preangerbode, De Locomotief, Java-bode* and *Het Nieuwsblad voor Sumatra*.[65] From March 1946, the coverage of the violence in *Het Dagblad* increasingly consisted of articles and letters about violence that had taken place (much) earlier. Under the headline 'Mass graves discovered', for example, in November 1946 the newspaper reflected on the violence that had occurred in late 1945. The Military Police (Militaire Politie, MP) had discovered the following:

> More light has been shed on one of the large scale murders, committed during the *bersiap* period in the months of October, November and December of last year in Batavia. [...] mass graves [...] of the people, who in that period were first kidnapped from their homes or the street by frenzied and bloodthirsty rogues, and then slaughtered in beastly fashion. The graves are located in an old Japanese trench just off the main road to Tangerang, on the way to Slipi camp.[66]

A count in the database of digitized Dutch newspapers that were published in the Netherlands and Indonesia between 17 August 1945 and 27 December 1949 shows that the word 'bersiap' was mentioned 516 times in that period.[67]

Table 4: number of articles in digitized Dutch-language newspapers in the Netherlands and Indonesia in which the term 'bersiap' appears, 1945-1949 (reference date 10 October 2021).

Year	Number of mentions of 'bersiap' in newspaper articles
1945	0
1946	13
1947	128
1948	181
1949	194
Total	516

Source: Delpher

When considering the distribution of these numbers over time, we should be aware that the frequency could be strongly influenced by a few attention-grabbing events, whereby a large number of articles could be reduced to a single report. For example, the murder of the Indo-European Jonathans family was widely reported in the news, no doubt fuelled by the scale and gruesome nature of the violence that was used:

> The remains of the Jonathans family were found in a well in Kampong Rawah Mangoen. This family, consisting of eleven male and seven female members, was massacred during the *bersiap* period.[68]

This discovery not only attracted the attention of editors in Jakarta, Bandung and Surabaya, but also in the Netherlands, who reproduced the same press release.

That 'bersiap' did not yet feature in newspapers in 1945 can be explained by the fact that the fierce outbreaks of violence did not take place until late in that year. In 1946, there were 13 mentions, and in 1947 128, in which 'bersiap' mainly features in the context of 'targeting Europeans', the 'fate of Indo-Europeans', and the murder of the Indo-European Jonathans and Portier families. The newspaper reporting emphasized that Indo-Europeans had been severely affected during the first phase of the Indonesian Revolution, something that was also underlined by several MPs in the House of Representatives. The term 'bersiap' was also used in the sense of 'robbery with murder', but also as a much broader indication of violence against various groups of victims. In addition to the 'Ambonese', the following were named: 'Dutch, English, Chinese, Indonesians and Arabs',[69] as well as 'Europeans, Chinese and Indonesians who did not sympathize sufficiently with the Republic';[70] it was also mentioned that 'village heads [*loerahs*] were killed, prominent villagers were kidnapped and peaceful peasants [*tanis*] attacked'.[71]

Around the time of the second Dutch military offensive, 'Operation Kraai', in late 1948 and early 1949, the term 'bersiap' was explicitly used in the Dutch press to refer to a period of revolutionary violence, and thus functioned as a warning. Newspapers wrote about the danger of a 'second *bersiap*' and a 'new *bersiap* period', and emphasized that a 'repetition of *bersiap*' must be prevented. These warnings were directly related to the political situation: as a consequence of the Linggadjati Agreement (November 1946), the United States of Indonesia (Verenigde Staten van Indonesië, VSI) had to be established by 1 January 1949. In various articles, journalists expressed the fear that the Republic of Indonesia would dominate the other federal states in this construction, and that:

> a new *bersiap* would begin, much larger than the one that raged at the turn of the year, three years ago. [...] The coming *bersiap*, organized on a much larger scale and prepared much more intensively than the first, would plunge the archipelago into a pool of misery.[72]

Another commonly-heard term is 'psychosis', something with which the violence was associated:

> 1 January: the start of a new *bersiap* period? A massive attack on the Dutch troops does not seem to be the intention; we expect something more in the direction of a second so-called 'bersiap' period. The first *bersiap* period will be remembered all too well by anyone who was in Indonesia in the period between October and December 1945. Thousands of murders were committed back then, usually by people who were guided solely by the general murder-psychosis of the time.[73]

The newspapers do not present the *bersiap* period as a reason for the second military action. In late December 1948, the RVD and DLC information services pursued a strict media strategy in which journalists were told that 'not only is war being waged here, but the focus is on the economic and social relations and conditions'.[74]

THE ROUND TABLE CONFERENCE

The ongoing political developments resulted in negotiations between the Netherlands and Indonesia during the Round Table Conference (RTC), which was held in The Hague between late August and early November 1949. The outcomes of the conference again raised concerns that were expressed in Dutch papers with recollections of the *bersiap* period. A correspondent from *De Telegraaf*, who had attended the RTC and returned to his post in Jakarta, wrote that the Dutch, Indo-Dutch and Moluccans were hardly enthusiastic about the results of the conference:

> Hanging over the Dutch community is the shadow of an uncertain future and a nameless fear of the repetition of the shocking November

days of 1945, the infamous 'bersiap' period, when so many Dutch and pro-Dutch Indonesians fell victim to terrorists.[75]

Other newspapers, such as the social democratic-leaning but independent newspaper *Het Parool* and the Catholic trade union paper *de Volkskrant*, also mentioned *bersiap*, but in this case to express their fear that a refusal to ratify the outcomes of the RTC would provoke to international censure, loss of face for the Indonesian leaders and, not least, a lack of direction for the Netherlands and Indonesia. For example, *Het Parool* reported on the 'lengthy and tiring' debate in the House of Representatives, in which the MPs eventually voted in approval of the transfer of sovereignty. The newspaper wrote that 'if the results of the RTC were rejected, one could expect a catastrophe worse than the infamous *bersiap* period in 1945'.[76] According to *de Volkskrant*, refusal to ratify the RTC results would immediately give rise to 'chaos and repetition of *bersiap* 1945', and would reignite the distrust between the countries.[77] The right-wing paper *De Telegraaf* reported that great concerns prevailed among the Europeans in Indonesia, caused by the uncertainty:

> The question that almost everyone is asking, is: are peace and order guaranteed in the time immediately after the transfer of sovereignty, or will we get a second *bersiap* period? (*Bersiap* means: 'attack', and *bersiap* period refers to the time just after the Japanese capitulation when thousands of Europeans were murdered by Indonesians who were whipped up into a hysterical state.)[78]

Strikingly, the author of this article considered it necessary to explain the term *bersiap*, indicating that the term was not in common parlance in late 1949, after four years of war. Furthermore, the writer borrowed a term from the field of psychology to define *bersiap*: in addition to the aforementioned 'psychosis', 'hysteria' was introduced as a driver of the violence by Indonesians against Europeans.

Concern was also expressed in *Het Nieuwsblad van het Zuiden*, which published an article with the telling headline: 'When the red-and-white flag is raised, the Dutch bite the bullet'. The article was about an administrator at a sugar company who had decided to stay in Indonesia after the transfer of sovereignty. This 'young man' stood by his decision, even after TNI leaders, according to the paper, distributed pamphlets in which 'a second *bersiap* was wished upon the Dutch'.[79] The liberal *Algemeen Handelsblad* reported on the economic interests at stake for the Netherlands. The newspaper saw Indonesia as an 'enormous potential field of activity if peace and order prevail', and wrote anxiously:

> That strife, often bitter strife, will break out appears almost certain, and a country that is pillaged by extremist desperados will be unable to develop. Will the Westerners be left alone? The white population in Indonesia is unlikely to survive a second *bersiap* period; and that would put an end to the economic influence of the Dutch. Questions, nothing but questions.[80]

Based on the reporting in Dutch newspapers, the term *bersiap* was thus used more and more frequently towards the end of 1949. As such, the term mainly functioned as a time designation for the period of violence in the first phase of the Indonesian Revolution. Importantly, *bersiap* was not used as a revenge motive for past violence or as justification for the later use of force by Dutch troops, but rather as a spectre: the possibility of a 'second *bersiap*'. In Dutch papers, *bersiap* served as a warning: the fear that walking away from the negotiations with the Republic of Indonesia might lead to a 'second or new *bersiap*'. After all, the first and second Dutch military offensives had provoked renewed violence on the Indonesian side.

'FOREIGNERS AND MINORITIES'

In contrast to newspapers published in the Netherlands, Dutch-language papers that were published in Indonesia covered multiple perspectives on the transfer of sovereignty. These newspapers also reported the opinions of Republican Indonesians. For example, this is shown by an article about a lecture given by the journalist Mohammed Tabrani, who described the Dutch and Indo-Europeans who would settle in the young nation as 'foreigners and minorities', respectively; terms that the editors of *De Nieuwe Courant* in Surabaya adopted in their coverage.

Furthermore, these newspapers took a more moderate position on the possibility of the outbreak of a 'second *bersiap*' after the transfer of sovereignty. In late 1949, the *Nieuwe Courant* reported on meetings between the Dutch, Indo-Europeans and Moluccans with Indonesians, where they jointly discussed the near future. One of the speakers on such an occasion was the above-mentioned Tabrani, editor-in-chief of the newspaper *Indonesia Merdeka*. After his lecture, a member of the audience mentioned the great fear of a second *bersiap* period. Tabrani was asked whether the future United States of Indonesia (Republik Indonesia Serikat, RIS) would offer sufficient guarantees for the protection of 'minorities and foreigners'. According to *Nieuwe Courant*, Tabrani admitted that there had indeed been a 'fear psychosis as a result of the events in the past'. He believed that these events were the result of a political conflict. Tabrani pointed out that in a revolution, as well as the good elements who want to stand up for their country's rights, 'the mob' comes out of hiding: 'Now that the conflict has been resolved, everyone must cooperate to fight and suppress this mob.'[81]

A few days later, Indonesian perspectives were again addressed in the same paper in an article about a speech by Colonel Sungkono, addressed to the country's 'minorities'. Sungkono also acknowledged the 'fear psychosis', but believed that anxiety about a 'second *bersiap* period' was unfounded. According to Sungkono, the 'first *bersiap* period' could be regarded as a natural phenomenon, for the birth of every new state was accompanied by a revolution.[82] Despite the concerns that were aired at the meeting, the article otherwise suggests a relaxed atmosphere. It describes how people stayed for some time after the lecture 'in pleasant conversation, while enjoying a cool drink'.

In early December 1949, *De Locomotief* wrote about a well-attended meeting organized by the Semarang department of the Indo-European Alliance (Indo-Europees Verbond, IEV). At this meeting, 'Indo-Europeans and stayers [*blijvers*]' expressed their confidence, through a resolution, in the government of the RIS. The newspaper also suggested that people should no longer fear a *bersiap* period, for if Indonesia were free, there would be no reason for one. 'This is confirmed by the Indonesian side, where there is a general sympathy for the minorities,' wrote *De Locomotief*.[83]

A first, modest inventory of Indonesian newspapers that were published in the early phase of the revolution provides more insight into how Indonesians experienced and interpreted this time. A reflection piece in the newspaper *Merah-Poetih* from late October 1945 describes the previous period of war and international conflict as extremely difficult. The newspaper considered the situation at that time as a transition period ('masa pantjaroba') between 'wartime' ('masa perang') and 'peacetime' ('masa damai').[84] In March 1946, the newspaper *Gelora Rakjat* described Indonesia's predicament as follows: 'We are living in the age of the bloody revolution.'[85] The author of this article also used the term 'transition period' ('djaman pantjaroba') to describe the situation in which Indonesia found itself. He also called on the readers to keep calm, because 'those who are not able to calm their hearts will surely suffer hardships and sorrow in this era of transition!'[86]

Considering all of the above – the military information and information from the Dutch government, military magazines, journalistic reporting, film productions, diaries and memoirs of veterans, and Indies, Dutch and Indonesian newspapers about the period 17 August 1945-27 December 1949 – we can conclude that it was not until 1948 and 1949 that the term 'bersiap' assumed a clear place in the public domain. At the time of the extreme violence, in the period between late 1945 and late March 1946, as well as shortly afterwards, 'bersiap' was not yet a common term. Other terms associated with the violence of this period, such as 'rampokker', 'p(e)loppor' and 'extremist', were used much more frequently to report on and write about the (extreme) violence and the opposition. This observation is more than a matter of terminology: whilst the term 'bersiap' implies a more or less comprehensive process, the use of pejorative and stereotypical terms to describe the perpetrators suggests that the violence was interpreted as individual and irregular actions. This may partly explain why the extreme violence by the Indonesian side in the earliest phase of the Indonesian Revolution was not presented as the (main) reason for the deployment of the Dutch military in Indonesia. Indeed, that deployment had long been anticipated. As early as 1942, it had been the main objective of the Dutch authorities to restore colonial authority by recapturing what had previously been the Dutch East Indies.

Appendix 1. Entries in NIMH diaries database[87]

Keyword	No. of hits	1945	1946	1947	1948	1949	1950 and beyond
Rampok [raid, rob]	83	2	2	8	37	12	22
Rover [robber]	66	2	10	23	8	17	6
Roven [to rob]	5		2	1		1	1
Pelopper [fighter]	93		1	11	13	64	4
Plopper [fighter]	84		1	10	14	59	
Pemoeda [pemuda]	15	0	5	5	3	2	
Terreur [terror]	14	2	2	2	6	2	
Extremist	65	1	38	13	9	3	
Terrorist	5		1	1	1	2	
Bersiap	2		1			1	
Terrorisme [terrorism]							
Extremisme extremism	1					1	
Bende [gang]	287	2	12	75	112	87	9

V.
TO CONCLUDE

Conclusions

The extreme violence that broke out after the proclamation of Indonesian independence, which became known in the Netherlands as the *bersiap* period, came as an utter shock to the great majority of Dutch, Indo-Europeans and Moluccans who had lived through the Japanese occupation in or outside the prisoner-of-war and civilian camps. For many, the news of the Japanese surrender on 15 August 1945 was literally a matter of life and death. The fact that this message was followed, two days later, by the announcement that the Republic of Indonesia had proclaimed its independence was barely comprehensible to them. Many found it completely inconceivable that Indonesians would turn against the Dutch regime, and that they would be willing to take up arms to defend the young Republic. For example, J.J.C.H. van Waardenburg, a former internee from Bangkinang men's camp in Padang (Central Sumatra), wrote about a 'minor incident on the fourth day after the liberation':

> On that day, we were ordered to lower the national flag. We refused, of course. By the way, the reason for the request – that the Dutch flag might vex our brown brothers – struck us as so absurd that we couldn't stop laughing. Vex the people, ha ha, those people with whom we were on the friendliest terms! Who offered their goods for sale from early in

the morning until late at night, and who were only interested in making money.¹

Mieke van Hoogstraten made a similar observation on 29 August 1945. As a young woman, she was interned in Halmaheira camp in Semarang (Central Java), where she worked as a nurse. In her diary, she noted how after the Japanese surrender, the former cook, whom they called 'Annie' and who had 'served' their family for twelve years, had gone in search of her former employer:

> A few days after the peace, she turned up by the fence of our house, quite by chance, and it was a moving reunion after such a long time. She had come all the way from Surabaya and had finally found us. [...] All of the Javanese were so friendly, they smiled at us and watched us. I think we were the first *blandas* [whites] they had seen in a long time! [...] But there was no feeling of hostility or suchlike from those Javanese. And our good Annie was overjoyed to have us back.²

In these diaries, we can read between the lines that there had been a shift in relations since the pre-war days, between those who represented the former colonial administration and the Indonesians. Although Indonesian nationalism had grown stronger after 1900, it had been harshly suppressed by the colonial regime from the outset. Nationalist leaders had been exiled, weakening the movement; moreover, many Indonesians dared not express their nationalist sentiments for fear of possible reprisals. For many in the upper and middle classes of the colonial regime, the proclamation of the Republic of Indonesia and the desire to defend it by force, even with extreme violence, was not only completely unexpected, but also utterly inexplicable. In some later studies, cultural explanations were given for the outbursts of violence, in which that violent aspect was attributed to the allegedly more vicious character or cruel nature of Asian peoples. Historian Herman Bussemaker used the metaphor of a volcano, for example:

> Our study indeed points to an undercurrent of violence among the otherwise very docile and friendly native Javanese and Sudanese. In their national character, the volcanism of their mountains became explicit, as it were; with a period of long rest and dormant volcanic activity that is then roughly and explosively interrupted by short bursts

of excessive natural violence. The national character has learned to live with that. But this, of course, is a crude generalization.[3]

Although in that last sentence, Bussemaker does put his own analysis in perspective, his 'explanation' is a painful example of a colonial way of thinking about Indonesians rooted in racism and paternalism that was thus still very much alive, even in 2005. In their book *Talen van geweld* [*Languages of violence*], Remco Raben and Peter Romijn describe the principle that underlies this as 'colonial dissociation'.[4] In their view, the conflict between the Indonesian nationalists and the Netherlands was fuelled by a clash of worldviews. The Indonesians' was a world of resistance and the will to determine their own fate as a sovereign nation. The Dutch were guided by colonial impulses of prejudice, paternalism and control. This led to a serious lack of insight into the actual situation. The Dutch could see the proclamation of Indonesian independence only as a Japanese fabrication, and in doing so erroneously assumed that the majority of the Indonesian population would be on the Dutch side, whilst they underestimated the capacities of Indonesia in terms of leadership and combat power. This colonial framework also created a blind spot when it came to its own performance, for example with regard to the use of violence by the Dutch regime in earlier periods. The use of brute force to subject the Indonesian people to Dutch authority may have led to the much-remarked submissive and friendly attitude of the Indonesians, but there was a failure to understand that this was a forced and by no means voluntary choice, as the events after 17 August 1945 would emphasize.

In *The sound of violence*, we have attempted to expose a number of these misconceptions. Although the extreme violence came out of the blue, as it were, for almost the entire colonial upper and middle class, it did in fact form part of a continuity of violence. It fitted into a long pattern of colonial violence: from the colonial Dutch East Indies (until 1942), through the Japanese occupation (1942-1945) to the Indonesian Revolution (1945-1949). Following Peter Romijn, who argues in *De lange Tweede Wereldoorlog* [*The long Second World War*] that the war, as far as the Dutch were concerned, began with the German invasion in May 1940 and only ended on 27 December 1949 with the transfer of sovereignty to Indonesia, we argue that not only should the Japanese conquest of the Dutch East Indies be seen as foreign oppression, but so also should the violence-based presence of the Netherlands in the preceding centuries.[5] That is why we addressed the periods of Dutch and Japanese rule as one; we wished to show that the attitude of Indonesians to 'foreign elements' in their country (as they are described in the Indonesian historiography) should be viewed in the context of resistance to a colonial structure in which violence was constantly used in order to maintain a society of 'superiors, inferiors and most inferior'.

For the Indo-Europeans, Dutch and Dutch Moluccans who lived through and commemorated the events, the extremely violent first months of the Indonesian Revolution took on significance as the *bersiap* period, and would become known as such in Dutch history and society. In doing so, these communities attempted to give a place to the atrocities they had experienced in late 1945 and early 1946, and that they had passed down to subsequent generations of children and grandchildren. From this perspective, the *bersiap* period is seen as 'violence against the Dutch and everything that was Dutch'. Following on from this, it has long been common in Dutch history and society to interpret this outburst of violence as a 'racial conflict' or 'ethnic conflict'; something that is understandable if one's personal experience or inherited memory is one of 'death to all *blandas* [whites]'. But a broader analysis of the violence shows that it was by no means only ethnically motivated, nor was it directed only against Indo-Europeans, Dutch and Moluccans. The Japanese, Indonesians, British, British Indians and Chinese also fell victim to what was often horrific violence. Indeed, the picture is even more complex: Indo-Europeans, Dutch and Moluccans were not only the victims of Indonesian extreme violence, but they themselves also used violence; they sometimes instigated violence, for example when they took provocative action against Indonesian civilians. By describing the group from the colonial upper and middle classes exclusively as victims, we overlook the fact that this group also included perpetrators of violence, and that some of them were both victims and perpetrators.

The extreme violence against Indo-Europeans, Dutch and Moluccans cannot be viewed as an isolated phenomenon, separate from the wider colonial and simultaneously revolutionary context in which these acts of violence took place. They formed part of a dynamic of violence that also produced large numbers of victims in other groups. That is why we argue that this period should be seen as the first phase of the Indonesian Revolution. In contrast to the picture that is commonly presented in the Dutch historiography, our book shows that the violence in this era undoubtedly targeted not only Indo-European, Dutch and Moluccan groups, but also various other communities, and that these violent acts, depending on the community concerned, also continued with varying intensity after March 1946. The *bersiap* period is thus interpreted or reinterpreted as an integral part of the war of independence or war of decolonization. This does justice to the many, sometimes contradictory, forms, expressions and motives of violence that became interlinked at that time.

With this observation, it is time to answer the question of how the various warring parties related to one another in the first phase of the Indonesian Revolution, and how this influenced the violence against civilians and captured fighters. Unlike the traditional historiography on the so-called *bersiap* period, we also considered the violence against civilians and captured fighters on islands other than Java and Sumatra. That is because an analysis of the violence in the rest of the archipelago can contribute to our understanding of the extreme violence on Java and Sumatra, as it reveals general patterns and characteristics. It is clear that local circumstances played a major role in the origin, nature and direction of the violence. To gain a better understanding of the circumstances in which the violence against civilians and captured fighters took place, by way of an analytical framework, we divided the archipelago into three constellations of power.

In the first constellation of power there was one dominant party, roughly speaking. This was the case on the islands in the eastern part of the archipelago, with the exception of Bali and parts of South Sulawesi. There, the Allies – in this case, the Australians and the Dutch – had the upper hand militarily and politically. In the second constellation of power, on Java and Sumatra, there were several national and international competing power blocks: nationalist Indonesians, Dutch, Japanese and British. These power blocks were not monolithic, of course, but contained all kinds of factions and individuals with what were sometimes opposing interests. In the third constellation of power (parts of Java and Sumatra), none of these power blocks was able to enforce its authority effectively, and local armed Indonesian groups fought one another for power.

In the eastern archipelago, the Australians arrived soon after the Japanese surrender, Indonesian nationalism was weakly developed, the Indonesian population was small, and the Japanese cooperated with the Allies. Furthermore, there were no large groups of young men who had received semi-military training from the Japanese, meaning that there was less potential for violence. Moreover, certain regions and islands, such as Minahassa (North Sulawesi) and Ambon, were traditionally oriented towards the Netherlands. All of this meant that the violence there was mainly perpetrated by Dutch soldiers against nationalist Indonesians and Japanese prisoners of war. Parts of South Sulawesi, Kalimantan and Bali formed exceptions to this.

On South Sulawesi, nationalist Indonesians disputed Allied authority to a greater degree than on the other islands. Here, there was a dynamic of violence in which both *pemuda* and KNIL soldiers acted provocatively and used extreme violence, meaning that dozens of civilians were killed on both sides in the first months after the Japanese surrender. On Kalimantan, Chinese and Indonesian armed groups initially used a lot of violence against civilians due to provocative actions by the Chinese, who did not want to support the Republic of Indonesia, but the nationalist China of General Chiang Kai-shek. Here, too, the first KNIL units used excessive violence against the civilian population. On Bali, many mutual scores were settled; it was also the only island outside Java and Sumatra where the Japanese military cracked down on nationalist Indonesian armed groups.

On Java and Sumatra, various factors contributed to the creation of an extremely violent situation from October 1945, in which the violence was used in all directions and took multiple forms. Indonesians, Japanese, British and Dutch attempted to establish their authority on the island, but none was sufficiently dominant to impose their will by force, or they were simply not prepared to pay the price in human lives required by such hegemony. Indonesian nationalism was most developed on Java and Sumatra. Moreover, the late arrival of the Allies gave the nationalist movement an opportunity to grow in strength. The landing of the British and Dutch on Java on 29 September 1945 and on Sumatra on 10 October 1945 resulted in the escalation of an already tense situation. Reports and rumours about atrocities went back and forth, contributing to an atmosphere of distrust and fear.

The key role played by the Japanese – who could tip the balance of power in favour of the Allies or the Indonesian side – meant that the Japanese on Sumatra and Java became more involved than elsewhere in the extreme violence, both as perpetrators and as victims. On the whole, there were also many more civilian casualties there, because there were more potential targets present; Java was the most densely populated island in Indonesia. Moreover, most Indo-Europeans on Java were more vulnerable, because – unlike on the other islands – they had not been interned by the Japanese during the Second World War, and were thus unable to stay in the relative safety of the internment camps after the Japanese surrender.

In those places where neither the Allies nor the Japanese or the Republic were able to assert their power (the third power constellation), there was often a violent social revolution by local Indonesian alliances. Scores were settled with anyone associated with the colonial elite or with whom they had outstanding grievances.

Reviewing the violence against civilians and captured fighters in the first months of the Indonesian Revolution across the archipelago as a whole, we are struck by several patterns. First, it was often the arrival of the Allies that led to an escalation of the violence. Although the British and Australians were often welcomed by the Indonesian population at first, the Dutch were regarded with distrust from the outset. The patronizing attitude of many Dutch who had left the Japanese internment camps and who wanted to pick up the threads of their pre-war lives again, as though nothing had happened, and the provocative and violent actions of armed groups on the Dutch side and of the first KNIL units, confirmed Indonesian suspicions that the Netherlands wanted to restore colonial rule. When the actions of the British and the Australians subsequently gave Indonesians the impression that they were helping the Dutch to restore colonial power, they also became the targets of Indonesian extreme violence.

Furthermore, we are struck by the half-hearted attitude of the military and civilian authorities on all sides: they often took insufficient action to curb or prevent extreme violence by their armed groups and units, an attitude that sometimes stemmed from impotence, at other times from opportunism. Extreme violence by the British and Japanese military was condoned by the leadership – and, in the case of the British after November 1945, even became policy – while Sukarno and the Indonesian political and military leadership were ambiguous, at the very least, about the extreme violence used by *pemuda* and armed groups. Although they did not order the killings, as far as is known, the nationalist leaders appear to have condoned them to a greater or lesser degree, and sometimes used them opportunistically for political gain. At the local level, in any case, Dutch sources suggest that the violence sometimes appears to have been coordinated.

The Australians and the British, but also Dutch observers, held the armed groups on the Dutch side and the first KNIL units jointly responsible for the dynamic of violence. It was no accident that the Australians on South Sulawesi and the British on Sumatra and Java removed Westerling's KNIL units and police force from Makassar, Medan and Jakarta, respectively. On the Dutch side, too, the authorities sometimes appear to have had an ambiguous attitude to the extreme violence by armed groups and regular units. Sometimes, admittedly, they were unable to act, but on the other hand, the actions of the first KNIL units and the Dutch armed groups – which included former prisoners of war – also formed part of a long colonial military tradition of intimidating the population with a superior show of force and violence. Moreover, the armed groups filled a gap – only a limited number of KNIL servicemen were present, after all – and could counterbalance the Indonesian violence and what the Dutch saw as the passive British response. However, the scale of the extreme violence in this early phase of the Indonesian Revolution by Dutch armed groups and units, which were far outnumbered, was more limited than the Indonesian violence used by *pemuda* and Indonesian armed groups.

Against the background of the three power constellations described above, it is important to note that Indonesian loyalties and positions could be fluid during the first phase of the Indonesian Revolution; they had the option of joining the armed group or party that appeared to be winning, and then shifting to another power block if this proved a better option. Furthermore, we can identify different motives for the Indonesian violence. First, there were anti-colonial and political motives directed against those both from inside and outside the archipelago who represented the colonial administration, who desired a return to the colonial regime and system, who threatened the independence of Indonesia, who had failed to throw in their lot (unambiguously) with the Republic of Indonesia, or who were suspected – rightly or wrongly – of this. Second, there were economic and social motives. Poverty, unemployment, poor education and limited future prospects, in many respects outcomes of the colonial system, encouraged violence against the more wealthy and privileged in colonial society. Often these acts of violence were perpetrated and justified under the banner of Indonesian independence. Third, there were criminal and opportunistic motives for violence, such as revenge, envy and personal reasons, both on the part of collectives (gangs) and individuals, which also took place under the guise of defending Indonesian sovereignty. As a result, anti-colonial and politically motivated violence was mixed with other forms of violence. This amalgam produced an extremely violent situation, with undirected and random violence that claimed many civilian lives.

For the first generation of Indo-Europeans, Dutch and Moluccans, the battle-cry of 'bersiap' can understandably evoke traumatic and harmful memories, even today. Its effects are still visible in later generations. Indeed, over the decades, the memories of this period have gained an increasingly important place in the Dutch historiography and society, whereby an emphatic link is drawn between the Indonesian violence and the deployment of the Dutch armed forces. It must be noted that this picture is not supported by our research.

The extreme violence in this period was not the primary reason for the Netherlands to deploy troops in Indonesia; the decision to reoccupy the archipelago, as it was described at the time, was taken before the proclamation of Indonesian independence, and even before the Japanese surrender. It was for other reasons, such as prestige and economic interests, that the Dutch government wanted to restore colonial rule in Indonesia by whatever means, after which a slow 'process of decolonization' would ensue under Dutch leadership. But this early extreme violence did provide a very useful framework for demonizing the opponent(s) in Indonesia and calling for order and recovery, which necessitated the deployment of Dutch troops in the archipelago; and this happened continuously, in texts and images that presented a hostile picture of terrorists and *rampokkers*. In short, the argument that *'bersiap* violence' was the specific reason for sending Dutch troops to Indonesia may fit seamlessly into the old, wider notion of the duty to restore authority and bring order and peace, but there are no grounds for this in the historical events themselves.

Epilogue
The resonance of the sound of violence

'I knew the word "tjintangen" before I was familiar with the concept of "bersiap"', said the journalist Hans Moll.[1] As this quote indicates, the extreme violence during the earliest phase of the Indonesian Revolution, as well as its designation as the *bersiap* period, were unfamiliar topics in the Dutch public domain for many years. More openness gradually emerged, most recently culminating in the fierce discussion that erupted in early January 2022 around guest curator Bonnie Triyana and Rijksmuseum Amsterdam's plan to scrap the word *bersiap* from the 'Revolusi' exhibition, which focused on the Indonesian struggle for independence.[2] This sparked parliamentary questions, the initiation of legal proceedings against Rijksmuseum Amsterdam, and a public debate in which not only traditional advocates of the broad Indo-Dutch community made themselves heard, but also numerous other voices.[3] The discussion did not go unnoticed in Indonesia.[4] The recent debate is in stark contrast to the invisibility of *bersiap* in the public domain in the first three decades after 1950. This changed in the 1980s, when freedom was created in Dutch society to discuss memories of the war, which were no longer confined to the private sphere. Increasing attention was also paid to the possible impact of the war at the psychological level, in the form of trauma.⁵ The Dutch government also became aware of this problem, and developed support for people who had suffered health damage during the Second World War. This resulted, among other things, in the Benefit Act for Civilian War Victims 1940-1945 (*Wet uitkering burger-oorlogsslachtoffers 1940-1945*, Wubo) in 1985.⁶ The founding of the self-help organization Children of the Japanese Occupation and Bersiap 1941-1949 (Kinderen uit de Japanse Bezetting en Bersiap 1941-1949, KJBB) in 1988 was a turning point in this social context.⁷ The year 1988 was also significant for the public visibility of the Dutch Indo commemorative community, because it saw the founding of the Indies Monument 1941-1945 in The Hague and the National Indies Monument 1945-1962 in Roermond, bringing the war years of the Japanese occupation and the Indonesian Revolution to the attention of a wider audience.

In addition to self-help organizations, memorials and legislation, *bersiap* entered the public domain through scholarly studies. In that same, significant year of 1988, the Epilogue was published to Loe de Jong's series *Het Koninkrijk der Nederlanden in de Tweede Wereldoorlog* [*The Kingdom of the Netherlands in the Second World War*].⁸ In this, De Jong wrote about the early Indonesian Revolution and its impact on the Indo-Dutch community. He mentioned the motive of revenge, for example in relation to the actions of KNIL soldiers on South Sulawesi in April 1946. The latter had tortured *pemuda* and other Indonesian resistance groups with electricity, and shot them during staged attempts to escape. According to De Jong, they were 'KNIL servicemen who had lost relatives in the *bersiap* actions'.⁹ He believed that there were strong indications that the initiative for 'excesses' was mainly taken by individual soldiers who, 'for whatever reason (in the case of relatives of victims of the *bersiap* terror, the need to take revenge could play a role), were more inclined than others to take excessive action'.¹⁰

Significantly, by doing this, this historian of Dutch national history not only introduced the term 'bersiap' to the Dutch people, but he also placed it in the context of revenge actions by individual KNIL soldiers. The Dutch public had purchased De Jong's history in their masses; no fewer than 2.7 million copies were sold.¹¹ Although not every owner of the series will have read it in its entirety or even partially, it is clear that De Jong's work formed part of a wider social trend in which attention was paid to the violence in the earliest phase of the revolution, which was discovered (or rediscovered) in the public domain as the '*bersiap* period'. One year later, De Jong's Epilogue was followed by the book *Bersiap in Bandoeng* by cultural anthropologist Mary van Delden, the first study to present a local analysis of the violence in this period.[12]

The social changes of the 1980s also became manifest in a new genre of first-hand accounts: this period saw the first works of Indo-Dutch remembrance literature. The 1980s and 1990s saw the publication of a wave of war memoirs about the Japanese occupation. Former internees, the vast majority of whom were of Dutch origin – a consequence of the Japanese internment policy – published their memories of the Japanese prisoner-of-war or civilian camps in so-called 'camp memoirs'. Most of them ended on or shortly after the date of the Japanese surrender (15 August 1945), on the grounds that 'the war' ended at that point.[13] Many egodocuments still paid little attention to what would increasingly become known as the *bersiap* period, at most as the aftermath of the Japanese occupation.

The 1980s also saw the memoirs of 'Indies veterans' come to light, peaking in the 1990s.[14] We can mention a number of reasons for this. There was the 'retirement effect': veterans had completed their working lives and any children had grown up and left home. Now they had time to reflect on their lives, including the war in Indonesia, and had an opportunity to write their memoirs. In addition, there was more after-care for veterans in the form of a veterans' policy and the founding of veterans' organizations.

The veterans' memoirs reveal a striking phenomenon. Memoirs published in recent decades provide explicit and shocking descriptions of violence in the earliest phase of the revolution. This is in contrast to the content of the veterans' diaries, which also described murders, looting and raping by Indonesians, but rarely went into detail. One example of such a detailed description can be found in the 2008 memoirs of Marijn de Jonge, commander of the 4th panzer squadron of the Huzaren van Boreel regiment:

> The Dutch and Indo-Dutch were dragged from their homes and often murdered after being tortured dreadfully. Men were surrounded by a crowd and slaughtered with bamboo spears and machetes, children were impaled on bamboo spears in front of their mothers, women were raped by dozens of men and then, if they were still alive, murdered. Whole families were sometimes buried alive. The abuse was often of a sadistic nature: the bodies of men were found with their cut-off genitals in their mouths, of women with mutilated breasts and bamboo spears in their vaginas. Sometimes the bodies were tied to a door and

thrown into a river where they floated with the current, others were thrown into wells or into shallow mass graves.[15]

These kinds of explicit descriptions of violence are less common in diaries.[16] One is also struck that in the memoirs, reports of similar acts of violence appear multiple times, as though the authors copied passages from each another. Although the diaries reveal that the authors were convinced of the Dutch need to intervene, due to the violence in the colony, they did not usually explain this. The authors considered the necessity of the intervention to be self-evident. By contrast, in the memoirs, which were written (much) later, it is stated frequently and explicitly that the extreme violence in the first phase of the Indonesian Revolution was the reason for the presence of the Dutch army in the archipelago.[17] In his 2008 memoirs, F.C. Hazekamp put it as follows:

> Should we have left the country in chaos in 1946, after rescuing the people from the concentration camps? We had a historical responsibility there. Belgium evacuated the Congo, Portugal Angola, practically without a transition period. This resulted in total and lasting chaos, both at the time and today [2006].[18]

Through the 'rediscovery' of *bersiap* in the public domain, various projects and publications were produced with the aim of keeping memories of *bersiap* alive.[19]

Although extreme Indonesian violence during the earliest phase of the Indonesian Revolution did form an additional reason to deploy Dutch troops, since the 1980s and 1990s, the term 'bersiap' has gained significance as a justification after the event. This *post facto* legitimization often features in the memoirs of veterans. In part through the involvement of successive generations of children, grandchildren and great-grandchildren, the *bersiap* period, which was initially known only to a relatively small commemorative community, has become a permanent yet disputed term in the Dutch historiography and in the public debate about the war of independence in Indonesia.

Notes

Prologue – Resonance of violence

1. S.M. Jalhay, *Allen zwijgen. Van merdeka en Andjing-Nica tot APRA*. Hillegom: Gevana [1989], 70.
2. In chapter 1, we explain how the different communities in the archipelago were classified by the Dutch colonial administration. These classifications emerged in a colonial context and have colonial overtones. For that reason, we do not use terms such as 'Foreign Orientals [Vreemde Oosterlingen]' and 'Natives [Inlanders]', as they have derogatory connotations. In the context of the Dutch East Indies, the concepts 'European' and 'Indo-European' are also colonial constructions; the term 'Dutchman [Nederlander]' had no formal meaning. Needless to say, the Dutch fell under the category 'European'. 'Indo-Europeans' were also considered to be 'European' if they were recognized by their father. In this book, we use the concepts 'Europeans' and 'Dutch' interchangeably, and 'Indo-Europeans' are also seen as belonging to the category of 'Dutch'. For the sake of readability, we do not always refer to Indo-Europeans, Chinese, Dutch, Moluccans, Menadonese, Timorese and Indonesians who were (allegedly) on the Dutch side, but limit the terms to the main groups of Indo-Europeans, Dutch and Moluccans, and Chinese and Indonesians.
3. Yaichiro Shibata, 'Surabaya after the surrender', in: Anthony Reid and Oki Akira, *The Japanese experience in Indonesia. Selected memoirs of 1942-1945*, Athens: Ohio University, 1986, 341-374 (361-362).
4. *Nieuwe Courant* (Surabaya), 21 December 1949.
5. William Frederick, 'Shadow of an Unseen Hand. Some Patterns of Violence in the Indonesian Revolution, 1945-1949', in: Freek Colombijn and J. Thomas Lindblad (eds), *Roots of Violence in Indonesia. Contemporary Violence in Historical Perspective*. Leiden: KITLV Press, 2002, 143-172, note 2; Henk Beekhuis, Herman Bussemaker, Paula de Haas, Ton Lutter, *Geïllustreerde Atlas van de Bersiapkampen in Nederlands-Indië, 1945-1947*. Bedum: Profiel, 2009, 7.
6. Sheri Lynn Gibbings and Fridus Steijlen, 'Colonial Figures: Memories of Street Traders in the Colonial and Early post-Colonial Periods', in: *Public History Review*, vol. 19, 2012, 63-85 (69).
7. Tjalie Robinson, *Tjies*. The Hague: H.P. Leopolds Uitgeversmaatschappij, 1958.

8   Our thanks to Abdul Wahid for his suggestion that we review other terms for violence during the early phase of the Indonesian Revolution.
9   Our thanks to Oktoriza Dhia, email dated 15 January 2021. Retrieved from: *Kamus Besar Bahasa Indonesia* (KBBI) (Great Dictionary of the Indonesian Language); Dendy Sugono (ed.), *Kamus Besar Bahasa Indonesia*, Jakarta: Pusat Bahasa, 2008, 284; Eko Endarmoko, *Thesaurus Bahasa* Indonesia, Jakarta: Gramedia Pustaka Utama, 2007, 130.
10 Hans Moll, *Sluipschutters in de tuin. Een Indische geschiedenis*. Zutphen: Walburg Pers, 2021, 170.
11 Interview with Father Josephus van Beek by To de Boer, 28 October 1978, KDC KMM-26. Father Van Beek died shortly after the interview on 26 February 1979.
12 Robert Cribb, *Gangsters and Revolutionaries. The Jakarta's People's Militia and the Indonesian Revolution.* Jakarta/Kuala Lumpur: Equinox Publishing, 2009 (first edition 1991), 65.
13 Anton Lucas, *One soul, one struggle. Region and Revolution in Indonesia.* Sydney: Allen & Unwin, 1991, 155.
14 Anton Lucas, *One soul, one struggle. Region and Revolution in Indonesia.* Sydney: Allen & Unwin, 1991, 104-105.
15 *De Avondpost*, 2 February 1913.
16 *De Java-bode, nieuws, handels- en advertentieblad voor Nederlands-Indië*, 18 June 1878. *Frikadel* is a kind of meatloaf. See also: *De Locomotief, Samarangsch handels- en advertentieblad*, 19-8-1880.
17 Hendri F. Isnaeni, 'Cincang masa perang', in: *Historia*, 27 July 2011. See: https://historia.id/politik/articles/cincang-masa-perang-vVNkv/page/2, consulted on 21-10-2021.

1. Bersiap in broader context

1   Following Harry Poeze and Mary van Delden, see also: Harry A. Poeze, 'Walking the tightrope: internal Indonesian conflict, 1945-1949', in: Bart Luttikhuis and Dirk A. Moses, (eds), *Colonial counterinsurgency and mass violence. The Dutch Empire in Indonesia*, Routledge, London/New York 2014. Also in: *Journal of Genocide Studies*, vol. 14, no. 3-4, 2012, 176-197, and Mary van Delden, 'De andere kant van de Bersiap', as a series of articles in *Pelita Nieuws*, 2017.
2   Database of *bersiap* victims, ODGOI. The details in this database were entered in accordance with what was written in the sources. If there was no further specification of the time period, a note such as 'beginning of the Merdeka period' was recorded. The children Robert and Johanna did not belong to the couple Lothar and Miene Engelenburg. See: https://oorlogsverhalen.com/oorlogsverhalen/roos-engelenburg/, accessed on 14 January 2022.
3   See: https://www.hansvervoort.nl/article/1003/Dodentocht-in-de-bergen, consulted on 14 January 2022.
4   Pia van der Molen, *Research rapport documentaire tweeluik Archief van Tranen*. No place: Pia Media, 2011-2012. See also: https://pia-media.nl/projecten/archief-van-tranen-project/, consulted on 14 January 2022.
5   Database of *bersiap* victims, ODGOI. The details in this database were entered in accordance with what was written in the sources. If there was no further indication of the time, a note such as 'bersiap' was recorded.
6   Database of *bersiap* victims, ODGOI.
7   Report ODO, E.Ch. Wernink, 9-3-1948, National Archives of the Netherlands, reference number 2.10.62, inv. no. 2053; Letter J.W.F. Meeng, 13-12-1948: NIOD, Netherlands East Indies Collection, reference number 400, inv. no. 891.
8   Informant report, drawn up by F.M. Loth, 26-2-1948: NIOD, Netherlands East Indies Collection, reference number 400, inv. no. 891.
9   Copy of a statement signed by Dulsaid Gondongan on 10-4-1948: NIOD, Netherlands East Indies Collection, reference number 400, inv. no. 891.

10   Statement by Dulsaid Gondongan on 10-4-1948: NIOD, Netherlands East Indies Collection, reference number 400, inv. no. 891.
11   Herman Bussemaker, *Bersiap! Opstand in het paradijs. De Bersiap-periode op Java en Sumatra 1945-1946*. Zutphen: Walburg Pers, 2005, 268; informant report M. Asdjojo, drawn up by G. von Kriegenbergh on 12-01-1948, NIOD, Netherlands East Indies Collection, reference number 400, inv. no. 891. A witness statement reports another version: that the two *pemuda* who were responsible for the murders in Tumpang were arrested by the general police in Tumpang and sent to the general police in Malang, who released them two days later. Excerpt from statement by Tjoa Boen Tek, 23-09-1947, NIOD, Netherlands East Indies Collection, reference number 400, inv. no. 891. This is probably a reference to the Republican police. See: Letter E.L. Souweine on behalf of the head of NEFIS, external office Surabaya to Investigation Service for the Deceased in Surabaya 25-11-1947, NIOD, Netherlands East Indies Collection, reference number 400, inv. no. 891.
12   E.L. Souweine, deputy head NEFIS B.K. Soerabaia to the Investigation Service for the Deceased 25-11-1947: NIOD, Netherlands East Indies Collection, reference number 400, inv. no. 891. See also: NA, NEFIS/CMI, reference number 2.10.62, inv. no. 2022.
13   Letter J.F.C. Otten, head of the field service department to the chief of police in Surabaya, 26-2-1948: NIOD, Netherlands East Indies Collection, reference number 400, inv. no. 891.
14   Witness statement A.J.F. Moormann, drawn up by W.J. v.d. Griend, 6-12-1946, NA, NEFIS, reference number 2.10.62, inv. no. 2022.
15   S.M.E. Moormann, a relative of the victims, recorded in a statement on 13-1-1947 that he believed that Bambang Sumandi was responsible for the 39 murders in Tumpang. The authors were unable to find this statement in the archives. Letter J.W.F. Meeng, 10-5-1947, NA, NEFIS, reference number 2.10.62, inv. no. 2022.
16   Witness statement C.E. de Jong-Brouwer, drawn up by J.W.F. Meeng, 27-12-1946, NA, NEFIS, reference number 2.10.62, inv. no. 2022. These two families were the De Jong family and the Flissinger family.
17   M.C. van Daalen Wetters, 'Verslag over de "Indonesische gevangenschap" etc. doorgebracht te Malang v/m 13 October 1945 t/m 13 Juni 1946', NIMH, reference number 509, inv. no. 76, 17-7-1946.
18   Statement informants J.M. Nilsen, E. Deeleman-Bonebakker, C.J.J. Veerman, J.J. Geul, M.C. van Noppen, J.R. Ungerer-Bos, drawn up by A.J. Laurs, no date, National Archives of the Netherlands, reference number 2.10.37.02, inv. no. 17, dossier Extremists in Malang.
19   Letter G.W. Lamers, 26-6-1947, NA: NEFIS, reference number 2.10.62, inv. no. 2022.
20   Nur Hadi and Sutopo, *Perjuangan total brigade IV. Pada perang kemerdekaan di karesidenan Malang*. Malang: Brawijaya, 1997, 44-45.
21   R. Rezia Hudiyanto, *Pemerintah kota masyarakat bumiputra kota Malang, 1914-1950*. Yogyakarta: Universitas Gadjah Mada 2009, Mashuri, *Daerah Malang selatan pada masah perang kemerdekaan 1947-1949*. Depok: Universitas Indonesia, 2004.
22   Pelita Archive, Sociale rapportage in het kader van de oorlogswetten, dossier 0764078-WUB.
23   Pelita Archive, Sociale rapportage in het kader van de oorlogswetten, dossier 0470414.WUB. In the book *Vogelvrij* [Outlawed], published in 1984 and one of the few publications from that decade about the situation outside the camps, the murders in and around Tumpang were also addressed, bringing them back into the public domain. *Vogelvrij* is based on a war diary, in which the Tumpang murders were a topic of discussion among Indo-Europeans. See: M. Moscou-de Ruyter, *Vogelvrij. Het leven buiten de kampen 1942-1945*. Weesp: Fibula-van Dishoeck, 1984, 203.
24   Following Harry Poeze and Mary van Delden, see also: Harry A. Poeze, 'Walking the tightrope: internal Indonesian conflict, 1945-1949', in: Bart Luttikhuis and Dirk A. Moses, ed., *Colonial counterinsurgency and mass violence. The Dutch Empire in Indonesia*, Routledge, London/New York 2014. Also in: *Journal of Genocide Studies*, vol. 14, no. 3-4, 2012, 176-197 and Mary van Delden, 'De andere kant van de Bersiap', as a series of articles in *Pelita Nieuws*, 2017.

25 Marieke Bloembergen, *Uit zorg en angst. De geschiedenis van de politie in Nederlands-Indië.* Amsterdam/Leiden: Boom/KITLV, 2009; Henk Schulte Nordholt, *Een staat van geweld.* Rotterdam: EUR, 2000.
26 Christian Gerlach, 'Introduction: extremely violent societies', in: Extremely Violent Societies. Mass Violence in the Twentieth-Century World. Cambridge: Cambridge University Press, 2010, 1-2.
27 Taomo Zhou, *Migration in time of revolution. China, Indonesia and the Cold War.* Ithaca and London: Cornell University Press, 2018, 19.
28 Rémy Limpach, *De brandende kampongs van generaal Spoor*, Boom, Amsterdam 2016, 265-270. On the actions of Westerling and the Depot Speciale Troepen, see: 270 ff.
29 William Frederick, 'The killing of Dutch and Eurasians in Indonesia's National Revolution (1945-1949): a "Brief genocide" reconsidered', in: *Journal of Genocide Research*, vol. 14, no. 3/4 (2012), 359-380, (367-368).

2. Violence from above: the colonial context of violence in Indonesia

1 Ethan Mark, *Japan's occupation of Java in the Second World War. A Transnational History.* London/New York: Bloomsbury, 2018, 84.
2 Ethan Mark, *Japan's occupation of Java in the Second World War. A Transnational History.* London/New York: Bloomsbury, 2018, 84.
3 Ethan Mark, *Japan's occupation of Java in the Second World War. A Transnational History.* London/New York: Bloomsbury, 2018, 84.
4 'Indonesian "Republic" refuses to deal with Dutch alone', in: *New York Times*, 5-10-1945. NIMH, 509, inv. no. 35.
5 'Dutch fear clash with Indonesians', in: *New York Times*, 2-10-1945. NIMH, 509, inv. no. 35.
6 Sutan Sjahrir, *Onze strijd.* Amsterdam: Vrij Nederland, 1946, 20.
7 Serge Andréfouët, Mégane Paul, A. Riza Farhan, 'Indonesia's 13558 islands: A new census from space and a first step towards a One Map for Small Islands Policy', in: *Marine Policy*, vol. 135, 2022. https://doi.org/10.1016/j.marpol.2021.104848.
8 Piet Hagen, *Koloniale oorlogen in Indonesië. Vijf eeuwen verzet tegen vreemde overheersing.* Amsterdam: Arbeiderspers, 2018, 885-906.
9 See also: Petra Groen, Anita van Dissel, Mark Loderichs, Rémy Limpach, Thijs Brocades Zaalberg, *Krijgsgeweld en kolonie. Opkomst en ondergang van Nederland als koloniale mogendheid 1816-2010.* Amsterdam: Boom, 2021.
10 'Indonesian "Republic" refuses to deal with the Dutch alone' in: *New York Times*, 5-10-1945. NIMH, 509, inv.nr. 35.
11 Piet Hagen, *Koloniale oorlogen in Indonesië. Vijf eeuwen verzet tegen vreemde overheersing.* Amsterdam: Arbeiderspers, 2018, 814.
12 Derived from: Reggie Baay, *Het kind met de Japanse ogen.* Amsterdam: Arbeiderspers, 2018.
13 A. van Marle, 'De groep van Europeanen in Nederlands-Indië, iets over ontstaan en groei', in: *Indonesië*, vol. 5, no. 2, 1951, 97-121.
14 Kees Groeneboer, *Weg tot het Westen. Het Nederlands voor Indië 1600-1950.* Leiden: KITLV, 1993, 474-477.
15 Gijs Beets, *Demografische aspecten van de bevolking van Nederlands-Indië 1945-1950. Demografische hand-out.* The Hague: Netherlands Interdisciplinary Demographic Institute (NIDI), 2018.
16 *Volkstelling 1930 van Nederlandsch-Indië.* Batavia: 1933-1936.
17 Mary Somers Heidhues, 'Anti-Chinese Violence in Java during the Indonesian Revolution, 1945-1949', in: *Journal of Genocide Research*, vol. 14, no. 3-4, 2012, 381-401 (382).
18 Cees Fasseur, 'Hoeksteen en struikelblok. Rassenonderscheid en overheidsbeleid in Nederlands-Indië', in: *Tijdschrift voor Geschiedenis*, vol. 105, no. 2, 1992, 218-242.
19 *Volkstelling 1930 van Nederlandsch-Indië.* Batavia: 1933-1936.

20 Interview with *bapak* Hartawan, Wawancara Sejarah Lisan, Badan Arsip, Propinsi Jawa Timur, 2002.
21 NIMH, memoirs of C. van Reijnoudt, 3-3 RI, North Sumatra, Medan, 28 October 1946.
22 Sudjarwo, 'Portret diri pemuda dalam Revolusi kita', in: *Prisma*, 8 August 1981, 22.
23 Henk Schulte Nordholt, 'A genealogy of violence', in: Freek Colombijn and J. Thomas Lindblad (eds), *Roots of Violence in Indonesia. Contemporary Violence in Historical Perspective*. Leiden: KITLV Press, 2002, 33-62, here 36.
24 Henk Schulte Nordholt, 'A genealogy of violence', in: Freek Colombijn and J. Thomas Lindblad (eds), *Roots of Violence in Indonesia. Contemporary Violence in Historical Perspective*. Leiden: KITLV Press, 2002, 33-62, here 37.
25 Petra Groen, 'Colonial warfare and military ethics in the Netherlands East Indies, 1816-1941', in: *Journal of Genocide Studies*, vol. 14, no. 3-4, 2012, 277-296, here 292.
26 Piet Hagen, *Koloniale oorlogen in Indonesië. Vijf eeuwen verzet tegen vreemde overheersing*. Amsterdam: Arbeiderspers, 2018, 25.
27 Piet Hagen, *Koloniale oorlogen in Indonesië. Vijf eeuwen verzet tegen vreemde overheersing*. Amsterdam: Arbeiderspers, 2018, 31.
28 Remco Raben, 'Epilogue: on genocide and mass violence in colonial Indonesia', in: Bart Luttikhuis and Dirk Moses, *Mass violence and the end of the Dutch colonial empire*, 2012, 487.
29 Remco Raben, 'Epilogue: on genocide and mass violence in colonial Indonesia', in: Bart Luttikhuis and Dirk Moses, *Mass violence and the end of the Dutch colonial empire*, 2012, 487.
30 Remco Raben, 'Epilogue: on genocide and mass violence in colonial Indonesia', in: Bart Luttikhuis and Dirk Moses, *Mass violence and the end of the Dutch colonial empire*, 2012, 485-502.
31 Petra Groen, Anita van Dissel, Mark Loderichs, Rémy Limpach, Thijs Brocades Zaalberg, *Krijgsgeweld en kolonie. Opkomst en ondergang van Nederland als koloniale mogendheid 1816-2010*. Amsterdam: Boom, 2021, 27-28.
32 Robert Cribb, *Gangsters and Revolutionaries. The Jakarta People's Militia and the Indonesian Revolution 1945-1949*. Jakarta: Equinox Publishers, 2009 (first edition 1991).
33 Piet Hagen, *Koloniale oorlogen in Indonesië. Vijf eeuwen verzet tegen vreemde overheersing*. Amsterdam: Arbeiderspers, 2018, 31.
34 Thijs Brocades Zaalberg en Bart Luttikhuis, 'Extreem geweld tijdens dekolonisatieoorlogen in vergelijkend perspectief, 1945-1962', in: BMGN – *Low Countries Historical Review*, vol. 135, no. 2. 2020, 34-51 (40).
35 Violence took multiple forms: it was exercised by force of arms, but there was also 'soft violence'. The latter included the Protestant and Catholic missionaries who attempted to spread their version of Christianity among the archipelago's population, and in doing so used practices such as removing children from their parents and surroundings by putting them in boarding schools and orphanages. See: Geertje Mak, Marit Monteiro and Liesbeth Wesseling, 'Child separation. (Post)Colonial Policies and Practices in the Netherlands and Belgium', in: BMGN – *Low Countries Historical Review*, vol. 135, no. 3-4 (special issue) 2020, 4-28.
36 A comparison with population percentages produces the following figures: 43 per cent Javanese in the KNIL (46 per cent of the population), 20 per cent (Indo-)Europeans (0.40 per cent of the population), 14 per cent Menadonese (0.47 per cent of the population), 11 per cent Ambonese (0.38 per cent of the population), 4 per cent Sundanese (14.25 per cent of the population), 3 per cent Timorese (0.72 per cent of the population) and others. See: Marc Lohnstein, *Royal Netherlands East Indies Army 1936-1942*. Oxford: Osprey Publishing, 2018, 5.
37 Piet Hagen, *Koloniale oorlogen in Indonesië. Vijf eeuwen verzet tegen vreemde overheersing*. Amsterdam: Arbeiderspers, 2018, 31.
38 Riyadi Gunawan, 'Jagoan dalam Revolusi kita', in: *Prisma*, 8 August 1981, 41-50 (42-43).
39 Marieke Bloembergen, *Uit zorg en angst. De geschiedenis van de politie in Nederlands-Indië*. Amsterdam/

Leiden: Boom/KITLV, 2009, 352.

40 Marieke Bloembergen, *Uit zorg en angst. De geschiedenis van de politie in Nederlands-Indië*. Amsterdam/Leiden: Boom/KITLV, 2009, 356.

41 Elsbeth Locher-Scholten, 'Interraciale ontmoetingen naar sekse in Nederlands-Indië. De onmacht van het getal', in: Esther Captain, Marieke Hellevoort, Marian van der Klein (eds), *Vertrouwd en vreemd. Ontmoetingen tussen Nederland, Indië en Indonesië*. Hilversum: Verloren, 2000, 15-21.

42 Petra Groen, 'Colonial warfare and military ethics in the Netherlands East Indies, 1816-1941', in: *Journal of Genocide Studies*, vol. 14, no. 3-4, 2012, 277-296, here 291-292.

43 Audrey R. Kahin, ed., *Regional dynamics of the Indonesian revolution. Unity from diversity*, University of Hawaii Press, Honolulu 1985, 3-4.

44 Between 1921 and 1932, Hatta studied at the business school in Rotterdam; between 1929 and 1931, Sjahrir studied law in Leiden. See: Harry A. Poeze et al., *In het land van de overheerser I. Indonesiërs in Nederland 1600-1950*. Dordrecht/Providence: Foris Publications, 1986.

45 Audrey R. Kahin, ed., *Regional dynamics of the Indonesian revolution. Unity from diversity*, University of Hawaii Press, Honolulu 1985, 4-5; Lambert Giebels, *Soekarno, Nederlands onderdaan. Een biografie 1901-1950*. Amsterdam: Bert Bakker, 1999.

46 Petra Groen, 'The war in the Pacific', in: Peter Post et al. (eds), *The encyclopedia of Indonesia in the Pacific War*, Brill, London/Boston 2010, 6-20 (7).

47 Ken'ichi Goto, *Tensions of empire. Japan and Southeast Asia in the colonial and postcolonial world*, Ohio University Press/Singapore University Press, Athens (Ohio)/Singapore 2003, 287.

48 Ken'ichi Goto, *Tensions of empire. Japan and Southeast Asia in the colonial and postcolonial world*, Ohio University Press/Singapore University Press, Athens (Ohio)/Singapore 2003, 287.

49 Petra Groen, 'The war in the Pacific', in: Peter Post et al. (eds), *The encyclopedia of Indonesia in the Pacific War*, Brill, London/Boston 2010, 6-20 (13).

50 Ethan Mark, *The Japanese Occupation of Indonesia in the Second World War: A Transnational History*, New York/London: Brill, 2018, 79.

51 Ken'ichi Goto, 'Indonesia during the Japanese occupation', in: Peter Post et al. (eds), *The encyclopedia of Indonesia in the Pacific War*, London/Boston: Brill, 2010, 31-46 (45).

52 Ethan Mark, *The Japanese Occupation of Indonesia in the Second World War: A Transnational History*, New York/London: Brill, 2018, 75.

53 See also: Esther Captain, *Achter het kawat was Nederland. Indische oorlogservaringen en –herinneringen 1942-1995*. Kampen: Kok, 2002.

54 Dora van Velden, *De Japanse interneringskampen voor burgers gedurende de Tweede Wereldoorlog*. Franeker: Wever, 1985, 4th edition), 55.

55 H.W. van den Doel, *Afscheid van Indië. De val van het Nederlandse imperium in Azië*, Prometheus, Amsterdam 2000, 63.

56 Marieke Bloembergen, *Uit zorg en angst. De geschiedenis van de politie in Nederlands-Indië*. Amsterdam/Leiden: Boom/KITLV, 2009, 352.

57 Shigeru Sato, 'Occupation: administration and policies. Introduction', in: Peter Post et al. (eds), *The encyclopedia of Indonesia in the Pacific War*, London/Boston: Brill, 2010, 61.

58 Peter Post, 'Policing society', in: Peter Post et al. (eds), *The encyclopedia of Indonesia in the Pacific War*, London/Boston: Brill, 2010, 154-156.

59 Ken'ichi Goto, 'Indonesia during the Japanese occupation', in: Peter Post et al. (eds), *The encyclopedia of Indonesia in the Pacific War*, London/Boston: Brill, 2010, 31-46 (40-41).

60 Ethan Mark, *The Japanese Occupation of Indonesia in the Second World War: A Transnational History*, New York/London, Bloomsbury Press, 2018, 219.

61 Ethan Mark, *The Japanese Occupation of Indonesia in the Second World War: A Transnational History*, New York/London, Bloomsbury Press, 2018, 16.

62 Richard McMillan, *The British occupation of Indonesia 1945-1946. Britain, The Netherlands and the Indonesian revolution*, London/New York, Routledge 2005, 2-3.
63 Dora van Velden, *De Japanse interneringskampen voor burgers gedurende de Tweede Wereldoorlog*. Franeker: Wever, 1985, 23-24.
64 Ken'ichi Goto, *Tensions of empire. Japan and Southeast Asia in the colonial and postcolonial world*, Ohio University Press/Singapore University Press, Athens (Ohio)/Singapore 2003, 287.
65 Henk van den Doel, *Afscheid van Indië*, 64.
66 Ethan Mark, *The Japanese Occupation of Indonesia in the Second World War: A Transnational History*, Bloomsbury Press, New York/London 2018, 219.
67 Robert Cribb, 'Institutions', in: Peter Post et al. (eds), *The encyclopedia of Indonesia in the Pacific War*, London/Boston: Brill, 2010, 103.
68 Gusti Anan, 'Sumatra's regional governments', in: Peter Post et al. (eds) *The encyclopedia of Indonesia in the Pacific War*, Brill, London/Boston 2010, 61-71 (62).
69 Gusti Anan 'Sumatra's regional governments', in: Peter Post et al. (eds) *The encyclopedia of Indonesia in the Pacific War*, London/Boston: Brill, 2010, 61-71 (66).
70 Gusti Anan 'Sumatra's regional governments', in: Peter Post et al. (eds) *The encyclopedia of Indonesia in the Pacific War*, London/Boston: Brill, 2010, 61-71 (70).
71 Gin Eat Ooi, 'Of "permanent possession"-territories under the imperial Japanese navy', in: Peter Post et al. (eds), *The encyclopedia of Indonesia in the Pacific War*, Brill, London/Boston 2010, 71-86.
72 Ken'ichi Goto, 'Indonesia during the Japanese occupation', in: Peter Post et al., (eds), *The encyclopedia of Indonesia in the Pacific War*, Brill, London/Boston 2010, 31-46 (45).
73 Ken'ichi Goto, *Tensions of empire. Japan and Southeast Asia in the colonial and postcolonial world*, Ohio University Press/Singapore University Press, Athens (Ohio)/Singapore 2003, 233-235.
74 Muhammad Yuanda Zara, *Voluntary participation, state involvement: Indonesian propaganda in the struggle for maintaining independence, 1945-1949*. PhD thesis University of Amsterdam: 2016.
75 Ken'ichi Goto, 'Indonesia during the Japanese occupation', in: Peter Post et al. (eds), *The encyclopedia of Indonesia in the Pacific War*, Brill, London/Boston 2010, 31-46 (35).
76 Ken'ichi Goto, 'Indonesia during the Japanese occupation', in: Peter Post et al. (eds), *The encyclopedia of Indonesia in the Pacific War*, London/Boston: Brill, 2010, 31-46 (39, 41); Shigeru Sato, 'Romusha's', in: Peter Post et al. (eds) *The encyclopedia of Indonesia in the Pacific War*, London/Boston: Brill, 2010, 197-201 (200).
77 Sutan Sjahrir, *Onze strijd*. Amsterdam: Vrij Nederland, 1946, 23.
78 Ethan Mark, *The Japanese Occupation of Indonesia in the Second World War: A Transnational History*, New York/London: Bloomsbury, 2018, 162, 165, 173-179.
79 Robert Cribb, 'Institutions', in: Peter Post et al. (eds), *The Encyclopedia of Indonesia in the Pacific War*, London/Boston: Brill, 2010, 110.
80 H.W. van den Doel, *Afscheid van Indië*, 65-66.
81 Sudjarwo, 'Portret diri pemuda dalam Revolusi kita', in: *Prisma*, 8 August 1981, 27.
82 H.W. van den Doel, *Afscheid van Indië. De val van het Nederlandse imperium in Azië*, Prometheus, Amsterdam 2000, 66.
83 Mestika Zed, 'Giyugun – The indigenous defense force in Sumatra', in: *The encyclopedia of Indonesia in the Pacific War*, London/Boston: Brill, 2010, 128-132 (128-129).
84 H.W. van den Doel, *Afscheid van Indië. De val van het Nederlandse imperium in Azië*, Prometheus, Amsterdam 2000, 66.
85 Shigeru Sato, 'The PETA', in: Peter Post et al., (eds), *The Encyclopedia of Indonesia in the Pacific War*, Brill, London/Boston 2010, 132-145 (132-133).
86 Shigeru Sato, 'The PETA', in: Peter Post et al., (eds), *The encyclopedia of Indonesia in the Pacific War*, Brill, London/Boston 2010, 132-145 (132-133 and 144).

87 Shigeru Sato, 'The PETA', in: Peter Post et al, (eds), *The encyclopedia of Indonesia in the Pacific War*, Brill, London/Boston 2010, 132-145 (136); Ken'ichi Goto, 'Indonesia during the Japanese occupation', in: Peter Post et al., (eds), *The encyclopedia of Indonesia in the Pacific War*, Brill, London/Boston 2010, 31-46 (38).
88 Shigeru Sato, 'The PETA', in: Peter Post et al., (eds), *The encyclopedia of Indonesia in the Pacific War*, Brill, London/Boston 2010, 132-145 (132-133).
89 Shigeru Sato, 'The PETA', in: Peter Post et al., (eds), *The encyclopedia of Indonesia in the Pacific War*, Brill, London/Boston 2010, 132-145 (138).
90 Interview with *bapak* Hartawan, Wawancara Sejarah Lisan, Badan Arsip, Propinsi Jawa Timur, 2002. Original translation from Indonesian to Dutch by Esther Captain and Ireen Hoogenboom.
91 H.W. van den Doel, *Afscheid van Indië. De val van het Nederlandse imperium in Azië*, Prometheus, Amsterdam 2000, 66.
92 Robert Cribb, 'Institutions', in: Peter Post et al. (eds), *The Encyclopedia of Indonesia in the Pacific War*, London/Boston: Brill, 2010, 102-113 (107).
93 Shigeru Sato, 'Relocation of labor and the romusha's issue', in: Peter Post et al. (eds), *The Encyclopedia of Indonesia in the Pacific War*, London/Boston: Brill, 2010, 245-261 (252).
94 Aiko Kurasawa, 'Social change', in: Peter Post et al. (eds), *The Encyclopedia of Indonesia in the Pacific War*, London/Boston: Brill, 2010, 282-290 (285). The *tonarigumi* system was later renamed as the administrative system to denote neighbourhoods, terms that are still in use in Indonesia today (rukun tetangga (RT)/rukun kampung (RK); neighbourhood association/district association).
95 P.J. Suwarno, 'Romusha's from Yogyakarta', in: Peter Post et al. (eds), *The encyclopedia of Indonesia in the Pacific War*, London/Boston: Brill, 2010, 201-212 (206).
96 Interview with *bapak* Hartawan, Wawancara Sejarah Lisan, Badan Arsip, Propinsi Jawa Timur, 2002. Original translation from Indonesian to Dutch by Esther Captain and Ireen Hoogenboom.
97 Ken'ichi Goto, 'Indonesia during the Japanese occupation', in: Peter Post et al., (eds), *The encyclopedia of Indonesia in the Pacific War*, Brill, London/Boston 2010, 31-46, here 37.
98 Ethan Mark, *The Japanese Occupation of Indonesia in the Second World War: A Transnational History*, Bloomsbury Press, New York/London 2018, 2 (proofs). The research programme 'Food, famine and decolonization in Indonesia, 1940-1950' at Wageningen University & Research researches the relationship between food distribution and warfare, and tests the hypothesis that widespread hunger both catalyzed and accelerated the decolonization process.
99 William Bradley Horton, 'Comfort Women', in: Peter Post et al., (eds), *The encyclopedia of Indonesia in the Pacific War*, Brill, London/Boston 2010, 184-197.
100 William Bradley Horton, 'Comfort Women', in: Peter Post et al., (eds), *The encyclopedia of Indonesia in the Pacific War*, Brill, London/Boston 2010, 188, 190, 195; Bart van Poelgeest, 'Oosters stille dwang. Tewerkgesteld in de Japanse bordelen van Nederlands-Indië', in: *ICODO-Info*, vol. 10, no. 3, 1993, 13-21.
101 Ken'ichi Goto, 'Indonesia during the Japanese occupation', in: Peter Post e.a., (eds), *The encyclopedia of Indonesia in the Pacific War*, Brill, London/Boston 2010, 31-46 (38).
102 Sudjarwo, 'Portret diri pemuda dalam Revolusi kita', in: *Prisma*, 8 August 1981, 25.
103 Benedict Anderson, *Java in a Time of Revolution. Occupation and Resistance 1944-1946*. Ithaca/London: Cornell University Press, 1972, 49.
104 Robert Cribb, *Gangsters and Revolutionaries. The Jakarta People's Militia and the Indonesian Revolution 1945-1949*. Jakarta: Equinox Publishers, 2009 (first edition 1991) 50.
105 Sudjarwo, 'Portret diri pemuda dalam Revolusi kita', in: *Prisma*, 8 August 1981, 23.
106 Benedict Anderson, *Java in a Time of Revolution. Occupation and Resistance 1944-1946*. Ithaca/London: Cornell University Press, 1972, 39-48.
107 Benedict Anderson, *Java in a Time of Revolution. Occupation and Resistance 1944-1946*. Ithaca/London: Cornell University Press, 1972, 424.

108 Francis Palmos, *Surabaya 1945: Sacred Territory. Revolutionary Surabaya as the Birthplace of Indonesian Independence*. Perth: PhD thesis University of Western Australia, 2011. Also published as: Frank Palmos, *Surabaya 1945: Sakral Tanahku, the founding of the Indonesian Republic*. Jakarta: Obor, 2016. See also: Anthony Reid, *The Indonesian National Revolution, 1945 1950*. Hawthorn: Vic. Longmans 1974, 54.
109 Aiko Kurasawa, 'Social change', in: Peter Post et al., (eds), *The encyclopedia of Indonesia in the Pacific War*, Brill, London/Boston, 282-290 (287).
110 Aiko Kurasawa, 'Social change', in: Peter Post et al., (eds), *The encyclopedia of Indonesia in the Pacific War*, Brill, London/Boston, 282-290 (287).
111 Ken'ichi Goto, 'Indonesia during the Japanese occupation', in: Peter Post et al., (eds), *The encyclopedia of Indonesia in the Pacific War*, Brill, London/Boston 2010, 31-46 (38).
112 William Frederick, 'The Aftermath', in: Peter Post et al. (eds), *The encyclopedia of Indonesia in the Pacific War*, London/Boston: Brill, 2010, 46-60 (46).
113 William Frederick, 'The Aftermath', in: Peter Post et al. (eds), *The encyclopedia of Indonesia in the Pacific War*, London/Boston: Brill, 2010, 46-60 (47).

3. Rising tensions

1 The preparations for independence had already begun: on 31 May 1945, the committee set up by the Japanese, the Badan Penyelidik Usaha Persiapan Kemerdekaan (BPUPK), the Investigating Committee for Preparatory Work for Independence, met for the first time. Benedict R. O'G. Anderson, *Java in a time of revolution. Occupation and resistance 1944-1946*, Cornell University Press, Ithaca/London 1972, 69-70; Han Bing Siong, 'Sukarno-Hatta versus de *Pemuda* in the first months after the surrender of Japan (August-November 1945)', in: *Bijdragen tot de Taal-, Land- en Volkenkunde* 156, (2000), no. 2, Leiden, 233-273, here 235.
2 Anderson, *Java in a time of revolution*, 71; Siong, 'Sukarno-Hatta', 235.
3 Bob Hering, *Soekarno. Founding father of Indonesia 1901-1945*, KITLV Press, Leiden 2002, 366-367; Harry Poeze, *Verguisd en vergeten. Tan Malaka, de linkse beweging en de Indonesische Revolutie, 1945-1949*, volume I, KITLV Uitgeverij, Leiden 2007, 6.
4 Hering, *Soekarno*, 367-369; Poeze, *Verhuisd en vergeten*, 6; Nishijima Shigetada, 'The independence proclamation in Jakarta', in: Anthony Reid and Oki Akira (eds), *The Japanese experience in Indonesia. Selected memoirs of 1942-1945*, Ohio University, Athens (Ohio) 1986, 299-324, here 315-317.
5 Poeze, *Verguisd en vergeten*, 7.
6 S. Woodburn Kirby, *The war against Japan*, V, *The surrender of Japan*, Her Majesty's Stationary Office, London 1969, 224.
7 Peter Dennis, *Troubled days of peace. Mountbatten and South East Asia Command, 1945-1946*, Manchester University Press, Manchester, 1987, 5; Ken'ichi Goto, 'Indonesia during the Japanese occupation', in: Post, Peter, et al., eds, *The encyclopedia of Indonesia in the Pacific War*, Brill, London/Boston 2010, 31-46, here 45; William H. Frederick, 'The aftermath', in: Post, Peter, et al., eds, *The encyclopedia of Indonesia in the Pacific War*, Brill, London/Boston 2010, 46-60, here 47.
8 Richard McMillan, *The British Occupation of Indonesia 1945-1946. Britain, the Netherlands and the Indonesian Revolution*, London/New York: Routledge, 2005, 10; Van den Doel, *Afscheid van Indië*, 75.
9 McMillan, Richard, *British Occupation*, 3; Elly Touwen-Bouwsma and Petra Groen, 'Inleiding', in: Elly Touwen-Bouwsma and Petra Groen, *Tussen Banzai en Bersiap. De afwikkeling van de Tweede Wereldoorlog in Nederlands-Indië*, Sdu Uitgevers, The Hague 1996, 9-24, here 14.
10 Dennis, *Troubled days of peace*, 12-13; P.M.H. Groen, *Marsroutes en dwaalsporen. Het Nederlands militair-strategisch beleid in Indonesië 1945-1950*, Sdu uitgevers, The Hague 1991, 21.
11 Kirby, *The war against Japan*, V, 237 and 245; Touwen-Bouwsma and Groen, 'Inleiding', 18.
12 Ken'ichi Goto, *Tensions of empire. Japan and Southeast Asia in the colonial and postcolonial world*, (Ath-

ens (Ohio)/Singapore 2003) 190-192; Mary C. van Delden, *De Republikeinse kampen in Nederlands-Indië, oktober 1945-mei 1947. Orde in de chaos?*, self-published, Kockengen 2007, 72-73 and 75.

13 W.G.J Remmelink, 'The emergence of the new situation: the Japanese army on Java after the surrender', in: *Militaire Spectator*, vol. 148 (1978), 49-66, here 53.

14 Shigeru Sato, 'The PETA', in: Peter Post et al., eds, *The encyclopedia of Indonesia in the Pacific War*, Brill, London/Boston 2010, 132-145, here 144; Ken'ichi Goto, *Tensions of empire. Japan and Southeast Asia in the colonial and postcolonial world*, Ohio University Press/Singapore University Press, Athens (Ohio)/Singapore 2003, 283.

15 Van Delden, *Republikeinse kampen*, 80; Herman Bussemaker, *Bersiap! Opstand in het paradijs. De Bersiap-periode op Java en Sumatra 1945-1946.* Zutphen: Walburg Pers, 2005, 36-37; Elly Touwen-Bouwsma and Petra Groen, 'Van banzai tot bersiap', in: *Tussen banzai en bersiap. De afwikkeling van de Tweede Wereldoorlog in Nederlands-Indië*, 18; no author, Table showing the principal events and incidents since the cessation of hostilities', no date, NIOD, IC, inv. no. 1942; Han Bing Siong, 'Captain Huyer and the massive Japanese arms transfer in East Java in October 1945', in: *Bijdragen tot de taal-, land- en volkenkunde / Journal of the Humanities and Social Sciences of Southeast Asia*, 2003, vol.159 (2-3), 291-350, here 301; letter from Lieutenant Governor General (Van Mook) to Minister of Overseas Territories (Logemann), 29-11-1945, in: S.L van der Wal, P.J. Drooglever and M.J.B. Schouten (eds), *Officiële bescheiden betreffende de Nederlands-Indonesische betrekkingen 1945-1950*, volume 2. Digitally available at: resources.huygens.knaw.nl/indonesischebetrekkingen1945-1969/. Consulted on: 5-10-2021, no. 107, 208. Cited hereinafter as: *NIB*, volume x, no. x, p. x; Bart van Poelgeest, 'Figuranten op het Indische toneel. De Japanners in Nederlands-Indië, 1946-1949', in: Elly Touwen-Bouwsma and Petra Groen, *Tussen banzai en bersiap. De afwikkeling van de Tweede Wereldoorlog in Nederlands-Indië*, Sdu Uitgevers, The Hague 1996, 95-107, here 96-97.

16 No author, Table showing the principal events and incidents since the cessation of hostilities', no date, NIOD, IC, inv. no. 1942.

17 No author, 'The Allied occupation of the Netherlands East Indies September 1945-November 1946', National Archives (Kew), no date, 10, WO 203/2681.

18 Bussemaker, *Bersiap!*, 291.

19 Bussemaker, *Bersiap!*, 290-291.

20 Van den Doel, *Afscheid van Indië*, 79-80; Groen, *Marsroutes en dwaalsporen*, 18-20.

21 Anderson, *Java in a time of revolution*, 91 and 110.

22 As quoted in: Poeze, *Verguisd en vergeten*, I, 50.

23 Anderson, *Java in a time of revolution*, 113-115.

24 Van den Doel, *Afscheid van Indië*, 78-79.

25 Anderson, *Java in a time of revolution*, 115-117.

26 Anton Lucas, *One soul, one struggle. Region and revolution in Indonesia*, Allen & Unwin, Sydney 1991, 79-80; Van Delden, *Republikeinse kampen*, 83

27 Letter from Lt. H. Faber to Major-general F.G.L. Weijerman, NICA chief of staff in Ceylon, 22-9-1945, National Archives of the Netherlands, The Hague, General Secretary of the Netherlands Indies Government and the Archives deposited there, reference number 2.10.14, inventory number 5679; Lucas, *One soul one struggle*, 79; Robert Cribb, *Gangsters and revolutionaries. The Jakarta People's Militia and the Indonesian Revolution 1945-1949*, Equinox Publishing, Jakarta/Kuala Lumpur 2009, 61; diary E.M. Stok 03-10-1945, National Archives of the Netherlands, The Hague, Collection 301 E.M. Stok, reference number 2.21.183.80, inventory number 9.

28 On 1 September, Sukarno called on Indonesians everywhere to display the Republican flag and use 'merdeka' as a national greeting. Van Delden, *Republikeinse kampen*, 83.

29 William H. Frederick, *Visions and heat. The making of the Indonesian revolution*, Athens (Ohio), Ohio University Press 1989, 198; Mary C. van Delden, *Bersiap in Bandoeng. Een onderzoek naar geweld in de*

periode van 17 augustus 1945 tot 24 maart 1946, self published, Kockengen 1989, Report dr. Waibel about his stay in Salatiga from 27 September 1945–15 February 1946 04-03-1946, 5, NL-HaNA, General Secretary of the Netherlands Indies Government, 2.10.14, inv. no. 3044; Cribb, *Gangsters and revolutionaries*, 61-62.

30 Anderson, *Java in a time of revolution*, 124.
31 Cribb, *Gangsters and revolutionaries*, 61.
32 Elly Touwen-Bouwsma, 'De opvang van de burgergeïnterneerden op Java en Sumatra (15 augustus 1945–15 april 1946', in: Elly Touwen-Bouwsma and Petra Groen, *Tussen Banzai en Bersiap. De afwikkeling van de Tweede Wereldoorlog in Nederlands-Indië*, Sdu Uitgevers, The Hague 1996, 25-42, here 30-31.
33 Anderson, *Java in a time of revolution*, 129-130.
34 Cribb, *Gangsters and revolutionaries*, 58; Touwen-Bouwsma and Groen, 'Inleiding', 21-22; Touwen-Bouwsma, 'De opvang van burgergeïnterneerden op Java en Sumatra', 25.
35 Van den Doel, *Afscheid van Indië*, 61 and 80.
36 Diary L.R. Oldeman and E.M.C Oldeman-Duyfjes, 02-09-1945, NIOD, Netherlands East Indies diaries and egodocuments, reference 401, inventory number 232.
37 'Dutch East Indies are handicapped. High officials think Queen's Commonwealth Promise is dependent on security', in: *New York Times*, 5-9-1945, Netherlands Institute of Military History (NIMH), The Hague, Decolonization of the Dutch East Indies (1945-1950), reference number 509, inventory number 35.
38 H.W. van den Doel, *Afscheid van Indië*, 62-63.
39 As quoted in: Tom van den Berge, *H.J. van Mook 1894-1965. Een vrij en gelukkig Indonesië*, Uitgeverij THOTH, Bussum 2014, 204.
40 Letter from Ch.O. van der Plas to H.J. van Mook, 18-9-1945, NL-HaNA, General Secretary of the Netherlands Indies Government, 2.10.14, inv. no. 2987.
41 Report A.I.D. Prentice no date, Netherlands Institute of Military History (NIMH), The Hague, Decolonization of the Dutch East Indies (1945-1950), reference number 509, inventory number 229.
42 McMillan, *British occupation of Indonesia*, 73.
43 Mohammad Hatta, *Indonesian patriot. Memoirs*, edited by C.L.M. Penders, Gunung Agung, Singapore 1981, 247.
44 Bussemaker, *Bersiap!*, 199-200; Frederick, *Visions and heat*, 200-201; W. Meelhuisen, *Revolutie in Soerabaja. 17 augustus–1 december 1945*, Walburg Pers, Zutphen 2000, 72-77.
45 Van Delden, *Bersiap in Bandoeng*. 1989, 97; daily reports Kempeitai Semarang, 10-9-1945 (English translation: Seatic), NIOD, Netherlands East Indies Collection, reference number 400, inv. no. 704; Lucas, *One soul one struggle*, 79-81.
46 Anton Lucas, *One soul one struggle*, 79.
47 79.
48 Anthony Reid, *The blood of the people. Revolution and the end of traditional rule in northern Sumatra*, Oxford University Press, Kuala Lumpur/Oxford/New York/Melbourne 1979, 153-156; diary Major M.J. Knottenbelt 4-10-1945, NIOD Netherlands East Indies Collection 401, Indies diaries and egodocuments, inventory number 24.
49 Reid, *Blood of the people*, 156-157.
50 J.A. de Moor, *Westerling's oorlog. Indonesië 1945-1950*, Uitgeverij Balans, Amsterdam, 1999, 103.
51 Sartono Kartodirdjo, Marwati Djoened Poesponegoro and Nugroho Notosusantoso (eds), *Sejarah Nasional Indonesia*, Volume 6: *Zaman Jepang dan Zaman Republik Indonesia*, Balai Pustaka, Jakarta 1975 (republished 2008), 178.
52 CONICA J.C.C. Haar, General and political overview of the period 10-20 November 1945, 23-11-1945, 12, NL-HaNA, General Secretary of the Netherlands Indies Government, 2.10.14, inv. no. 3165.
53 Geoffrey Robinson, *The dark side of paradise. Political violence in Bali*, Cornell University Press, Ithaca/

London 1995, 117; Anne-Lot Hoek, *De strijd om Bali. Imperialisme, verzet en onafhankelijkheid 1846-1950* (Amsterdam 2021), 134.
54 Hoek, *De strijd om Bali*, 140.
55 Ibid., 140-141.
56 Telegram from the Heemskerck to NOIC C-in-C N.F.E.I. Abraham Crynssen. Taff, no date, NL-HaNA, General Secretary of the Netherlands Indies Government, 2.10.14, inv. no. 3678. See for date: No author, 'Table showing the principal events and incidents since the cessation of hostilities', no date, NIOD, 1C, inv. no. 1942.
57 Hoek, *De strijd om Bali*, 141.
58 Bussemaker, *Bersiap!*, 86-87.
59 Limpach, *De brandende kampongs*, 184; Bussemaker, *Bersiap!*, 193-294.
60 *Public Peace Intelligence Bulletin* no. 5, 23-9-1945, 3, Japanese 16th Army Headquarters, NIOD, Netherlands East Indies Collection, reference number 400, inv. no. 706.
61 MacMillan, *The British occupation of Indonesia*, 16.

4. Power constellations

1 See, for example: Audrey R. Kahin, ed., *Regional dynamics of the Indonesian revolution. Unity from diversity*, University of Hawaii Press, Honolulu 1985. Harry A. Poeze, 'Walking the tightrope: internal Indonesian conflict, 1945-1949', in: Bart Luttikhuis and Dirk A. Moses, eds, *Colonial counterinsurgency and mass violence. The Dutch Empire in Indonesia*, Routledge, London/New York 2014, 176-197, 194.
2 Audrey R. Kahin, 'Overview', in: Audrey R. Kahin, ed., *Regional dynamics of the Indonesian revolution. Unity from diversity*, University of Hawaii Press, Honolulu 1985, 265-284, here 277-278.
3 Kahin, 'Overview', 278-279.
4 See, for example: report W.C. Schoevers, 07-05-1947, NA, 2.10.14, inv. no. 4952; Abu Hanifah, *Tales of a revolution*, Angus and Robertson, Sydney/London (etc.) 1972, 178-179; McMillan, *British occupation*, 70; J.A. Stevens and Ben Grevedamme, *Vrij; een verzameling foto's uit Indië van den foto-journalist van den Marine-Voorlichtingsdienst Luit. ter zee 3e kl. J.A. Stevens met brieven van Ben Grevedamme* (Deventer 1946) 11.
5 See page 130

5. The Eastern archipelago: Allied dominance

1 P.J. Drooglever, *Een daad van vrije keuze. De Papoea's van westelijke Nieuw-Guinea en de grenzen van het zelfbeschikkingsrecht*, Boom, Amsterdam 2005, 73; William H. Frederick, 'The aftermath', in: Post, Peter, et al., eds, *The encyclopedia of Indonesia in the Pacific War*, Brill, London/Boston 2010, 46-60, here 47.
2 Geoffrey Robinson, *The dark side of paradise. Political violence in Bali*, Cornell University Press, Ithaca/London 1995, 97 and 177, 122. See also Anne-Lot Hoek, *De strijd om Bali. Imperialisme, verzet en onafhankelijkheid 1846-1950*, Amsterdam 2021.
3 Frederick, 'The aftermath', 47.
4 Rémy Limpach and Petra Groen, 'De oorlog met de Republiek Indonesië 1945-1950/1962', in: Petra Groen, Anita van Dissel, Mark Loderichs, Rémy Limpach and Thijs Brocades Zaalberg, *Krijgsgeweld en kolonie. Opkomst en ondergang van Nederlands als koloniale mogendheid 1816-1920*, Boom, Amsterdam 2021, 309-350, here 310.
5 Letter from Lieutenant Governor General (Van Mook) to the Minister of Overseas Territories (Logemann), 29-11-1945, in: S.L van der Wal, P.J. Drooglever and M.J.B. Schouten (eds), *Officiële bescheiden betreffende de Nederlands-Indonesische betrekkingen 1945-1950*, volume 2. Available online at: resources.huygens.knaw.n/lindonesische betrekkingen19451969/. Consulted on: 5-10-2021, no. 107, 208. Hereinafter cited as: *NIB*, volume x, no. x, p. x; Bart van Poelgeest, 'Figuranten op het Indische toneel. De Japanners in Nederlands-Indië, 1946-1949', in: Elly Touwen-Bouwsma and Petra Groen, *Tussen banzai*

en bersiap. De afwikkeling van de Tweede Wereldoorlog in Nederlands-Indië, Sdu Uitgevers, The Hague 1996, 95-107, here 96-97.

6   In December 1945, the Japanese troops on Bali abandoned their initially passive attitude to the pro-Republican Balinese, presumably under British pressure. In response, the Balinese armed forces undertook a simultaneous attack on all Japanese military installations in the night of 13 December 1945. The attack was a total failure, and the Republican armed forces were subsequently expelled from the major towns. Robinson, *The dark side of paradise*, 117-118.

7   L. van Poelgeest, *Japanse besognes. Nederland en Japan 1945-1975*, Sdu Uitgevers, The Hague 1999, 38 and 43; Drooglever, *Een daad van vrije keuze*, 93.

8   Brigadier F. Chilton, Report on the operations of Makassar Force 22 September 1945 to 20 December 1945, 31-12-1945, 5, Australian War Memorial (AWM) 52 8/2/21/38 War Diary 21 Infantry Brigade December 1945.

9   Chilton, Report, 6.

10 Barbara S. Harvey, 'South Sulawesi: puppets and patriots', in: Audrey R. Kahin, ed., *Regional dynamics of the Indonesian revolution. Unity from diversity*, University of Hawaii Press, Honolulu 1985, 207-235, here 231n; Limpach, *Brandende kampongs*, 253.

11 *NIB*, volume II, no. 107 (p. 208) and no. 112 (p. 221).

12 Richard Chauvel, 'Ambon: not a revolution but a counterrevolution', in: Audrey R. Kahin, ed., *Regional dynamics of the Indonesian revolution. Unity from diversity*, University of Hawaii Press, Honolulu 1985, 236-264, here 245.

13 Gin Eat Ooi, 'Of "permanent possession"-territories under the imperial Japanese navy', in: Peter Post et al., eds, *The encyclopedia of Indonesia in the Pacific War*, Brill, London/Boston 2010, 71-86, here 82-83.

14 A.H. Nasution, *Sekitar perang kemerdekaan Indonesia*, Jil. I, Proklamasi, Angkasa, Bandung 1977, 425; Richard Chauvel, 'Ambon: not a revolution but a counterrevolution', in: Audrey R. Kahin, ed., *Regional dynamics of the Indonesian revolution. Unity from diversity*, University of Hawaii Press, Honolulu 1985, 236-264, here 245; J.H.J. Brendgen, *Belevenissen van een K.N.I.L.-officier in de periode 1942-1950. Belevenissen vóór en bij politiele acties*, Self-publication [Haarlem] 1980, 47.

15 C.O. NICA L.G. Boldingh, 04-11-1945, monthly report of the CONICA Ambon for the month of October 1945, NA, 2.10.14, inv. no. 3165.

16 J.P.K. van Eechoud, Political report New Guinea, 1-11-1945, 51, NA, 2.10.14, inv. no. 3263; C. CONICA J.C.C. Haar, General and political overview of the period 10-20 November 1945, 23-11-1945, 3, NA, 2.10.14, inv. no. 3165; P.J. Drooglever, *Een daad van vrije keuze. De Papoea's van westelijke Nieuw-Guinea en de grenzen van het zelfbeschikkingsrecht*, Boom, Amsterdam 2005, 94.

17 J.P.K. van Eechoud, Political report New Guinea, 1-11-1945, 1, NA, 2.10.14, inv. no. 3263; P.J. Drooglever, *Een daad van vrije keuze. De Papoea's van westelijke Nieuw-Guinea en de grenzen van het zelfbeschikkingsrecht*, Boom, Amsterdam 2005, 93-94.

18 J.P.K. van Eechoud, Political report New Guinea 20-12-1945, 5, NA, 2.10.14, inv. no. 3265

19 J.P.K. van Eechoud, Political report New Guinea 20-12-1945, 3, NA, 2.10.14, inv. no. 3265; J.P.K. van Eechoud, Political report New Guinea 9-3-1946, 2, NA, 2.10.14, inv. no. 3265.

20 Ooi Keat Gin, *Post-war Borneo, 1945-1950. Nationalism, empire and state-building*, London/New York 2013, 49-55.

21 Gin, *Post-war Borneo*, 59-61.

22 C. CONICA C.C. de Rooy, General and political overview of the period 1-10 November 1945, 11-11-1945, 9, NL-HaNA, General Secretary of the Netherlands Indies Government, 2.10.14, inv. no. 3165.

23 Gin, *Post-war Borneo*,72; CONICA J.C.C. Haar, General and political overview of the period 10-20 November 1945, 23-11-1945, 12, NL-HaNA, General Secretary of the Netherlands Indies Government, 2.10.14, inv. no. 3165; C. CONICA C.C. de Rooy, General and political overview of the period 1-10 November 1945, 11-11-1945, 9, NL-HaNA, General Secretary of the Netherlands Indies Government,

2.10.14, inv. no. 3165.
24   Abdul Haris Nasution, *Sekitar Perang Kemerdekaan Indonesia*, I, Bandung 1977, 413-414; Ansar Rachman, et al., *Tandjungpura Berdjuang: Sedjarah Kodam XII/Tandjungpura Kalimantan Barat*, Pontianak, 1970, 103; Hassan Basry, *Kisah Gerila Kalimantan Dalam Revolusi Indonesia 1945-1949*, Bandjarmasin 1961, 71. See also https://en.wikipedia.org/wiki/Zhonghua_minzu.
25   Nasution, *Sekitar*, I, 414-415; *Republik Indonesia Propinsi Kalimantan*, Jakarta 1953, 132; Gin, *Post-war Borneo*, 74.
26   Memo on archival research on data concerning excesses committed by Dutch soldiers in Indonesia between 1945 and 1950 (*Excessennota*), The Hague, 2 June 1969, Appendix 5: Overview of data relating to excesses found in the government archives under investigation, 1. See also Limpach, *Brandende kampongs*, 577.
27   *Excessennota*, Appendix 5, 1.
28   Limpach, *Brandende kampongs*, 216.
29   Petra Groen, 'Koortsachtig imperialisme 1894-1914', in: Petra Groen, Anita van Dissel, Mark Loderichs, Rémy Limpach and Thijs Brocades Zaalberg, *Krijgsgeweld en kolonie. Opkomst en ondergang van Nederlands als koloniale mogendheid 1816-1920*, Boom, Amsterdam 2021, 135-159. Harvey, 'South Sulawesi', 208-211.
30   Harvey, 'South Sulawesi', 212 and 224.
31   Brigadier F. Chilton, Report on the operations of Makassar Force 22 September 1945 to 20 December 1945, 31-12-1945, 17-18, AWM 52 8/2/21/38 War Diary 21 Infantry Brigade December 1945.
32   Letter from Moertedjo to Major General Ivan Dougherty, 12-10-1945, AWM 52, 8/2/21/36, War Diary 21 Infantry Brigade October 1945 Appendix 31; Major General F. Chilton, Report on the operations of Makassar Force 22 September 1945 to 20 December 1945, 31-12-1945, 10, AWM 52 8/2/21/38 War Diary 21 Infantry Brigade December 1945. See also: Anthony Reid, 'Australia's hundred days in South Sulawesi', in: D. Chandler and M.C. Ricklefs, eds, *Nineteenth and twentieth century Indonesia. Essays in honour of professor J.D. Legge*, Monah University, Clayton, Victoria 1986, 201-224, here 210.
33   H.A.M. Daeng api, *Menyingkap Tabir Sejarah Budaya di Sulawesi Selatan*. Jakarta: Yayasan Bhinneka Tunggal Ika. 1988, 226. See also: Lahadjdji Patang. *Sulawesi dan Pahlawannja*. Jakarta: Yayasan Kesejahteraan Generasi Muda Indonesia. 1967, 106-107; Mattalatta, Andi. *Meniti Siri' dan Harga Diri: Catatan dan Kenangan*. Jakarta: Khasanah Manusia Nusantara. 2003, 173.
34   Manai Sophiaan. *Hari-hari Pertama Pendaratan NICA di Sulawesi Selatan*, memoir article in *Sulawesi dan Pahlawannja*. Jakarta: Yayasan Kesejahteraan Generasi Muda Indonesia. 1967, 174; H.A.M. Daeng Rapi. *Menyingkap Tabir Sejarah Budaya di Sulawesi Selatan*. Jakarta: Yayasan Bhinneka Tunggal Ika. 1988, 227; Andi Mattalatta, *Meniti Siri' dan Harga Diri: Catatan dan Kenangan*. Jakarta: Khasanah Manusia Nusantara. 2003, 173.
35   Abdul Haris Nasution. *Sekitar Perang Kemerdekaan Indonesia I*. Bandung: Disjarah-AD & Penerbit Angkasa. 1977, 442; Manai Sophiaan. *Apa Yang Masih Teringat*. Jakarta: Yayasan Mencerdaskan Kehidupan Bangsa. 1991, 68-69; Manai Sophiaan. *Hari-hari Pertama Pendaratan NICA di Sulawesi Selatan*, memoir article in *Sulawesi dan Pahlawannja*. Jakarta: Yayasan Kesejahteraan Generasi Muda Indonesia. 1967, 174; Lahadjdji Patang. *Sulawesi dan Pahlawannja*. Jakarta: Yayasan Kesejahteraan Generasi Muda Indonesia. 1967, 106-107; Mohammad Saleh La Hade. 'Korban 40.000 Jiwa di Sulawesi Selatan dan artinya bagi perjuangan Kemerdekaan Republik Indonesia', article in *Seminar Sejarah Perjuangan Rakyat Sulawesi Selatan Menentang Penjajahan Asing*. Jakarta: Departemen Pendidikan dan Kebudayaan, 1983, 371; Muhammad Natzir Said. *Korban 40.000 Jiwa di Sulawesi Selatan: S.O.B. 11 Desember 1946 Penyebab Banjir Darah dan Lautan Api*. Bandung: Alumni. 1985, 39-41; Andi Mattalatta. *Meniti Siri' dan Harga Diri: Catatan dan Kenangan*. Jakarta: Khasanah Manusia Nusantara. 2003, 173; H. Ahmad Masiara Daeng Rapi, *Menyingkap Tabir Sejarah Budaya di Sulawesi Selatan*. Jakarta: Yayasan Bhinneka Tunggal Ika. 1988, 226-227.

36 Brigadier F. Chilton, Report on the operations of Makassar Force 22 September 1945 to 20 December 1945, 31-12-1945, 13 AWM 52 8/2/21/38 War Diary 21 Infantry Brigade December 1945; Muhammad Natzir Said. *Korban 40.000 Jiwa di Sulawesi Selatan: s.o.b. 11 Desember 1946 Penyebab Banjir Darah dan Lautan Api*. Bandung: Alumni. 1985, 40; Mohammad Saleh La Hade, 'Korban 40.000 Jiwa di Sulawesi Selatan dan artinya bagi perjuangan Kemerdekaan Republik Indonesia', article in *Seminar Sejarah Perjuangan Rakyat Sulawesi Selatan Menentang Penjajahan Asing*. Jakarta: Departemen Pendidikan dan Kebudayaan, 1983, 371; Manai Sophiaan, *Hari-hari Pertama Pendaratan NICA di Sulawesi Selatan*, memoir article in *Sulawesi dan Pahlawannja*. Jakarta: Yayasan Kesejahteraan Generasi Muda Indonesia. 1967, 174-175; Abdul Harris Nasution, *Sekitar Perang Kemerdekaan Indonesia I*. Bandung: Disjarah-AD & Penerbit Angkasa. 1977, 442.
37 Memorandum [G.J.] Wolhoff and [H.J.] Koerts for the CONICA Makassar [C. Lion Cachet], 14-10-1945, 1, Special Collections Leiden University. Collection Willem IJzereef D H 1284, inv. no. 11.
38 AWM 52 8/3/27/101, War Diary 2/27 Infantry Battalion October 1945, 15-10-1945; Willem IJzereef, *De Zuid-Celebes affaire. Kapitein Westerling en de standrechtelijke executies*, De Bataafsche Leeuw, Dieren 1984, 25.
39 Telegram MAKFORCE to LANDOPS 16-10-1945, AWM 52, 8/3/14/90, War Diary 2/14 Infantry Battalion October 1945; Report Enthoven Commission no date, 4, NA, 2.03.01, inv. no. 12007.
40 Database *bersiap* victims ODGOI.
41 Sarita Pawiloy. *Sejarah Perjuangan Angkatan '45 di Sulawesi Selatan*. Ujung Pandang: Dewan Harian Daerah Angkatan '45 Propinsi Sulawesi Selatan, 113. See note 326 for the Indonesian sources that only mention the murders on 2 October 1945 and the following days.
42 AWM 52, 8/3/14/90, War Diary 2/14 Infantry Battalion October 1945, 19-10-1945.
43 Instruction Major L.E. Walcott [16-10-1945], AWM 52, 8/2/21/36, War Dairy 21 Infantry Brigade October 1945, Appendix 35.
44 C. Giebel, *Morotai. De bevrijding van de Grote Oost en Borneo*, Wever, Franeker 1976, 140; Willem IJzereef, *De Zuid-Celebes affaire. Kapitein Westerling en de standrechtelijke executies*, De Bataafsche Leeuw, Dieren 1984, 25.
45 McMillan, *British occupation of Indonesia*, 22-23; J.A. de Moor, *Westerling's oorlog. Indonesië 1945-1950*, Uitgeverij Balans, 1999, Amsterdam, 104-107.
46 Memorandum [G.J.] Wohlhoff and [H.J.] Koerts for the CONICA Makassar [C. Lion Cachet], 14-10-1945, 8-9, Special Collections Leiden University. Collection Willem IJzereef D H 1284, inv. no. 11. See also: Ch.A. Rosheuvel, *Van west naar oost. De rol van de Curaçaose Rode-Kruiscolonne in het voormalige Nederlands Oost-Indië*, Walburg Pers, [Zutphen] 1989, 256.
47 C. Giebel, *Morotai. De bevrijding van de Grote Oost en Borneo*, Wever, Franeker 1976, 140. See also 117 and 124.
48 Petra Groen, 'Colonial warfare and military ethics in the Netherlands East Indies, 1816-1941', in: Bart Luttikhuis and Dirk A. Moses, eds, *Colonial counterinsurgency and mass violence. The Dutch Empire in Indonesia*, Routledge, London/New York 2014, 25-44, here 40-42; no author, 'Slotbeschouwing', in: Petra Groen, Anita van Dissel, Mark Loderichs, Rémy Limpach and Thijs Brocades Zaalberg, *Krijgsgeweld en kolonie. Opkomst en ondergang van Nederlands als koloniale mogendheid 1816-1920*, Boom, Amsterdam 2021, 309-350, here 504.
49 Limpach, *Brandende kampongs*, 65-73. For a contemporary source that mentions some of these explanations, see: J.P.K. van Eechoud, Political report New Guinea 20-12-1945, 3 and Political report New Guinea 9-3-1946, 2.
50 AWM 52, 8/3/27/101, War Diary 2/27 Infantry Battalion October 1945, 29-10-1945.
51 Anthony Reid, 'Australia's hundred days in South Sulawesi', in: D. Chandler and M.C. Ricklefs, eds, *Ninteenth and twentieth century Indonesia. Essays in honour of professor J.D. Legge*, Monah University, Clayton, Victoria 1986, 201-224, here 215.

52 Proclamation Brigadier F.O. Chilton 29-10-1945, AWM 52 8/2/21/38 War Diary 21 Infantry Brigade December 194.
53 Limpach, *Brandende kampongs*, 187-188.
54 AWM 52 8/3/27/101, War Diary 2/27 Infantry Battalion October 1945, 20-10-1945 and 21-10-1945; Report C. Lion Cachet 21-10-1945, NA 2.10.14, inv. no. 3165. For intimidation and violence against Indo-Europeans and Chinese by pro-Republican Indonesians in Gorontalo, see: C. CONICA C.C. de Rooy, General and political overview of the period 1-10 November 1945, 11-11-1945, 6, NA, 2.10.14, inv. no. 3165.
55 AWM 52, 8/3/27/101 War Diary 2/27 Infantry Battalion October 1945, 4-10-1945.
56 IJzereef, *De Zuid-Celebes affaire*, 28-29.
57 Harvey, 'South Sulawesi', in: Kahin, *Regional dynamics*, 214-215; IJzereef, *De Zuid-Celebes affaire*, 29-51; Limpach, *Brandende kampongs*, 70-71, 250-251.
58 Harvey, 'South Sulawesi', in: Kahin, *Regional dynamics*, 214-215; IJzereef, *De Zuid-Celebes affaire*, 29-51; Limpach, *Brandende kampongs*, 251-252.
59 IJzereef, *De Zuid-Celebes affaire*, 25-51; Harvey, 'South Sulawesi', in: *Regional dynamics*, 214-217. Limpach, *Brandende kampongs*, 252. On 1 February 1946, the Australians handed over command to the 80th British Indian Infantry Brigade. By mid-July 1946, all civilian and military power was back in Dutch hands. Limpach, *Brandende kampongs*, 252-253.
60 Idwar Anwar and Andi Nur Fitri, *Ensiklopedi Sejarah Luwu*, Komunitas Kampung Sawrigading & Pemkot Kab. Luwu, Palopo 2005, 414.
61 Limpach, *Brandende kampongs*, 253.

6. Java and Sumatra: rival international power blocks

1 Rémy Limpach and Petra Groen, 'De oorlog met de Republiek Indonesië 1945-1950/1962', in: Petra Groen, Anita van Dissel, Mark Loderichs, Rémy Limpach and Thijs Brocades Zaalberg, *Krijgsgeweld en kolonie. Opkomst en ondergang van Nederland als koloniale mogendheid 1816-1920*, Boom, Amsterdam 2021, 309-350, here 310-311; Anthony Reid, *The blood of the people. Revolution and the end of traditional rule in northern Sumatra*, Oxford University Press, Kuala Lumpur/Oxford/New York/Melbourne 1979, 158; Van den Doel, *Afscheid van Indië*, 93-94.
2 McMillan, *British Occupation*, 17-18 and 113-116; Limpach and Groen, 'De oorlog met de Republiek Indonesië 1945-1950/1962', 311.
3 Letter F.C.C. Schokking 23-11-1945, NA, 2.10.36.15, inv. no. 9.
4 Abu Hanifah, *Tales of a revolution*, Angus and Robertson, Sydney/London (etc.) 1972, 183.
5 Abu Hanifah, *Tales of a revolution*, Angus and Robertson, Sydney/London (etc.) 1972, 174, 176 and 190.
6 Lucas, *One soul one struggle*, 138; Van den Doel, *Afscheid van Indië*, 90.
7 Report no. 1 by Lieutenant Commander A.J. Leland to Captain E. Tyndale Cooper, 3-11-1945, NIMH, Decolonization of the Dutch East Indies (1945-1950) (reference number 509), inv. no. 219. See also the reception of British troops in Surabaya: memoires of Major General L.H.O. Pugh, 6-9, NIMH, Decolonization (509), inv. no. 1771.
8 McMillan, *British occupation of Indonesia*, 37, 38 and 116; copy Report no. 2 by Lieutenant Commander A.J. Leland to Captain E. Tyndale Cooper, 8-11-1945, NIMH, 509, inv. no. 219; Limpach, *Brandende kampongs*, 232.
9 Mestika Zed, 'Bab 6 Perjuangan dan diplomasi', in: Mestika Zed, Mukhlis PaEni (eds), *Indonesia dalam Arus Sejarah*, VI, *Perang dan revolusi*, Jakarta 2012, 194-249, 203, translation Taufik Hanafi. Lucas, *One soul one struggle*, 139. See also: Anderson, *Java in a time of revolution*, 138.
10 'Belanda memboesoekan di mata internasional', in: *Merah-Poetih*, 18-10-1945. See also: 'Tentara Serikat dipakai Untuk mengebui mata', in: *Merdeka. Soera Rakjat Repoeblik Indonesia*, 03-10-1945; 'NICA

terus mengacaukan', in: *Merdeka. Soera Rakjat Repoeblik Indonesia*, 06-10-1945; 'Sampai dimana praktek-praktek NICA', in: *Merdeka*, 09-10-195; 'Kejahatan serdadu NICA CS makin memuncak', in: *Merdeka*, 16-10-1945.

11 Excerpt from letter A.J.L. to J.L. 5-11-1945, NIMH, 509, inv. no. 219.

12 Sheri Lynn Gibbings and Fridus Steijlen, 'Colonial figures: memories of street traders in the colonial and early post-colonial periods', in: *Public history review*, volume 19 (2012), 63-85, 77n; email Paul van Geldere to Esther Captain 15-08-2020; Cribb, *Gangsters and revolutionaries*, 80.

13 Henk Schulte Nordholt, *Een staat van geweld*, inaugural address held on 22 June 2000 ESHCC, Rotterdam 2000, 13-14. Also: Henk Schulte Nordholt, 'A genealogy of violence', in: Freek Colombijn and Thomas J. Lindblad, eds, *Roots of violence in Indonesia*, KITLV Press, Leiden 2002, 33-61, here 41.

14 Zara, *Indonesian propaganda*, 178-182 and 325.

15 Bussemaker, *Bersiap!*, 214-215, 244 and 260; Zara, *Indonesian propaganda*, 178-182 and 325; email Anda Zara to author 15-05-2020; Marjolein van Pagee, *Bung Tomo: War Crimimal or Hero? Dutch and Indonesian Views on the Violence in Surabaya 1945*. Leiden: Master's Thesis, 2018, 60, 61.

16 'Makloemat Pemerintah Repoeblik Indonesia', in: *Berita Repoeblik Indonesia*, 17-11-1945.

17 Limpach, *Brandende kampongs*, 238-239.

18 Jacques Semelin, *Purify and destroy. The political uses of massacre and genocide*, Columbia University Press, New York 2007, 293. See also 295-296. On the role of rumours in the normalization of violence, see also: Robert Cribb, 'Misdaad, geweld en uitsluiting in Indonesië', in: Els Bogaerts and Remco Raben, *Van Indië tot Indonesië*, Boom, Amsterdam 2007, 13-30, here 31-48, here 45

19 Sri Margana et al., *Gelora di tanah raja: Yogyakarta pada masa revolusi 1945-1949* Yogyakarta 2017 86; John R.W. Smail, *Bandung in the early revolution, 1945-1946: A Study in the Social History of the Indonesian Revolution*, (Ithaca/New York 1964) 84, 90, 94, 97; Cribb, *Gangsters and Revolutionaries*, 60-62; Mary Margaret Steedly, *Rifle Reports: A Story of Indonesian Independence* (Berkeley 2013) 119 and 127; Anderson, *Java in a Time of Revolution*, 108, 118 and 185.

20 Siauw Tiong Djin, *Siauw Giok Tjhan. Bicultural leader in emerging Indonesia* (Clayton 2018) 39-40, Smail, *Bandung*, 90.

21 Harry Poeze and Henk Schulte Nordholt, *Merdeka. De strijd om de Indonesische onafhankelijkheid en de ongewisse opkomst van de Republiek 1945-1950* (Amsterdam 2022) 107-108; John R.W. Smail, *Bandung in the early revolution, 1945-1946: A Study in the Social History of the Indonesian Revolution* (Ithaca/New York 1964) 84, 90, 94, 97; Cribb, *Gangsters and Revolutionaries*, 60-62; Mary Margaret Steedly, *Rifle Reports: A Story of Indonesian Independence* (Berkeley 2013) 119 and 127; Anderson, *Java in a Time of Revolution*, 108, 118 and 185.

22 Y. Yogaswara, 'Lahirnya badan-badan perjuangan dan BKR [Barisan Keamanan Rakjat] di kota Bandung sampai timbulnya MDPP/MPPP [Markas Daerah Perjoangan Pertahanan Priangan/Majelis Persatuan Perjuangan Priangan]', seminar sejarah nasional 10-13 November 1981, Jakarta 1981, 15-16; Van Delden, *Bersiap in Bandoeng*, 75-76, 81-82.

23 John R.W. Smail, *Bandung in the Early Revolution, 1945-1946: A Study in the Social History of the Indonesian Revolution*, (Ithaca/New York 1964) 84, 90, 94, 97; Cribb, *Gangsters and Revolutionaries*, 60-62; Mary Margaret Steedly, *Rifle Reports: A Story of Indonesian Independence* (Berkeley 2013) 119 and 127; Anderson, *Java in a Time of Revolution*, 108, 118 and 185.

24 Cribb, *Revolutionaries and gangsters*, 58; Anderson, *Java in a time of revolution*, 130 and 170; Zara, *Indonesian propaganda*, 182; Audrey R. Kahin, 'Introduction', in: *Regional Dynamics of the Indonesian Revolution. Unity from Diversity*. Honolulu: University of Hawaii Press, 1985, 1-21, here 12-13.

25 Muhammad Yuanda Zara, *Voluntary participation, state involvement: Indonesian propaganda in the struggle for maintaining independence, 1945-1949*, dissertation UvA 2016, 178.

26 Anderson, *Java in a time of revolution*, 121-122, 130-131; Poeze, *Verguisd en vergeten*, 104.

27 Letter Sukarno to the Supreme Commander of the Farther East regions 30-9-1945, 3, NA, 2.10.14, inv.

no. 5445.
28 Muhammad Yuanda Zara, *Voluntary participation, state involvement: Indonesian propaganda in the struggle for maintaining independence, 1945-1949*, dissertation UvA 2016, 178-179.
29 'Table showing the principal events and incidents since the cessation of hostilities', no date, NIOD, IC, inv. no. 1942.
30 This document was later translated into English. No author, copy of 'Table showing the principle events since the cessation of hostilities', 1947, NIOD, IC (reference number 400), inv. no. 1942; no date, copy of excerpt report Intel. & loyalty research No. 145., 05-06-1946, National Archives, The Hague, Attorney General of the Supreme Court of the Dutch East Indies, reference number 2.10.17, inventory number 65; in a report by the Red Cross in Bandung, the date of the murder of the Japanese in Garut is given as 9 October 1945; no author, report by Red Cross in Bandung, included with letter by B. Sorgdrager, head of department II of NEFIS to the attorney general in Batavia. 14-08-1947, NL-HaNA, Attorney General Supreme Court of the Dutch East Indies, 2.10.17, inv. no. 65.
31 Abu Hanifah, *Tales of a revolution*, Angus and Robertson, Sydney/London (etc.) 1972, 178.
32 Report W.C. Schoevers, 07-05-1947, NA, 2.10.14, inv. no. 4952.
33 W.G.J. Remmelink, 'The emergence of the new situation: the Japanese army on Java after the surrender', in: *Militaire Spectator*, volume 148 (1978), 49-66, here 57.
34 *Sejarah Nasional*, 174; Anderson, *Java in a time of revolution*, 123.
35 Van Schaik, *Malang. Beeld van een stad*, 62; Van Delden, *Bersiap in Bandoeng*, 100; *Sejarah Nasional*, 174; Lucas, *One soul one struggle*, 95-98.
36 Shigeru Sato, 'The PETA', in: Peter Post et al., eds, *The encyclopedia of Indonesia in the Pacific War*, Brill, London/Boston 2010, 132-145, here 143.
37 Frederick, *Visions and heat*, 218.
38 Frederick, *Visions and heat*, 211 and 213-214. For information about the new *priyayi*, see 34 ff.
39 W.G.J. Remmelink, 'The emergence of the new situation: the Japanese army on Java after the surrender', in: *Militaire Spectator*, volume 148 (1978), 49-66, here 60; Han Bing Siong, 'Captain Huyer and the massive Japanese arms transfer in East Java in October 1945', I; in: *Bijdragen tot de taal-, land- en volkenkunde / Journal of the Humanities and Social Sciences of Southeast Asia*, 2003, Vol. 159 (2-3), 291-350, here 327-329. The significance of these weapons transfers and Huijer's role in them is an issue of debate among historians. See also: Bussemaker, *Bersiap!*, 211-214; Frederick, *Visions and heat*, 230n.
40 Van Delden, *Bersiap in Bandoeng*, 73, 100 and 105.
41 W.G.J Remmelink, 'The emergence of the new situation: the Japanese army on Java after the surrender', in: *Militaire Spectator*, volume 148 (1978), 49-66, here 62. According to Van Delden, *Bersiap in Bandoeng*, 107.
42 Van Delden, *Bersiap in Bandoeng*, 107-108.
43 W.G.J. Remmelink, 'The emergence of the new situation: the Japanese army on Java after the surrender', in: *Militaire Spectator*, volume 148 (1978), 49-66, here 62-63; see Van Delden, *Bersiap in Bandoeng*, 78.
44 Groen, 'Patience and bluff', 104 and 111.
45 Han Bing Siong, 'The secret battle of major Kido', 399; Groen, 'Patience and bluff', 109-110, 111 and 113.
46 Han Bing Siong, 'The secret battle of major Kido', 402-404. The Japanese military code of honour probably played a role in Kido's refusal as well. Earlier batches of weapons had been older KNIL weapons that were used by PETA. Now it was a matter of handing over Japanese weapons bearing the imperial emblem. This was a mortal sin, as every Japanese soldier had to fight to the death. Kido therefore decided to take action against the Indonesians, should this prove inevitable.
47 Groen, 'Patience and bluff', 112-113.
48 Groen, 'Patience and bluff', 113-116; W.G.J. Remmelink, 'The emergence of the new situation: the Japanese army on Java after the surrender', in: *Militaire Spectator*, volume 148 (1978), 49-66, here 62-63;

Miyamoto Shizuo, 'Army problems in Java after the surrender', in: Anthoy Reid and Oki Akira, *The Japanese experience in Indonesia. Selected memoirs of 1942-1945*, Ohio University, Athens (Ohio) 1986, 325-340, here 336-337.

49 Indonesian victims: see Groen, 'Patience and bluff', 118 Japanese victims: No author, 'List of Japanese dead, wounded and missing in Java on 10 Feb [1946]', NA, 2.10.62, inv. no. 3867; Ken'ichi Goto, *Tensions of empire. Japan and Southeast Asia in the colonial and postcolonial world*, Ohio University Press/Singapore University Press, Athens (Ohio)/Singapore 2003, 171.

50 'Patience and bluff', 114-117; Ken'ichi Goto, *Tensions of empire. Japan and Southeast Asia in the colonial and postcolonial world*, Ohio University Press/Singapore University Press, Athens (Ohio)/Singapore 2003, 173-174. Report D.H.W. Soltau, 19-10-1945, in: Han Bing Siong et al., eds, *Geschiedenis van de vijfdaagse strijd in Semarang 14-19 october 1945*, Stichting Reünisten HBS-Semarang, Rijswijk 1995, 163. See also: 'Sejarah pertempuran lima hari di Semarang' (translated into Dutch), in: Han Bing Siong et al., eds. *Geschiedenis van de vijfdaagse strijd in Semarang 14-19 october 1945*, Stichting Reünisten HBS-Semarang, Rijswijk 1995, 37; Han Bing Siong, 'Het geheim van majoor Kido', in: Han Bing Siong et al., eds, *Geschiedenis van de vijfdaagse strijd in Semarang 14-19 october 1945*, Stichting Reünisten HBS-Semarang, Rijswijk 1995, 120-122.

51 No author, 'Table showing the principal events and incidents since the cessation of hostilities', no date, NIOD, IC, inv. no. 1942; Anderson, *Java in a time of revolution*, 148-149. Reid and Akira suspect that this attack was a reaction to the Japanese recapture of Bandung on 10 October 1945. Yaichiro Shibata, 'Surabaya after the surrender', in: Anthoy Reid and Oki Akira, *The Japanese experience in Indonesia. Selected memoirs of 1942-1945*, Ohio University, Athens (Ohio) 1986, 341-374, here 369n.

52 Lucas, *One struggle one soul*, 95-96; Michael C. Williams, 'Banten: "Rice debts will be repaid with rice, blood debts with blood"', in: Audrey R. Kahin, ed., *Regional dynamics of the Indonesian revolution. Unity from diversity*, University of Hawaii Press, Honolulu 1985, 55-81, here 63; for the Japanese death toll in the incidents in Pekalongan, Serang and Rangkasbitung, see No author, 'Table showing the principal events and incidents since the cessation of hostilities', no date, NIOD, IC, inv. no. 1942.

53 Reid, *Blood of the people*, 157.

54 F. Asbeck Brusse 6-10-1945, NL-HaNA, Attorney General Supreme Court of the Dutch East Indies, 2.10.17, inv. no. 1038; Cribb, *Gangsters and revolutionaries*, 63; Frederick, *Visions and heat*, 233; M.C. Van Daalen Wetters, 'Verslag over de "Indonesische gevangenschap" etc. doorgebracht te Malang v/m 13 October 1945 t/m 13 Juni 1946', 17-7-1946, 3-4, NIMH, 509, inv. no. 76; Van Schaik, *Malang*, 262; Van Delden, *Bersiap in Bandoeng*, 101; Mary C. van Delden, *De Republikeinse kampen in Nederlands-Indië, oktober 1945-mei 1947. Orde in de chaos?*, self-publication, Kockengen 2007, 141.

55 Van Delden, *De Republikeinse kampen*, 149-150.

56 The question of whether it is plausible that the internments in the Republican camps were organized centrally is discussed in chapter 7.

57 The *totoks* had already been interned in camps during the Japanese occupation, but they had then left them and had returned to their pre-war homes in Republican territory. Van Delden, *De Republikeinse kampen*, 149-152 and 160.

58 Report R.J. Prins, 06-10-1946, NA, 2.10.62, inv. no. 2030.

59 Bussemaker, *Bersiap!*, 111. For the history of the incident in Depok, see also: Nonja Peters, *The Christian slaves of Depok: a colonial tale unravels*, Newcastle upon Tyne 2021.

60 Frederick, *Visions and heat*, 242; Bussemaker, *Bersiap!*, 216.

61 Witness statement H.R.H. van Affelen van Saemsvoort, recorded by J.W.F. Meeng, 26-11-1947, NA. 2.10.62, inv.no. 2039; Statement L. Sinsu-Andries, recorded by J.W.F. Meeng, 29-11-1947, NA, 2.10.62, inv. no. 2039.

62 Statement F.H.H. Holtkamp, recorded by J.W.F. Meeng, 25-10-1947, NA. 2.10.62, inv. no. 2039.

63 Statement L. Sinsu-Andries, recorded by J.W.F. Meeng, 29-11-1947, 2, NA, 2.10.62, inv. no. 2039.

64 Frederick, *Visions and heat*, 242.
65 Transcript of interview with Captain Lieutenant physician ret. W.J.M.W. Timmers, recorded by Mrs A.M. van Lynden-Bloem, NIMH, Collection Sweep. Egodocuments Dutch East Indies, 1945-1950 (reference number 545), inv. no. 661.
66 William Frederick, 'Shadow of an Unseen Hand. Some Patterns of Violence in the Indonesian Revolution, 1945-1949', in: Freek Colombijn and J. Thomas Lindblad (eds), *Roots of Violence in Indonesia. Contemporary Violence in Historical Perspective*. Leiden: KITLV Press, 2002, 143-172, 150-153.
67 Witness statement Koesen, recorded by J.W.F. Meeng, 21-10-1947, NA, 2.10.62, inv. no. 2044.
68 Report M.R. Vrijens, 6-8-1947, National Archives of the Netherlands,The Hague, Netherland Forces Intelligence Service (NEFIS) and Central Military Intelligence Service (CMI) in the Dutch East Indies, reference number 2.10.62, inventory number 2035. According to Nasution, however, the Indo-Europeans were murdered in the prison. Abdul Haris Nasution, *Sekitar Perang Kemerdekaan Indonesia*, 1, Disjarah-AD & Penerbit Angkasa. Bandung 1977, 345.
69 Vaandrig Claessens, Report Status 1 Mission 28 Aug.–14 Dec. 1945, no date, 3-4, NIMH, 509, inv. no. 214; Michael van Langenberg, 'East Sumatra: accommodating an Indonesian nation within a Sumatran residency', in: Audrey R. Kahin, ed., *Regional dynamics of the Indonesian revolution. Unity from diversity*, University of Hawaii Press, Honolulu 1985, 113-143, here 132.
70 J.A. de Moor, *Westerling's oorlog. Indonesië 1945-1950*, Uitgeverij Balans, 1999, Amsterdam, 99-105; Limpach, *Brandende kampongs*, 184.
71 Edisaputra, *Lintasan dan Cukilan Perjuangan Kemerdekaan Se-Sumatera dan Kalimantan Barat*, Bina Satria 1945, Medan 1977, 69-70. For a slightly different version of the events, see: Tim Khusus Perencanaan dan Pelaksana Pembangunan Tatengger di Propinsi Daerah Tingkat I Sumatera Utara, *Perjuangan Menegakkan dan Mempertahankan Kemerdekaan Republik Indonesia di Sumatera Utara*, Jil. 3, (*1945–1949*), Tim tsb., Medan 1996, 48-51; Reid, *Blood of the people*, 159.
72 According to Indonesian publications, the Dutch RAPWI officer J.C. Groenenberg was killed in the incident in Medan. He actually died in an attack on Hotel Siantar in Pematang Siantar two days later. Edisaputra, *Lintasan dan Cukilan*, 71; Tim Khusus Perencanaan dan Pelaksana, *Perjuangan Menegakkan*, 51. For victim number, see also: Reid, *The blood of the people*, 159-160; De Moor, *Westerling's Oorlog*, 5.
73 Vaandrig Claessens, 'Rapport Status 1 Mission 28 Aug.–14 Dec. 1945', 4, no date NIMH, 509, inv. no. 214.
74 Vaandrig Claessens, 'Rapport Status 1 Mission 28 Aug.–14 Dec. 1945', 5, no date NIMH, 509, inv. no. 214.
75 Edisaputra, *Lintasan dan Cukilan Perjuangan Kemerdekaan Se-Sumatera dan Kalimantan Barat*, Bina Satria 1945, Medan 1977, 71.
76 Hans Vervoort, 'Een feestelijke moordpartij', www.hansvervoort.nl. Consulted 5 July 2021; Vaandrig Claessens, 'Rapport Status 1 Mission 28 Aug.–14 Dec. 1945', 5-6, no date NIMH, 509, inv. no. 214; Reid, *Blood of the people*, 160; No author, 'Intelligence received from the field report No. 18', 27-10-1945, NA, 2.10.14, inv. no. 3590. The Indonesian account of the number of victims is questionable. In *Lintasan dan Cukilan*, 71, Edisaputra writes that five soldiers from the Royal Netherlands Army (KL) and twelve from the KNIL were killed. These numbers are not confirmed by other sources. Moreover, at that time there were no soldiers from the Royal Netherlands Army on Sumatra.
77 Pia van der Molen and Michiel Praal, Research report documentary *Archief van Tranen*, 2011, 62. See: www.pia-media.nl/projecten/documenten-research.
78 KDC, KMM, 75-647, Jan van der Pol, Bandung.
79 Cribb, *Gangsters and revolutionaries*, 65; McMillan, *British occupation of Indonesia*, 63; Bussemaker, *Bersiap!*, 86-87, 112-113, 129-130 and 204; Limpach, *Brandende kampongs*, 183-184 and 186-187.
80 Bussemaker, *Bersiap!*, 112.
81 Limpach, *Brandende kampongs*, 188 and 194; Bussemaker, *Bersiap!*, 113.

82 Gielt Algra et al., *Militaire ooggetuigen Nederlands-Indië 1941-1949: beleving, terugblik en doorwerking* (Utrecht 2021) 137-138.
83 Algra, *Militaire ooggetuigen*, 137.
84 Social report A81214. WUV, archive Stichting Archief Pelita.
85 War Diairies for 1st Patialas, War Diary for November 1945, entry for 20 November, National Archives (Kew), WO 172/7827, quoted in: McMillan, *British occupation of Indonesia*, 86. See also pages 22-23 and 87; Excerpt letter Lieutenant Commander A.J. Leland. to J. Leland, 25-10-1945, NIMH, 509, inv. no. 219. For a Dutch report, see: Giebel, *Morotai*, 150.
86 Johan Fabricius, *Hoe ik Indië terugvond*, The Hague 1947, 57-58.
87 J.A.A. van Doorn and W.J. Hendrix, *Ontsporing van geweld. Het Nederlands-Indonesische conflict*, Zutphen 2021, 127.
88 Limpach, *Brandende kampongs*, 187-188 and 194; S.M. Jalhay, *Allen zwijgen. Van merdeka en Andjing-Nica tot APRA*, Gevana, Hillegom (1989), 93, 103-104 and 138 ; C.E.L. Helfrich, *Memoires van C.E.L. Helfrich, luitenant-admiraal b.d.*, II, *Glorie en tragedie* (Amsterdam 1950) 268; Bussemaker, *Bersiap!*, 87.
89 McMillan, *British occupation of Indonesia*, 22-23 en 63.
90 Limpach, *Brandende kampongs*, 65.
91 J.A. de Moor, *Westerling's oorlog. Indonesië 1945-1950*, Uitgeverij Balans, 1999, Amsterdam, 104-107; Limpach, *Brandende kampongs*, 232.
92 *NIB*, no. 114, 184n.
93 'British-Indian Army Lands in Batavia Zone', in: *Nippon Times*, 3-10-1945.
94 This stands for: 'We Indonesians have no quarrel with anyone except the Dutch.' Excerpt letter Sukarno to Philip Christison 9-10-1945, 1-2, NA, 2.10.14, inv. no. 5445.
95 McMillan, *British Occupation*, 23.
96 McMillan, *British Occupation*, 26-27. Number of internees from: Groen, 'Patience and bluff', 96.
97 McMillan, *British occupation*, 44; Frederick, *Visions and heat*, 258-259.
98 Frederick, *Visions and heat*, 278-279.
99 McMillan, *British occupation*, 53-56; William Frederick, 'The killing of Dutch and Eurasians in Indonesia's National Revolution (1945-1949): a "brief genocide" reconsidered', *Journal of Genocide Research* 14-3/4 (2012), 359-380, here 371.
100 49th Indian Infantry Brigade, 'A report on the ambush of a RAPWI-convoy in Sourabaya', no date, Appendix N bij majoor P.L.H. Barber namens lt.-gen. G.O. C.-in-C. HQ AFNEI, HQ AFNEI Intelligence Review Period Oct 45-Nov 46, 25-11-1946, Netherlands Institute of Military History (NIMH), The Hague, Decolonization of the Dutch East Indies (1945-1950), reference number 509, inventory number 163; Bussemaker, *Bersiap!*, 231; Frederick, 'The killing of Dutch and Eurasians', 365.
101 49th Indian Infantry Brigade, 'A report on the ambush of a RAPWI-convoy in Sourabaya'; Bussemaker, *Bersiap!*, 231.
102 49th Indian Infantry Brigade, 'A report on the ambush of a RAPWI-convoy in Sourabaya'.
103 Bussemaker, *Bersiap!*, 229-234 Frederick, *Visions and heat*, 261; McMillan, *British occupation*, 44-45; Henk Itzig Heine, 'Aanvulling op het rapport van het Gubeng-transport', unpublished 2008, 59.
104 Limpach, *Brandende kampongs*, 238-239.
105 McMillan, *British occupation*, 70; Limpach, *Brandende kampongs*, 238-239.
106 Excerpt from letter A.J.L. to J.L. 20-11-1945, NIMH, 509, inv. no. 219
107 Secret report H.S. Edersheim, 7-12-1945, NL-HaNA, NEFIS and CMI, 2.10.62, inv. no. 992.
108 Transcript of statement by O. Brouwer von Gonzenbach 18-10-1947, drawn up by C.A.M. Brondgeest, NL-HaNA, NEFIS and CMI, 2.10.62, inv. no. 2058.
109 Reid, *Blood of the people*, 166.
110 Reid, *Blood of the people*, 165-168.

111 Reid, *Blood of the people*, 168.
112 Takao Fusayama, *A Japanese memoir of Sumatra, 1945-1946. Love and hatred in the liberation war*, Ithaca, New York, Cornell Modern Indonesia Project, Southeast Asia Program, Cornell University 1993, 70-76. This reading is confirmed by a Dutch source: C.O. AMACAB (name illegible), fortnightly report period 1-15 January '46, 5-2-1946, NL-HaNA, NEFIS and CMI, 2.10.62, inv. no. 725, 13. Indonesian sources also report dozens of Japanese victims in this period: Legiun Veteran Republik Indonesia Propinsi Sumatera Utara, *Veteran Pejuang Kemerdekaan dan Legiun Veteran R.I. Sumatera Utara*. Legiun Veteran R.I. Sumatera Utara Medan 2001, 178; Biro Sejarah, *Medan Area Mengisi Proklamasi*, PRIMA, Medan 1976, 620.
113 M. Kassim and Amir Taat Nasution, *Peristiwa Berdarah Serangan Tentara Jepang 13 Desember 1945 di Tebing Tinggi (Sumatera Utara)*, Universitas Medan Area Medan 1992, 70-80; Biro Sejarah, *Medan Area Mengisi Proklamasi*, PRIMA, Medan 1976, 620-621 and 623-625. Other Indonesian sources give a slightly different account of the events, with a different date (9 or 11 December), or with several Japanese who were killed or two trains that were stopped. Legiun Veteran, *Veteran Pejuang Kemerdekaan*, 179; Biro Sejarah, *Medan Area Mengisi Proklamasi*, PRIMA, Medan 1976, 620-621 and 623-625; Legiun Veteran, *Veteran Pejuang Kemerdekaan*, 178-179; Reid, *Blood of the people*, 169. However, it is rather unlikely that a second train was stopped at Tebing Tinggi. That is because the Swedish missionary Ostrom, who is said to have been on the train and was killed with some Japanese, was only murdered when he arrived at the station to take a train back to Medan. Moreover, he was alone. See the report by his wife: Vera Edborg Ostrom, *O bok su. The story of Egon Ostrom known to the Chinese as 'O Bok Su,' an ambassador to the kingdom of God*, Paul Foss Press, Minneapolis, Minnesota, 1949, 106-109.
114 Kassim and Nasution, *Peristiwa*, 90-109; Biro Sejarah, *Medan Area*, 622 and 625-626; Fusayama, *Japanese memoir*, 81-82.
115 C. Brondgeest, 'Rapport van Sumatra No. 1', 26-12-1945, NL-HaNA, NEFIS and CMI, 2.10.62, inv. no. 715; C.O. AMACAB, fortnightly report period 1-15 January 1946, 5-2-1946, NL-HaNA, NEFIS and CMI, 2.10.62, inv. no. 725, 10-11.
116 Legiun Veteran, *Veteran Pejuang Kemerdekaan*, 181; Kassim and Nasution, *Peristiwa*, 104, 140 and 143.
117 No author, 'Sumatra killings reported', in: *New York Times*, 22-12-1945; Brondgeest, 'Rapport van Sumatra No. 1', 26-12-1945, NL-HaNA, NEFIS and CMI, 2.10.62, inv. no. 715; C.O. AMACAB, fortnightly report period 1-15 January 1946, 5-2-1946, NL-HaNA, NEFIS and CMI, 2.10.62, inv. no. 725, 10-11; Biro Sejarah, *Medan Area*, 623 and 626-627; Michael van Langenberg, *National Revolution in North Sumatra: Sumatera Timur and Tapanuli, 1942-1950* (unpublished PhD dissertation, 1976), 345; Reid, *Blood of the people*, 169.
118 Interrogation report A.E. Leclair, drawn up by Sgt. Knuttel and G.N. Ch. Janssen Andeweg, 28-6-1946, NL-HaNA, NEFIS and CMI, 2.10.62, inv. no. 2393; Fusayama, *A Japanese memoir of Sumatra*, 68.
119 Anthony Reid, *The blood of the people*, 169; Van Langenberg, *National revolution*, 348-349.
120 Harry A. Poeze, 'Walking the tightrope: internal Indonesian conflict, 195-1949', in: Bart Luttikhuis and Dirk A. Moses, eds, *Colonial counterinsurgency and mass violence. The Dutch Empire in Indonesia*, Routledge, London/New York 2014, 176-197, here 194; M.C. Ricklefs, *A history of modern Indonesia since c. 1300*, MacMillan, London 1993, 218. For the use of the term 'social revolution', see for example: Anderson, *Java in a time of revolution*, 332-369 and various chapters in Audrey R. Kahin, ed., *Regional dynamics of the Indonesian revolution. Unity from diversity*, University of Hawaii Press, Honolulu 1985. Harry A. Poeze, 'Walking the tightrope: internal Indonesian conflict, 1945-1949', in: Bart Luttikhuis and Dirk A. Moses, eds, *Colonial counterinsurgency and mass violence. The Dutch Empire in Indonesia*, Routledge, London/New York 2014, 176-197, here 194.
121 Mestika Zed, 'Masa Bersiap', in: Taufik Abdullah, A.B. Lapian, Mestika Zed, Mukhlis PaEni (eds), *Indonesia dalam Arus Sejarah*, VI, *Perang dan revolusi*, Ichtiar Baru Van Hoeve. Jakarta 2012, 202-210, here 202. Translation from Indonesian to English by Taufik Hanafi; Limpach, *Brandende kampongs*, 166.

122 Michael C. Williams, 'Banten: "Rice debts will be repaid with rice, blood debts with blood", in: Audrey R. Kahin, ed., *Regional dynamics of the Indonesian revolution. Unity from diversity*, University of Hawaii Press, Honolulu 1985, 55-81, here 55-57.
123 Williams, 'Banten', 59-64.
124 Williams, 'Banten', 63-65; Abdul Haris Nasution, *Sekitar Perang Kemerdekaan Indonesia*, jilid 2, *Diplomasi atau Bertempur*, Disjarah AD & Penerbit Angkasa Bandung 1977, 520-521.
125 Nasution, *Sekitar Perang Kemerdekaan Indonesia*, 522-523.
126 Halwany Michrob and A. Mudjahid Chudari, *Catatan Masa Lalu Banten*, Penerbit Saudara, Serang 1993, 342-347 and 369-370; Matia Madijah, *Kisah Seorang Dokter Gerilya dalam Revolusi Kemerdekaan di Banten*, Penerbit Sinar Harapan, Jakarta 1986, 63-64; Departemen Penerangan, *Propinsi Djawa Barat*, Kementerian Penerangan, Jakarta 1953, 150-151. However, Nasution does mention an order by the resident to release all prisoners, which would have led to many murders in the residency of Serang. Former prisoners also mistreated guards and overseers. Nasution, *Sekitar Perang Kemerdekaan Indonesia*, 522.
127 Transcript of letter from Ed. Franzen to Mr Busselaar 16-02-1948, NL-HaNA, Attorney General of the Supreme Court of the Dutch East Indies, 2.10.17, inv. no. 65.
128 Letter from Ed. Franzen to Mr Busselaar 16-02-1948, NL-HaNA, NEFIS and CMI, 2.10.62, inv. no. 2029; P. Busselaar, report 12-02-1948, NA, 2.10.62, inv. no. 2029.
129 Williams, 'Banten', 65-71; Nasution, *Sekitar Perang Kemerdekaan Indonesia*, 520-525.
130 Anton Lucas, *One soul, one struggle. Region and revolution in Indonesia*. Sydney: Allen & Unwin, 69-70, 95-96, 105-106, 139-140, 182 and 253-254.
131 Report M.R. Vrijens (field office NEFIS Cirebon) 01-08-1947, NL-HaNA, NEFIS and CMI, 2.10.62, inv. no. 2037; Lucas, *One soul*, 140-141. According to Lucas, eleven Van Wijk children were arrested, four of whom escaped.
132 Report M.R. Vrijens (field office NEFIS Cirebon) 01-08-1947, NL-HaNA, NEFIS and CMI, 2.10.62, inv. no. 2037; No author, 'Het drama van Balapoelang. Hoe het recht van een ieder om vrij te leven door de Republiek verkracht werd', in: *Algemeen Indisch Dagblad*, 19-08-1947 ; Lucas, *One struggle*, 141.
133 Anton Lucas, *One soul, one struggle. Region and revolution in Indonesia*. Sydney: Allen & Unwin, 202-213.
134 Harry A. Poeze, 'Walking the tightrope: internal Indonesian conflict, 195-1949', in: Bart Luttikhuis and Dirk A. Moses, eds, *Colonial counterinsurgency and mass violence. The Dutch Empire in Indonesia*, Routledge, London/New York 2014, 176-197, 187.
135 Reid, *The Blood of the People*, 195-197 and 210.
136 Reid, *The Blood of the People*, 198-205.
137 Eric Morris, 'Aceh: social revolution and the Islamic vision', in: Audrey R. Kahin, ed., *Regional dynamics of the Indonesian revolution. Unity from diversity*, University of Hawaii Press, Honolulu 1985, 82-110, here 93-96; Reid, *The Blood of the People*, 207- 211.
138 Reid, *Blood of the people*, 218-227.
139 Michael van Langenberg, 'East Sumatra: accommodating an Indonesian nation within a Sumatran residency', in: Audrey R. Kahin, ed., *Regional dynamics of the Indonesian revolution. Unity from diversity*, University of Hawaii Press, Honolulu 1985, 113-143, here 123-124. Harry A. Poeze, 'Walking the tightrope: internal Indonesian conflict, 1945-1949', in: Bart Luttikhuis and Dirk A. Moses, eds, *Colonial counterinsurgency and mass violence. The Dutch Empire in Indonesia*, Routledge, London/New York 2014, 176-197, here 186-187; Reid, *Blood of the people*, 230-245.
140 Van den Doel, *Afscheid van Indië*, 126-127 and 130-131.
141 No author, 'The Allied occupation of the Netherlands East Indies September 1945–November 1946', no date, National Archives (Kew), 67, WO 203/2681; Cribb, *Gangsters and revolutionaries*, 67; McMillan, *British occupation of Indonesia*, 60-63; Van den Doel, *Afscheid van Indië*, 118.

142 No author, 'The Allied occupation of the Netherlands East Indies September 1945–November 1946', no date, National Archives (Kew), 67, WO 203/2681.
143 Van Delden, *Bersiap in Bandoeng*, 162-164 and 168-170; McMillan, *British occupation*, 67-69.
144 Mary C. van Delden, *De Republikeinse kampen in Nederlands-Indië, oktober 1945–mei 1947. Orde in de chaos?*, self-publication, Kockengen 2007, 293; Wim Willems, *De uittocht uit Indië 1945-1995*, Uitgeverij Bert Bakker, Amsterdam 2001, 28 and 47.
145 Van Delden, *Republikeinse kampen*, 149-150, 305, 311, 331-332.
146 Bart van Poelgeest, 'Figuranten op het Indische toneel. De Japanners in Nederlands-Indië, 1946-1949', in: Elly Touwen-Bouwsma and Petra Groen, *Tussen banzai en bersiap. De afwikkeling van de Tweede Wereldoorlog in Nederlands-Indië*, Sdu Uitgevers, The Hague 1996, 95-107, here 100.
147 Van den Doel, *Afscheid van Indië*, 127-130; Groen, *Marsroutes en dwaalsporen*, 34.
148 William Frederick, 'The killing of Dutch and Eurasians in Indonesia's National Revolution (1945-1949): a "Brief genocide" reconsidered, *Journal of Genocide Research* 14-3/4 (2012), 359-380, here 367-368.
149 Taomo Zhou, *Migration in time of revolution. China, Indonesia and the Cold War*. Ithaca/London: Cornell University Press, 2018; Mary Somers Heidhues, 'Anti-Chinese violence in Java during the Indonesian Revolution, 1945-1949', *Journal of Genocide Research* 14:3-4 (2012) 381-401, 387.
150 Limpach, *De brandende kampongs*, 265-270. For the actions of Westerling and the special forces, see: 270 ff.

7. The organization of Indonesian violence

1 AMW 52, 8/3/14/90, War Diary 2/14 Infantry Battalion October 1945, 19-10-1945.
2 Maarten van der Bent, 'Verslaglegging bersiap in *Het Dagblad*, 23 oktober 1945–30 maart 1946', 01-10-2019; Maarten van der Bent, 'Analyse van *Het Dagblad*, 23 oktober 1945 tot en met 30 maart 1946', 01-10-2019.
3 See for example: Abdul Haris Nasution. *Sekitar Perang Kemerdekaan Indonesia* jilid 2 *Diplomasi atau Bertempur* (Bandung: 1977) 522-523; Andi Mattalatta, *Meniti Siri' dan Harga Diri: Catatan dan Kenangan* (Jakarta 2003) 173 Edisaputra, *Sumatera Dalam Perang Kemerdekaan, Perlawanan Rakyat Semesta Menentang Jepang, Inggris, dan Belanda* (Jakarta 1987) 192.
4 The NEFIS dossiers on the murders in the first months of the Indonesian Revolution can be found in the following, among others: NL-HaNA, NEFIS en CMI, 2.10.62, inv. nos. 2022-2059 and NIOD, Netherlands East Indies Collection (reference number 400), inv. nos. 376-891.
5 Analysis Chrissy Flohr NEFIS- reports 28 July 2021.
6 M.R. Vrijens, Verslag 'Moord op de Europeanen te Tjibatoe', 13-11-1947, NL-HaNA, NEFIS and CMI, 2.10.62, inv. no. 2045; report interview Tojib, drawn up by M.R. Vrijens, 13-11-1947, NL-HaNA, NEFIS and CMI, 2.10.62, inv. no. 2045; 'Lijst der medemoordenaars behoorende bij het rapp. 'TOJIB', NL-HaNA, and CMI, 2.10.62, inv. no. 2045.
7 No author, transcript of excerpt report Intel. & Loyalty survey No. 145, 05-06-1946, NL-HaNA, Attorney General Supreme Court Dutch East Indies, 2.10.17, inv. no. 65.
8 Memorandum Ch.O. van der Plas, 11-11-1945, NL-HaNA, General Secretary of the Netherlands Indies Government, 2.10.14, inv. no. 2988. For other examples of the possible coordination of the killings, see also: statement Shimizu Hitoshi 2-12-1945, 3, NL-HaNA, General Secretary of the Netherlands Indies Government, 2.10.14, inv. no. 2212; report no. 9 by Lieutenant Commander A.J. Leland to Captain E. Tyndale Cooper, 26-12-1945, NIMH, Decolonization of the Dutch East Indies 1945-1950, 509, 509, inv. no. 219; report Ch.O van der Plas, Batavia, 4-10-1945, NL-HaNA, General Secretary of the Netherlands Indies Government, 2.10.14, inv. no. 2988; report no author, Bandung 27-9-1945, NL-HaNA, General Secretary of the Netherlands Indies Government, 2.10.14, inv. no. 2988.
9 Frederick, 'The killing of Dutch and Eurasians', 372; G. Roger Knight, 'Death in Slawi: The "Sugar Factory Murders", Ethnicity, Conflicted Loyalties and the Context of Violence in the Early Revolution in

Indonesia, October 1945', *Itinerario*, 41;3 (2017), 606-626, 618; Robert Cribb, 'The brief genocide of Eurasians in Indonesia, 1945/46', in: A. Dirk Moses, (ed.), *Empire, colony, genocide: Conquest, occupation, and subaltern resistance in world history* (New York/Oxford 2008), 424-439, 425.

10 It is not exactly clear which organization or militia this was. 'Indonesians declare war', in: *Nippon Times*, 15-10-1945, 1; 'Belanda memboesoekan Indonesia dimata internasional', in: *Merah Poetih*, 18-10-1945.
11 'NICA menganiaya Umat Islam, Indonesia' and 'Seruan Umat Islam: Fie Sabielillah', in: *Merdeka*, 12-10-1945.
12 'Soekarno shows up: call cabinet meeting', in: *Nippon Times*, 19-10-1945, 1.
13 No author 'Strategie der "Republiek". Hatta verbiedt de oorlogsterminologie', in: *Nieuwsgier*, 20-10-1945 no. 51, 1.
14 No author, 'Uit het Republikeinsche kamp', in: *Nieuwsgier*, 20-10-1945 no. 51, 4.
15 Transcript letter Sukarno to Philip Christison 9-10-1945, 3-4, NA, 2.10.14, inv. no. 5445; no author (R.B. Quack), Minutes, RAPWI meeting 8-10-1945, NA, 2.10.14, inv. no. 3021.
16 Bussemaker, *Bersiap!*, 130; no author (P.J. Schippers), Minutes RAPWI meeting 6-10-1945, NA, 2.10.14, inv. no. 3021; memorandum M. Klaassen for lieutenant governor general H.J. van Mook, 10-10-1945, NA, 2.10.14, inv. no. 3021; daily report 8-10-1945, NA, 2.10.14, inv. no. 3021.
17 Copy Report by Wing Commander T.S. Tull O.B.E. on operation Salex Mastiff Mid-Java 10 September to 15 December 27-12-1945, 11, NIMH, Decolonization of the Dutch East Indies 1945-1950, 509, inv. no. 220.
18 Van Delden, *Bersiap in Bandoeng*, 110.
19 Chairul Riza, *Radio Pemberontakan dan Perannya dalam Revolusi Kemerdekaan di Surabaya 1945-1947*. Surabaya: Universitas Airlangga, 2006, 48; Suhario Padmodiwiryo, translated by Frank Palmos, *Revolution in the city of heroes. A memoir of the battle that sparked Indonesia's national revolution*, NUS Press, Singapore 2016, 130-131; Bussemaker, *Bersiap!*, 214-215.
20 There were just 4,500 *totoks* among the 46,000. In early October 1945, shortly before the internment began, the majority of *totoks* were still in the former Japanese internment camps. Van Delden, *De Republikeinse kampen*, 149-150.
21 Van Delden, *De Republikeinse kampen*, 152.
22 Van Delden, *De Republikeinse kampen*, 151-152.
23 Bussemaker, *Bersiap!*, 217.
24 Limpach, *De brandende kampongs*, 140.
25 Copy Report no. 1 from Lieutenant Commander A.J. Leland to Captain E. Tyndale Cooper, 3-11-1945, NIMH, Decolonization of the Dutch East Indies 1945-1950, 509, inv. no. 219; Robert Cribb, 'The brief genocide of Eurasians in Indonesia, 1945/46', in: Moses, ed., *Empire, colony, genocide. Conquest, occupation, and subaltern resistance in world history*, Berghahn Books, New York/Oxford 2008, 424-439, 425; Van Delden, *De Republikeinse kampen*, 137-138; J.D. Legge, *Sukarno; A political biography*, Singapore 2003, 232-233.
26 'Soekarno eischt discipline. "Eigenmachtig optreden leidt tot anarchie"', in: *De Nieuwsgier* 31-10-1945 (no. 61), 2.
27 Soetan Sjahrir, *Onze strijd*, Perhimpoenan Indonesia/Vrij Nederland, Amsterdam 1946, 16.
28 Lieutenant colonel L. van der Post, translation of parts of minutes of Indonesian Council of Ministers November and December 1945, 19-12-1945, 2-5, National Archives (Kew), WO 203/5573 South East Asia Command, Netherlands East Indies: administrative and political matters, Dec. 1945.
29 Transcript letter Sukarno to Philip Christison 9-10-1945, 3-4, NA, 2.10.14, inv. no. 5445. Also available in NIB, I, no. 160, 285-290; letter Mohammad Hatta to R.C.M. King, 11-10-1945, NA, 2.10.14, inv. no. 5545.
30 Transcript letter Sukarno to Philip Christison 9-10-1945, 3-4, NA, 2.10.14, inv. no. 5445. in NIB, I, no. 160, 285-290.

31 Letter Mohammad Hatta to R.C.M. King, 11-10-1945, NA, 2.10.14, inv. no. 5545.
32 Foreign Broadcast Intelligence Service, Military Intelligence Division, War Department, Daily reports foreign radio broadcasts Far Eastern section no. 31, 13-2-1946, Southeast Asia, Netherlands East Indies, E2, NIMH, 509, inv. no. 470.
33 Suhario Padmodiwiryo, translated by Frank Palmos, *Revolution in the city of heroes. A memoir of the battle that sparked Indonesia's national revolution*, NUS Press, Singapore 2016, 130-131; Bussemaker, *Bersiap!*, 214-215.
34 Marjolein van Pagee, *Bung Tomo: War Crimimal or Hero? Dutch and Indonesian Views on the Violence in Surabaya 1945*. Leiden: Master's thesis, 2018, 59-60.
35 William Frederick, 'Shadow of an Unseen Hand. Some Patterns of Violence in the Indonesian Revolution, 1945-1949', in: Freek Colombijn and J. Thomas Lindblad (eds), *Roots of Violence in Indonesia. Contemporary Violence in Historical Perspective*. Leiden: KITLV Press, 2002, 143-172, here 150-154.
36 Letter G.H. Evers, head of department II NEFIS, 28-4-1948, NA, (NEFIS) 2.10.62, inv. no 2064; Daily report NEFIS headquarters 20-1-1945 NA, (NEFIS) 2.10.62, inv. no. 2820; Daily report NEFIS headquarters 20-1-1945 NA, (NEFIS) 2.10.62, inv. no. 2820; Collection of papers, received on 2-9-1947 from lt. col. Agerbeek. Presumably from ALI, Kepala Kampong Pasar Baroe, Goenoeng Sahari. NA, NEFIS (2.10.62), inv. no. 5169.
37 Report M.R. Vrijens (field office NEFIS Cirebon) 01-08-1947, NA, 2.10.62, inv. no. 2037.
38 Interrogation Slamet-Depok, drawn up on 12-05-194 by J. v. der Valk (field office NEFIS Semarang), NA, 2.10.17, inv. no. 65. See also: 'Drie doodstraffen wegens moord te Semarang', in: *Het Dagblad*, 28-08-1948.
39 Record of interrogation of Jatin, drawn up by J. van der Valk (field office NEFIS Semarang) 11-05-1946, NA, 2.10.17, inv. no. 65. For the name of the branch of Angkatan Moeda, see: statement by Oei Ing Bing 08-05-1946, attached to report Th.N. Helsloot 09-05-1946, NA, 2.10.17, inv. no. 65.
40 Interrogation Slamet-Depok., drawn up on 12-05-194 by J. v. der Valk (field office NEFIS Semarang), NA, 2.10.17, inv. no. 65.
41 Frederick, *Visions and heat*, 240. Some eyewitness reports, however, ascribe a more active role to the *pemuda*. For example, one of the guards reportedly called out: 'Saudara-saudaran ini ANDJING-NICA' ('Brothers, here are the NICA dogs'). Witness statement A.Ph. de Bruyn, recorded by J.W.F. Meeng, 30-9-1947 NA, 2.10.62, inv. no. 2051.

8. Estimates of casualty numbers

1 Ulbe Bosma, Remco Raben and Wim Willems, *De geschiedenis van de Indische Nederlanders*, Uitgeverij Bert Bakker, Amsterdam 2008, 12.
2 For a more detailed discussion of social divisions during the Dutch colonial period, see chapter 3.
3 Memo Ch.O. van der Plas to Idenburg and Kerstens, 21-12-1945, NA, 2.10.14, inv. no. 2644.
4 Memo Ch.O. van der Plas to Idenburg and Kerstens, 21-12-1945, NA, 2.10.14, inv. no. 2644; Minutes of fifth meeting of the Anglo-Dutch Publicity Committee 22-12-1945, NA, 2.21.266, inv. no. 214.
5 'British push on in Surabaya fight', in: *New York Times*, 16-11-1945.
6 R. de Bruin, Memo 'Opsporingsdienst Overledenen (O.D.O.)', 19-12-1958, NIOD, IC, inv. no. 2458, 1.
7 'O.D.O. een Sociaal Belang. Detective-werk in vaag verleden', in: *Nieuwe Courant*, 20-11-1948. The *Nieuwe Courant* also mentions a branch in Medan, but, according to a statement in the same paper almost a year later by C.D. van der Harst, head of the ODO, this branch never materialized. 'Bezuinigingswee. O.D.O. bijkantoren opgeheven', in: *Nieuwe Courant*, 05-09-1945. The ODOreports in the National Archives of the Netherlands and NIOD only mention investigations in the Indonesian archipelago on Java, Sumatra and Madura, with one exception: an investigation into the murder of American pilots at Una una on Sulawesi (see the archives of NEFIS, access number 2.10.62, inv. no. 2025). There was also an investigative service for the deceased that fell under the Troepencommando Siam/Dutch Military Mission

Bangkok. Under the leadership of the Allied War Graves Unit, this service was charged with tracing the graves of deceased Dutch prisoners of war and establishing war cemeteries in Kanchanaburi and Chungkai. See (the description of the inventory of) the archives of the Troepencommando Siam/Dutch Military Mission Bangkok in the National Archives of the Netherlands in The Hague (reference number 2.13.108).
8   NEFIS archives (reference numbers 2.10.62 and 2.10.37.02) in the National Archives of the Netherlands and the Netherlands East Indies Collection (reference 400) in NIOD.
9   Muhammad Yuanda Zara, *Voluntary participation, state involvement: Indonesian propaganda in the struggle for maintaining independence, 1945-1949*, thesis University of Amsterdam 2016, 183, 185-186 and 189-190.
10 Memo Ch.O. van der Plas to Idenburg and Kerstens, 21-12-1945, NA, 2.10.14, inv. no. 2644; memorandum no author no date, NA, 2.21.266, inv. no. 208; memorandum attached to letter from director of Justice Department to the Minister of Overseas Territories 16-1-1946, NA, 2.10.14, inv. no. 4218, 2.
11 See *Nederlands-Indonesische Betrekkingen*, volume 12, 30, no. 24, note 3, 82, no. 49 note 2, and 110, no. 68, note 1.
12 Code telegram DIRVO to Ministry of Foreign Affairs (Buza), NA, Buza Code archives (2.05.117), inv. no. 22595.
13 H.J. van Mook, *The stakes of democracy in South-east Asia*, Allen & Unwin, London 1950, 210n.
14 L. de Jong, *Het Koninkrijk der Nederlanden in de Tweede Wereldoorlog*, volume 11c, Martinus Nijhoff, Leiden 1986, 598.
15 NIOD, Card collections L. de Jong for *Het Koninkrijk der Nederlanden in de Tweede Wereldoorlog* volume 12, chapter 7; L. de Jong, *Het Koninkrijk der Nederlanden in de Tweede Wereldoorlog*, volume 12, second half, *Epiloog*, Martinus Nijhoff, Leiden 1988, 744-745.
16 L. de Jong, *Het Koninkrijk der Nederlanden in de Tweede Wereldoorlog*, volume 12, second half, *Epiloog*, Martinus Nijhoff, Leiden 1988, 1141-1143.
17 Bussemaker, *Bersiap!*, 342.
18 Herman Bussemaker, 'Bersiap in cijfers', 3 September 2012, at: www.javapost.nl. Bussemaker assumed that there were 50,000 internees; 1 per cent of this is 500. Although he writes that this was an excess mortality rate of 1 per cent over the period November 1945–May 1946, he probably made a mistake here, for that is seven months, not five.
19 Herman Bussemaker, 'Bersiap in cijfers', 3 September 2012, at: www.javapost.nl.
20 Mary C. van Delden, 'Bersiapkampen boden schuilplaats in de chaos', in: *Trouw*, 15-08-2012; Mary van Delden, 'Het Rode Kruis kende de waarheid', 14 September 2012, at: www.javapost.nl.
21 Bert Immerzeel, 'Bersiap: de werkelijke cijfers', 7 February 2014, at: www.javapost.nl.
22 Bert Immerzeel, 'Het vuur van de bersiap', *Java Post*, 24 January 2019, at: www.javapost.nl.
23 Robert, Cribb, 'The brief genocide of Eurasians in Indonesia, 1945/46', in: Moses, ed., *Empire, colony, genocide. Conquest, occupation, and subaltern resistance in world history*, Berghahn Books, New York/Oxford 2008, 424-439, here 436.
24 Okke Norel, *En, ...hoe was het daarbuiten? Buiten de Japanse kampen en in de bersiap (1941-1949). Een te weinig gestelde vraag. Een bibliografie*, self-publication, Winterswijk 2001, 15.
25 William Frederick, 'The killing of Dutch and Eurasians in Indonesia's National Revolution (1945-1949): a "Brief genocide" reconsidered', *Journal of Genocide Research* 14-3/4 (2012), 359-380, here 369.
26 Frederick, 'The killing of Dutch and Eurasians', 368-369.
27 Meindert van der Kaaij, 'De Bersiap: een vergeten golf van etnisch geweld', in: *Trouw*, 18-11-2013.
28 Bert Immerzeel, 'Bersiap: de werkelijke cijfers', 7 February 2014, at: www.javapost.nl
29 The monthly reports by the Deceased Persons Investigation Service from December 1946 and from March 1947 to December 1949 can be found at NIOD, in the Netherlands East Indies Collection (reference number 400), inventory number 892. Remarkably enough, this latter series is complete, with the

exception of the May 1947 report used by William H. Frederick. However, this monthly report can be found in the National Archives of the Netherlands, in the archives of the Attorney General to the Supreme Court of the Dutch East Indies (1936) 1945-1949 (1969) (reference number 2.10.17), inv. no. 65.

30 J. Wetters, 'Verslag van de Opsporingsdienst van Overleden (O.D.O.) over de maand december 1949', NIOD, IC, inv. no. 892.
31 Minister for Overseas Territories J.A. Jonkman, *Handelingen der Tweede Kamer*, 03-02-1948, 1325.
32 'Slachtoffers van extremisten', in: *Nieuwe Courant*, 03-05-1947.
33 Bert Immerzeel, 'Bersiap in cijfers', 3 September 2012, at: www.javapost.nl.
34 Jeroen Kemperman, 'De slachtoffers van de Bersiap, 16 mei 2014', at: www.niod.nl.
35 Robert, Cribb, 'The brief genocide of Eurasians in Indonesia, 1945/46', in: Moses, ed., *Empire, colony, genocide. Conquest, occupation, and subaltern resistance in world history*, Berghahn Books, New York/Oxford 2008, 424-439, here 436.
36 Martin Mennecke, 'Genocide en het internationaal recht', in Barbara Boender and Wichert ten Have (eds), *De holocaust en andere genociden. Een inleiding*, Amsterdam University Press, Amsterdam 2012, 145-162, here 149.
37 William Frederick, 'The killing of Dutch and Eurasians', 376.
38 Remco Raben, 'On genocide and mass violence in colonial Indonesia', in: *Journal of Genocide Research*, (2012) 14:3-4, 485-502, here 492.
39 Raben, 'On genocide', 492 and 499.
40 Raben, 'On genocide', 499.
41 A. Dirk Moses, *The problems of genocide. Permanent security and the language of transgression*, Cambridge University Press, Cambridge 2021.
42 www.oorlogsgravenstichting.nl/geschiedenis
43 For the statutes of the War Graves Foundation, see: https://oorlogsgravenstichting.nl/assets/upload/documenten/Statuten%20OGS%202014(1).pdf.
44 Renske Krimp, *De doden tellen. Slachtofferaantallen van de Tweede Wereldoorlog en sindsdien*, National Committee for 4 and 5 May, Amsterdam 2016, 53-55.
45 For the ODO reports, see the archives of the Netherlands Forces Intelligence Service (NEFIS) (reference number 2.10.62) in the National Archives of the Netherlands and the Netherlands East Indies Collection (reference number 400) at NIOD. Lists of victims' names can also be found in the archives of the General Secretariat (reference number 2.10.14) and the archives of the Attorney General (reference number 2.10.17) in the National Archives of the Netherlands.
46 For a detailed account of the compilation of the file of victims, see the document by Ron Habiboe in the archives of the ODGOI at NIOD.
47 Leo van Bergen, *Een menslievende en nationale taak. Oorlog, kolonialisme en het Rode Kruis in Nederlandsch-Indië 1870-1950*, Soesterberg 2004, 7.
48 The archives of Information Office A of the Red Cross can be found in the National Archives of the Netherlands, under reference number 2.19.286. The correspondence about the fate of persons during the Japanese occupation and the *bersiap* period in Indonesia can be found in inventory numbers 36-39, and the card index boxes with the names of people who went missing and were murdered during the *bersiap* period in the inventory numbers 297-300.
49 For an explanation of the work of the Pelita Foundation, see: www.pelita.nl. For an explanation of war-related acts: Elly Touwen-Bouwsma, *Op zoek naar grenzen. Toepassing en uitvoering van de wetten voor oorlogsslachtoffers*, Amsterdam 2010.
50 The gender is unknown for a significant number of the dead (610), and for a small proportion (27) we know only that they were children.
51 The 1,824 who are likely to have been civilians come from the registered file of the War Graves Foundation, in which a soldier's rank is always mentioned. If no rank is mentioned, we can therefore assume

that the person was a civilian. The breakdown also includes a large group (372) for whom it is not known whether they were soldiers or civilians.

52 No author (Headquarters Japanese 16th Army), 'Document II', 12-12-1945, NIMH, 509, inv. no. 78.
53 Miyamoto Shizuo, *Jawa Shusen Shoriki* (an account of post-war affairs on Java), Jawa Shusen Shoriki Kankokai, Tokyo 1973, 363, as quoted in: W.G.J Remmelink, 'The emergence of the new situation: the Japanese army on Java after the surrender', in: *Militaire Spectator*, volume 148 (1978), 49-66, here 64.
54 Email from J. Snellen van Vollenhoven to Onno Sinke, 04-04-2021. More data may be available at Japan's National Institute for Defence Studies: www.nids.mod.go.jp/english/.
55 S. Woodburn Kirby, *The war against Japan*, V, *The surrender of Japan*, Her Majesty's Stationary Office, London 1969, 544, Appendix 31. McMillan, *British occupation*, 73 mentions slightly different numbers: 620 killed, 1,331 wounded and 402 missing.
56 McMillan, *British occupation*, 73.
57 L. de Jong, *Het Koninkrijk der Nederlanden in de Tweede Wereldoorlog*, 12, second half, *Epiloog*, Martinus Nijhoff, Leiden 1988, 865n; email Jeroen Kemperman (NIOD) to author 17-02-2021.
58 P. Groen, *Marsroutes en dwaalsporen* 262 (attachment 14).
59 Gert Oostindie, *Soldaat in Indonesië 1945-1950. Getuigenissen van een oorlog aan de verkeerde kant van de geschiedenis*, Prometheus, Amsterdam 2015, 26; Rémy Limpach, *De brandende kampongs van generaal Spoor*, Boom, Amsterdam 2016, 57. On p. 766, Limpach discusses the historians who have made crude estimates, potentially of much more than 100,000 or 150,000 fatalities, without mentioning a source.
60 Gert Oostindie, *Soldaat in Indonesië 1945-1950. Getuigenissen van een oorlog aan de verkeerde kant van de geschiedenis*, Prometheus, Amsterdam 2015, 26; Remco Raben, 'Epilogue. On genocide and mass violence in colonial Indonesia', in: Bart Luttikhuis and Dirk A. Moses, eds, *Colonial counterinsurgency and mass violence. The Dutch Empire in Indonesia*, Routledge, London/ New York 2014, 329-347, here 331.
61 Vincent Houben, 'A torn soul. The Dutch public discussion on the colonial past in 1995', in: *Indonesia*, no. 63 (April 1997), 47-66, here 49.
62 Adrian Vickers, *A history of modern Indonesia*, Cambridge University Press, New York 2013, 105.
63 Bussemaker, *Bersiap!*, 330-331.
64 Christiaan Harinck, Nico van Horn and Bart Luttikhuis, 'Wie telt de Indonesische doden? Onze vergeten slachtoffers', in: *De Groene Amsterdammer*, no. 30, 26-07-2017.
65 https://www.kitlv.nl/wp-content/uploads/2017/07/Overzicht-doden-versie-14-juli-2017.pdf
66 https://www.kitlv.nl/wp-content/uploads/2017/07/Overzicht-doden-versie-14-juli-2017.pdf
67 J.P.K. van Eechoud, Political report New Guinea 20-12-1945, 3, NA, 2.10.14, inv. no. 3265.
68 For Java, this concerns the number of people killed by the military on the Dutch side in the period between 11 October 1945 and 28 March 1946, with the exception of December 1945. For Bali/Lombok it concerns the number of victims in the period 1 March-28 March 1946 (the reporting period was from 1 March, but Dutch troops only landed in Bali on 2 March 1946). For Sumatra, it concerns the period between 8 February and 28 March 1946, for Borneo/Kalimantan from 12 January to 28 March 1946. https://www.kitlv.nl/wp-content/uploads/2017/07/Overzicht-doden-versie-14-juli-2017.pdf
69 Ricklefs, *A history of modern Indonesia*, 217.
70 McMillan, *British occupation of Indonesia*, 73.
71 Harry A. Poeze, 'Walking the tightrope: internal Indonesian conflict, 195-1949', in: Bart Luttikhuis and Dirk A. Moses, eds, *Colonial counterinsurgency and mass violence. The Dutch Empire in Indonesia*, Routledge, London/New York 2014, 195.
72 Email Abdul Wahid (Universitas Gadjah Mada) to author, 11-09-2020.
73 Marwati Djoened Poesponegoro and Nugroho Notosusanto, *Sejarah Nasional Indonesia*, IV (4th edition, Jakarta 1993).
74 Marwati Djoened Poesponegoro and Nugroho Notosusanto, *Sejarah Nasional Indonesia*, IV (4th edition, Jakarta 1993), 103-104.

75 Sarita Pawiloy, 'Arus Revolusi di Sulawesi Selatan' (no place 1987), 113 and 318.
76 Hario Kecik, *Pertempuran Surabaya*, Abhiseka Dipantara, Yogyakarta 2012, iii.
77 Hario Kecik, *Pertempuran Surabaya*, Abhiseka Dipantara, Yogyakarta 2012, 59.
78 The Taman Makam Pahlawan fall under the administrative responsibility of the Ministry of Social Affairs (Kementerian Sosial).
79 We are extremely grateful to Ron Habiboe for mapping out the Indonesian sources containing information about the number of Indonesians who died during the war of independence in Indonesia. The following paragraphs on this topic are based on the report that he made on 08-03-2021. This report is in the possession of the authors.
80 The Heroes' Cemeteries, which are spread over the different islands, give the following overview: Sumatra: Aceh (1x), Bengkulu (1x), Jambi (1x), Riau (7x); Sulawesi: West Sulawesi (7x), South Sulawesi (9x), Central Sulawesi (5x), North Sulawesi (1x), Sulawesi Gorontalo (2x); Kalimantan: West Kalimantan (8x), South Kalimantan (1x) and Central Kalimantan (1x); Java: West Java (2x), Yogyakarta (6x), Jakarta (Kalibata, National Heroes' Cemetery). A separate list of the cemeteries mentioned is available. For a number of provinces, no data were included in this overview. This concerns the provinces of Bali, Nusa Tenggara Barat (NTB), Nusa Tenggara Timur (NTT), Maluku, Maluku Utara and Papua. The website concerned was taken down before these data could be recorded. These data may be added later.
81 It should also be noted that the Heroes' Cemetery in Kalibata (Jakarta) also contains the graves of Japanese volunteers who fought on the side of the Indonesian nationalists after the Japanese surrender on 15 August 1945, and lost their lives in the struggle. Kiyoyuki Hatakeyama, Masayasu Hosaka (2004), Rikugun Nakano Gakko Shusen Hishi, Shinchosha, 675-676. https://en.wikipedia.org/wiki/Kalibata_Heroes_Cemetery, consulted on 26-01-2022.
82 The website of the LVRI is available at: www.veteranri.go.id. Of particular importance for additional research is Veteran Anumerta Pejuang Kemerdekaan Republik (the posthumous fighters for the independence of the Republic of Indonesia). These are Indonesians who actively contributed to the Indonesian Revolution, but lost their lives in that period and are registered as recipients of the Tanda Kehormatan Veteran Republik Indonesia (Honours of Veterans of the Republic of Indonesia).
83 Provincial or district (kabupaten) departments: Sumatra (101): Aceh (14x), Noord-Sumatra (23x), West Sumatra (12x), Riau (10x), Riau archipelago (4x), Jambi (6x), Bengkulu (5x), Bangka Belitung (2x), South Sumatra (14x) and Lampung (11x). Java (109): Banten (6x), DKI Jakarta (12x), West Java (21x), Central Java (32x), D.I. Yogyakarta (5x), East Java (33x). Kalimantan (35): East Kalimantan (9x), West Kalimantan (8x), Central Kalimantan (6x) and South Kalimantan (12x). Sulawesi (54): Gorontalo (4x), North Sulawesi (11x), Central Sulawesi (6x), South/West Sulawesi (27x) and Southeast Sulawesi (6x). Moluccas (4), Papua (11), Bali (9), Nusa Tenggara Barat (NTB) (6) and Nusa Tenggara Timur (NTT) (5).
84 Mary Somers Heidhues, 'Anti-Chinese violence in Java during the Indonesian Revolution, 1945-49', in: Bart Luttikhuis and Dirk A. Moses, eds, *Colonial counterinsurgency and mass violence. The Dutch Empire in Indonesia*, Routledge, London/New York 2014, 155-175, here 160-161.
85 Mary Somers Heidhues, 'Anti-Chinese violence in Java during the Indonesian Revolution, 1945-49', in: Bart Luttikhuis and Dirk A. Moses, eds, *Colonial counterinsurgency and mass violence. The Dutch Empire in Indonesia*, Routledge, London/New York 2014, 155-175, here 170. According to her, the violence on Sumatra was worse than that on Java, but complex power relations and ethnic rivalries made it impossible for her to include Sumatra in her article. See 171, note 2.
86 Database bersiap victims ODGO1.
87 Some Sino-Indonesian sources may also contain valuable information on the number and backgrounds of Chinese victims. Following the student association for *peranakan* Chinese students, Chung Hua Hui, founded in 1911, associations were also founded for *peranakan* Chinese at the local level. For example, the Chung Hua Tsung association assembled a team in Batavia to investigate the fate of the Chinese victims during the first Dutch offensive (also known as the first 'Police Action') in 1947. To date, it

is unknown how far these associations have been subsumed into existing (Chinese) organizations and whether relevant data on the *bersiap* period have been preserved in their archives.

88 Tjamboek Berdoeri, 'Indonesia dalem Api dan Bara', (2nd edition; Jakarta 2004), 362-365.
89 Pramudya Ananta Tur, et al., *Kronik Revolusi Indonesia*, Jilid I (1945), (Jakarta 1999), 138.

9. The significance of *bersiap* in the Indonesian War of Independence

1   L. de Jong, *Het Koninkrijk der Nederlanden in de Tweede Wereldoorlog, Epilogue (second half)*. The Hague; Sdu, 1988, 728.
2   Letter Tj. De Cock Buning, 19-9-1946, NA, 2.10.37.02, inv. no. 14.
3   *De Excessennota: nota betreffende het archiefonderzoek naar de gegevens omtrent excessen in Indonesië begaan door Nederlandse militairen in de periode 1945-1950. Ingeleid door Jan Bank*. The Hague, Sdu, 1995, appendix 7, III-1. See also: Letter W.L.G. Lemaire to head of the Government Information Service, 1-8-1946, NA, 2.10.37.02, inv. no. 14.
4   *De Excessennota: nota betreffende het archiefonderzoek naar de gegevens omtrent excessen in Indonesië begaan door Nederlandse militairen in de periode 1945-1950. Ingeleid door Jan Bank*. The Hague, Sdu, 1995 (1st edition 1969), appendix 7, III-1.
5   There were also cases of soldiers taking revenge on Indonesians after their wives were murdered. They included Sergeant Vrijens of NEFIS; see letter from the attorney general to the Supreme Court of the Dutch East Indies to Th. van der Laan, the representative of the attorney general at RECOMBA, 12-8-1947, NA, 2.10.17, inv. no. 65. Sometimes no penalty was imposed: see NA 2.10.58, inv. no. 2613.
6   Rémy Limpach, *De brandende kampongs van Generaal Spoor*. Amsterdam: Boom, 2016, 68-69.
7   Florence Imandt, *'De onverbloemde waarheid'? Interne legervoorlichting met betrekking tot Indonesië 1945-1950, en de relatie met moreel*. Doctoral thesis in Social History, Erasmus University Rotterdam, 1988, 56.
8   Our thanks to Jonathan Verwey, head of the expert centre at Museum Bronbeek, email 18 March 2020.
9   Florence Imandt, *'De onverbloemde waarheid'? Interne legervoorlichting met betrekking tot Indonesië 1945-1950, en de relatie met moreel*. Doctoral thesis in Social History, Erasmus University Rotterdam, 1988, 32.
10 J.A.A. van Doorn, *Gevangen in de tijd. Over generaties en hun geschiedenis*. Amsterdam: Boom, 2002, 32.
11 J.A.A. van Doorn, *Gevangen in de tijd. Over generaties en hun geschiedenis*. Amsterdam: Boom, 2002, 32-33.
12 Rémy Limpach, *De brandende kampongs van Generaal Spoor*. Amsterdam: Boom, 2016, 127.
13 Wim Willems, *Tjalie Robinson. Biografie van een Indo-schrijver*. Amsterdam: Bert Bakker, 2008, 201; Lilian Ducelle, *'Doe maar gewoon, dan doe je al Indisch genoeg'. Het journalistieke werk van Lilian Ducelle, bezorgd en ingeleid door Marjolein van Asdonck*. Amersfoort: Moesson, 2008, 138.
14 *Wapenbroeders* is available online at: https://www.indiegangers.nl/index.php/digiboek/category/45-wp.
15 Our thanks to Jonathan Verwey, head of the centre of expertise at Museum Bronbeek, email exchange between 1 and 18 March 2020, 19 January 2021 and 30 January 2022.
16 In October 1945, *Pen Gun* (published 1945-1946) had a print run of 140,000 copies, of which 80,000 were military subscriptions and 60,000 copies for private sale. See: Florence Imandt, *'De onverbloemde waarheid'? Interne legervoorlichting met betrekking tot Indonesië 1945-1950, en de relatie met moreel*. Rotterdam: doctoral thesis Erasmus Universiteit Rotterdam, 1988, 64.
17 E.H. s'Jacob, 'Om de eenheid van het koninkrijk. Onze opdracht eischt ervaring, behoedzaamheid en beleid', in: *Pen Gun*, 11 April 1946.
18 H.L., 'Nederland en de Japanse erfenis', in: *Pen Gun*, 22 August 1946.
19 E.H. s'Jacob, 'Tekort aan onderscheidingsvermogen. Nederland heeft in den Archipel zijn taak – maar ook zijn historisch recht', in: *Pen Gun*, 2 November 1945.

20 E.H. s'Jacob, 'Een zuiveringsactie en haar aspecten', in: *Pen Gun*, 1 March 1946.
21 Email from Jonathan Verwey, 1 March 2021.
22 Rémy Limpach, *De brandende kampongs van Generaal Spoor*. Amsterdam: Boom, 2016, 611. See also, for example, *De Klewang*, vignette with the weekly list of the fallen.
23 Rémy Limpach, *De brandende kampongs van Generaal Spoor*. Amsterdam: Boom, 2016, 592. Louis Zweers, *De gecensureerde oorlog. Militairen versus media in Nederlands-Indië 1945-1949*. Zutphen: Walburg Pers 2013.
24 On this, see also the forthcoming study: Esther Zwinkels, *De klewang van vrouwe Justitia*. Amsterdam: AUP, 2022.
25 J.A. de Moor, Generaal Spoor. *Triomf en tragiek van een legercommandant*. Amsterdam: Boom, 2011, 142-143.
26 J.A. de Moor, Generaal Spoor. *Triomf en tragiek van een legercommandant*. Amsterdam: Boom, 2011, 163.
27 J.A. de Moor, Generaal Spoor. *Triomf en tragiek van een legercommandant*. Amsterdam: Boom, 2011, 192.
28 J.A. de Moor, Generaal Spoor. *Triomf en tragiek van een legercommandant*. Amsterdam: Boom, 2011, 196.
29 P.M.H. Groen, *Marsroutes en dwaalsporen. Het Nederlands militair-strategisch beleid in Indonesië 1945-1950*. The Hague: Sdu, 1991, 52.
30 Photo Minahassa (North Sulawesi): Image database WWII – NIOD 52386, photo Timor: Image database WWII – NIOD 56405.
31 On 30 March 1946, the RVD issued a memorandum in which it analysed the information situation in Indonesia and set out its long-term vision. See: A.C.M. Houwer, *Propaganda en politiek. De regeringsvoorlichtingsdienst in Nederlands-Indië 1945-1950*. Utrecht: doctoral thesis, Utrecht University: 1986, 15, 20.
32 A.C.M. Houwer, *Propaganda en politiek. De regeringsvoorlichtingsdienst in Nederlands-Indië 1945-1950*. Utrecht: doctoral thesis, Utrecht University: 1986, 21.
33 Johan Fabricius, *Hoe ik Indië terugvond*. The Hague: Leopolds, 1947, 12.
34 Johan Fabricius, *Hoe ik Indië terugvond*. The Hague: Leopolds, 1947, 12.
35 Johan Fabricius, *Hoe ik Indië terugvond*. The Hague: Leopolds, 1947, 46.
36 Rosihan Anwar, *Sejarah Kecil 'Petite Histoire' Indonesia*. Jakarta: Penerbit Buku Kompas, 2015, 27-35.
37 Johan Fabricius, *Hoe ik Indië terugvond*. The Hague: Leopolds, 1947, 47.
38 Louis Zweers, *De gecensureerde oorlog. Militairen versus media in Nederlands-Indië 1945-1950*. Zutphen: Walburg Pers, 2013, 182.
39 J.A. Stevens and Ben Grevendamme, *Vrij*. Deventer: De IJsel, 1946, 13. The book contains texts based on letters written by Ben Grevedamme.
40 Alfred van Sprang, *En Soekarno lacht..!* The Hague: W. van Hoeve 1946, 20.
41 Depher – radio bulletins, consulted on 8 October 2021. The search term 'terror' could also relate to other events, in the Netherlands or elsewhere.
42 Alfred van Sprang, *En Soekarno lacht..!* The Hague: W. van Hoeve 1946, 73.
43 Johan Fabricius, *Hoe ik Indië terugvond*. The Hague: Leopolds, 1947, 118.
44 René Kok, Erik Somers, Louis Zweers, *Koloniale oorlog 1945-1949. Van Indië naar Indonesië*. Amsterdam: Carrera, 2015, 14-15.
45 NA, 2.21.266, inv. no. 214, minutes of twelfth meeting of the Anglo-Dutch Publicity Committee, 9-3-1946.
46 Louis Zweers, *De gecensureerde oorlog. Militairen versus media in Nederlands-Indië 1945-1950*. Zutphen: Walburg Pers, 2013, 186.
47 Gerda Jansen Hendriks, *Een voorbeeldige kolonie. Nederlands-Indië in 50 jaar overheidsfilms, 1912-1962*. Amsterdam: University of Amsterdam, 2016, 239.

48 Gerda Jansen Hendriks, *Een voorbeeldige kolonie. Nederlands-Indië in 50 jaar overheidsfilms, 1912-1962*. Amsterdam: University of Amsterdam, 2016, 214.
49 On the one hand, this can be explained by the fact that they were in a majority compared to the personnel of the Royal Navy (Koninklijke Marine, KM) and the Royal Netherlands East Indies Army (Koninklijk Nederlands-Indisch Leger, KNIL); and, on the other hand, because of their new experiences, they were more inclined to record what they had gone through in a diary than KNIL-servicemen. Literacy rates also played a role. Memoirs, correspondence and published diaries are not included in the NIMH Diaries Project.
50 Henrike Vellinga, 'Wij hadden daar een historische verantwoordelijkheid': de Bersiap-periode (1945-1946) in memoires en dagboeken van Nederlandse militairen, thesis Leiden University 2020.
51 See appendix 1, with thanks to Thirza van Hofwegen.
52 Report Thirza van der Hofwegen, 'Trefwoorden NIMH en KITLV databases', 2021.
53 Jot Polmans, *De brutale reis. De eerste tocht naar een nieuwe wereld*. Meppel: Roelofs van Goor, 1947, 47.
54 In the period between the end of 1945 and the end of 1949, two servicemen used this term. On 11 December 1946, C.W. van Bijsterveld of the 3-9 RI company (West Java) wrote about a prisoner who had been a member of a *laskar rakjat* (people's militia), who had said that he had been called to action with the 'code signal Bersiap'. On 20 April 1949, H. van der Sluis from the 1-2 RVA company (West Java) wrote that a wanted murderer from the *bersiap* period had been captured. NIMH Diaries Project 'Dutch military personnel in Indonesia 1945-1949', quote from: Nederlands Instituut voor Militaire Historie (NIMH), The Hague, 509, inv. no. 1292, Diary C.W. van Bijsterveld, 11 December 1946; NIMH, 545, inv. no. 135, Diary H. Van der Sluis, 20 April 1949.
55 The paper was edited by Willem Belonje, who was critical of the nationalists' striving for independence on the grounds that Indonesians were far capable of standing on their own two feet. Before the war, Belonje had been the editor-in-chief of *Het Nieuws van den Dag voor Nederlandsch-Indië* (1938-1942), and before that, editor-in-chief of the *Indische Courant* (1925-1936). The anti-Republican course he pursued with *Het Dagblad*, a government-financed newspaper, got him into trouble with Lieutenant Governor General Van Mook, who was seeking a rapprochement with the Indonesian nationalists. In early May 1946, Belonje was fired. He returned to the Netherlands, where he worked for a lobbying group, the Nationaal Comité Handhaving Rijkseenheid (the national committee for the preservation of national unity). See: Gerard Termorshuizen and Anneke Scholte, 'Realisten en reactionairen. Een geschiedenis van de Indisch-Nederlandse pers, 1905-1942', in: G.P.A. Termorshuizen, *Tropenstijl. Amusement en verstrooiing in de (post)koloniale pers*. Leiden: KITLV Press, 2011, 541-545.
56 *Het Dagblad*, 21 January 1946.
57 *Het Dagblad*, 23 October 1945.
58 The column 'De eindelooze rij' appeared in *Het Dagblad* on 3, 4, 5, 8, 10, 14 and 17 December 1945 and on 3 January 1946.
59 *Het Dagblad*, 18 February 1946.
60 *Het Dagblad*, 22 February 1946.
61 Research report Maarten van der Bent, 'Verslaglegging bersiap in *Het Dagblad*, 23 oktober 1945 tot en met 30 maart 1946', 2019.
62 *Het Dagblad*, 8 February 1946.
63 'There are also the rumours about *pemuda* concentrations in the East and in the South of the Indonesian part of the city [Bandung]. More to the South, further away from the demarcation line, in the vicinity of Sitoenaeur and Tegallega, people urge each other on with "bersiap"'; in: *Het Dagblad*, 16 February 1946.
64 *Algemeen Indisch Dagblad*, 10 September 1947.
65 *Nieuwe Courant*, first post-war edition on Delpher (www.delpher.nl): 19 January 1946; *De Preangerbode*, first post-war edition on Delpher: 2 January 1947; *De Locomotief: Samarangsch handels- en advertentie-blad*, first post-war edition on Delpher: 2 September 1947; *Het Nieuwsblad voor Sumatra*, first

post-war edition on Delpher: 1 July 1948; *Java-Bode: nieuws, handels- en advertentieblad voor Nederlandsch-Indië*, first post-war edition on Delpher: 24 September 1949.
66   *Het Dagblad*, 16 November 1946.
67   An analysis of Dutch-language digitized papers that were published in Indonesia between 17 August 1945 and 27 December 1949, included in the Delpher database of Dutch newspapers, books and journals, reference date 10 October 2021. Although many newspapers that were published in Indonesia in this period are included in Delpher, the database is far from complete. The project is ongoing and new scans are being added, meaning that the numbers are dynamic.
68   In: *Het Dagblad* (Jakarta) on 26 and 29 April 1947; see also: *Algemeen Indisch Dagblad* (Bandung), 2 May 1947; *Nieuwe Courant* (Surabaya), 6 May 1947; *Provinciale Drentsche en Asser Courant* (Assen), 8 May 1947.
69   *De Standaard* (Amsterdam), 26 July 1947.
70   *Nieuwe Apeldoornsche Courant* (Apeldoorn), 23 August 1947.
71   *Het Dagblad* (Jakarta), 27 February 1948.
72   *Nieuw Nederland* (Amsterdam), 13 January 1949.
73   *De Maasbode* (Rotterdam), 18 December 1948.
74   Louis Zweers, *De gecensureerde oorlog. Militairen versus media in Nederlands-Indië 1945-1950*. Zutphen: Walburg Pers, 2013, 223.
75   *De Telegraaf* (Amsterdam), 11 November 1949.
76   *Het Parool* (Amsterdam), 9 December 1949.
77   *De Volkskrant* (Amsterdam), 10 November 1949.
78   *De Telegraaf* (Amsterdam), 8 November 1949.
79   *Het Nieuwsblad van het Zuiden* (Tilburg), 21 December 1949.
80   *Algemeen Handelsblad* (Amsterdam), 24 December 1949.
81   *De Nieuwe Courant* (Surabaya), 21 December 1949.
82   *De Nieuwe Courant* (Surabaya), 24 December 1949.
83   *De Locomotief* (Semarang), 5 December 1949.
84   *Merah-Poetih*, 27 October 1945. With thanks to Muhammad Anda Zara for the details on Indonesian papers during the revolution.
85   'Kita hidoep didjaman repoloesie-darah' (old spelling), in: *Gelora Rakjat*, 30 March 1946.
86   'Mereka jang tidak koeasa menenangkan hatinja, pasti akan menderita kesoelitan dan kesoekaran dalam djaman pantjaroba ini!' (old spelling), in: *Gelora Rakjat*, 30 March 1946.
87   NIMH database, Diary Project Dutch military personnel in Indonesia 1945-1949.

Conclusions

1   NIOD Netherlands East Indies Collection 401, Indies diaries inventory number 176: diary of J.J.C.H. van Waardenburg, Bangkinang camp, Padang, Central Sumatra, 221. The precise date of this diary entry is not mentioned.
2   NIOD Netherlands East Indies Collection 401, Indies diaries inventory number 57, diary of Mieke van Hoogstraten, Halmaheira camp, Semarang, Central Java, 29 August 1945.
3   Herman Bussemaker, *Bersiap! Opstand in het paradijs. De Bersiap-periode op Java en Sumatra 1945-1946*. Zutphen: Walburg Pers, 2005, 18.
4   Remco Raben and Peter Romijn, *Talen van geweld. Stilte, informatie en misleiding in de Indonesische onafhankelijkheidsstrijd 1945-1949*. Amsterdam: AUP, to be published in mid-2022.
5   Peter Romijn, *De lange Tweede Wereldoorlog. Nederland 1940-1949*. Amsterdam: Balans, 2020; C.J. Lammers, *Vreemde overheersing. Bezetting en bezetten in sociologisch perspectief*. Amsterdam: Bert Bakker, 2005.

Epilogue – The resonance of the sound of violence

1 Hans Moll, *Sluipschutters in de tuin. Een Indische geschiedenis*. Zutphen: Walburg Pers, 2022, 170.
2 Bonnie Triyana, 'Schrap de term "Bersiap" want die is racistisch', in: NRC, 10 January 2022; Michiel Maas, 'Het Indonesische geweld kwam niet uit de lucht vallen', in: *de Volkskrant*, 15 January 2022.
3 House of Representatives, report 2022Z00031; for complaints filed against Rijksmuseum Amsterdam by the Federation of Dutch Indos (Federatie Indische Nederland, FIN), see https://www.federatie-indo.nl/22-01-11/, consulted on 30 January 2022; for complaints by foundation KUKB, see https://kukb.nl/artikelen/stichting-k-u-k-b-doet-aangifte-tegen-het-rijksmuseum, consulted on 30 January 2022.
4 Aboeprijadi Santoso, '"Bersiap": negeren van het Nederlandse kolonialisme', in: *Jakarta Post*, 20 January 2022, see: https://javapost.nl/2022/01/23/bersiap-negeren-van-het-nederlandse-kolonialisme, consulted on 30 January 2022. Historian Abdul Wahid had focused on *bersiap* back in 2013: Abdul Wahid, 'The untold story of the Surabaya battle of 1945', in: *Jakarta Post*, 12 November 2013.
5 Jolande Withuis, *Erkenning. Van oorlogstrauma naar klaagcultuur*. Amsterdam: De Bezige Bij, 2002.
6 Elly Touwen-Bouwsma, *Op zoek naar grenzen. Toepassing en uitvoering van de wetten voor oorlogsslachtoffers*. Amsterdam: Boom, 2010, 193.
7 Amber Vosveld, *De Vereniging Kinderen uit de Japanse Bezetting en Bersiap 1941-1949*. Amsterdam: dissertation, University of Amsterdam, 2008.
8 L. de Jong, *Het Koninkrijk der Nederlanden in de Tweede Wereldoorlog*, Epilogue (second half). The Hague; Sdu, 1988, 718.
9 L. de Jong, *Het Koninkrijk der Nederlanden in de Tweede Wereldoorlog*, 12c, second half, Epilogue, Leiden: Martinus Nijhoff, 1988, 1016. In a footnote, De Jong refers to the *Excessennota*, appendix 5, 6 and 7.
10 L. de Jong, *Het Koninkrijk der Nederlanden in de Tweede Wereldoorlog*, 12c, second half, Epilogue, Leiden: Martinus Nijhoff, 1988, 1032. In a footnote, De Jong refers to Van Doorn and Hendrix, *Ontsporing van geweld*, 253.
11 Pieter Lagrou, 'Loe de Jong, of de professionele strategieën van een publieke intellectueel in Koude Oorlogstijd', in: *BMGN – Low Countries Historical Review*, vol. 130, no. 3, 2015, 79-90 (82).
12 Mary van Delden, *Bersiap in Bandoeng; een onderzoek naar geweld in de periode van 17 augustus 1945 tot 24 maart 1946*. Kockengen: self-publication, 1989.
13 Esther Captain, *Achter het kawat was Nederland. Indische oorlogservaringen en -herinneringen 1942-1995*. Kampen: Kok, 2002.
14 The database of the KITLV was consulted for this, which consists of 659 published egodocuments, written by 1,362 military personnel from the Royal Netherlands Army (Koninklijke Landmacht, KL), the Royal Navy (Koninklijke Marine, KM) and the Royal Netherlands East Indies Army (Koninklijk Nederlands-Indisch Leger, KNIL). The KNIL (and thereby Indonesian servicemen) is very underrepresented in this corpus. See: Gert Oostindie, *Soldaat in Indonesië 1945-1950. Getuigenissen van een oorlog aan de verkeerde kant van de geschiedenis*. Amsterdam: Prometheus, 2015, 311. For the most recent list: https://www.kitlv.nl/wp-content/uploads/2020/01/Lijst-met-gepubliceerde-egodocumenten-Indieveteranen-7-januari-2020.pdf.
15 M. de Jonge, *Mijn Ruiters. Ervaringen als commandant van het 4e Eskadron Pantserwagens Huzaren van Boreel tijdens de politionele acties (1947-1949) in toenmalig Nederlands-Indië*. Zierikzee: foundation Cultureel Erfgoed De Jonge, 2008, 38.
16 Henrike Vellinga, *'Wij hadden daar een historische verantwoordelijkheid': de Bersiap-periode (1945-1946) in memoires en dagboeken van Nederlandse militairen*, dissertation Leiden University 2020, 8.
17 Henrike Vellinga, *'Wij hadden daar een historische verantwoordelijkheid': de Bersiap-periode (1945-1946) in memoires en dagboeken van Nederlandse militairen*, dissertation Leiden University 2020, 7.
18 F.C. Hazekamp, *Twee broers, twee luitenants in Indië. Verslag van de militaire diensttijd van de broers Ted en Frans Hazekamp in Engeland en Nederlands Oost-Indië*. No place, no publisher, 2008, 50.

19 They include the multimedia project 'Archief van tranen [archive of tears]' by Pia van der Molen, see: https://pia-media.nl/projecten/archief-van-tranen-project/, consulted on 15 June 2021; the documentary 'Buitenkampers' of 2013 by director Hetty Naaijkens-Retel Helmrich drew 10,000 paying cinema-goers.

List of abbreviations

Abbreviation	Dutch/Indonesian	English
Aneta	*Algemeen Nieuws- en Telegraaf-Agentschap*	General News and Telegraph Agency
ANP	*Algemeen Nederlands Persbureau*	General Netherlands News Agency
API	*Angkatan Pemuda Indonesia*	Indonesian Young Generation
ARP	*Anti Revolutionaire Partij*	Anti-Revolutionary Party
BBC		British Broadcasting Corporation
BKK	*Buitenkampkinderen*	Children who spent the war outside the internment camps
BKR	*Badan Keamanan Rakyat*	People's Security Agency, 22 August–5 October 1945
BNS	*Bevelhebber Nederlandse Strijdkrachten*	Commander of the Dutch Armed Forces
CHU	*Christelijk Historische Unie*	Christian Historical Union
CONICA		Commanding Officer Netherlands Indies Civil Administration

CPN	*Communistische Partij Nederland*	Communist Party of the Netherlands
DLC	*Dienst voor Legercontacten*	Army Contacts Service
ELS	*Europeesche Lagere School*	European Elementary School
FIN	*Federatie Indische Nederlanders*	Federation of Dutch Indos
GKI	*Gerakan Pramuka Indonesia*	Scouting movement of Indonesia
Grayak	*Grayan Rakyat*	People's Movement
GBP3D	*Gabungan Badan Perjuangan Tiga Daerah*	Federation of Resistance Organizations of the Three Regions
HCS	*Hollandsch Chineesche School*	Dutch Chinese School
HIS	*Hollandsch-Inlandsche School*	Dutch School for Natives
HVK	*Hoge Vertegenwoordiger van de Kroon*	High Representative of the Crown
IEV	*Indo-Europeesch Verbond*	Indo-European Alliance
INOG	*Indische Naoorlogse Generatie*	Indo-Dutch Post-war Generation
IPPHOS		Indonesia Press Photo Services
IV	*Indische Vorming*	Indies training
IVG	*Inlichtingen- en Veiligheidsgroepen*	Intelligence and Security Groups
IIB	*Indisch Instructie Bataljon*	Indies Instruction Battalion
KDC	*Katholiek Documentatie Centrum*	Catholic Documentation Centre
KITLV	*Koninklijk Instituut voor de Taal-, Land- en Volkenkunde*	Royal Netherlands Institute of Southeast Asian and Caribbean Studies
KJBB	*Kinderen uit de Japanse Bezetting en Bersiap 1941-1949*	Children of the Japanese Occupation and *Bersiap* 1941-1949
KBBI	*Kamus Besar Bahasa Indonesia*	Great Dictionary of the Indonesian Language
KL	*Koninklijke Landmacht*	Royal Netherlands Army
KM	*Koninklijke Marine*	Royal Netherlands Navy
KMM	*KomMissie Memoires*	Memoirs archive, Catholic Documentation Centre
KNI	*Komité Nasional Indonesia*	Indonesian National Committee
KNIL	*Koninklijk Nederlands-Indisch Leger*	Royal Netherlands East Indies Army
KNIP	*Komité Nasional Indonesia Pusat*	Central Indonesian National Committee

KNP	*Katholieke Nationale Partij*	Catholic National Party
KVP	*Katholieke Volkspartij*	Catholic People's Party
KUKB	*Komite Utang Kehormatan Belanda*	Committee of Dutch Debts of Honour
LSK	*Luchtstrijdkrachten*	Airborne Forces
LVD	*Legervoorlichtingsdienst*	Army Information Service
LVRI	*Legiun Veteran Republik Indonesia*	Veterans' Legion of the Republic of Indonesia
MP	*Militaire Politie*	Military Police
NA	*Nationaal Archief*	National Archives of the Netherlands
NEFIS		Netherlands East Indies Forces Intelligence Service
NICA		Netherlands Indies Civil Administration
NIMH	*Nederlands Instituut voor Militaire Historie*	Netherlands Institute for Military History
NIOD	*Nederlands Instituut voor Oorlogs-, Holocaust- en Genocidestudies*	NIOD Institute for War, Holocaust and Genocide Studies
NPO	*Nederlandse Padvinders Organisatie*	Netherlands Scouting Organization
ODGOI	*Onafhankelijkheid, Dekolonisatie, Geweld en Oorlog in Indonesië*	Independence, Decolonization, Violence and War in Indonesia
ODO	*Opsporingsdienst van Overledenen*	Investigation Service for the Deceased
OVW	*Oorlogsvrijwilliger*	War Volunteer
Parindra	*Partai Indonesia Raya*	Great Indonesia Party
PETA	*(Sukerela Tentara) Pembela Tanah Air*	Volunteer Defenders of the Homeland
PID	*Politieke Inlichtingendienst*	Political Intelligence Service
PKI	*Partai Komunis Indonesia*	Communist Party of Indonesia
PKO	*Pendjaga Keamanan Oemoem*	Public Security Guard
PNI	*Partai Nasional Indonesia*	Indonesian National Party
PNI (new PNI)	*Pendidikan Nasional Indonesia*	Indonesian National Education
Putera	*Pusat Tenaga Rakjat*	Centre of the People's Power
PvdA	*Partij van de Arbeid*	Labour Party
PvdV	*Partij van de Vrijheid*	Freedom Party

RAPWI		Recovery of Allied Prisoners of War and Internees
RI	*Republik Indonesia*	Republic of Indonesia
RI	*Regiment Infanterie*	Infantry Regiment
RIOD	*Rijksinstituut voor Oorlogsdocumentatie*	National Institute for War Documentation
RIS	*Republik Indonesia Serikat*	United States of Indonesia
RT	*Rukun Tetangga*	Neighbourhood association
RTC		Round Table Conference
RVD	*Regeringsvoorlichtingsdienst*	Government Information Service
RW	*Rukun Warga*	Civic association
SACSEA		Supreme Allied Commander South East Asia
SI	*Sarekat Islam*	Islamic Union
SMGI	*Stichting Mondelinge Geschiedschrijving Indonesië*	Foundation for the Oral Historiography of Indonesia
TNI	*Tentara Nasional Indonesië*	Indonesian National Armed Forces
TKR	*Tentara Keamanan Rakyat*	People's Security Army, 5 October 1945–1 January 1946
VARA	*Vereeniging van Arbeiders Radio Amateurs*	Association of Worker Radio Amateurs
UN		United Nations
VSI	*Verenigde Staten van Indonesië*	United States of Indonesia
VP	*Veldpolitie*	Field Police
Wubo	*Wet uitkeringen burger-oorlogsslachtoffers*	Benefit Act for Civilian War Victims

Glossary

adat	tradition, lore
anjing	dog
anjing Jepang	Japanese dog (derogatory)
arit	sickle, grass-cutter
asrama	lodging, hostel
Asrama Angkatan Baru Indonesia	Asrama of the New Generation Indonesia
Asrama Indonesia Merdeka	Independent Indonesia Asrama
badan perjuangan	armed group
bambu runcing	bamboo spear
barang	luggage, goods
barisan	troop, armed group, corps
Barisan Pelopor	Vanguard Corps
Barisan Soekarela	Volunteer Corps
Barisan Wanita	Women's Corps
bergolak	turmoil
Boedi Oetomo	'Prime Philosophy'
bunuh	kill, murder, do away with
camat	deputy district head

Departemen Pendidikan dan Kebudayan	Ministry of Education and Culture
dessa	village
dewan rakyat	people's council
gadis-gadis penghibur	comfort girl
Gakutotai (Japanese)	Student corps
Gabungan Badan Perjuangan Tiga Daerah	Federation of Resistance Organizations of the Three Regions
gang	alley, narrow street
gedek	fence (bamboo)
gedoran	bang, knock (on door)
geger (Javanese)	commotion
Gerakan Pramuka Indonesia	Indonesian scouting movement
geledah	search
Hari Proklamasi	Proclamation Day
heiho (Japanese)	Indonesian auxiliary, in Japanese service
Hizbullah	Party of Allah
ibukota	capital city
Indonesia dalam arus sejarah	Indonesia through the course of history
jaman (zaman)	era
- Jaman Bersiap	*Bersiap* era
jawara	gang leader
jugun ianfu (Japanese)	comfort girl
kali	river
kampong	district, neighbourhood
Kamus Besar Bahasa Indonesia	Great Dictionary of the Indonesian Language
kedaulatan rakyat	sovereignty of the people
Kempeitai (Japanese)	Japanese military police
golok	Javanese cleaver (machete)
kongsi	club, union
kyai	teacher, (Islamic) spiritual leader
laskar	militia
- rakyat	people's militia
lurah	village head, mayor
markas (besar)	(head)quarters
masa	time, period
- masa bersiap	*Bersiap* period

-masa damai	peacetime
-masa pancaroba	transition, era of transition
-masa perang	wartime
menggedor	looting
merah-putih	red and white (Indonesian flag)
merdeka	independent, free
muezzin	caller to prayer
musuh (moesoeh)	enemy
padi	rice (plant)
pangreh praja	Indonesian administrator
pasar	market
Partai Indonesia Raya	Great Indonesia Party
pejuang	freedom fighter
pemuda	youngster, young Indonesian fighter
-muda	young
perang	war
- perang diplomasi	diplomatic war
- perang fisik	physical war
peranakan	child of the nation; Chinese period born in Indonesia/Indies
pergerakan	movement (nationalism)
Perhimpoenan Indonesia	Indonesian Association
pribumi kotor	'dirty native' (derogatory)
pusaka	heirloom
- k(e)ris pusaka	family dagger (passed from generation to generation)
Raden Mas	Javanese noble title: man of rank
Rakyat (Rakjat, Rayat)	people
rampok	robber
perampokan	plundering
revolusi fisik	physical revolution
revolusi sosial	social revolution
romo (Javanese)	pastor, clergyman
romusha (Japanese)	forced labourer
Rukun Tetangga (rt)	neighbourhood association
Rukun Kampung (rw)	district association
Sejarah Nasional Indonesia	National History of Indonesia
siap	ready, prepared

~siaga	ready for action
slof	flip-flop, sandal
Tamam Makam Pahlawan	Military cemetery for (national) heroes
tani	farmer
tempo dulu (doeloe)	good old days
cincang (tjingtjangen)	to chop into pieces, butcher
totok	European of Dutch origin (lit. pure, pure-blood, thoroughbred)
tong	'bong' (onomatopoeia)
tongtong	drum to sound alarm, signal
ulama	(Islamic) spiritual leader
wedana	district head on Java, administrative offices

Sources

LITERATURE

Adams, Cindy, *Sukarno. An autobiography. As told to Cindy Adams*. The Bobbs-Merrill Company, Inc, Indianapolis/Kansas City/New York 1965.

Anderson, Benedict, *Java in a time of revolution. Occupation and resistance 1944-1946*. Cornell University Press: Ithaca and London 1972.

Andréfouët, Serge, Mégane Paul, A. Riza Farhan, 'Indonesia's 13558 islands: A new census from space and a first step towards a One Map for Small Islands Policy' in: *Marine Policy*, vol. 135, 2022.

Anwar, Idwar and Andi Nur Fitri, *Ensiklopedi Sejarah Luwu*. Komunitas Kampung Sawrigading & Pemkot Kab. Luwu, Palopo 2005.

Anwar, Rosihan, *Sejarah Kecil 'Petite Histoire' Indonesia*. Jakarta: Penerbit Buku Kompas, 2015.

Baay, Reggie, *Het kind met de Japanse ogen*. Amsterdam: Arbeiderspers, 2018.

Basry, Hassan, *Kisah Gerila Kalimantan Dalam Revolusi Indonesia 1945-1949*, Bandjarmasin 1961.

Beekhuis, Henk, Herman Bussemaker, Paula de Haas and Ton Lutter, *Geïllustreerde Atlas van de Bersiapkampen in Nederlands-Indië, 1945-1947*. Bedum: Profiel, 2009.

Beets, Gijs, *Demografische aspecten van de bevolking van Nederlands-Indië 1945-1950. Demografische hand-out*. The Hague: Nederlands Interdisciplinair Demografisch Instituut (NIDI), 2018.

Berdoeri, Tjambroek, *Indonesia dalem Api dan Bara*. Jakarta: Elkasa, 2004.

Berge van den, Tom. 'Indonesisch geweld tegen de burgerbevolking in West-Java, 1945-1949. Een verkenning' in: *Leidschrift*, vol. 31, no. 3, 57-77.

Berge van den, Tom, *H.J. van Mook 1894-1965. Een vrij en gelukkig Indonesië*, Bussum: Thoth, 2014.

Bergen van, Leo, *Een menslievende en nationale taak. Oorlog, kolonialisme en het Rode Kruis in Nederlandsch-Indië 1870-1950*, Soesterberg: Aspekt, 2004.

Berkel van, M., *Welk verhaal telt? De oorlog in Nederlands-Indië/Indonesië 1942-1949 in het geschiedenisonderwijs*. Amsterdam: National Committee for 4 and 5 May, 2017.

Bloembergen, Marieke, *Uit zorg en angst. De geschiedenis van de politie in Nederlands-Indië*. Amsterdam/Leiden: Boom/KITLV, 2009.

Bosma, Ulbe, Remco Raben and Wim Willems, *De geschiedenis van de Indische Nederlanders*. Amsterdam: Bert Bakker, 2008.

Brocades Zaalberg, Thijs and Bart Luttikhuis, 'Extreem geweld tijdens dekolonisatieoorlogen in vergelijkend perspectief, 1945-1962' in: *BMGN - Low Countries Historical Review*, vol. 135, no. 2, 2020, 34-51.

Broeshart, A.C. et al., *Soerabaja. Beeld van een stad*. Purmerend: Asia Maior, 1994.

Bussemaker, Herman, *Bersiap! Opstand in het paradijs. De Bersiap-periode op Java en Sumatra 1945-1946*. Zutphen: Walburg Pers, 2005.

Bijl, Paul, 'Colonial Memory and Forgetting in the Netherlands and Indonesia' in: *Journal of Genocide Research*, 14(3-4), 2012, 441-461.

Captain, Esther and Guno Jones, *Oorlogserfgoed overzee. De erfenis van de Tweede Wereldoorlog in Aruba, Curaçao, Indonesia en Suriname*. Amsterdam: Bert Bakker, 2010.

Captain, Esther, *Achter het kawat was Nederland. Indische oorlogservaringen en –herinneringen 1942-1995*. Kampen: Kok, 2002.

Chauvel, Richard, 'Ambon: not a revolution but a counterrevolution', in: Audrey R. Kahin, ed., *Regional dynamics of the Indonesian revolution. Unity from diversity*, Honolulu: University of Hawaii Press, 1985, 236-264.

Chauvel, Richard, *Nationalists, soldiers and seperatists. The Ambonese islands from colonialism to revolt 1880-1950*. Leiden: KITLV Press, 1990.

Colombijn, Freek, 'A cultural practice of violence in Indonesia: lessons from history', in: Dewi Fortuna Anwar et al., *Violent internal conflicts in Asia Pacific: histories, political economies and policies*, Jakarta: Yayasan Obor Indonesia, LIPI, LASEMA-CNRS and KITLV-Jakarta, 2005.

Colombijn, Freek, and Thomas J. Lindblad, *Roots of violence in Indonesia. Contemporary violence in historical perspective*. Leiden: KITLV Press, 2002.

Cribb, Robert, 'Jakarta: Cooperation and Resistance in an Occupied City' in: *Regional Dynamics of the Indonesian Revolution. Unity from Diversity*. Honolulu: University of Hawaii Press, 1985, 179-205.

Cribb, Robert, 'A Revolution Delayed: The Indonesian Republic and the Netherlands Indies, August-November 1945' in: *The Australian Journal of Politics and History*, vol. 32, no. 1, 72-86.

Cribb, Robert, *Gangsters and revolutionaries. The Jakarta People's Militia and the Indonesian Revolution 1945-1949*. Jakarta/Kuala Lumpur: Equinox Publishing, 2009 (first edition 1991).

Cribb, Robert, 'The brief genocide of Eurasians in Indonesia, 1945/46', in: Dirk A. Moses, ed., *Empire, colony, genocide. Conquest, occupation, and subaltern resistance in world history*, Berghahn Books, New York/Oxford 2008, 424-439.

Cribb, Robert, 'Misdaad, geweld en uitsluiting in Indonesië', in: Els Bogaerts and Remco Raben, *Van Indië tot Indonesië*, Boom, Amsterdam 2007, 13-30.

Daeng Rapi H.A.M, . *Menyingkap Tabir Sejarah Budaya di Sulawesi Selatan*. Jakarta: Yayasan Bhinneka Tunggal Ika, 1988.

Delden van, Mary C., 'De andere kant van de Bersiap', series of articles in *Pelita Nieuws*, 2017.

Delden van, Mary C., 'Bersiapkampen boden schuilplaats in de chaos', in: *Trouw*, 15-08-2012.

Delden van, Mary C., 'Het Rode Kruis kende de waarheid', 14 September 2012, at: www.javapost.nl

Delden van, Mary C., *De republikeinse kampen in Nederlands-Indië oktober 1945-mei 1947. Orde in de chaos?* Kockengen: self-publication, 2007.

Delden van, Mary C., *Bersiap in Bandoeng. Een onderzoek naar geweld in de periode van 17 augustus 1945 tot 24 maart 1946*, Kockengen: self-publication, 1989.

Delden van, Mary C. van, 'Orde in de chaos? De internering in en evacuatie van uit de Republikeinse kampen', in: Wim Willems and Jaap de Moor (eds), *Het einde van Indië*, Amsterdam: Bert Bakker, 1995, 188-207.

Dennis, Peter, *Troubled days of peace. Mountbatten and South East Asia Command, 1945-1946*, Manchester: Manchester University Press, 1987.

Dirk Moses, A., *The problems of genocide. Permanent security and the language of transgression*. Cambridge University Press, Cambridge 2021.
Doel, H.W. van den, *Afscheid van Indië. De val van het Nederlandse imperium in Azië*, Prometheus, Amsterdam 2000.
Doorn van, J.A.A., *Gevangen in de tijd. Over generaties en hun geschiedenis*. Amsterdam: Boom, 2002.
Doorn van, J.A.A., *De laatste eeuw van Indië. Ontwikkeling en ondergang van een koloniaal project*. Amsterdam: Bert Bakker, 1995.
Doorn van, J.A.A and W.J. Hendrix, *Ontsporing van geweld. Over het Nederland/Indisch/Indonesisch conflict*. Rotterdam: Universitaire Pers, 1970.
Droogleever, P.J., *Een daad van vrije keuze. De Papoea's van westelijk Nieuw-Guinea en de grenzen van het zelfbeschikkingsrecht*. Boom/Instituut voor Nederlandse Geschiedenis, Amsterdam/The Hague 2005.
Ducelle, Lilian, *'Doe maar gewoon, dan doe je al Indisch genoeg'. Het journalistieke werk van Lilian Ducelle, bezorgd en ingeleid door Marjolein van Asdonck*. Amersfoort: Moesson, 2008.
Dulm van, J., W.J. Krijgsveld, H.J. Leegemaate, H.A.M. Liesker, G. Wijers, *Geïllustreerde Atlas van de Japanse kampen in Nederlands-Indië, 1945-1947*. Purmerend: Asia Maior, 2000.
Fasseur, Cees, 'Hoeksteen en struikelblok. Rassenonderscheid en overheidsbeleid in Nederlands-Indië' in: *Tijdschrift voor Geschiedenis*, vol. 105, no. 4. 2, 1992, 218-242.
Foray, Jennifer L., 'A Unified Empire of Equal Parts: The Dutch Commonwealth Schemes of the 1920s-1940s' in: *The Journal of Imperial and Commonwealth History*, vol. 21, no. 2, 259-284.
Frakking, Roel, '"Who wants to cover everything, covers nothing": the organization of indigenous security forces in Indonesia, 1945-1950' in: *Journal of Genocide Research*, vol. 14, no. 3-4, 2012, 337-358.
Frederick, William, 'The killing of Dutch and Eurasians in Indonesia's National Revolution (1945-1949): a "Brief genocide reconsidered"' in: *Journal of Genocide Research*, vol. 14, no. 3-4, 2012, 359-380.
Frederick, William H., Hans Antlöv and Stein Tønnesson, 'The man who knew too much: Ch.O. van der Plas and the future of Indonesia, 1927-1950' in: *Imperial policy and Southeast Asian nationalism 1930-1957*, Surrey: Curzon Press, 1995, 34-62.
Frederick, William, 'Shadow of an Unseen Hand. Some Patterns of Violence in the Indonesian Revolution, 1945-1949' in: Freek Colombijn and J. Thomas Lindblad (eds), *Roots of Violence in Indonesia. Contemporary Violence in Historical Perspective*. Leiden: KITLV Press, 2002, 33-62.
Frederick, William H., *Visions and heat. The making of the Indonesian revolution*. Athens: Ohio University Press 1989.
Gerlach, Christian, 'Introduction' in: *Extremely Violent Societies. Mass Violence in the Twentieth-Century World*. Cambridge: Cambridge University Press, 2010, 1-14.
Giebel,C., *Morotai. De bevrijding van de Grote Oost en Borneo*, Franeker: Wever, 1976.
Giebels, Lambert. *Soekarno, Nederlandsch onderdaan. Een biografie 1901-1950*, Amsterdam: Bert Bakker, 1999.
Goor van, J. (ed.), *The Indonesian Revolution*. Conference Papers Utrecht, 17-29 June 1986. Utrecht: Utrechtse Historische Cahiers, 1986, vol. 7, no. 2/3.
Gotō Ken'ichi, *Tensions of Empire: Japan and Southeast Asia in the Colonial and Postcolonial World*, Singapore: University Press Singapore 2003.
Gotō Ken'ichi, 'Caught in the middle: Japanese attitudes toward Indonesian independence in 1945', in: *Journal of Southeast Asian Studies*, vol. 27, no. 1, 1996, 37-48.
Groen, Petra, Anita van Dissel, Mark Loderichs and Rémy Limpach, Thijs Brocades Zaalberg, *Krijgsgeweld en kolonie. Opkomst en ondergang van Nederland als koloniale mogendheid 1816-2010*. Amsterdam: Boom, 2021.
Groen, Petra, 'Colonial warfare and military ethics in the Netherlands East Indies, 1816-1941', in: *Journal of Genocide Studies*, vol. 14, no. 3-4, 2012, 277-296.
Groen, P.M.H., *Marsroutes en dwaalsporen. Het Nederlands militair-strategisch beleid in Indonesië 1945-1950*. 's-Gravenhage: SDU, 1991.

Groen, P.M.H., '"Patience and bluff": de bevrijding van de Nederlandse burgergeinterneerden op Midden-Java (augustus-december 1945)', in: *Mededelingen van de Sectie Militaire Geschiedenis, Landmachtstaf*, no. 8, 1985, 91-154.

Groeneboer, Kees, *Weg tot het Westen. Het Nederlands voor Indië 1600-1950*. Leiden: KITLV, 1993, 474-477.

Gunawan, Riyadi, 'Jagoan dalam Revolusi kita' in: *Prisma*, 8 August 1981, 41-50.

Haas, Paula de, *Indo-Europeanen in Malang buiten de Japanse kampen, 9 maart 1942-31 juli 1947*, thesis Leiden, December 1992.

Hadi, Nur and Sutopo, *Perjuangan total brigade IV. Pada perang kemerdekaan di karesidenan Malang*. Malang: Brawijaya, 1997.

Hagen, Piet, *Koloniale oorlogen in Indonesië. Vijf eeuwen verzet tegen vreemde overheersing*. Amsterdam/Antwerp: De Arbeiderspers, 2018.

Han Bing Siong, 'Sukarno-Hatta versus de *Pemuda* in the first months after the surrender of Japan (August-November 1945)', in: *Bijdragen tot de Taal-, Land- en Volkenkunde*, vol. 156, no. 2, 2000, 233-273.

Han Bing Siong, 'Captain Huyer and the massive Japanese arms transfer in East Java in October 1945', in: *Bijdragen tot de taal-, land- en volkenkunde / Journal of the Humanities and Social Sciences of Southeast Asia*, vol. 159, no. 2-3, 2003, 291-350.

Han Bing Siong, 'The Indonesian need of arms after the proclamation of independence', in: *Bijdragen tot de taal-, land- en volkenkunde / Journal of the Humanities and Social Sciences of Southeast Asia*, vol. 157, no. 4, 2001, 799-830.

Han Bing Siong, 'The secret of major Kido; The battle of Semarang, 15-19 October 1945', in: *Bijdragen tot de taal-, land- en volkenkunde / Journal of the Humanities and Social Sciences of Southeast Asia*, vol. 152, no. 3, 1996, 382-428.

Han Bing Siong, *Geschiedenis van de vijfdaagse strijd in Semarang, 14-19 October 1945*, Rijswijk : Stichting Reünisten HBS Semarang 1995.

Hanifah, Abu, *Tales of a revolution*, Sydney/London: Angus and Robertson, 1972.

Harinck, Christiaan, Nico van Horn and Bart Luttikhuis, 'Wie telt de Indonesische doden?', in: *De Groene Amsterdammer*, no. 30, 26 July 2017.

Harvey, Barbara S., 'South Sulawesi: puppets and patriots', in: Audrey R. Kahin, ed., *Regional dynamics of the Indonesian revolution. Unity from diversity*, Honolulu: University of Hawaii Press, Honolulu 1985, 207-235.

Harsono, Ganis, *Recollections of an Indonesian diplomat in the Sukarno era* (eds C.L.M. Penders and B.B. Hering). St. Lucia: University of Queensland Press, 1977.

Hasan, Sabriah. *Andi Makkasau. Menakar harga 40.000 jiwa*. Yogyakarta: Penerbit Ombak, 2010.

Hatta, Mohammad (ed. C.L.M. Penders), *Indonesian patriot. Memoirs*. Singapore: Gunung Agung, 1981.

Heidhues, Mary Somers *Golddiggers, farmers, traders in the 'Chinese Districts' of West Kalimantan, Indonesia*. Ithaca/New York: Cornell University, 2003.

Heidhues, Mary Somers, 'Anti-Chinese violence in Java during the Indonesian Revolution, 1945-49', in: Bart Luttikhuis and Dirk A. Moses, eds, *Colonial counterinsurgency and mass violence. The Dutch Empire in Indonesia*. London and New York: Routledge 2014, 155-175.

Hering, Bob, *Soekarno. Fouding father of Indonesia 1901-1945*. Leiden: KITLV Press, 2002.

Hoek, Anne-Lot, *De strijd om Bali. Imperialisme, verzet en onafhankelijkheid 1846-1950*. Amsterdam: De Bezige Bij, 2021.

Houben, Vincent, 'A torn soul. The Dutch public discussion on the colonial past in 1995', in: *Indonesia*, vol. 63, 1997, 47-66.

Houwer, A.C.M., *Propaganda en politiek. De regeringsvoorlichtingsdienst in Nederlands-Indië 1945-1950*. Utrecht: Utrecht University, 1986.

Hudiyanto, R. Rezia, *Pemerintah kota masyarakat bumiputra kota Malang, 1914-1950*. Yogyakarta: Universitas Gadjah Mada, 2009.

Ibrahim, Julianto, *Bandit dan pejuang di simpang Bengawan: kriminalitasdan kekerasan masa revolusai di*

Surakarta. Wonogiri: Bina Citra Pustaka, 2004.
IJzereef, Willem, *De Zuid-Celebes affaire. Kapitein Westerling en de standrechtelijke executies*. Dieren: De Bataafsche Leeuw, 1984.
Imandt, Florence, *'De onverbloemde waarheid'? Interne legervoorlichting met betrekking tot Indonesië 1945-1950, en de relatie met moreel*. Erasmus University Rotterdam, 1988.
Immerzeel, Bert, 'Bersiap: de werkelijke cijfers', in: *Javapost*, 7 February 2014.
Immerzeel, Bert, "Het vuur van de bersiap", in: *Java Post*, 24 January 2019.
Isnaeni, Hendri F., 'Cincang masa perang', in: *Historia*, 27 July 2011.
s'Jacob, E.H., 'Om de eenheid van het koninkrijk. Onze opdracht eischt ervaring, behoedzaamheid en beleid', in: *Pen Gun*, 11 April 1946.
s'Jacob, E.H., 'Een zuiveringsactie en haar aspecten', in: *Pen Gun*, 1 March 1946.
s'Jacob, E.H., 'Tekort aan onderscheidingsvermogen. Nederland heeft in den Archipel zijn taak - maar ook zijn historisch recht', in: *Pen Gun*, 2 November 1945.
Jansen Hendriks, G., *Een voorbeeldige kolonie. Nederlands-Indië in 50 jaar overheidsfilms 1912-1962*. Amsterdam: University of Amsterdam, 2014.
Jansen Hendriks, Gerda, '"Not a colonial war": Dutch film propaganda in the fight against Indonesia, 1945-1949', in: Bart Luttikhuis and A. Dirk Moses (eds), *Colonial counterinsurgency and mass violence. The Dutch empire in Indonesia*. Routledge: London and New York, 198-213.
Jong de, J.J.P., *Avondschot. Hoe Nederland zich terugtrok uit zijn Aziatisch imperium*. Amsterdam: Boom, 2011.
Jong de, J.J.P., 'De bersiap-periode', in: P.J. Drooglever, ed., *Indisch intermezzo. Geschiedenis van de Nederlanders in Indonesië*. Amsterdam: De Bataafsche Leeuw, 1991, 81-99.
Jong de, Loe, *Het Koninkrijk der Nederlanden in de Tweede Wereldoorlog*. The Hague: SDU, 1969-1996.
Kaaij van der, Meindert, 'De Bersiap: een vergeten golf van etnisch geweld', in: *Trouw*, 18-11-2013.
Kahin, Audrey R., 'Introduction' in: *Regional Dynamics of the Indonesian Revolution. Unity from Diversity*. Honolulu: University of Hawaii Press, 1985, 1-21.
Kahin, Audrey R., 'West Sumatra: Outpost of the Republic', in: Audrey R. Kahin, ed., *Regional dynamics of the Indonesian revolution. Unity from diversity*. University of Hawaii Press, Honolulu 1985, 145-176.
Kartodirdjo, Sartono, Marwati Djoened Poesponegoro and Nugroho Notosusantoso (eds), *Sejarah Nasional Indonesia*. Volume 6: *Zaman Jepang dan Zaman Republik Indonesia*. Jakarta: Balai Pustaka, 1975 (reissued 2008).
Kecik, Hario, *Pertempuran Surabaya*. Yogyakarta Abhiseka Dipantara, 2012.
Kementerian Penerangan (Indonesia), *Republik Indonesia: Propinsi Sulawesi*, Kementerian Penerangan, Djakarta 1953.
Kemperman, Jeroen, 'De slachtoffers van de Bersiap, 16 mei 2014', at: www.niod.nl
Keppy, Peter. *Sporen van vernieling. Oorlogsschade, roof en rechtsherstel in Indonesië 1940-1957*. Amsterdam: Boom, 2006.
Knight, G. Roger, 'Death in Slawi: The "Sugar Factory Murders", Ethnicity, Conflicted Loyalties and the Context of Violence in the Early Revolution in Indonesia, October 1945' in: *Itinerario*, vol. 41, no. 3, 606-626.
Kok, René, Erik Somers and Louis Zweers, *Koloniale oorlog 1945-1949. Van Indië naar Indonesië*. Amsterdam: Carrera, 2015.
Krimp, Renske. *De doden tellen. Slachtofferaantallen van de Tweede Wereldoorlog en sindsdien*. Amsterdam: National Committee for 4 and 5 May, 2016.
Kwisthout, Jan-Karel, *De Mardijkers van Tugu en Depok: vrijmaking, bevrijding en merdeka*. Zoetermeer: Lecturium Uitgeverij. 2018
L., H., 'Nederland en de Japanse erfenis' in: *Pen Gun*, 22 August 1946.
Lagrou, Pieter, 'Loe de Jong, of de professionele strategieën van een publieke intellectueel in Koude Oorlogstijd' in: *BMGN – Low Countries Historical Review*, vol. 130, no. 3, 2015, 79-90.
Langenberg, Michael van, 'East Sumatra: accommodating an Indonesian nation within a Sumatran residency',

in: Audrey R. Kahin, ed., *Regional dynamics of the Indonesian revolution. Unity from diversity.* Honolulu: University of Hawaii Press, 1985, 113-143.

Legge, J.D., *Sukarno; A political biography.* Singapore: Archipelago Press, 2003.

Limpach, Remy, *De brandende kampongs van generaal Spoor.* Amsterdam: Boom, 2016.

Locher-Scholten, Elsbeth, 'Interraciale ontmoetingen naar sekse in Nederlands-Indië. De onmacht van het getal' in: Esther Captain, Marieke Hellevoort and Marian van der Klein (eds), *Vertrouwd en vreemd. Ontmoetingen tussen Nederland, Indië en Indonesië.* Hilversum: Verloren, 2000, 15-21.

Lohnstein, Marc, *Royal Netherlands East Indies Army 1936-1942.* Oxford: Osprey Publishing, 2018.

Lucas, Anton, *One soul one struggle. Region and revolution in Indonesia.* Sydney: Allen and Unwin, 1991.

Lynn Gibbings, Sheri and Fridus Steijlen, 'Colonial Figures: Memories of Street Traders in the Colonial and Early post-Colonial Periods' in: *Public History Review*, vol. 19, 2012, 63-85.

Maas, Michiel, 'Het Indonesische geweld kwam niet uit de lucht vallen' in: *De Volkskrant*, 15 January 2022.

Mak, Geertje, Marit Monteiro and Liesbeth Wesseling, 'Child separation. (Post)Colonial Policies and Practices in the Netherlands and Belgium' in: *BMGN – Low Countries Historical Review*, vol. 135, no. 3-4 (special issue), 2020, 4-28.

Mark, Ethan, *The Japanese Occupation of Indonesia in the Second World War: A Transnational History.* Bloomsbury Press, New York/London 2018.

Marle van, A., 'De groep van Europeanen in Nederlands-Indië, iets over ontstaan en groei' in: *Indonesië*, vol. 5, no. 2, 1951, 97-121.

Mattalatta, Andi. *Meniti Siri' dan Harga Diri: Catatan dan Kenangan.* Jakarta: Khasanah Manusia Nusantara. 2003.

Mashuri, *Daerah Malang selatan pada masah perang kemerdekaan 1947-1949.* Depok: Universitas Indonesia, 2004.

Meelhuisen, W., *Revolutie in Soerabaja. 17 augustus-1 december 1945.* Zutphen: Walburg Pers, 2000.

McGregor, Katherine E., *History in Uniform. Military Ideology and the Construction of Indonesia's Past.* Leiden: KITLV Press, 2007.

McMillan, Richard, *The British Occupation of Indonesia 1945-1946. Britain, the Netherlands and the Indonesian Revolution.* London and New York: Routledge, 2005.

Mennecke, Martin, 'Genocide en het internationaal recht', in Barbara Boender and Wichert ten Have (eds), *De holocaust en andere genociden. Een inleiding.* Amsterdam: Amsterdam University Press, 2012, 145-162.

Molen, Pia van der, *Researchrapport documentaire tweeluik Archief van Tranen.* No place: Pia Media, 2011-2012.

Mook, H.J. van, *The stakes of democracy in South-east Asia.* London: Allen & Unwin.

Moor, J.A. de, *Generaal Spoor. Triomf en tragiek van een legercommandant.* Amsterdam: Boom, 2011.

Moor, J.A. de, *Westerling's oorlog. Indonesië 1945-1950.* Amsterdam: Uitgeverij Balans, 1999.

Nasution, A.H., *Sekitar perang kemerdekaan Indonesia,* Jil. I, Proklamasi, Angkasa, Bandung 1977.

Natzir Said, Muhammad. *Korban 40.000 Jiwa di Sulawesi Selatan: S.O.B. 11 Desember 1946 Penyebab Banjir Darah dan Lautan Api.* Bandung: Alumni, 1985.

Nish, Ian, 'British-Japanese dilemmas in South East Asia after 1945', in: Hugo Dobson and Kosuge Nobuko (eds), *Japan and Britain at war and peace.* Routledge: London and New York 2009, 69-81.

Norel, Okke, *En, ...hoe was het daarbuiten? Buiten de Japanse kampen en in de bersiap (1941-1949). Een te weinig gestelde vraag. Een bibliografie.* Winterswijk: self-publication, 2001.

Ooi Keat Gin, *Post-war Borneo, 1945-1950. Nationalism, empire and state-building.* London and New York: Routledge, 2013.

Oostindie, Gert, *Soldaat in Indonesië 1945-1950. Getuigenissen van een oorlog aan de verkeerde kant van de geschiedenis.* Amsterdam: Prometheus, 2016.

Padmodiwiryo, Suhario, *Memoar Hario Kecik. Autobiografi seorang mahasiswa prajurit,* Jakarta: Yayasan Obor, 1995.

Padmodiwiryo, Suhario, (translated by Frank Palmos), *Revolution in the city of heroes. A memoir of the battle that sparked Indonesia's national revolution*. NUS Press: Singapore, 2016

Pagee van, Marjolein, *Bung Tomo: War Crimimal or Hero? Dutch and Indonesian Views on the Violence in Surabaya 1945*. Leiden: Master's thesis Leiden University, 2018.

Palmos, Frank, *Surabaya 1945: Sakral Tanahku*, Jakarta: Yayasan Pustaka Obor Indonesia, 2016.

Palmos, Francis, *Surabaya 1945: Sacred Territory. Revolutionary Surabaya as the Birthplace of Indonesian Independence*. Perth: PhD thesis University of Western Australia, 2011.

Patan, Lahadjdji, *Sulawesi dan Pahlawannya*. Jakarta: Yayasan Kesejahteraan Generasi Muda Indonesia, 1967.

Pawiloy, Sarita. *Sejarah Perjuangan Angkatan '45 di Sulawesi Selatan*. Ujung Pandang: Dewan Harian Daerah Angkatan '45 Propinsi Sulawesi Selatan, 1987.

Pawiloy, Sarita, *Arus Revolusi di Sulawesi Selatan*, No date: Gita Karya, 1987.

Poelgeest van, L., *Japanse besognes. Nederland en Japan 1945-1975*.The Hague: SDU, 1999.

Poelgeest van, Bart, 'Figuranten op het Indische toneel. De Japanners in Nederlands-Indië 1946-1949', in: Elly Touwen-Bouwsma and Petra Groen (eds), *Tussen Banzai en Bersiap. De afwikkeling van de Tweede Wereldoorlog in Nederlands-Indië*. The Hague: SDU, 1996, 95-107.

Poelgeest van, Bart, 'Oosters stille dwang. Tewerkgesteld in de Japanse bordelen van Nederlands-Indië.' in: *ICODO-Info*, vol. 10, no. 3, 1993, 13-21.

Poeze, Harry A., 'Walking the tightrope: internal Indonesian conflict, 195-1949', in: Bart Luttikhuis and Dirk A. Moses, eds, *Colonial counterinsurgency and mass violence. The Dutch Empire in Indonesia*. London and New York: Routledge, 2014, 176-197.

Poeze, Harry A, *Verguisd en vergeten. Tan Malaka, de linkse beweging en de Indonesische revolutie, 1945-1949*, volume I. Leiden: KITLV Uitgeverij, 2007.

Poeze, Harry A. et al., *In het land van de overheerser I. Indonesiërs in Nederland 1600-1950*. Dordrecht/Providence: Foris Publications, 1986.

Post, Peter, and Elly Touwen-Bouwsma, *Japan, Indonesia and the war. Myths and reality*. Leiden: KITLV Press, 1997.

Purwanto, Bambang, 'Oude en nieuwe stadsbeelden. Veranderingen in de Indonesische stedelijke symboliek' in: Els Bogaerts and Remco Raben (eds), *Van Indië tot Indonesië*. Amsterdam: Boom, 2007, 65-76.

Purwanto, Bambang, *Yogyakarta pada masa Jepang: menulis sejarah kehidupan sehari-hari dan historiografi yang manusiawi*. Yogyakarta: paper for the seminar 'Tinjauan historis sosio kultural Yogyakarta pada masa pendudukan Jepang' in Museum Benteng Yogyakarta, 2009.

Raben, Remco and Peter Romijn, *Talen van geweld. Stilte, informatie en misleiding in de Indonesische onafhankelijkheidsstrijd 1945-1949*. Amsterdam: AUP, 2022.

Raben, Remco, 'Epilogue: on genocide and mass violence in colonial Indonesia', in: in: Bart Luttikhuis and A. Dirk Moses (eds), *Colonial counterinsurgency and mass violence. The Dutch empire in Indonesia*. Routledge: London and New York, 485-502.

Raben, Remco, 'Hoe wordt men vrij? De lange dekolonisatie van Indonesië', in: Els Bogaerts and Remco Raben (eds), *Van Indië tot Indonesië*. Amsterdam: Boom, 2007, 13-25.

Raben, Remco (ed.), *Beelden van de Japanse bezetting in Indonesië. Persoonlijke getuigenissen en publieke beeldvorming in Indonesië, Japan en Nederland*. Zwolle: Waanders, 1999.

Rachman, Ansar, et al., *Tandjungpura Berdjuang: Sedjarah Kodam XII/Tandjungpura Kalimantan Barat*, Pontianak: no publisher, 1970.

Reid, Anthony, *The Indonesian national revolution, 1945-1950*. Hawthorn: Longman, 1974.

Reid, Anthony, *The blood of the people: revolution and the end of traditional rule in northern Sumatra*. Singapore: NUS Press, 2014.

Reid, Anthony, 'Australia's hundred days in South Sulawesi', in: D. Chandler and M.C. Ricklefs (eds), *Ninteenth and twentieth century Indonesia. Essays in honour of professor J.D. Legge*. Clayton: Monash University, 1986, 201-224.

Reid, Anthony and Oki Akira, *The Japanese experience in Indonesia. Selected memoirs of 1942-1945*. Athens:

Ohio University Press, 1986.

Remmelink, W.G.J., 'The emergence of the new situation: the Japanese army on Java after the surrender' in: *Militaire Spectator*, vol. 148, no. X, 1978, 49-66.

Ricklefs, M.C., *A History of Modern Indonesia*. London: Macmillan, 1981.

Riza, Chairul, *Radio Pemberontakan dan Perannya dalam Revolusi Kemerdekaan di Surabaya 1945-1947*. Surabaya: Universitas Airlangga, 2006.

Robinson, Geoffrey, *The dark side of paradise. Political violence in Bali*. Ithaca/London: Cornell University Press, 1995.

Robinson, Tjalie. *Tjies*. The Hague: H.P. Leopolds Uitgeversmaatschappij, 1958.

Romijn, Peter, *De lange Tweede Wereldoorlog. Nederland 1940-1949*. Amsterdam: Balans, 2020.

Saleh La Hade, Mohammed. 'Korban 40.000 Jiwa di Sulawesi Selatan dan artinya bagi perjuangan Kemerdekaan Republik Indonesia, article in *Seminar Sejarah Perjuangan Rakyat Sulawesi Selatan Menentang Penjajahan Asing*. Jakarta: Departemen Pendidikan dan Kebudayaan, 1983.

Scagliola, Stef, *Last van de oorlog. De Nederlandse oorlogsmisdaden in Indonesië en hun verwerking*. Amsterdam: Balans, 2002.

Scagliola, Stef, '"Cleo's 'unfinished business": Coming to terms with Dutch war crimes in Indonesia's war of independence' in: *Journal of Genocide Research*, vol. 14, no. 3-4, 419-439.

Schaik, A. van, *Malang. Beeld van een stad*. Asia Maior: Purmerend 1996.

Schulte Nordholt, Henk, 'A genealogy of violence' in: Freek Colombijn and J. Thomas Lindblad (eds),. *Roots of Violence in Indonesia. Contemporary Violence in Historical Perspective*. Leiden: KITLV Press, 2002, 33-62.

Schulte Nordholt, Henk, 'Een staat van geweld', Inaugural address Erasmus University Rotterdam, Rotterdam, 2000.

Semelin, Jacques, *Purify and destroy. The political uses of massacre and genocide*. New York: Columbia University Press, 2007.

Shibata, Yaichiro, 'Surabaya after the surrender', in: Anthoy Reid and Oki Akira, *The Japanese experience in Indonesia. Selected memoirs of 1942-1945*. Athens: Ohio University, 1986, 341-374.

Smit, Herman, *Gezag is gezag. Kanttekeningen bij de houding van de gereformeerden in de Indonesische kwestie*. Hilversum: Verloren, 2006.

Shigetada, Nishijima, 'The independence proclamation in Jakarta', in: Anthony Reid and Oki Akira (eds), *The Japanese experience in Indonesia. Selected memoirs of 1942-1945*. Athens: Ohio University, 1986, 299-324.

Shizuo, Miyamoto, 'Army problems in Java after the surrender', in: Anthony Reid and Oki Akira (eds), *The Japanese experience in Indonesia. Selected memoirs of 1942-1945*. Athens: Ohio University, 1986, 325-340.

Siauw Tiong Djin, *Siauw Giok Tjhan. Bicultural leader in emerging Indonesia*. Clayton: Monash University Publishing, 2018.

Sjahrir, Soetan. *Onze strijd*. Amsterdam: Perhimpoenan Indonesia/Vrij Nederland, 1946.

Sophiaan, Manai. *Apa Yang Masih Teringat*. Jakarta: Yayasan Mencerdaskan Kehidupan Bangsa, 1991.

Sophiaan, Manai. *Hari-hari Pertama Pendaratan NICA di Sulawesi Selatan*, memoir article in *Sulawesi dan Pahlawan2nja*. Jakarta: Yayasan Kesejahteraan Generasi Muda Indonesia, 1967.

Spector, Ronald H., *In the ruins of empire. The Japanese surrender and the battle for postwar Asia*. New York: Random House, 2008.

Spoor-Dijkema, Mans, *Achteraf kakelen de kippen. Herinneringen aan Generaal KNIL S.H. Spoor, Legercommandant in Nederlands-Indië 30 januari 1946-25 mei 1949, opgetekend door zijn weduwe*. Amsterdam: De Bataafsche Leeuw, 2004.

Steedly, Mary Margaret, 'The Golden Bridge' in: *Rifle Reports. A story of Indonesian Independence*. Oakland: University of California Press, 2013, 22-42.

Sudjarwo, 'Portret diri pemuda dalam Revolusi kita' in: *Prisma*, 8 August 1981, 22.

Termorshuizen, G.P.A., *Tropenstijl. Amusement en verstrooiing in de (post)koloniale pers*. Leiden: KITLV Press, 2011.

Touwen-Bouwsma, Elly, *Op zoek naar grenzen. Toepassing en uitvoering van de wetten voor oorlogsslachtoffers*. Amsterdam: Boom, 2010.

Touwen-Bouwsma, Elly, 'De opvang van de burgergeïnterneerden op Java en Sumatra (15 augustus 1945-15 april 1946)', in: Elly Touwen-Bouwsma and Petra Groen (eds), *Tussen Banzai en Bersiap. De afwikkeling van de Tweede Wereldoorlog in Nederlands-Indië*. The Hague: SDU, 1996, 25-42.

Triyana, Bonnie, 'Schrap de term 'Bersiap' want die is racistisch' in: *NRC*, 10 January 2022.

Velden van, Dora, *De Japanse interneringskampen voor burgers gedurende de Tweede Wereldoorlog*. Franeker: Wever, 1985.

Vellinga, Henrike, *'Wij hadden daar een historische verantwoordelijkheid': de Bersiap-periode (1945-1946) in memoires en dagboeken van Nederlandse militairen*, thesis Leiden University 2020.

Vickers, Adrian, *A history of modern Indonesia*. New York: Cambridge University Press, 2013.

Vosveld, Amber, *De Vereniging Kinderen uit de Japanse Bezetting en Bersiap 1941-1949*. Amsterdam: University of Amsterdam, 2008.

Wahid, Abdul, 'The untold story of the Surabaya battle of 1945' in: *Jakarta Post*, 12 November 2013.

Williams, Michael C., 'Banten: "Rice debts will be repaid with rice, blood debts with blood', in: Audrey R. Kahin, (ed)., *Regional dynamics of the Indonesian revolution. Unity from diversity*. Honolulu: University of Hawaii Press, 1985, 55-81.

Williams, Michael Charles, *Communism, religion and revolt in Banten*. Athens: Ohio University, 1990.

Westerbeek, Loes, 'Indische Identity in Australia' in: Nonja Peters (ed.) *The Dutch Down Under 1606-2006*. Sydney: Wolters Kluwer: 2006, 254-275.

Willems, Wim, *Tjalie Robinson. Biografie van een Indo-schrijver*. Amsterdam: Bert Bakker, 2008.

Withuis, Jolande. *Erkenning. Van oorlogstrauma naar klaagcultuur*. Amsterdam: De Bezige Bij, 2002.

Woodburn Kirby, S., *The war against Japan*, V, *The surrender of Japan*, London: Her Majesty's Stationary Office, 1969.

Zara, Muhammad Yuanda, '"Trust me, this news is indeed true": representations of violence in Indonesian newspapers during the Indonesian revolution, 1945-1948', in: Bart Luttikhuis and Dirk A. Moses, (eds), *Colonial counterinsurgency and mass violence. The Dutch Empire in Indonesia*. London and New York: Routledge, 2014, 214-239.

Zara, Muhammad Yuanda, 'Gallant British-indians, Violent Indonesians: British-indonesian Conflict in Two British Newspapers, The Fighting Cock and Evening News (1945-1946)' in: *Patrawidya, seri penerbitan penelitian sejarah dan budaya*, vol. 16, no. 4, 2015, 515-528.

Zara, Muhammad Yuanda, *Voluntary participation, state involvement: Indonesian propaganda in the struggle for maintaining independence, 1945-1949*. Amsterdam: PhD thesis, University of Amsterdam, 2016.

Zhou, Taomo, *Migration in time of revolution. China, Indonesia and the Cold War*. Ithaca and London: Cornell University Press, 2018.

Zweers, Louis, *De gecensureerde oorlog. Militairen versus de media in Nederlands-Indië 1945-1949*. Zutphen: Walburg Pers 2013.

Egodocuments

Berduri, Tjamboek, (pseudonym of Kwee Thiam Tjing), *Indonesia dalem Api dan Bara*. Jakarta: Elkasa, 2004.

Brendgen, J.H.J., *Belevenissen van een K.N.I.L-officier in de periode 1942-1950. Belevenissen vóór en bij politiële acties*. Haarlem: self-publication, 1980.

Fabricius, Johan, *Hoe ik Indië terugvond*. The Hague: Leopolds, 1947.

Fusmama, Takao, *A Japanese memoir of Sumatra, 1945-1946: Love and hatred in the liberation war*. Ithaca/New York: Cornell University, 1993.

Hazekamp, F.C., *Twee broers, twee luitenants in Indië. Verslag van de militaire diensttijd van de broers Ted en Frans Hazekamp in Engeland en Nederlands Oost Indië*. No place, no publisher, 2008.

Jalhay, S.M., *Allen zwijgen. Van merdeka en Andjing-Nica tot APRA*. Hillegom: Gevana, 1989.

Jonge de, M., *Mijn Ruiters. Ervaringen als commandant van het 4e Eskadron Pantserwagens Huzaren van Boreel tijdens de politionele acties (1947-1949) in toenmalig Nederlands-Indië*. Zierikzee: Stichting Cultureel Erfgoed De Jonge, 2008.

Moll, Hans, *Sluipschutters in de tuin. Een Indische geschiedenis*. Zutphen: Walburg Pers, 2021.

Moscou-De Ruiter, M., *Vogelvrij*. Weesp: Fibula van Dishoeck, 1984.

Polmans, Jot, *De brutale reis. De eerste tocht naar een nieuwe wereld*. Meppel: Roelofs van Goor, 1947.

Peters, Nonja, *The Christian Slaves of Depok. A Colonial Tale Unravels*. Newcastle upon Tyne: Cambridge Scholars Publishing, 2021.

Peters, Nonja. *Depok. De droom van Cornelis Chastelein*. Volendam: LM Publishers, 2019.

Saveur, Martje. *Het koffertje van mijn moeder. Herinneringen aan Indië*. Bloemendaal: Schaep14, 2017.

Sprang van, Alfred, *En Soekarno lacht..!* 's-Gravenhage: W. van Hoeve, 1946.

Stevens, J.A. and Ben Grevedamme, *Vrij; een verzameling foto's uit Indië van den foto-journalist van den Marine-Voorlichtingsdienst Luit. ter zee 3^e kl. J.A. Stevens met brieven van Ben Grevedamme*. Deventer: no publisher, 1946.

Toer, Pramoedya Ananta, et al., *Kronik Revolusi Indonesia*, Jilid I (1945). Jakarta: Gramedia 1999.

Wiersema, Bert. *De vergeten strijd van '45-'50*. Barneveld: De Vuurbaak, 1998.

Newspapers
American
New York Times, 5 September 1945, 5 October 1945.

Dutch and Indo-Dutch
Algemeen Handelsblad, 24 December 1949.
Algemeen Indisch Dagblad, 2 May 1947, 10 September 1947.
Avondpost, 2 February 1913.
Dagblad, passim.
Java-bode, nieuws, handels- en advertentieblad voor Nederlands-Indië.
Locomotief, Samarangsch handels- en advertentieblad, 5 December 1949.
Maasbode (Rotterdam), 18 December 1948.
Nieuw Nederland, 13 January 1949.
Nieuwe Apeldoornsche courant, 23 August 1947.
Nieuwe Courant, 3 and 6 May 1947, 20 November 1948, 21 and 24 December 1949.
Nieuwsblad van het Zuiden, 21 December 1949.
Nieuwsblad voor Sumatra, 1 July 1948.
Nieuwsgier, 20 October 1945.
Parool, 9 December 1949.
Preangerbode, 2 January 1947.
Provinciale Drentsche en Asser Courant, 8 May 1947.
Standaard, 26 July 1947.
Telegraaf, 8 and 11 November 1949.
Volkskrant, 10 November 1949.

Indonesian
Asia Raya, 1942-1945.
Atjeh Sinbun, 1942-1943, 1945.
Bali Sinbun, August 1945.
Banteng, November 1945.
Berdjoeang, November 1945.

Berita Gunseikanbu, September 1945.
Berita Indonesia, 1945-1946.
Berita Repoeblik Indonesia, 1945-1946.
Djawa Baroe, 1943-1945.
Djiwa Repoeblik, 1945.
Gelora Rakjat, 1946.
Merah Poetih, 18 and 27 October 1945.
Merdeka, 12 October 1945.
Mimbar Merdeka, 1946.
Minggoean Merdeka, 1946.
Nippon Times, 15 October 1945.

Archives and collections

Australian War Memorial (AWM), Canberra
Collection 52: 2nd Australian Imperial Force (AIF) and Citizen Military Forces (CMF) unit war diaries, 1939-1945

Netherlands Institute for Sound and Vision, Hilversum

Museum Brawijaya, Malang

Centre des Archives diplomatiques de La Courneuve, Parijs
Série Asie-Océanie, Sous-série Indonésie, Période 1944–1955, Cote 129QO

Catholic Documentation Centre (KDC), Nijmegen
Collection 75: KomMissie Memoires (KMM)

Leiden University Library
Special Collections: Collection Willem IJzereef
Database of Dutch incidents of violence, based on systematic research in 659 published egodocuments (2017), Royal Netherlands Institute of Southeast Asian and Caribbean Studies (KITLV), limited access for copyright and privacy reasons. For access: kitlv@kitlv.nl
Oral History Archive, Indonesian Oral Historiography Foundation (Stichting Mondelinge Geschiedschrijving Indonesië, SMGI), Royal Netherlands Institute of Southeast Asian and Caribbean Studies

National Archives, Kew, London (NA Kew)
War Office 203: South East Asia Command: Military Headquarters Papers, Second World War

National Archives of the Netherlands, The Hague (NA)
Collection 2.19.286: Dutch Red Cross Information office, department A and registered archives relating to the Dutch East Indies
Collection 2.03.01: Ministries of War and General Affairs (Ministeries voor Algemeene Oorlogvoering van het Koninkrijk (AOK) en van Algemene Zaken (AZ)): Prime Minister's Office (Kabinet van de Minister-President (KMP))
Collection number 2.13.197: Ministry of Defence, Protestant and Roman Catholic Pastoral Care Services (Ministerie van Defensie, Diensten Protestantse en Rooms-Katholieke Geestelijke Verzorging)
Collection 2.10.62: Netherlands Forces Intelligence Service [NEFIS] and Central Military Intelligence Service (Centrale Militaire Inlichtingendienst [CMI]) in the Dutch East Indies

Collection 2.10.37.02: Netherlands Forces Intelligence Service (NEFIS) 1945-1950
Collection 2.21.266: Ch.O. van der Plas
Collection 2.10.17: Attorney General to the Supreme Court of the Dutch East Indies (Procureur-Generaal bij het Hooggerechtshof van Nederlands-Indië)
Collection 2.10.14: General Secretariat of the Dutch East Indies Government and its registered Archives (Algemene Secretarie van de Nederlands-Indische Regering en de daarbij gedeponeerde Archieven)
Collection 2.13.132: Ministry of Defence: Armed groups in the Dutch East Indies
Collection 2.10.36.15: Ministry of the Colonies: Indies Archive, Series V

Netherlands Institute for Military History (NIMH), The Hague
Collection 509: Decolonization of the Dutch East Indies (1945-1950)
Collection 545: Egodocuments Dutch East Indies 1945-1950 (Sweep collection)
Collection 557: Psychological care in the armed forces

Netherlands Institute for War Documentation (NIOD), Amsterdam
Collection 400: Indies Collection (Indische Collectie, IC)
Collection 401: Dutch East Indies diaries and egodocuments
Digital database Indonesian newspapers 1942-1947
ODGOI project: Witnesses & Contemporaries, database of *bersiap* victims

Pelita Foundation, Diemen, the Netherlands
Social reports in context of the Victims of Prosecution Benefits Act (Wet Uitkering Vervolgingsslachtoffers, WUV) and the Civilian War Victims Benefits Act (Wet Uitkering Burgeroorlogsslachtoffers, WUBO)

Utrecht Archives (HUA), Utrecht
Collection 1133: General Deputation for the Mission, Mission Office, Mission Centre and Related Institutions of the Reformed Churches in the Netherlands

REFERENCE WORKS/SOURCE PUBLICATIONS

Post, Peter, et al., eds, *The encyclopedia of Indonesia in the Pacific War*. London and Boston: Brill, 2010.
De excessennota: nota betreffende het archiefonderzoek naar de gegevens omtrent excessen in Indonesië begaan door Nederlandse militairen in de periode 1945-1950. Ingeleid door Jan Bank. The Hague: SDU, 1995.
Officiële bescheiden betreffende de Nederlands-Indonesische betrekkingen 1945-1950 (NIB).
Volkstelling 1930 van Nederlandsch-Indië. Batavia: 1933-1936.

WEBSITES

https://en.wikipedia.org/wiki/Kalibata_Heroes_Cemetery
https://www.federatie-indo.nl/22-01-11/
https://historia.id/politik/articles/cincang-masa-perang-vVNkv/page/2
https://javapost.nl/
https://www.kitlv.nl/wp-content/uploads/2020/01/Lijst-met-gepubliceerde-egodocumenten-Indieveteranen-7-januari-2020.pdf
https://www.kitlv.nl/wp-content/uploads/2017/07/Overzicht-doden-versie-14-juli-2017.pdf
https://kukb.nl/artikelen/stichting-k-u-k-b-doet-aangifte-tegen-het-rijksmuseum
https://www.oorlogsgravenstichting.nl/geschiedenis
https://oorlogsverhalen.com/oorlogsverhalen/roos-engelenburg/
https://pia-media.nl/projecten/archief-van-tranen-project/
https://www.hansvervoort.nl/article/1003/Dodentocht-in-de-bergen
https://www.veteranri.go.id

Acknowledgements

We benefitted greatly from the insightful and expert comments from Elly Touwen-Bouwsma, Harry Poeze, Rémy Limpach, Bert Immerzeel, Esther Zwinkels, Frank van Vree, Gert Oostindie and Ben Schoenmaker, who read (parts of) the manuscript. We are also grateful to Anne-Lot Hoek, Maaike van der Kloet and Azarja Harmanny for their advice, and to Abdul Wahid and Muhammad Yuanda Zara for interesting discussions that sharpened the focus of our research. Our research was also enriched by discussions with Henk Beekhuis, Mary van Delden, Trudy Mooren and Harry Poeze.

We would like to express our great appreciation for our Indonesian colleagues who took part in the regional studies project: Bambang Purwanto, Abdul Wahid, Satrio Dwicahyo, Yulianti, Uji Nugroho Winardi, Taufik Ahmad, Galuh Ambar, Maiza Elvira, Farabi Fakih, Aprianti Harahap, Sarkawi B. Husain, Julianto Ibrahim, Tri Wahyuning M. Irsyam, Gayung Kasuma, Erniwati Nur, Mawardi Umar and Muhammad Yuanda Zara. Our discussions with you broadened our view of the events during the Indonesian Revolution and opened up new lines of research. We would also like to thank our Dutch colleagues, with whom we made two trips to Indonesia: Martijn Eickhoff, Anne van der Veer, Roel Frakking, Anne Lot-Hoek, Ireen Hoogenboom, Hans Meijer and Henk Schulte Nordholt.

We are grateful to the editorial board and to Robert Cribb, Petra Groen, Jan Hoffenaar and Henk Schulte Nordholt of the Scientific Advisory Committee for their critical comments and valuable suggestions on earlier versions of this manuscript.

We would also like to thank our interns and research assistants for their crucial support and friendly collaboration during the research. In Indonesia: Muhammad Alif Ichsan, Oktoriza Dhia, Tia Farahdiba and Antonia Asta Gaudi. In the Netherlands: Bastiaan van den Akker, Maarten van den Bent, Nuranisa Halim, Thirza van Hofwegen and John Soedirman.

We thank our translators: Tia Farahdiba, Taufiq Hanafi and John Soedirman.

We are very grateful to Ron Habiboe and Chrissy Flohr for the boundless dedication and great commitment they showed to the end when compiling the file of victims on the Dutch side. Marijn Versteegen, Daanjan Wisselink and Maarten van der Bent also made a major contribution to its compilation, by painstakingly recording and processing the information on the victims in the archives.

A book is not complete without illustrations. We are therefore particularly grateful to Ellen Klinkers, who tenaciously and enthusiastically tracked down the illustrations for this book and for our chapter in the joint volume, *Beyond the pale*.

Onno Sinke

I would like to express my great appreciation to Annelieke Drogendijk, the director of the ARQ Centre of Expertise on War, Persecution and Violence, who enabled me to focus on this research for more than four years. The research took much more time and energy than I initially anticipated. Despite this, she always supported me and stood by me with advice. Thank you to Grace Leksana, Indah Utami and Martijn Eickhoff, who assisted me in word and deed during my exploratory trip to Malang. Grace and Indah ensured that my stay in the city was extremely pleasant.

Paul and Kieke Arlman and Monique van Beers made it possible for me to work as much as I could during the lockdowns.

I am very grateful to my parents-in-law for the helping hand they gave in everyday life, especially in the last stages. Finally, my family: the dynamics surrounding the research, the trips to Indonesia and the workload also had an impact on family life. I am therefore very grateful to my wife for making everything possible. My two young children provided a welcome distraction from the research.

Esther Captain

I should like to thank Gert Oostindie, director of the KITLV until 13 December 2021, who generously allowed me to devote many more hours than previously anticipated to this research programme. His successor, Diana Suhardiman, and David Kloos, gave me all the support I needed in the key concluding phase of the research.

I held the workshop 'Memory landscapes' in Yogyakarta with Martijn Eickhoff and Eveline Buchheim: I thank them for the great cooperation, and the students of Universitas Gadjah Mada for their enthusiasm and expertise. It is such a shame that the planned workshops in Depok, Malang and Medan could not go ahead due to the pandemic.

For almost 25 years, the house of my father Armand (+ 2003) in Kramat, Jakarta – now the house of my aunt Enny Kewas (+ 2018) and cousin Ricky Nelson Kewas – has been a warm home. The same goes for Yogyakarta, where Laine Berman and Athonk Sapto Raharjo welcomed me back into their home.

Balance is important, both in research and in life. I am very grateful to everyone who contributed to this project at an academic, physical and mental level.

My sister, Ingrid, along with Daniël and Maxime, sent support and sunshine from Aruba. My mother and Gerard provided empathy closer to home. My thanks to you all!

Guno Jones was an essential discussion partner when it came to every aspect of postcolonial research.

Dirk Staat knows all about the heavy burden of researching extreme violence in Indonesia. Having shared this burden with him for more than four years, it is now time for some lightness again.

About the authors

Dr. Esther Captain is a historian and works as a senior researcher at KITLV/Royal Netherlands Institute of Southeast Asian and Caribbean Studies in Leiden. She is endowed professor Intergenerational Impact of Colonialism and Slavery at Utrecht University. She is currently involved in a research program on the role of the House of Orange-Nassau in Dutch colonial history.

Dr. Onno Sinke is a historian and works as a researcher for the Netherlands Institute for Military History in The Hague. During the research for this book he was seconded to the KITLV/Royal Netherlands Institute of Southeast Asian and Caribbean Studies in Leiden.

Index

3A Movement see Gerakan Tiga-A

Abraham Crijnssen, Hr.Ms. (schip) 77
Aceh 34, 38, 83, 84, 131, 135, 136
Aceh-oorlog (1873-1912) 15, 38
Aek Pamienke (kamp) 68
Agence France-Presse 194
Algemeen Handelsblad (dagblad) 207
Algemeen Indisch Dagblad (dagblad) 203
Algemeen Nederlands Persbureau (ANP) 191, 194, 195
Algemeen Nieuws- en Telegraaf Agentschap (Aneta) 191, 200
Allied Military Administration Civil Affairs Branch 155 (see: Netherlands Indies Civil Administration (NICA))
Almujah, H. 137
Ambarawa 109, 113, 125, 138
Ambas 144
Ambon 22, 40, 46, 47, 51, 58, 89, 90, 94, 99, 198, 217
America United Press 194

AMRI see: Angkatan Muda Republik Indonesia
Andir (airfield) 111
Andjing Nica (KNIL Battalion Infantry V) 122
Aneta *zie:* Algemeen Nieuws- en Telegraaf Agentschap
Angkatan Muda 113
Angkatan Muda Republik Indonesia (AMRI) 138, 150
Angkatan Muda Tionghoa 106
Angkatan Pemuda Indonesia (API) 70, 71, 106, 107, 134
Anglo-Dutch Publicity Committee 195, 197
Angola 226
ANP see Algemeen Nederlands Persbureau
Ancol Canal 198, 201
API see Angkatan Pemuda Indonesia
Army Contacts Service (Dienst voor Legercontacten, DLC) 181, 188, 189, 191-195, 205, 264
Army Information Service (Legervoorlichtingsdienst, LVD) 188, 265

Asahan 78
Asrama Angkatan Baru Indonesia 60
Asrama Indonesia Merdeka 60
Australia 62, 68, 73, 157, 192, 194

Badan Keamanan Rakyat (BKR) 24, 54, 69, 109, 144, 176
Badan Pemuda Indonesia (BPI) 75, 119
Bahagian Penjerboean 151
Bahilang River 130
Balapulang 134, 135, 150
Bali 46, 47, 51, 54, 55, 67, 76, 77, 83, 87, 88, 89, 99, 108, 118, 119, 165, 175, 217, 218
Balikpapan 62, 76, 87, 91, 96
Banda Neira 44
Bandung 12, 13, 44, 50, 70, 74, 77, 101, 102, 104, 107, 109, 111, 112, 115, 120, 121, 125, 132, 138, 139, 146, 156, 162, 202, 204
Bangka 35, 165, 169
Bangkinang (camp) 213
Bangkok 139
Banjarmasin 91
Banten 83, 113, 131-134, 138
Banyumas 55
Barisan Mati 136
Barisan Pemuda Indonesia 120
Barisan Wanita 55
Barisan Pelopor 55
Baros (camp) 74
Batavia 22, 46, 102, 133, 193, 196, 200, 203
Battle of Medan (October 1945-April 1946) 119
Battle of Midway (4 June 1942) 54, 60

Battle of Semarang (14-19 October 1945) 113, 125
Battle om Surabaya (November 1945) 114, 125, 126, 128
Bauer, A. 120
BBC see British Broadcasting Corporation
Beek, J.B. van 14
Bekasi 128, 172, 174
Belawan 101, 124, 129
Belgium 226
Belitung 35, 133, 165, 169
Belonje, W. 200
Benefit Act for Civilian War Victims 1940-1945 (Wet Uitkeringen Burger-Oorlogslachtoffers 1940-1945, WUBO) 224, 266
Bengkulu 44
Berduri, T. 180
Bergen-Belsen 33
Berita Repoeblik Indonesia (dagblad) 106
Bernhard (Prince) 189
Besuki 111
Billiton Maatschappij 133
BKR see Badan Keamanan Rakyat
Blamey, T.A. 96
Bloembergen, M. 42
BNS see Commander of the Dutch Armed Forces
Bodjonegoro 19
Boer, J. 74
Boetzelaer, E.O. van 93
Bogodan see Keibodan
Bogor 22, 55, 101, 102, 125, 138, 139
Bokelaar (family) 122
Bondowoso 157
Bonn, E. 93

Bonthain 98
Boogaard, T. 20
Boon, J. see Robinson, T.
Borneo see Kalimantan
Bouwer, J. 194
Boven-Digul 33, 44
BPI see Badan Pemuda Indonesia
Brisbane 63
British Broadcasting Corporation 263
(BBC) 200, 262
Britisch Indian 18, 66, 101, 104, 120, 122, 126-129, 180
Bronbeek (Bandung) 112
Brondgeest, C.A.M. 75, 118
Bubutan prisons 115
Buchenwald 33
Budi Langgeng Budi Suworo 95
Bukittinggi 50
Buleleng 77
Bulu prison 113
Buru 51
Bussemaker, H. 121, 147, 159, 161, 163, 174, 214, 215, *253*
Buurman van Vreeden, D.C. 192

Cabinet of Schermerhorn 185
Cawang 122
Ceylon see Sri Lanka 139
Chambers, H.M. 131
Chiang Kai-shek 218
Children of the Japanese Occupation and Bersiap 1941-1949 (Kinderen uit de Japanse Bezetting en Bersiap 1941-1949, KJBB) 224
Chilton, F. 88, 97
China 35, 45, 65, 76, 92, 194, 218
Christison, A.F.P. 123, 124, 148

Cibatu 144
Cikampek 113, 172
Cilacap 46
Cilandak 108
Cilimus 118, 139
Cimahi 72, 122, 139
Ciomas 132
Cirebon 118, 139
Cock Buning, Tj. De 186
Coen, J.P. 48
Coenen (family) 22
Commander of the Dutch Armed Forces (Bevelhebber Nederlandse Strijdkrachten, BNS) 189
Combok 135, 136
Cribb, R. 14, 159-163
Cumberland, HMS (ship) 72, 78

Dagblad, Het (newspaper) 144, 200-203, *259*
Darmo (camp) 126
Daud, M. 135
Delden, M.C. van 147, 159, 225
Departement of Justice 186
Depok 23, 115, 116, 147, 195
Depot Speciale Troepen (DST, special forces) 28, 141, 175
Deuning-Anthonio, V. van 20, 23
Dewan Rakyat 133, 134
Displaced Persons Office 155
Djawa Hokokai 56
Djojoprajitno 151
DLC see Army Contacts Service (Dienst voor Legercontacten)
Doewet 151
Door duisternis tot licht (*Through darkness to light*, film) 196
Doorn, J.A.A. van 188, 189

Dougherty, I.N. 95, 96
DST see special forces (Depot Speciale Troepen)
Ducelle, L. 189
Dunki Jacobs, R. 116
Durensawit 150
Dutch Chinese School (Hollandsch-Chineesche School, HCS) 36
Dutch School for Natives (Hollandsch-Inlandsche School) 36

Eastern Broadcasting Service 156
Eechoud, J.P.K. van 90
ELS see European Elementary School (Europeesche Lagere School)
Ende 44
Engelenburg (family) 18-20
European Elementary School (ELS) 36, 264

Fabricius, J. 123, 193-195, 197, 199
Far East Department (Directie Verre Oosten) 157, 158
First Dutch offensive (21 July-5 August 1947) 28, 140, 256
Flohr (family) 150
Flores 44, 47, 51
Frederick, W.H. 28, 110, 140, 160-163
Fusayama, T. 129

Gabungan Badan Perjuangan Tiga Daerah (GBP3D) 135, 264
Gakutotai 55
Gani, A.K. 76

Garut 109, 144, *244*
GBP3D see Gabungan Badan Perjuangan Tiga Daerah
Gelora Rakjat (newspaper) 208
Genyem 90
Gerakan Pramuka Indonesia (GKI) 13, 264
Gerakan Tiga-A (3A Movement) 53
Gereke, H.F.M. 186
Gerlach, C. 27, 143
Germany 45
Giebel, C. 96
Giyugun 54, 68, 69
GKI see Gerakan Pramuka Indonesia
Gondongan, D. 23
Goossens (family) 20
Goto, K. 45
Government Information Service (Regeringsvoorlichtingsdienst, RVD) 193, 195-197, 200-205, 265
Great-Britain 17, 18, 27, 45, 65-68, 73, 74, 81-85, 88, 89, 91, 94, 98, 101-106, 114, 120-131, 138-146, 149, 172, 176, 178, 180, 216-220

Greater East Asia Co-Prosperity Sphere 45-50
Grevendamme, B. 194
Groen, P.M.H. 38, 173
Groene Amsterdammer, De (weekly) 174
Gubeng transport 126
Gunawan, R. 41
Gunseikanbu 50
Gunshireibu 50

Haar, J.C.C. 76
Haasen-van den Dungen Bille, F. van 22
Hagen, P.J. 33, 34, 38, 40
Halmaheira (camp) 214
Halmahera 51, 58
Hanifah 102
Harada, K. 49
Hardy, B. 127
Harinck, C.H.C. 174, 175
Hart, H. van der 161
Hartawan 36, 56, 58
Hasan, T.M. 75
Hatta, M. 32-34, 44, 51-53, 56, 62-64, 69, 74, 148, 149, *232*
Hawthorn, D.C. 97
Hazekamp, F.C. 226
HCS see Dutch Chinese School (Hollandsch-Chineesche School)
Heemskerck, Hr.Ms. Van (ship) 77
Heiho 55, 56, 67, 69
Heutsz, J.B. van 48
Hirohito (keizer) 60
Hiroshima 60
HIS see Dutch School for Natives (Hollandsch-Inlandsche School)
Historia (journal) 15
Hitler, A. 33
Hizbullah 55, 266
Hoek, A.-L. 77
Hollandia 62, 87, 90
Hoogstraten, M. van 214
Horn, N.A. van 174, 175
Hotel Siantar 119, 120, *246*
Houben, V. 173
Hughan, A.T. 22
Huijer, P.J.C. 111

IEV see Indo-European Alliance (Indo-Europees Verbond)
IIB see Indisch Instructie Bataljon
Ik zal handhaven (magazine) 191
Ikada Square 70, 71
Imamura, H. 31, 32, 47, 48
Immerzeel, B. 158, 159, 160, 161
Indies Instruction Battailon (Indisch Instructie Bataljon (IIB) 187, 264
Indies Monument 1941-1945 224
Indies Training squad (Indische Vorming, IV) 187
Indochina 65
Indo-Dutch Post-war Generation (Indische Naoorlogse Generatie, INOG) 264
Indo-European Alliance (Indo-Europeesch Verbond, IEV) 208, 264
Indonesia Merdeka (newspaper) 207
Indonesia Press Photo Service (IPPHOS) 194, 264
Indonesia Raya (nationalist song) 52
INOG see Indo-Dutch Post-war Generation
Investigation Service for the Deceased (Opsporingsdienst van Overledenen, ODO) 23, 155, 156, 159, 160, 161, 164, 166, 168, 265
IPPHOS see Indonesia Press Photo Service
Ismirah 36
Italy 45
IV see Indies Training squad (Indische Vorming, IV)

Iwabe, S. 111

Jacobs, G.F. 68
Jakarta 14, 22, 25, 31, 35, 37, 46, 48, 50, 52, 58, 59, 63, 66, 69, 71-73, 81, 83, 84, 93, 96, 101, 102, 104, 105, 108, 11, 112-113, 115, 121, 122, 123, 125, 132, 134, 138-140, 146, 149, 155-157, 159, 177, 179, 186, 188, 189, 192, 195, 198, 200, 202, 204, 205, 219
Jalhay, S.M. 11
Jansen Hendriks, G. 197
Japan 31, 32, 45-60, 62, 65, 67, 68, 72, 108, 172, 189
Jatin 151
Jatinegara-markt 104
Java-bode (newspaper) 15, 203
Java War (1825-1830) 38
Javapost (website) 159
Jayapura 90
Jonathans (family) 204
Jong, L. de 158, 173, 224
Jonge, M. de 225
Jonkman, J.A. 161, 196, 197
Journal of Genocide Research (journal) 163

Kahin, A. 84
Kakyo Leibotai 55
Kalimantan 35, 45-47, 50, 51, 57, 58, 62, 76, 81, 87, 88, 90-94, 96, 165, 168, 170, 175, 218
Kalisosok prison 115, 117, 151
Kaliung 109
Karoland 75
Kartawinata 202
Katholieke Illustratie (weekly) 191

Kebaktian Rakyat Indonesia Maluku (KRIM) 95
Kebaktian Rakyat Indonesia Sulawesi 106
Kecik, H. see Padmodiwirjo, S.
Kediri 108
Keibodan 54
Kelly, T.E.D. 124, 129
Kembang Kuning 18
Kempeitai 49, 53, 67, 71, 74, 90, 109, 111, 113, 132, 177
Kemperman, J.F. 161
Kido, S. 112, 113
Kiek, R.H.J. 194
Children of the Japanese Occupation and Bersiap 1941-1949 (Kinderen uit de Japanse Bezetting en Bersiap 1941-1949, KJBB) 224, 264
King, R.C.M. 148
Kisaran 129
KITLV see Royal Netherlands Institute of Southeast Asian and Carribean Studies (Koninklijk Instituut voor Taal-, Land- en Volkenkunde)
KJBB see Japanese Occupation and Bersiap 1941-1949 (Kinderen uit de Japanse Bezetting en Bersiap 1941-1949)
Klaassen, M. 202
Klaten 21
Kleffens, E.N. van 157
Klewang, De (magazine) 189, 190
KNI see Komité Nasional Indonesia
KNIL see Royal Netherlands East Indies Army (Koninklijk Nederlands-Indisch Leger, KNIL)

KNIP see Komite Nasional Indonesia Pusat
Kobuku, S. 49
Koerts, H.J. 96
Koiso, K. 55
Komité Nasional Indonesia (KNI) 69, 102, 111, 133, 146, 264
Komite Nasional Indonesia Daerah 110
Komite Nasional Indonesia Pusat (KNIP) 264
KomMissie Memoires 264
Koninklijk Instituut voor Taal-, Land- en Volkenkunde (KITLV) 174, 175, 264
Koninklijke Landmacht (KL) 198, 249, 264
Koninkrijk der Nederlanden in de Tweede Wereldoorlog, Het (series) 158, 173, 224
Korea 51, 58
Korps Marechaussee 38
Kota Baru 176
Krandji 115
Kriegenbergh (family) 20, 21, *229*
KRIM see Kebaktian Rakyat Indonesia Maluku 95
Kuningan 118, 120
Kuomintang 92
Kwee Thiam Tjing see Berduri, T.

Langkat 75, 137
Langsa 136
Lansdorp, J. 74
Laskar Bambu Runcing 136
Laskar Puteri 83
Laskar Rakyat Jawa Raya 138
Laskar Wanita 103 Latang 99

Latumahina 95
Lawson, J. 124
Lebak 132
Leeuw, J.W. de 164, 166, 179
Legiun Veteran Republik Indonesia (LVRI) 179, *248*
Leiden 117
Leland, A.J. 103, 128
Lichtspoor, Het (magazine) 191
Lijnis-Huffenreuter-Schröder, J.F. 21
Linggarjati Agreement (15 november 1946) 204
Limpach, R.P. 147, 173, 186, 191
Locher-Scholten, E.B. 43
Locomotief, De (newspaper) 203, 208
Logemann, J.H.A. 185
Lombok 47, 51, 175, *255*
Loriaux (family) 120
Lowokwaru prison 24
Luttikhuis, B.W. 174
Luwu 99
LVD see Army Information Service (Legervoorlichtingsdienst)
LVRI see Legiun Veteran Republik Indonesia

Mabuchi, I. 111
MacArthur, D. 65, 66
Madura 50, 54, 55, 115, 118, 147, 156, 165, 169, *252*
Maeda, T. 64
Magelang 113, 125, 135, 145, 148
Mahieu, V. see Robinson, T.
Makassar 81, 83, 84, 88, 93, 94-99, 219
Malaka, T. 137

Malang 18-25, 106, 109, 111, 114, 117, 140, 146, 180, 181, 202, *229*
Malay Peninsula 50, 117
Malik, A. 46, 69
Mallaby, A.W.S. 126, 177, 195
Mamat, C. 133
Maricaya 95
Mariso 94
Mark, E. 49, 58
Markas Dewan Pimpinan Perdjuangan (MDPP) 107
Masjumi 55, 56, 118, 146
Matraman 108
McMillan, R.D.S. 172
MDPP see Markas Dewan Pimpinan Perdjuangan
Medan 23, 67, 68, 70, 75, 77, 81, 84, 96, 101, 118, 119, 124, 129, 131, 137, 219, *246, 252*
Memorandum on excesses (Excessennota) 186
Mendur, A. 194
Mendur, F. 194
Merah Poetih (newspaper) 104, 208
Merauke 90
Merdeka (newspaper) 145, 146, 148
Merta, K. 77
Military Police (Militaire Politie, MP) 203, 265
Minahassa 89, 193, 217
Ministry of Foreign Affairs 157
Ministry of War 164
Ministry of Overseas Territories 187
Ministry of Social Affairs 164
Ministry of Information of the Republic Indonesia 195

Moll, H. 14, 223
Mook, H.J. van 62, 70, 73, 93, 157, 195, *259*
Moormann (familie) 21, *229*
Moritake, T. 68
Morotai 61, 87, 96
Motoshige, Y. 54
Mountbatten, L.F.A.V.N. (Lord) 65, 66, 68, 73, 101, 108, 123
Mussolini, B.A.A. 33

Nagano, M. 112
Nagasaki 60
Nakamura, J. 113
Nakashima, T. 129
Nasution, A.H. 129
National Archives of the Netherlands 156, 165, 166, 175, 265
National Indies Monument 1945-1962 224
National Institute of War Documentation (Rijksinstituut voor Oorlogsdocumentatie, RIOD) see NIOD, Institute for War, Holocaust and Genocide Studies
Naval Information Service (Marine Voorlichtingdsdienst) 194
Netherlands Institute for Military History (NIMH) 173, 265
Nederlandsche Dagbladpers 200
NEFIS see Netherlands Forces Intelligence Service
Netherlands East Indies Forces Intelligence Service (NEFIS) 23-25, 118, 128, 134, 144, 150, 156, 192, *229, 244, 263*
Netherlands Indies Civil Adminis-

tration (NICA) 62, 65, 70, 72, 75, 76, 88, 90-104, 115, 116, 119, 122, 133, 145, 155, 193, 265
Netherlands War Graves Foundation (Oorlogsgravenstichting) 164-166, 179, *253*
New York Times (newspaper) 32, 72, 155
Ngadireso 18-20, 23
New Guinea 19, 47, 62, 81, 87, 90, 99, 165, 175
Nieuwe Courant (newspaper) 12, 161, 203, 207, 208
Nieuwsblad van het Zuiden, Het (newspaper) 206
Nieuwsblad voor Sumatra, Het (newspaper) 203
NICA see Netherlands Indies Civil Administration
NIMH see National Institute for Military History
NIOD Institute for War, Holocaust en Genocide Studies 156, 161, 164-166, 171, 265
Noort, van (family) 19, 21
Norel, O. 160
Nusa Tenggara 170, *257*

ODO see Investigation Service for the Deceased (Opsporingsdienst van Overledenen)
Oe, K. 46
Ohsugi, M. 88
Oji paper factory 109
Oldeman, L.R. 72
Onafhankelijkheidsverklaring see Proklamasi
Oostindie, G.J. 173

Operation Kraai see Second Dutch military offensive
Operation Pounce (December 1945- January 1946) 138
Operation Product see First Dutch offensive

Pacet 120
Padang 58 67, 68, 101, 128, 130, 156, 213
Padmodiwirjo, S. 177
Pagee, M. van 105, 150
Pahlawan Center 177
Palembang 67, 68, 76, 101, 124
Palmos, F. 60
Palopo 94, 99
Panitia Persiapan Kemerdekaan Indonesia (PPKI) 63, 64
Panorama (weekly) 191
Papua battalion 90
Paré-Paré 96
Parindra see Partai Indonesia Raya
Parool, Het (newspaper) 206
Partai Indonesia Raya (Parindra) 265
Partai Komunis Indonesia (PKI) 44, 132, 137, 265
Partai Nasional Indonesia (Pendidikan Nasional Indonesia, PNI) 44, 137, 265
Labour Party (Partij van de Arbeid, PvdA) 196, 265
Pasuruan 20, 21
Pati 19
Patterson, W.R. 72, 78
Pawilo, S. 176
Pearl Harbor 45

Pekalongan 21, 74, 83, 113, 131, 134, 135, 138, 147, 150
Pelita Foundation 25, 165, 166
Pematang Siantar 118, 119
Pembela Tanah Air (PETA) 54, 55, 67-69, 117, 265
Pemuda Banteng Hitam 174
Pemuda Betawia 59
Pemuda Republik Indonesia (PRI) 107, 110, 115, 144, 151
Pemuda Sosialis Indonesia (Pesindo) 107, 118, 129, 130, 137
Pen Gun (magazine) 189-191, 257
Pendidikan Nasional Indonesia (PNI) 44, 137, 265
Pendjaga Keamanan Oemoem (PKO) 91, 92, 265
Pensiun Wilhelmina 118, 119
Perdjuangan kita (pamphlet) 148, 149
Perhimpunan Indonesia 59
Persatuan Perjuangan 137
Persatuan Ulama Seluruh Aceh (PUSA) 135
Pesindo see Pemuda Sosialis Indonesia
PETA see Pembela Tanah Air
Peudaya 136
PID see Political Intelligence Service (Politieke Inlichtingendienst)
Pidië 136, 137
PKI see Partai Komunis Indonesia
PKO see Pendjaga Keamanan Oemoem
Plas, C.O. van der 70, 72, 73, 123, 144, 156, 156, 195
Ploegman, W. 74

PNI see Partai Nasional Indonesia (Pendidikan Nasional Indonesia)
Pol, J. van der 120
Polisi Tentara Keamanan Rakyat (PTKR) 117, 150
Political Intelligence Service (Politieke Inlichtingendienst, PID) 42, 49, 265
Polman, J. 199
Polygoon 197, 199
Poncokusomo 20, 24
Pontianak 91, 92
Portier (family) 204
Portugal 226
PPKI see Panitia Persiapan Kemerdekaan Indonesia
Preanger Bontweverij 109
Preangerbode, De (newspaper) 203
Prentice, A.I.D. 73
PRI see Pemuda Republik Indonesia
Probolinggo 36
Proust, M. 11
PTKR see Polisi Tentara Keamanan Rakyat
Pudja, K. 77
PUSA see Persatuan Ulama Seluruh Aceh
Pusat Tenaga Rakyat (Putera) 54, 56, 265
Putera see Pusat Tenaga Rakyat
PvdA see Labour Party (Partij van de Arbeid)

Raben, R. 38, 163, 173, 215, 231
Radio Free Indonesia 149
Radio Pemberontakan Rakjat 105, 147

Radjamandala 202
Rangkasbitung 113, 132
Ratulangi, G.S.S.J. 95, 97, 98
RAPWI see Recovery of Allied Prisoners of War and Internees
Rawah Mangoen 204
Recovery of Allied Prisoners of War and Internees (RAPWI) 65, 68, 70, 74, 103, 104, 119, 120, 125, 128, 146, *246*, 265
Red Cross 117, 127, 167, 164, 165, 166, *244*
Reijnoudt, C. van 37
Rengasdengklok 64
Republik Indonesia Serikat (RIS) 208, 266
Riau 35
Rijksmuseum (Amsterdam) 223, *261*
RIS see Republik Indonesia Serikat
Robinson, G. 87
Robinson, T. 13, 189
Roermond 224
Romijn, P. 215
Round Table Conference (Ronde Tafel Conferentie, RTC. Den Haag, August-November 1949) 205, 206, 266
Roon-Koek, mevr. Van 13
Rooy, C.C. de 91
Rossum, van (family) 22
Royal Netherlands East Indies Army (Koninklijk Nederlands-Indisch Leger, KNIL) 19, 31, 39, 40-43, 46, 55, 62, 65, 66, 77, 88-94, 96-100, 102, 203, 112, 118-123, 141, 175, 176, 186-188, 190, 199, 218-220, 224, *231*, *244*, *246*, *259*, *261*, 264
Royal Netherlands Institute of Southeast Asian and Carribean Studies (Koninklijk Instituut voor Taal-, Land- en Volkenkunde, KITLV) 174, 175, 264
RTC see Round Table Conference (Ronde Tafel Conferentie)
Ruter (family) 22
RVD see Government Information Service (Regeringsvoorlichtingsdienst)

Sabaruddin, Z. 117, 150
Sacsea see Supreme Allied Commander South East Asia
Salatiga 70
Sama, St. M.J. 97
Saparua 90
Sarekat Islam (SI, Islamic Union) 44, 266
Scherius (family) 21, 23
Schipper (family) 21
Schreuder (family) 21
Schröder (family) 21, 23, 24
Schulte Nordholt, H. 38
SEAC see South East Asian Comand
Second Dutch military offensive ('Operation Kraai', December 1948-January 1949) 204, 207
Seinendan 54
Semarang 14, 23, 50, 52, 58, 74, 97, 101, 103, 104, 112, 113, 125, 128, 138, 150, 151, 156, 186, 208, 214
Semarang-Joana Stoomtram Maatschappij 113

Sémelin, J. 106
Semeru 20
Seram 51, 90
Serang 113, 132, 133, *245, 249*
Shibata, Y. 12, 111
SI see Sarekat Islam
Si Rengo Rengo (camp) 68
Siam see Thailand
Sidoarjo 150
Sigli 136
Simon (family) 18, 19
Simpang Society 115, 194
Sinapati 99
Sinar Baroe (newspaperd) 52
Singapore 50, 124, 139
Singaraja 55, 76
Singkawang 92
Sjahrir, S. 32, 33, 44, 52, 60, 138, 148, 149, 156, 193, *232*
Sjarifuddin, A. 146
Slamet-Depok 150, 151
Slipi 203
Somers Heidhues, M.F. 179
Sophiaan, M. 95, 97
South East Asian Command (SEAC) 62, 101
Soviet Union 45, 76
Spiegel, De (weekly) 191
Spoor, S.H. 93, 192
Sprang, A. van 194, 195, 197, 199
Sri Lanka 139
Staatsblad van Nederlandsch-Indië (gazette) 37
Stevens, J. 194, 197, 199
Subarjo 193
Sudirman 55, 110, 111, 149
Sudjarwo 37, 54
Suerbeck, H. 119

Sukabumi 102, 109
Sukarela Tentara Pembela Tanah Air 54
Sukarno 31-33, 44, 49, 51, 52, 53, 56, 62, 63-65, 69, 70, 71, 72, 107, 108, 124, 145-149, 180, 193, 195, 219, *236*
Sulawesi 39, 45-47, 50, 51, 62, 81-84, 88, 89, 94, 97, 98, 99, 103, 106, 140, 143, 144, 165, 168, 170, 175, 176, 193, 217, 219, 224
Sulu archipelago 51
Sumadi, B. 24, 25
Sumba 47, 51
Sumbawa 47, 51
Sungkono 208
Supreme Allied Commander South East Asia (SACSEA) 108, 266
Surabaya 12, 18-22, 50, 60, 66, 67, 70, 73-75, 77, 97, 101, 105, 110, 111, 114, 115, 117, 121, 125, 126-129, 138, 145, 147, 150, 154, 156, 157, 160, 176, 177, 178, 180, 194, 195, 204, 207, 214
Surakarta 44, 50, 69, 103, 109, 111, 112
Surutanga 99
Sutomo 105, 149
Syaranamual 95

Tabrani, M. 207, 208
Tahrir, A. 119
Taiwan 51, 58, 92
Taman Makam Pahlawan 177
Tanah-Abang 200
Tanalepe 202
Tangerang 140, 179, 203
Tangsé 136

Tandjong Priok 78, 200
Tarakan 62, 87, 91
Tebing Tinggi 129-131, 138, 176, *248*
Technical college in Bandung 44
Tegal 74, 134, 135, 150
Telegraaf, De (newspaper) 205, 206
Tentara Keamanan Rakyat (TKR) 84, 102, 126, 129-131, 134-136, 138, 140, 145, 150, 151, 202, 266
Tentara Nasional Indonesia (TNI) 206, 266
Tentara Rakyat Indonesia (TRI) 37, 145
Thailand *255*
The Hague 157, 188, 205, 224
Tiga Daerah affair 131, 147
Timmers, W.J.M.W. 117
Timor 46, 47, 51, 58, 165, 170, 193
Tiongkok 92
Tjarda van Starkenborgh Stachouwer, A.W.L. 31
TKR see Tentara Keamanan Rakyat
TNI see Tentara Nasional Indonesia
Toer, P.A. 180
Tokio 48-50, 56, 66
TRI see Tentara Rakyat Indonesia
Triyana, B. 223
Tromp, Hr.Ms. (ship) 72
Trouw (newspaper) 160, 201
Tull, T.S. 150
Tumpang 18, 20, 22-25, *229*

UN see United Nations
United Nations Security Council (Veiligheidsraad) 157
United Nations (UN) 157, 264

Dutch East Indies Company (Verenigde Oostindische Compagnie, VOC) 38, 40, 48
United States 45, 76
United States of Indonesia (VSI) 204, 208, 266

Vaderlandsche Club 115
Veen, F. van der 158
Verspoor, D. 194
Vervoort, H. 18
Vickers, A. 173
VOC see Dutch East Indies Company (Verenigde Oostindische Compagnie)
Volkskrant, de (dagblad) 206
Volksraad (1918) 43
VSI see United States of Indonesia

Waardenburg, J.J.C.H. van 213
Wapenbroeders (magazine) 189-191
Warunggunung 113, 132
Watesbelung 20
Wehmann, H. 122
Werff, van der (family) 2
Werfstraat prison see Kalisosok prison
Westerling, R.P.P. 28, 77, 118, 119, 141
Wetzel-Catharinus, E.W. 23
Wijk, F.M. van 134, 135
Wikana 63
Wilaja, J. 77
Winter, R.J. 22
Winter-van der Dungen Bille, H. 22
Wiryowinoto 36
Wlingi 22

299

Wohlhoff, G.J. 96
Wongsonegoro 113
Woodburn Kirby, S. 172
WUBO see Benefit Act for Civilian War Victims 1940-1945 (Wet Uitkeringen Burger- Oorlogsslachtoffers 1940-1945)

Yamato hotel 74

Yogyakarta 20, 69, 107, 109, 112, 138, 146, 176
Yonosewoyo 150

Zele. L., van see Ducelle, L.

Overview of publications resulting from the research programme Independence, Decolonization, Violence and War in Indonesia, 1945,-1950

Publications Amsterdam University Press

Gert Oostindie, Thijs Brocades Zaalberg, Eveline Buchheim, Esther Captain, Martijn Eickhoff, Roel Frakking, Azarja Harmanny, Meindert van der Kaaij, Jeroen Kemperman, Rémy Limpach, Bart Luttikhuis, Remco Raben, Peter Romijn, Onno Sinke, Fridus Steijlen, Stephanie Welvaart, Esther Zwinkels, *Over de grens. Nederlands extreem geweld in de Indonesische onafhankelijkheidsoorlog, 1945-1949*

Gert Oostindie, Thijs Brocades Zaalberg, Eveline Buchheim, Esther Captain, Martijn Eickhoff, Roel Frakking, Azarja Harmanny, Meindert van der Kaaij, Jeroen Kemperman, Rémy Limpach, Bart Luttikhuis, Remco Raben, Peter Romijn, Onno Sinke, Fridus Steijlen, Stephanie Welvaart, Esther Zwinkels, *Beyond the Pale. Dutch Extreme Violence in the Indonesian War of Independence*, 1945-1949

Abdul Wahid en Yulianti (red), *Onze Revolutie. Bloemlezing uit de Indonesische geschiedschrijving over de strijd voor de onafhankelijkheid, 1945-1949*

Esther Captain en Onno Sinke, *Het geluid van geweld. Bersiap en de dynamiek van geweld tijdens de eerste fase van de Indonesische revolutie, 1945-1946*

Esther Captain and Onno Sinke, *Resonance of Violence. Bersiap and the Dynamics of Violence in the First Phase of the Indonesian Revolution, 1945-1946*

Remco Raben en Peter Romijn, mmv Maarten van der Bent en Anne van Mourik, *Talen van geweld. Stilte, informatie en misleiding in de Indonesische onafhankelijkheidsoorlog, 1945-1949*

Remco Raben and Peter Romijn, with Maarten van der Bent and Anne van Mourik, *Tales of Violence. Dutch Management of Information in the Indonesian War of Independence, 1945-1949*

Jeroen Kemperman, Emma Keizer en Tom van den Berge, *Diplomatie en geweld. De internationale context van de Indonesische onafhankelijkheidsoorlog, 1945-1949*

Rémy Limpach, *Tasten in het duister. Inlichtingenstrijd tijdens de Indonesische onafhankelijkheidsoorlog, 1945-1949*

Rémy Limpach, *Stumbling in the Dark. The Battle for Intelligence in the Indonesian War of Independence, 1945-1949*

Azarja Harmanny, *Grof geschut. Artillerie en luchtstrijdkrachten in de Indonesische onafhankelijkheidsoorlog, 1945-1949*

Bambang Purwanto, Roel Frakking, Abdul Wahid, Gerry van Klinken, Martijn Eickhoff, Yulianti and Ireen Hoogenboom (eds), *Revolutionary worlds. Local perspectives and dynamics during the Indonesian independence war, 1945-1949*

Meindert van der Kaaij, *Een kwaad geweten. De worsteling met de Indonesische onafhankelijkheidsoorlog vanaf 1950*

Eveline Buchheim, Satrio Dwicahyo, Fridus Steijlen en Stephanie Welvaart, *Sporen vol betekenis. In gesprek met 'Getuigen & Tijdgenoten' over de Indonesische onafhankelijkheidsoorlog / Meniti Arti. Bertukar Makna bersama 'Saksi & Rekan Sezaman' tentang Perang Kemerdekaan Indonesia*

Van Rij en Stam. Rapporten van de Commissie van onderzoek naar beweerde excessen gepleegd door Nederlandse militairen in Indonesië, 1949-1954 (Bronnenpublicatie), ingeleid en bezorgd door Maarten van der Bent

Other publications

Thijs Brocades Zaalberg, Bart Luttikhuis en anderen, 'Extreem geweld tijdens dekolonisatieoorlogen in vergelijkend perspectief, 1945-1962' in: *BMGN – Low Countries Historical Review*, Volume 135 nr.2

Thijs Brocades Zaalberg en Bart Luttikhuis (eds), *Empire's Violent End. Comparing Dutch, British, and French Wars of Decolonization, 1945–1962.* Cornell University Press

For Product Safety Concerns and Information please contact our EU representative GPSR@taylorandfrancis.com
Taylor & Francis Verlag GmbH, Kaufingerstraße 24, 80331 München, Germany